ANCIENT LITERACY

ANCIENT

LITERACY

William V. Harris

Harvard University Press
Cambridge, Massachusetts
London, England

Copyright © 1989 by the President and Fellows of Harvard College
All rights reserved
Printed in the United States of America
10 9 8 7 6 5 4 3 2

First Harvard University Press paperback edition, 1991

Library of Congress Cataloging-in-Publication Data

Harris, William V. q(William Vernon)
  Ancient literacy / William V. Harris
    p. cm.
  Bibliography: p.
  Includes index.
  ISBN 0-674-03380-9 (alk. paper) (cloth)
  ISBN 0-674-03381-7 (paper)
    1. Classical languages—History.   2. Literacy—Greece—History.
  3. Literacy—Rome—History.   4. Civilization, Classical.
    5. Language and culture—Greece.   6. Language and culture—Rome.
I. Title.
PA53.H37   1989   89-7588
302.2'244'0938—dc20   CIP

In Memory of
Elizabeth Harris
(1910–1975)

Preface

Some Greeks knew how to write as early as the fourteenth century B.C., if not earlier. The script they used at that time was the Linear B syllabary (derived from Linear A, a script which was already in use in Crete by about 1700 B.C.), containing as many as ninety syllabic signs. Knowledge of this script appears to have been largely confined to a few specialists who were royal clerks, and the prime purposes for which it was used seem to have been the accounting and stock-taking of the Minoan and Mycenaean princes. In both mainland Greece and the islands knowledge of this script perished in the great period of destruction which brought Mycenaean civilization to an end in the twelfth century B.C., though scripts which descended from Linear B continued to be used in Cyprus until the third century. Thus by about 1100 almost all parts of Greece had once more become illiterate.

Such, in outline, is the agreed account of Greek literacy in the second millennium B.C., and it is widely believed that writing returned to Greece at some date not very long before 750 B.C. All recognize that the new alphabet, entirely unconnected with Linear B, developed out of Phoenician script. However the date when this occurred is now once again disputed. The earliest examples of the new Greek writing published up to the present (A. Heubeck, *Würzburger Jahrbücher für die Altertumswissenschaft* xii [1986], 7–20) are datable to roughly 800 (and another very early text which is rumoured to be in the course of publication is said not to be significantly earlier). It is an impressive fact that in spite of all the Greek archaeological discoveries of recent generations the Dipylon Vase, found in 1871, remained until a short time ago the earliest known text, or was at least as early as any other. (For some rivals see L. H. Jeffery, *Cambridge Ancient History* iii.l [3d ed., Cambridge, 1982], 828.) Some experts in Semitic philology, on the other hand, maintain that Greek script must have branched off from Phoenician script far earlier than this, in the twelfth or eleventh century. The form of their argument is that the kind of Phoenician script which was the antecedent of the Greek alphabet went out of use at that time (see in particular J. Naveh, *Early History of the Alphabet* [Jerusalem & Leiden, 1982]). This too is a cogent line of reasoning, even though our knowledge of Phoenician script in this period is based on no more than a small number of texts.

I am not qualified to adopt a wholly confident view about this question, but it hardly needs to be decided in a book about Greek and Roman literacy. If the hypothetical early date for the Greek alphabet could be established, we would apparently be confronted by a period of several centuries in which its use was very restricted indeed, and that would accord quite well with the argument put forward in Chapter 3 that literacy spread slowly in the eighth and seventh centuries. And we may suspect that some of the earliest extant Greek inscriptions represent rather evolved uses of writing, an argument which has occasionally been thought to push the creation of the Greek alphabet back far beyond 750. But the more conventional chronology does not on the other hand cause any difficulty to a historian of Greek literacy.

The subject of this study is in any case the literacy of the Greeks and Romans from the time when the former were first provably able to write a non-syllabic script, in the eighth century B.C., until the fifth century A.D.

The title *Ancient Literacy* may seem somewhat misleading, since the Greeks and Romans alone are the subject of this book. The choice was suggested by convenience, not by any belief that the Greeks and Romans are more entitled to have a history than the Sumerians or the ancient Egyptians. The book's title also reflects my opinion that the literacy of the Greeks and Romans is a single phenomenon, which had a beginning, a series of developments and a decline. At the same time I have not lost sight of the fact—indeed in Chapter 7 I have heavily emphasized it—that Greek and Roman literacy often existed in environments in which other cultures were alive or even dominant.

In preparing this study I have been assisted by a number of institutions, and I wish to offer warm thanks to all the officials concerned. The John Simon Guggenheim Memorial Foundation awarded me a fellowship, and All Souls College awarded me a visiting fellowship. Columbia University gave me a sabbatical leave, and the American Philosophical Society provided me with some travel funds. Several parts of the books were written in the hospitable environment of the

American Academy in Rome. May all five establishments continue to flourish.

I have also benefited from innumerable exchanges, some oral, some written, some with close friends, some with amicable scholars, some with anonymous listeners. The list of those I could name is very long, and reciting it I would run the risk of omitting some kind person who deserved to be mentioned and also the risk of seeming to invoke weighty authorities for my own protection. I intend to do neither of these things.

Of the many friends and acquaintances to whom I am indebted for information or for other help concerning this book I must, however, mention and thank the following: John Baines, Mary Beard, Malcolm Bell, John Bodel, Glen Bowersock, Peter Brown, P. A. Brunt, Guglielmo Cavallo, S. J. D. Cohen, Mireille Corbier, J. H. D'Arms, Diana Delia, M. Detienne, Richard Duncan-Jones, Andrea Giardina, J. F. Gilliam, Christian Habicht, Alan Hall, Ann Hanson, F. D. Harvey, Keith Hopkins, Nicholas Horsfall, Christopher Jones, Ludwig Koenen, John Lenz, Walther Ludwig, Ramsay MacMullen, Stella G. Miller, John Hine Mundy, Oswyn Murray, James Packer, Silvio Panciera, Christopher Parslow, Charles Radding, Eila Kaarina Rämö, L. Richardson, Jr., Ihor Ševčenko, Morton Smith, Heikki Solin, Raymond Starr, Susan Treggiari, Andrew Wallace-Hadrill.

The arrival in the mail of a potentially fascinating manuscript from an old friend does not always make a scholar's heart rejoice. The following friends deserve honour for having, without open complaint, read all or part of this book and for having improved it: Alan Boegehold (Providence), Alan Bowman (Oxford), Lucia Criscuolo (Bologna), Jerzy Linderski (Chapel Hill, North Carolina), Myles McDonnell (New York), Caroline Williamson (Bloomington, Indiana) and Klaas Worp (Amsterdam).

Years ago, when after a few months' work I was confident that I knew almost all there was to know about the literacy of the Romans, Averil Cameron more or less gently explained to me that I was not even asking the truly interesting questions (always of course a devastating criticism, when it comes from someone qualified to offer it). I recall her advice with great gratitude. I should also like to offer sincere thanks for careful reading and strenuous criticism to Glenn W. Most, *Aenipontanus atque idem Florentinus,* whose natural modesty forbids me to laud him in the terms he deserves. It is enough to say that with his avuncular concern for my interests he has encouraged me to complete a book which is likely to cause severe mental indigestion in philologists of less stature than himself.

The manuscript of this book was completed in January 1988, and I have been able to add references to only a few publications which came to my attention after that date.

William V. Harris

Contents

Abbreviations

The names of ancient writers and their works are abbreviated according to standard practices. In case of obscurity, see Liddell-Scott-Jones' *Greek-English Lexicon*, the *Oxford Latin Dictionary* or the *Oxford Classical Dictionary*. With some late-antique texts which are less known or are tiresome to locate I have added references to series (*CCSL, CSEL, PG, PL, SC*) in which they can be consulted. For papyrological publications which are easily recognizable by the initial P., the uncertain reader is referred to standard handbooks such as E. G. Turner, *Greek Papyri. An Introduction* (Oxford, 1968); and J. F. Oates, R. S. Bagnall, et al., *Checklist of Editions of Greek Papyri and Ostraca* (3d ed.) (*Bulletin of the American Society of Papyrologists* Suppl. 5, 1985). Periodicals are abbreviated as in *L'année philologique*, except as noted below.

AAASH	*Acta Antiqua Academiae Scientiarum Hungaricae*
Abh.Gött.	*Abhandlungen der Akademie der Wissenschaften in Göttingen, Phil.-hist. Klasse*
AE	*L'année épigraphique*
ANRW	*Aufstieg und Niedergang der Römischen Welt*, ed. H. Temporini, innumerable vols. (Berlin & New York, 1972–)
Arch.Stor.Pugl.	*Archivio storico pugliese*
ASNSP	*Annali della Scuola normale superiore di Pisa*
BACT	*Bulletin archéologique du Comité des travaux historiques*
BGU	*Aegyptische Urkunden aus den (Königlichen) Museen zu Berlin. Griechische Urkunden*
BMQ	*British Museum Quarterly*
Bull.Ep.	J. & L. Robert, *Bulletin épigraphique*, published annually in *REG*, reprinted separately
CAF	*Comicorum Atticorum Fragmenta*, ed. T. Kock
CCSL	*Corpus Christianorum, Series Latina*
Cd'E	*Chronique d'Egypte*
CIG	*Corpus Inscriptionum Graecarum*
CIL	*Corpus Inscriptionum Latinarum*

CPIud	*Corpus Papyrorum Iudaicarum*
CPL	*Corpus Papyrorum Latinarum*
CRF	*Comicorum Romanorum Fragmenta*, ed. O. Ribbeck
CSEL	*Corpus Scriptorum Ecclesiasticorum Latinorum*
C.Th.	*Codex Theodosianus*
CVA	*Corpus Vasorum Antiquorum*
Dig.	*Digesta*
Diz.Ep.	*Dizionario epigrafico di antichità romane*, ed. E. de Ruggiero
D–K	H. Diels & W. Kranz (eds.), *Die Fragmente der Vorsokratiker* (8th ed., Berlin, 1956)
EAA	*Enciclopedia dell'arte antica*
EFH	*Entretiens [de la Fondation Hardt] sur l'antiquité classique*
ESAR	*Economic Survey of Ancient Rome*, ed. T. Frank
FCG	*Fragmenta Comicorum Graecorum*, ed. A. Meineke
FGrH	*Die Fragmente der griechischen Historiker*, ed. F. Jacoby
FHG	*Fragmenta Historicorum Graecorum*, ed. C. Müller
FIRA	*Fontes Iuris Romani Anteiustiniani*, ed. S. Riccobono et al.
HRR	*Historicorum Romanorum Reliquiae*, ed. H. Peter
HSCPh	*Harvard Studies in Classical Philology*
IG	*Inscriptiones Graecae*
IGRR	*Inscriptiones Graecae ad Res Romanas Pertinentes*
IGSK	*Die Inschriften der griechischen Städte Kleinasiens*
ILCV	*Inscriptiones Latinae Christianae Veteres*
ILLRP	*Inscriptiones Latinae Liberae Rei Publicae*
ILS	*Inscriptiones Latinae Selectae*, ed. H. Dessau
Inscr.It.	*Inscriptiones Italiae*
IRT	*The Inscriptions of Roman Tripolitania*
I.v.Priene	*Inschriften von Priene*
JIH	*Journal of Interdisciplinary History*
KAI	*Kanaanäische und aramäische Inschriften*, ed. H. Donner & W. Röllig
Marrou, *Histoire*	H. I. Marrou, *Histoire de l'éducation dans l'antiquité* (7th ed., Paris, n.d.)
MEFRA	*Mélanges d'archéologie et d'histoire de l'Ecole française de Rome, Antiquité*
Meiggs & Lewis, *GHI*	R. Meiggs & D. M. Lewis, *A Selection of Greek Historical Inscriptions* (Oxford, 1969)

Mem.Acc.Linc.	Memorie dell'Accademia nazionale dei Lincei
Mus.Helv.	Museum Helveticum
Not.Sc.	Notizie degli scavi di antichità
N.Th.	Leges Novellae ad Theodosianum Pertinentes, edited with C.Th.
O.Bodl.	Greek Ostraca in the Bodleian Library at Oxford, ed. J. G. Tait et al.
O. Mich.	Greek Ostraca in the University of Michigan Collection, ed. L. Amundsen
ORF³	Oratorum Romanorum Fragmenta, ed. H[enrica] (= Enrica) Malcovati, 3d ed.
PG	Patrologia Graeca
PL	Patrologia Latina
PSI	Papiri greci e latini (Pubblicazioni della Società italiana per la ricerca dei papiri . . .)
Publ.Soc.Fouad	Publications de la Société Fouad I de papyrologie
RE	Realencyclopädie der classischen Altertumswissenschaft, ed. Pauly—Wissowa—Kroll
Rev.arch.	Revue archéologique
Rev.Et.Aug.	Revue des études augustiniennes
RIB	The Roman Inscriptions of Britain
RLAC	Reallexikon für Antike und Christentum
S & C	Scrittura e Civiltà
SB	Sammelbuch griechischer Urkunden aus Aegypten, ed. F. Preisigke et al.; or Sitzungsberichte
SBAW	Sitzungsberichte der Bayerischen Akademie der Wissenschaften
SC	Sources chrétiennes
SEG	Supplementum Epigraphicum Graecum
Sel.Pap.	Select Papyri, ed. A. S. Hunt et al., Loeb Classical Library
SIG³	Sylloge Inscriptionum Graecarum, 3d ed.
SVF	Stoicorum Veterum Fragmenta, ed. H. von Arnim
Symb.Osl.	Symbolae Osloenses
TAM	Tituli Asiae Minoris
UPZ	Urkunden der Ptolemäerzeit, ed. U. Wilcken
W.Chr.	L. Mitteis & U. Wilcken (eds.), Grundzüge und Chrestomathie der Papyruskunde, vol. i
ZSS	Zeitschrift der Savigny-Stiftung, Romanistische Abteilung

PART ONE

Introduction

1   Levels of Greek and Roman Literacy

How many people could read, how many people could write in the Graeco-Roman world? These simple-seeming questions are the origin of this book. How widely were the capabilities of reading and writing diffused among the inhabitants of the classical Greek and Roman worlds, the rich and the poor, the free and the slaves, men and women, town-dwellers and country-people? Our inquiry will consider the entire period from the invention of the Greek alphabet to the fifth century A.D.; for literacy during this period was a single phenomenon, in the sense that, once having spread to a particular area, it seldom declined severely, at least until the third century A.D., and also in the sense that it was sustained by a continuous cultural tradition.

In every society which possesses writing, a line can be drawn between the literate and the illiterate population, and such lines are sometimes necessary. Of course any definition of literacy which draws such a line is bound to have an arbitrary element in it, and no single definition has succeeded in imposing itself. UNESCO made a useful attempt, suggesting that an illiterate should be defined as someone "who cannot with understanding both read and write a short simple statement on his everyday life."[1] But this definition was naturally not respected by the officials of all the countries which responded to UNESCO's most recent survey of world literacy (1977), the most culpable offenders being the officials of those industrialized countries that failed to provide accurate information.[2] There is no prospect whatsoever that UNESCO or anyone else will succeed in gaining acceptance for a single definition.

1. A 1958 UNESCO recommendation, cited in its *Statistics of Educational Attainment and Illiteracy 1945–1974* (UNESCO Statistical Reports and Studies no. 22, Paris, 1977), 12. The French version, by using the word "exposé," implies that quite a long "statement" was meant.

2. The value of the survey was also reduced by inadequate sampling methods and by the variety of the age-groups which were included.

To add to the confusion, English has the peculiarity that the words concerned, or to be more exact their adjectival forms "literate" and "illiterate," are commonly used to refer to general culture instead of to basic literacy (this appears to be much commoner in the case of "illiterate"). There are illiterate scholars; but they are not the subject of this book.

Historians as well as sociologists have employed differing definitions of literacy. The availability of signature evidence, for example in marriage registers, has been not only useful but irresistible. Hence some who have investigated the history of literacy in the modern world have treated the ability to write one's name as the important or even as the sole criterion of literacy[3]—in spite of the fact that, in cultures in which signatures have been important, they have for some people been virtually the only writing accomplishment. Such people are obviously barred from most of the advantages of writing and often from those of reading. Nor are the people who were called upon to sign (for instance) marriage registers likely to have been random members of a community. In this study we shall certainly pay attention to any information which we can find about who could and who could not subscribe a document, but we shall not treat this accomplishment as the single most vital one.

Other historians in turn have defined literacy by reference to reading ability,[4] which is normally more widespread, and sometimes has been much more widespread, than the ability to write.

UNESCO's definitional line appears to be better placed than signing ability or reading ability, since it requires that the literate person should possess a more active skill than reading, and possess it to a truly useful extent. But even this definition is a matter of crude con-

3. E.g., L. Stone, *P & P* xlii (1969), 98–99; M. Sanderson, *P & P* lvi (1972), 75; K. A. Lockridge, *Literacy in Colonial New England* (New York, 1974), esp. 7–13; R. W. Beales, *JIH* ix (1978–79), 93–102; D. Cressy, *Literacy and the Social Order. Reading and Writing in Tudor and Stuart England* (Cambridge, 1980). For arguments in favour of a close correlation between signing ability and literacy in a wider sense see also F. Furet & W. Sachs, *Annales E.S.C.* xxix (1974), 715–721. But it remains unclear, for instance, what the ratio was, in eighteenth-century England, of those able to sign marriage registers to those in the general population who were able to write something more elaborate. For some scepticism about the evidential value of signatures see P. Collinson, *Times Literary Supplement*, 8 January 1981, 31.

4. E.g., C. Cipolla, *Literacy and Development in the West* (Harmondsworth, 1969), 14–15.

venience, and in reality there are infinite gradations of literacy for any written language.[5] Although no study of a large population can busy itself with all the gradations of literacy to be found there, we should at least try to avoid an excessively sharp polarity of literacy and illiteracy. At least we must concern ourselves with a category of *semi-literates*, persons who can write slowly or not at all, and who can read without being able to read complex or very lengthy texts. These semi-literates are inevitably an amorphous group, but we shall catch glimpses of them throughout this study.

In some cultures non-writing readers, those possessed of one skill but not the other, have made up a broad stratum. To take a non-modern example, a recent book seems to maintain that in mediaeval England reading ability and writing ability were quite independent of each other.[6] We shall certainly have to be on guard for the possibility that the difference between reading and writing levels was actually very great among the Greeks and Romans. There is, however, no especial reason to think that those who could truly read and truly *not* write were numerous.

Just as there is obscurity in the modern terminology of literacy, so there was in the ancient terminology. Like the word *illiterate*, Greek *agrammatos* and Latin *illitteratus* seem to veer between the meanings "uncultured" and "incapable of reading and writing." Even the expression *litteras (ne)scire*, "(not) to know letters," may refer to lack of culture rather than to illiteracy in the narrow sense.[7] In documentary contexts all Greek and Latin expressions concerning "knowing letters" refer to literacy in the narrow sense,[8] but in literary contexts there is

5. This is well brought out by I. S. Kirsch & A. Jungeblut, *Literacy: Profiles of America's Young Adults* (Educational Testing Service Report no. 16-PL-02, Princeton, 1986).

6. M. T. Clanchy, *From Memory to Written Record: England, 1066–1307* (Cambridge, Mass., 1979), 183, supports his point of view by referring to, among other things, the physical difficulty of writing with parchment and quills; but although this matter of materials requires attention, reading could also, in antiquity at least, be physically harder than it is for us.

7. As Sen. *Suas.* vii.13 shows: "qui patrem tuum [i.e., Cicero] negabat litteras scire" (hence E. de Ruggiero & M. Sordi were mistaken in *Diz.Ep.* [1964] s.v. "littera," 1421).

8. Greek examples are legion: see below, p. 141. For Latin see *FIRA* iii no. 150 (a) and (b); and the document edited by F. Sbordone, *RAAN* li (1976), 145–147. See also Paulus, quoted at second hand in Dig. xxvii.1.6.19 ("eius qui se neget litteras scire").

ambiguity by the time of Plato and Xenophon,[9] and it continues into late antiquity.[10] Aristotle even uses the word *agrammatos* about animals, to mean "unable to utter articulate sounds."[11] Latin *illitteratus* must originally have meant "illiterate" in a narrow sense, with *litteratus* meaning the converse—and it so happens that the younger Seneca says something close to this.[12] But such primitive clarity, if it ever existed, may already have been lost by the second century B.C.,[13] and by Cicero's time *litteratus* commonly meant "cultivated," and *illitteratus* could mean "lacking in culture."[14] Even when it is clear that an ancient literary text is referring to basic literacy and not to some higher level of education, it is very seldom clear how much knowledge a person needed to qualify as "knowing letters." Such expressions have to be interpreted case by case. The occasional papyrus texts which show people who are said to be illiterate subscribing their names[15] suggest that something more than signature-writing ability may often have been needed to earn such a description.

9. It appears that in Pl. *Tim.* 23a *agrammatos* refers to the inability to read or write, and in Xen. *Mem.* iv.2.20 to a more general lack of culture.

10. Cf. R. A. Kaster, *TAPhA* cxiii (1983), 343.

11. *Hist.An.* i.1.488a33.

12. Sen. *De ben.* v.13.3: "quaedam, etiam si vera non sunt, propter similitudinem eodem vocabulo comprehensa sunt . . . sic inlitteratum non ex toto rudem, sed ad litteras altiores non perductum." But although he treats the more general meaning as an extension of the narrower meaning, he does not actually say that the latter was earlier (something which he could hardly have known for sure without a historically organized dictionary). Suet. *De gramm.* 4 says that *litteratus* had once been a word for *grammaticus;* but against this see E. W. Bower, *Hermes* lxxxix (1961), 462–477.

13. In Cato, *Orig.* fr. 31 (*HRR* i.64) *inliterati* probably has a narrow sense. Whether it does in Caecilius Statius (flor. 200–170) line 60 (*CRF* ii.51), as supposed by H. Grundmann, *Archiv für Kulturgeschichte* xl (1958), 15, is unclear. Another unclear passage is Lucilius 649 Marx = 674 Warmington ("et tu idem inliteratum me atque idiotam diceres"), where Grundmann 16 takes *inliteratum* to refer to lack of culture, interpreting it by means of the next line, which may not, however, have been the next line in the original. Grundmann supposes that the narrower meaning lasted longest in practical and technical writings, but there is no reason to think that it ever died out; in late antiquity, with basic literacy to some extent in retreat, this meaning is fairly common.

14. Cic. *De orat.* ii.6.25. See further Grundmann 16–18.

15. *P.Oxy.* xxxiii.2676 (151 A.D.), with the comments of H. C. Youtie, *GRBS* xii (1971), 254; the *agrammatos* wrote Αμοιτας Διονυσιου επιδεχομαι. A comparable case in Syriac:*P.Dura* 28. In *P.Petaus* 11, the village scribe Petaus proved that a colleague of his was not illiterate by asserting that he was able to sign; but (not to mention the textual problem, on which cf. Youtie 240 n.8) this may well have been special pleading.

The Greek and Latin terminology of literacy ought by rights to provide some useful information about the conceptual world of the Greeks and Romans, but in fact the implications are unclear. We might, for instance, suspect that the absence of *agrammatos* or any other word for "illiterate" from fifth-century Greek, and the ambiguities just mentioned, are signs that the Greeks and Romans generally regarded the acquisition of basic literacy as not very important in itself. There is probably some truth in this proposition, as we shall see; yet it is not a conclusion which can safely be drawn from the terminology, since *illiterate* (and *unlettered*) were ambiguous words in the nineteenth century—as indeed they still are—even though plenty of attention was being devoted to the diffusion of basic literacy.

We shall obviously never know in a clear-cut numerical way how many people were literate, semi-literate, or illiterate in the Graeco-Roman world in general, or even in any particular milieu within it. Some scholars, however, have reacted to this fact in a most misguided fashion by avoiding numerical estimates altogether and thereby perpetuating the sort of vagueness exemplified by the historian who wrote that the Roman Empire was "tolerably literate."[16] Not much more meaning can be found in assertions that there was a large or small amount of literacy in some part of the ancient world, and such assertions have seriously vitiated almost all research on the subject. It may be useful to undertake the risky task of estimating the numerical limits within which the literacy of some of the more accessible of ancient populations must have fallen, even if the limits turn out to be very broad ones.

At the very least we must decide where to place the Greeks and Romans with respect to mass literacy, and with respect to what may be called "scribal literacy" and "craftsman's literacy." By the former term I mean the sort of literacy which predominated in ancient Near Eastern cultures and in the Minoan and Mycenaean worlds, literacy restricted to a specialized social group which used it for such purposes as maintaining palace records;[17] and which also predominated in western Europe from late antiquity until at least the twelfth cen-

16. Cipolla, *Literacy and Development* 38. G. Cavallo's important work on aspects of Roman literacy has been somewhat marred by his unwillingness to put any of his estimates of the extent of literacy even tentatively into numerical terms; see his contribution to *Alfabetismo e cultura scritta nella storia della società italiana. Atti del seminario tenutosi a Perugia il 29–30 marzo 1977* (Perugia, 1978), 120, etc.

17. On the extent of literacy in dynastic Egypt see J. Baines & C. J. Eyre, *Göttinger Miszellen* lxi (1983), 65–96; and Baines, *Man* xviii (1983), esp. 584–586.

tury.[18] By craftsman's literacy I mean not the literacy of an individual craftsman but the condition in which the majority, or a near-majority, of skilled craftsmen are literate, while women and unskilled labourers and peasants are mainly not, this being the situation which prevailed in most of the educationally more advanced regions of Europe and North America from the sixteenth to the eighteenth century.

Our almost complete lack of evidence which could be converted into statistics about ancient literacy may, however, have a beneficial side effect, for it will ensure that we pay ample attention to social class. Historians investigating the extent of literacy in other cultures often seem to have as their final aim a percentage figure, broken down by gender perhaps, for literacy within a total population. The result may in practice be less informative than facts about whether literacy prevailed in specific social strata.

To a scholar who approaches Greek and Roman literacy from some other period of history or from the social sciences, it may seem obvious that nothing in the nature of mass literacy can ever have existed in the ancient world. Such has not, however, been the view taken by most of the classical scholars who have written on the subject. Though judgements have normally been vague about numbers, they have given a definite impression of optimism, even extreme optimism.

For example, the most thorough study of literacy in classical Athens concludes that "the great majority of Athenian citizens" were literate in the fifth and fourth centuries,[19] though "many of the inhabitants of the country districts of Attica, and many Athenian women, will have been illiterate or semi-literate"[20] (thus this view approaches self-contradiction). Almost the only scholar who has ever argued for a markedly different view about the extent of literacy in classical Athens was Hasebroek, who maintained that Athenian commerce in the fourth century still relied heavily on oral procedures.[21] But the con-

18. This is described as "professional literacy" by M. B. Parkes in D. Daiches & A. Thorlby (eds.), *The Mediaeval World* (London, 1973), 555–556.

19. F. D. Harvey, *REG* lxxix (1966), 628.

20. Harvey 629. M. Stubbs, *Language and Literacy. The Sociolinguistics of Reading and Writing* (London, 1980), 27, asserts that "in Athens in 500 B.C. it is probable that a majority of the citizens could read the laws which were posted round the city" (and it is indicative of common procedure that he refers to two authorities neither of whom has the slightest acquaintance with the evidence), though he knows literacy well enough to see that this would have made the place a historical exception.

21. J. Hasebroek, *Hermes* lviii (1923), 393–425. Cf. the brief statement by Wilamowitz in U. von Wilamowitz-Moellendorff et al., *Staat und Gesellschaft der*

sensus of expert opinion about Athens is clear, and similar opinions are sometimes expressed about Greece in general. Thus a recent book asserts that "in the period 750–650 writing became widespread in Greece"—and it is true that there was now *some* writing in many places—so that "archaic Greece was a literate society in a modern sense."[22] It has even been suggested that the rugged Spartans were pretty generally literate.[23]

With regard to the Roman Empire, a similarly optimistic view has long prevailed. In Marquardt's standard handbook on Roman private life, for example, it is said that "reading and writing were learned by a great part of the population not only in Rome but in the whole Roman Empire."[24] One of the first scholars to give careful thought to problems concerning Roman literacy, A.-M. Guillemin, argued that there were few illiterates in Roman antiquity, "even among slaves."[25] The mass of graffiti at Pompeii so impressed H. H. Tanzer that she concluded enthusiastically that in that town "everybody could read and almost everybody could, and apparently did, write."[26] A scholar as well acquainted with documents as C. H. Roberts has claimed that literacy was widespread in the Near East during the first century A.D. "at almost all social levels."[27] Such views have been transmitted to those who cannot judge the matter for themselves.[28]

In the case of Roman Italy—a fragment, though an important fragment, of our subject—a somewhat more nuancé opinion has been offered by the palaeographer G. Cavallo.[29] He appears to admit that a

Griechen und Römer (2 ed., Leipzig & Berlin, 1923), 77–78. For the views of E. A. Havelock, who imagines an Athens progressing rapidly from very sparse to very extensive literacy about 430, see below, p. 94 n.135.

22. O. Murray, *Early Greece* (Brighton, 1980), 94, 96.

23. According to P. A. Cartledge, *JHS* xcviii (1978), 28, even "the humblest Spartan ranker" was not illiterate; but in most of the population knowledge of writing remained "rudimentary" (37).

24. J. Marquardt, *Das Privatleben der Römer* (2 ed., Leipzig, 1886), 96.

25. A.-M. Guillemin, *Le public et la vie littéraire à Rome* (Paris, 1937), 77.

26. H. H. Tanzer, *The Common People of Pompeii: A Study of the Graffiti* (Baltimore, 1939), 83.

27. In the *Cambridge History of the Bible* i (Cambridge, 1970), 48.

28. Thus R. Pattison, *On Literacy. The Politics of the Word from Homer to the Age of Rock* (Oxford, 1982), 63, believes that the Romans "engineered a system of mass reading and writing skills."

29. Cavallo in *Alfabetismo* and in M. Vegetti (ed.), *Oralità, scrittura, spettacolo* (Turin, 1983), 173–180 (where the geographical reference is variable but is often to

majority of the population was illiterate, and he gives a markedly low estimate of the level of literacy achieved by women in imperial Italy. Yet at the same time he maintains a studied vagueness about the numerical level of literacy, and he quotes with apparent approval the claims of another scholar that literacy levels were very high.[30]

A clearer and more significant exception to the general consensus is to be found in the work of H. C. Youtie on the Greek papyrus evidence.[31] The special significance of his conclusions is that, unlike almost everything else that can be said about the diffusion of literacy in the ancient world, they are based on a mass of documentation. A large number of miscellaneous papyrus documents from Hellenistic and Roman Egypt—something like 1,500 of them have been printed—mention explicitly that one or more of the principals was illiterate.[32] This evidence also enables us to see in some detail how literates, semi-literates and illiterates functioned in and on the edge of the Greek milieu in Egypt. Hence we may obtain some guidance about how literacy may have worked elsewhere in the Greek world—always, however, with the large proviso that the social structure of Ptolemaic and Roman Egypt was unique, that the Greek population there was to some extent privileged. Youtie concluded that at the level of artisans and farmers the majority of males were illiterate, and also that at this social level literate women were quite unusual. (The problem is that very many indeed of these people had Egyptian as their chief or only spoken language, so that they may well differ, with respect to literacy, from ordinary Greeks and Romans.) Thus the scholar who has published the most detailed research on literacy in this particular milieu is not among those who have given high estimates of the extent of literacy in the Roman world.

Our ability to discover how much literacy there was among the Greeks and Romans may, at first thought, seem slight; and by com-

---

Rome and Italy; he speaks of a high level of literacy, 173, but now recognizes that the majority was illiterate, 174).

30. Cavallo in *Alfabetismo* 121, citing A. Petrucci, *Studi medievali* x.2 (1970), 160, who has often written to a similar effect elsewhere.

31. H. C. Youtie, *Cd'E* lxxxi (1966), 127–143; *HSCPh* lxxv (1971), 161–176; *GRBS* xii (1971), 239–261; *ZPE* xvii (1975), 201–221, xix (1975), 101–108.

32. Unfortunately there has been no catalogue since E. Majer-Leonhard, ΑΓΡΑΜ-ΜΑΤΟΙ. *In Aegypto qui litteras sciverint qui nesciverint ex papyris graecis quantum fieri potest exploratur* (Frankfurt-a.-M., 1913) (530 items). R. Calderini, *Aegyptus* xxx (1950), 17–41, based her article on a catalogue of 556 additional items, which she did not publish.

parison with what can be found out about literacy in some European countries in the sixteenth and seventeenth centuries, not to mention the nineteenth, that is certainly true. But some progress is possible. In the first place, there has never been a determined attempt to collect and analyse the evidence that does exist, except for Athens and Sparta in the classical period and for Graeco-Roman Egypt; and even in these cases there is scope for improvement. A body of evidence exists, most but not all of it textual. Some of it is indirect, notably the evidence about elementary schooling; the implications for literacy of the discoverable facts about ancient schools have not previously been pursued. At all events, a consideration of all the relevant texts, including the papyrus texts, is plainly essential and ought to lead, even by itself, to a rejection of optimistic conclusions.[33]

The volume and variety of the surviving Greek and Latin inscriptions both being enormous, their significance for the history of literacy will be an urgent problem. When a learned periodical asked several scholars how inscriptions might contribute to our knowledge of the extent of literacy in the classical world,[34] most of the answers were vague—not surprisingly, for the matter is very difficult. We shall be considering several cities which harboured numerous inscriptions—classical Athens, imperial Rome, Pompeii—and diverse functions of epigraphical commemoration. Where inscriptions were put up, there was literacy; but how much there was remains to be investigated.[35]

However a type of comparative method is of crucial importance for discovering the extent of ancient literacy. This is not a matter of random embellishments of some otherwise unappealing hypothesis. A train of argument is involved, which in outline runs as follows. Investigation of the volume of literacy in other societies, and in particular of the growth of literacy in early-modern and modern Europe, has shown that writing ceases to be the arcane accomplishment of a small professional or religious or social elite *only* when certain preconditions are fulfilled and *only* when strong positive forces are present

33. Yet lack of awareness of literary texts is certainly not the main source of such views, which derive more from class vision and from the idealization of antiquity.

34. *S & C* v (1981), 265–312.

35. The degree of caution which is appropriate in detecting widespread literacy via inscriptions is suggested by a comparison with Kievan Russia (c. 1050–1200), where S. Franklin recounts that writing was used for a fairly wide variety of purposes, including graffito-writing (*Speculum* lx [1985], esp. 6–7), even though by early-modern or modern standards the level of literacy was obviously very low indeed (cf. Franklin 37).

to bring the change about. Such forces may be economic, social or ideological or any combination of these things. They may even be political, as in Japan after the Meiji Restoration, or in Cuba and Nicaragua, where recent political revolutions, carried through by people holding beliefs about the effects of the spread of literacy, have led to dramatic increases in the numbers of the basically literate. But without these preconditions and without such positive forces, literacy remains a restricted possession—a state of affairs which may seem perfectly acceptable even in a culture which is in a sense penetrated through and through by the written word. The following chapters will show that some of the vital preconditions for wide diffusion of literacy were always absent in the Graeco-Roman world, and that no positive force ever existed to bring about mass literacy.

Though important work had been done earlier, Lawrence Stone's 1969 article about the origins of mass literacy in England seems to have been the first systematic attempt in any country to explain such a phenomenon.[36] He attributed primary importance to three positive factors which at various periods from the sixteenth to the nineteenth century exercised a powerful impetus. One was, unsurprisingly, the invention and diffusion of the printing press; another was Protestantism, especially in its severer forms, with its insistence on the value of private reading of the Bible; another was the demand, created by incipient industrialization, for a more literate workforce. Important secondary factors were several in number. One which may turn out to be relevant in a comparison with the Graeco-Roman world was the willingness of philanthropists, and later of the state, to allocate resources to basic education.[37] The importance of each of these factors has naturally been debated, with the relationship between industrialization and literacy causing especial difficulty.[38] It is not necessary to my ar-

36. Stone, *P & P* xlii (1969), 69–139. He also discusses parallel events in Scotland and France.

37. This is a bald summary which neglects practically all the specific social changes which Stone described. It must also be said that his account varies somewhat from one section to another.

38. On the latter question cf. M. Sanderson, *P & P* lvi (1972), 75–104, and for further discussion and bibliography H. J. Graff, *The Literacy Myth: Literacy and the Social Structure in the Nineteenth-Century City* (New York, 1979), 225–226 = Graff (ed.), *Literacy and Social Development in the West: A Reader* (Cambridge, 1981), 255–256. The debate has been carried on to an excessive degree in terms of short-term effects, and too little attention has been paid to the interrelationship between literacy and the growth of complex commercial and transport systems in the wake of industrialization.

gument that these debates should be settled—though it would certainly be of interest to establish in more detail how far, for instance, an ideological force such as Protestantism can create literacy independently of economic, social and technical developments. It is clear in any case that the general approach is right: only as a result of large-scale positive forces can literacy spread beyond a small minority.

Other studies of the growth of literacy have argued for the importance of various other factors. The rise of mass literacy in eighteenth-century New England, so it has been maintained by a historian with a careful approach to causality, was due in large part to urbanization, or what he prefers to call (since the communities in question were small) "population density." What mattered, he suggests, was not, say, the growth of Boston from a population of 5,000 to 15,000, but the proliferation of small towns with populations in the range 500–1,000—the reason being that such communities made schools available whereas smaller ones did not.[39] In other places, rapid urbanization has sometimes had negative effects on levels of literacy, straining school facilities;[40] but it seems a safe enough generalization that very small settlements and truly rural patterns of living are a hindrance to elementary education and that, as towns form, literacy has at least more of an opportunity.

There was without doubt a vast diffusion of reading and writing ability in the Greek and Roman worlds, and the preconditions and the positive causes of this development can be traced. But there was no mass literacy, and even the level which I have called craftsman's literacy was achieved only in certain limited milieux. The classical world, even at its most advanced, was so lacking in the characteristics which produce extensive literacy that we must suppose that the majority of people were always illiterate. In most places most of the time, there was no incentive for those who controlled the allocation of resources to aim for mass literacy. Hence the institutional lacunae which would have impeded any movement towards mass literacy—above all, the shortage of subsidized schools—were confronted to no more than a slight extent.

39. Lockridge, *Literacy in Colonial New England* 57–71 (where he used the uncomfortable expression "social concentration"), and in *Annales E.S.C.* xxxii (1977), 505 = Graff, *Literacy and Social Development* 186. There was a school law which required every town with fifty families to maintain an elementary school (Lockridge 65–66); the impossibility of such a law anywhere in the ancient world is in itself instructive. In the background was of course the powerful influence of Puritanism.

40. Cf. Stone, *P & P* xlii (1969), 69.

Some helpful preconditions for the spread of literacy were plainly present. The invention of a short but efficient alphabet by certain Phoenicians and Greeks made the tasks of learning to read and write almost as easy as they could be. However, as subsequent events have repeatedly shown, widespread diffusion of this knowledge does not by any means automatically follow; the history of Western culture has passed through many centuries during which hardly anyone learned these skills although they are within the capacity of almost every five-year-old. (Conversely, almost everyone is literate in Japan, in spite of the complexity of its writing system—a fact which should lead us to reflect about what really constitutes an intellectually difficult task.)

The invention of the printing press in fifteenth-century Mainz did not lead to mass literacy in a rapid or simple fashion. However technology which is capable of producing vast numbers of texts at low cost is an essential precondition of a wide diffusion of literacy. In the ancient world this was lacking, notwithstanding the scholar who claimed that many Romans read newspapers.[41] Expert copyists were fast,[42] but the lack of inexpensive (and also of fresh and up-to-date) reading matter greatly limited the possible social range of literacy. How much it did so is a complex question which will recur again and again in this book. Scholars have often asserted, rather vaguely, that ancient cities were full of things to read,[43] and there is some truth in this claim; but it must not lead us to the assumption that the majority of city-dwellers were able to read for themselves (they were all, however, in a position to learn what was written in public), still less to the assumption that they could write. It is also true that by the time of Gutenberg reading and writing had become far commoner than in the early Middle Ages,[44] and literacy had risen far above its nadir of centuries before. In various parts of Europe a process of educational expansion had already been taking place over a period of as much as

41. R. Marichal in *L'écriture et la psychologie des peuples (XXIIᵉ semaine de synthèse)* (Paris, 1963), 208. He also claims that Roman administration was as paper-dominated as ours—which is at least a comprehensible view. The only mass-produced texts of antiquity were coin legends, and perhaps the makers' names on terracotta lamps; the implications of such texts will be discussed in due course.

42. T. Kleberg, *Buchhandel und Verlagswesen in der Antike* (Darmstadt, 1967), 31. The evidence cited is fragile: Mart. ii.1.5.

43. Cf. Tanzer, *Common People of Pompeii* 83; J. Vogt, *RhM* cxvi (1973), 137.

44. On book production in the centuries immediately before printing see, e.g., E. Eisenstein, *The Printing Press as an Agent of Change* (Cambridge, 1979), i.11–16; C. Bozzolo, D. Coq & E. Ornato, *S & C* viii (1984), 129–160. On the growth of education in the same period cf. A. T. Grafton, *JIH* xi (1980–81), 273–275.

three centuries. But no historical culture is known to have achieved more than a rather low level of craftsman's literacy without the printing press.

In antiquity some other technical conditions, though less radically different from those of the early-modern world, made reading and writing quite difficult to put to use. In many places, for large segments of the population, reasonably convenient writing materials were expensive; for the moment it is enough to cite the common use of cumbersome potsherds as evidence that good writing material was scarce. Another convenience the ancients lacked was that of eyeglasses: though optical lenses were not completely unknown in antiquity, those who had poor eyesight from childhood, if they survived at all, would have found that the functions of the written word were limited by that fact: what was written on the wall or on the book-roll might be very hard or impossible to make out.[45]

In every single early-modern or modern country which has achieved majority literacy, an essential instrument has been an extensive network of schools, normally a network of schools subsidized by religion or by the state, or a large-scale literacy campaign effectively sponsored by the state.[46] Naturally some knowledge of a given script can be transmitted with little or no help from schools.[47] Quite a high proportion of a country's literacy can be based on teaching within the family,[48] and we shall have to be alert to the possibility that it was there that

45. Quint. *Inst.* x.3.31 alludes to the difficulty which those with "visus infirmior" might have with waxed tablets, which were a common and relatively cheap writing material.

46. When H. J. Graff (in *Literacy and Social Development* 7) claims that "mass literacy was achieved in Sweden . . . without formal schooling," he is in fact referring to the achievement of mass *reading* ability (see E. Johansson, ibid. 152–154). Even on these terms the case of Sweden and Finland is entirely exceptional, for the government, by the Church Law of 1686 and other regulations, coerced all parents to teach their children to read, for religious reasons. Furthermore, there actually were quite a lot of schools in seventeenth- and eighteenth-century Sweden, as one would expect (Johansson 163 is obscure about this, but see his fig. 8.8, which also shows that majority writing ability came only after 1850 with mass schooling).

47. An instance well known in the literature on literacy is that of the Vai in Liberia, who use their own script as well as arabic and roman; the transmission of Vai script takes place almost entirely outside formal school settings (S. Scribner & M. Cole, *The Psychology of Literacy* [Cambridge, Mass., 1981], 65–68). It reaches some 20% of the adult male population (Scribner & Cole 63), and apparently very few women indeed.

48. Cf. Cipolla, *Literacy and Development* 25; T. W. Laqueur, *Oxford Review of Education* ii (1976), 256–260.

most Greeks and Romans learned to read and write. We must also be on the watch for unfamiliar ways of organizing children's instruction, for instance through part-time or itinerant teachers. Teachers who also had other occupations are in fact occasionally attested under the Roman Empire. But it is a normal and of course expectable feature of peoples who are advancing beyond craftsman's literacy that they should have very many schools, including schools in small settlements. We may cite here, from a plethora of evidence, the large sums of money given to educational foundations in early-modern England,[49] and both seventeenth-century Scottish and eighteenth-century Prussian legislation in favour of compulsory schooling.[50] A historian of literacy in eighteenth-century New England has argued that the growth of mass literacy there was heavily dependent on schooling.[51] Japan, even in the Tokugawa period (1603–1867), had some free education for the poor;[52] but it remained a society with only craftsman's literacy until after the Restoration of 1868, when schools proliferated. In early nineteenth-century Egypt all the important towns had many schools, with some charitable support; the level of male literacy in Cairo was between one-quarter and one-third (which implies a countrywide literacy level below 5%).[53] Majority literacy is perhaps not an utter impossibility without an extensive network of partly subsidized schools; but the onus is heavily on any historian who claims to have unearthed such a phenomenon.

Schools are not always necessary for the teaching of the alphabet, and in these early-modern societies a great deal of literacy was acquired not in schools but in the home. A system of schools is nevertheless crucial, for they vastly reinforce basic literacy as well as spreading it, and they are symptomatic of societies which give high importance to mass education.

The school systems of Graeco-Roman antiquity were for the most part quite puny. By the fifth century B.C. schools had certainly become

49. See Cressy, *Literacy and the Social Order* 164–165, on the period 1500–1659; and Stone, *P & P* lxii (1969), 114–115, for some brief remarks on eighteenth- and early nineteenth-century schools. On the density of schools in France in the sixteenth to eighteenth centuries see R. Chartier, M. M. Compère & D. Julia, *L'éducation en France du XVIme au XVIIIme siècle* (Paris, 1976), 45–85.

50. Cf. Stone 96.

51. Lockridge, *Literacy in Colonial New England* 57–58.

52. By the 1670s: R. P. Dore, *Education in Tokugawa Japan* (London, 1965), 244, etc.

53. G. J. G. de Chabrol de Volvic, in *Description de l'Egypte* xviii (2 ed., Paris, 1826), 62–65.

a commonplace feature of Greek town life, and the schools of such small places as Astypalaea and Mycalessus are vital indications of the condition of Greek culture at that time. There was little if any subsidization of schools (a phenomenon examined more closely in Chapter 4). In the Hellenistic era the more advanced kind of Greek city did in fact try the remarkable innovations of subsidized and even universal education. Such schemes apparently faded away under Roman power, and nowhere, under the Roman Empire, was there any elaborate network of schools. Given the general character of the evidence, it is admittedly hard to be confident that silence reflects a lack of the thing itself; there may, for instance, have been more village schools than the evidence suggests. Schoolmasters were probably paid so badly that elementary education must in many places have been as cheap as unsubsidized schools could be. But the root of the matter is exactly there: subsidies were few for basic education. They were almost entirely limited, as far as we know, to the more civilized and the more fortunate Hellenistic cities.

Cities were a crucial factor in themselves, and K. A. Lockridge's observations about "population density" in New England may turn out to be especially important. At all events it is plain that rural patterns of living are inimical to the spread of literacy. The Greeks and Romans themselves frequently associated ignorance, and specifically illiteracy, with rusticity.[54] The fact that this was a topos need not mean that it was to any serious degree unrealistic. As to how urbanized Greek and Roman populations were in the sense that is relevant here—that is, concentrated in actual physical agglomerations of some size (as distinct from places which merely had the constitutional form of cities)—this is an intractable question, the answer to which will obviously vary a great deal from period to period and from region to region. It could be said that the most important single invention of the classical world was the *polis* (an invention which partly depended, as we shall see, on writing). Throughout antiquity, however, there is no doubt that in general and by nineteenth-century or modern standards a rural pattern of living prevailed.

Whatever the precise effects of industrialization or of such economic changes as the creation of mass markets may have been on literacy at various times during the last two hundred years,[55] it is clear

54. Eur. *Thes.* 382 Nauck; Ps.-Lys. xx.11; Plin. *NH* xxv.6; Plu. *Arist.* 7; Quint. *Inst.* ii.21.16 (where the meaning of *illitteratus* is no doubt simply "uncultivated") (cf. *Inst.* v.11.19); Longus i.8.

55. It might be suggested that the main failure of recent historical writing about

that the structure of the Greek and Roman economy, and the demands of work within that economy, must have had a considerable effect on the level of literacy. The effect may even have been dominant, and it is in danger of being underestimated because the documents, notations, lists, labels and so on of everyday economic life were almost all ephemera which outside Egypt have survived in fairly small numbers.

Once again there were great variations of time and place within the Graeco-Roman world, with regard for example to the amount of trade and the amount of dependent labour. Of course we are bereft of statistics, and even matters of scale are hard to get right. It seems plain that complex commercial relations, especially when carried on over large distances, encourage the use of writing and give a practical value to literacy which it might otherwise lack. What was the scale of long-distance trade in a classical Greek city? Perhaps most of the documentary needs of such trade could be met by the literacy of a small number of specialized slaves. Yet we have reason to believe that many thousands of Athenian citizens were semi-literate (at least) by the time the ostracism law was introduced. It is possible—but not, I think, demonstrable—that they had had economic reasons for learning some reading and writing; Solon's encouragement of technical skills *(technai)* may be relevant here. What *is* practically speaking demonstrable is that no ancient state reached the point of economic complexity, attained when the Industrial Revolution took hold, at which semi-educated masses were thought to be indispensable to the state's economic well-being. Such conditions might in theory not have been far off in a few cities, in imperial Ostia for instance. And the economic affairs of individuals and of partnerships were sometimes complex: the Zeno papyri offer a ready example from the third century B.C.; the administration of any great Roman fortune would offer another. Outside the realm of purely economic activity, some ancient armies, and above all the Roman army under the principate, required at any given time the services of a considerable number of literates.

But we must distinguish between, on the one hand, an economy which provides a certain number of clerical jobs and gives some incentive, though not an overwhelming one, to an artisan or shopkeeper to read and write, and, on the other hand, an economy in which the mass literacy of its workers and its consumers is an integral feature. It

---

literacy has been that it has so far produced no convincing account of the interaction between *economic* change and the rise of either craftsman's literacy or mass literacy.

is obvious that the Greeks and Romans never went beyond the former of these situations. One only has to remember some of the things that were missing to see that there was no structural economic need for really widespread literacy: no printed advertising even of the kind that existed in the eighteenth century, no insurance, no timetables, not to mention "industrialized" written communication itself (which may be considered to have begun with mass circulation of the Bible in the sixteenth century).[56] Furthermore, the Greeks and Romans, like many other peoples, had a more or less constant supply of persons who could act as substitute writers and readers; hence no economic need for an advance beyond a certain level of craftsman's literacy is likely to have made itself felt.

The effects of the economic structure on levels of literacy are further complicated by two important questions which will recur from time to time in the following pages: the ideas of the Greeks and Romans about economic opportunity (and hence also about social mobility), and their attitudes towards child labour. For the moment we may formulate both matters briefly. Did parents expect that sending their children to school or otherwise teaching them to read and write would bring economic benefit? And did they do so at the social level where there was a choice to be made about elementary education? In general the answer to the latter question is likely to be negative; the relative lack of clerical opportunities for the free-born certainly points in that direction. With regard to child labour, little has been written,[57] and the facts are still quite obscure. Children who were slaves often worked from an early age, even five. There is little evidence that the children of the free poor worked, and it may be that in most cases their work was seasonal, part-time, or otherwise sporadic (it was perhaps only the Industrial Revolution which introduced the systematic exploitation of child labour outside the framework of slavery). In those parts of the Greek and Roman world where slaves were numerous, this fact may well have allowed a larger proportion of the children of the free to attend schools than would otherwise have been able to do so. It may be that few free-born children were kept completely out of school by their parents' unwillingness to forgo the results of their work; rather, as often happened in early-modern soci-

56. This is emphatically not to be taken as an endorsement of a primitivist view of the Graeco-Roman economy.

57. The one valuable discussion: K. R. Bradley, *Historical Reflections* xii (1985), 311–330.

eties, school attendance was for many people subordinate to the exigencies of the agricultural calendar.

Even these brief initial speculations about the economic system and its effects on ancient levels of literacy should make it clear that the system differed radically from those which are known to have fostered mass literacy.

Religious reasons have from time to time induced large numbers of people to learn to read. Even before the Reformation, proto-Protestant movements, such as that of the Lollards in England from the 1380s onwards, had some effect in this direction.[58] The scripture-reading requirements of Protestantism without doubt contributed heavily to the early growth of mass literacy in Scotland, New England and Lutheran Germany.[59] Switzerland's Protestant cantons and the Massachusetts Bay Colony made early attempts at introducing universal compulsory education, the latter as early as 1642.[60] The general thesis is scarcely affected if it is true, as has recently been argued, that in Germany the causal relationship between Protestantism and mass literacy was more delayed and more complex than had previously been thought.[61]

Most of those who have analysed this phenomenon have not paid enough attention to the effects on literacy of a certain Protestant tendency to insist on the personal striving of the individual. This notion is not irrelevant to our inquiry here; and we should ask whether any Greek or Roman theories or beliefs might likewise have induced people to learn to read and write. (The effects of early Christianity in this regard will be considered in Chapter 8.) And in fact there did exist a certain Greek notion, which could be called an ideology if only it could be shown that more people consciously subscribed to it, that all citizen males should learn to read and write. Where and when in classical Greece this idea first circulated is a problem to be discussed. It evidently circulated widely in a number of cities in the Hellenistic

58. M. Aston, *History* lxii (1977), esp. 355–356. For similar effects attributed to the Waldensians and the Hussites see H. Hajdu, *Lesen und Schreiben im Spätmittelalter* (Pécs, 1931), 12, 36.

59. Cf. Stone, *P & P* lxii (1969), 76–83; Lockridge, *Literacy in Colonial New England* 49–51, 97–101. The Scandinavian case is similar, though there only mass reading ability resulted.

60. Stone 80.

61. R. Gawthrop & G. Strauss, *P & P* civ (1984), 31–55. They situate the crucial developments in the eighteenth century.

period, eventually receiving an eloquent endorsement from Diodorus Siculus;[62] it lived on, to some extent, under the principate.

The lawgiver Charondas of Catana, says Diodorus, wrote an excellent law which previous lawgivers had neglected:

> He laid down that all the sons of the citizens should learn letters, with the city providing the pay of the teachers; for he assumed that people without means, who could not pay fees on their own, would otherwise be cut off from the finest pursuits. For this lawgiver rated writing [*grammatike*] above other forms of knowledge, and with very good reason . . . For who could compose a worthy encomium of literacy?

The basis and the practical effects of such ideas deserve investigation. Some effects there were, if, as seems likely, it was this factor which led to the known attempts, which took place in four Hellenistic cities, and by implication in a few others, to organize mass education. There were some later echoes, including a particularly clear one in Antonine Lycia. Furthermore, we must presume that this Greek notion had some private effects even when it did not lead to political or philanthropic action; individuals subscribed to it, and some no doubt acted accordingly.

But the force of this idea was never widespread, even among Greeks. It lacked a single clear rationale and was impeded by its failure to become an ideology. Even in Greek cities, where so much was politically disputed, elementary education very seldom seems to have been an important issue.

The available statistics concerning literacy in early-modern and modern times are of considerable importance for our inquiry. Like most social statistics, they are of limited reliability.[63] To obtain accurate statistics about literacy requires, among other things, a sensible definition of what it is and an army of conscientious census-takers. In recent times the United States has lacked both of these prerequisites,[64]

---

62. xii.12–13; more of this passage is quoted below, p. 26.

63. In *International Encyclopedia of the Social Sciences* (New York, 1968) s.v. "literacy," 415–416, H. H. Golden gives a brief account of the difficulties of constructing and of interpreting literacy statistics.

64. The Bureau of the Census attempts to deal with the matter by asking questions in writing. J. Kozol, *Illiterate America* (New York, 1985), 37, summarizes the story: the literacy question was dropped from the 1940 census on the grounds that most people were literate, and when it was reinstated in 1970, "instead of posing ques-

and consequently no one knows how many Americans are illiterate; it is very clear that the number is far higher than the Bureau of the Census has imagined; the only dispute can be about the size of the error.[65] The figures in Table 1 are a sample of the illiteracy rates of various countries and regions in which early-modern conditions have prevailed. In considering them we should take into account not only the backwardness of the places in question, but also their modernity (printing, school systems, and so on) with respect to the world of the Greeks and Romans. Such figures indicate not that the ancients were necessarily less literate than the Moroccans or Tunisians of the mid-twentieth century, but that the onus of proof is upon any scholar who asserts otherwise. The likely overall illiteracy level of the Roman Empire under the principate is almost certain to have been above 90%. Even for the most educated populations—which would mainly have been found, I think, in Greek cities in the fourth to first century B.C.—the range is to be sought, if we include women and country-people, far above 50%. To refine these hypothetical notions is one of the purposes of the following chapters.

Known statistics about literacy invite two further observations highly relevant to the ancient world. One is that we must be careful not to infer from the literacy of a craftsman the general literacy of the poor. Not only is the individual's typicality open to question, but more importantly skilled craftsmen in general are far more literate than the population as a whole. One investigator has estimated, for example, that in England in the period 1580–1700, when it is likely that far fewer than 20% of adults could read and write, goldsmiths were 75% signature-literate and bakers 73%.[66]

The second observation concerns gender. It has been a common fault of scholarly assertions about literacy in the ancient world to pay

---

tions about actual skills, the census simply asked adults how many years of school they had attended." Four grades of schooling were taken as proof of literacy, and, what is more, 80% of those who had *not* completed four grades were presumed to be able to read. On this basis it was announced that 99% of Americans were literate. For further proof of the Bureau's incompetence in this regard see Kozol 37–38; cf. also D. Harman, *Harvard Educational Review* xl (1970), 229–230.

65. For the argument that the number of adult Americans who are "functional" or "marginal" illiterates is "well above one third" see Kozol 8–10. See also R. S. Nickerson, *Visible Language* xix (1985), 312–313.

66. Cressy, *Literacy and the Social Order* 132–133. On literacy by occupation in eighteenth-century France see Chartier, Compère & Julia, *L'éducation en France* 101–105.

Table 1. Estimates of literacy, various countries

Place	Date	Definition of literacy	% illiteracy
Census-derived figures			
Morocco	1960	Able to write	86.2
Tunisia	1961	Able to write	84.5
Algeria	1948	Able to write	82.2
Egypt	1948	Able to write	80.1 [a]
Campania	1871	Able to read	80
Italy	1871	Able to read	69
Lazio	1871	Able to read	68
Greece (over age 65)	1951	Able to write	56.6
Portugal	1950	Able to write	44.1
Historians' estimates			
Russia	1850	Able to read	90–95
Spain	1857	Able to read	75

Sources: Morocco, Tunisia, Algeria, Egypt, Greece and Portugal: UNESCO, *Statistics of Educational Attainment and Illiteracy 1945–1974* (UNESCO Statistical Reports and Studies no. 22, Paris, 1977), table 6. Campania, Italy and Lazio: C. Cipolla, *Literacy and Development in the West* (Harmondsworth, 1969), 19, 127, derived from Italian censuses. Russia and Spain: estimates by Cipolla 115.

a. The true figure is likely to have been somewhat higher: cf. UNESCO, *Statistics* 218.

little or no attention to women. Some recent studies have attempted to rectify this,[67] and the following chapters will pursue the matter further. The point here is that in societies in which illiteracy is widespread, a higher proportion of women than of men is usually illiterate, and in traditional societies the difference can be great. Thus in rural Greece in 1951 the illiteracy rate among males was 14.9%, that among females 49.9%.[68] Greece at that time, however, was a country in rapid transition; more typical of an early-modern setting would be Sicily in 1871, with 79% male and 91% female illiteracy (Sardinia showed 81% and 92%).[69] There is of course no fixed ratio of male to female literacy, and wide variations are possible. When the illiteracy

67. On the literacy of Greek women see S. G. Cole in H. P. Foley (ed.), *Reflections of Women in Antiquity* (New York, 1981), 219–245.

68. UNESCO, *Statistics* 207.

69. Cipolla, *Literacy and Development* 18, from the census. For some similar cases see R. Houston, *Social History* viii (1983), 271–272. Reversals of the general pattern are very few and are probably related to migration: Ireland after 1891 (Cipolla 125), Cuba in 1953 (UNESCO, *Statistics* 159), Jamaica and Martinique in the same period (ibid. 165–166).

level is close to 100%, the ratio may in fact approach 1 : 1.[70] But the general presumption must be that in a world of craftsman's literacy, and certainly in a world of scribal literacy, notably fewer women than men will have been literate. How great the differences between male and female literacy were in various ancient settings will have depended on matters which will be discussed, as far as possible, in subsequent chapters.

How are we to avoid vagueness, in the absence of statistical evidence about Greek and Roman literacy? Literacy does not exist in the abstract, but is closely linked to other features of the social and cultural landscape. We can say that in such-and-such conditions, it is very improbable that a given population reached a level of literacy above 10%, or 25%, or 50%. Without subsidized schools, for example, and without powerful incentives for farmers, artisans and day-labourers to teach their children to read and write, literacy is likely to have remained below a certain level. No one, admittedly, would hypothesize that any particular ancient community was exactly like any statistically better-known modern one. And needless to say, we can reach only approximate conclusions in this fashion—bands of probability within which the truth is likely to fall. Such conclusions will often have to be set about with the scholar's usual adverbs of reservation. But the attempt to hypothesize numerical answers can and should be made.

70. Cf. Cipolla 56n.

2 The Functions of Literacy
in the Graeco-Roman World

Even if we could discover with far greater precision than is actually possible the extent of literacy among the Greeks and Romans, we would still not understand what part the written word played in their lives, or indeed understand fully why literacy reached a certain extent and went no further. We are thus led forward to a new set of questions.

These questions concern the circumstances in which the Greeks and Romans made use of the written word, and hence the functions of literacy. To what extent and in what circumstances did people cease to rely on oral communication or come to rely on the written word? The question can be applied to many different spheres of life—to literature and law, but also to historical memory, political propaganda, estate management, and military organization, to name only some of them. Modern discussion of this matter has concentrated on poetic composition, understandably; though there has been a certain amount of attention paid to other facets of the problem, such as the intermingling of oral and written legal procedures. One aim of this book is to sketch at least a rough initial map of what people did with writing; the detailed cartography of the subject will only be possible later.

Beyond the functions of literacy in Greek and Roman antiquity there lie still further questions about the extent to which Greek and Roman ways of thinking about the world became literate or remained oral. How did the use of writing influence patterns of thought? No one knows, and hardly anyone claims to know. On this great question of cultural history, the partial emergence of a literate culture and the partial eclipse of an oral culture, this study makes no claim to be systematic or comprehensive; nevertheless some suggestions will be advanced.

A few ancient texts enumerate some of the functions of the written word. In a brief aside in the *Politics* Aristotle divides the useful functions of "letters" into four categories: moneymaking, household management, instruction *(mathesis)*, and civic activities.[1] The passage of Diodorus quoted earlier justifies as follows the high importance he attaches to literacy:

> it is by means of this that the most important and the most useful of life's business is completed—votes, letters, testaments *[diathekai]*, laws, and everything else which puts life on the right track. For who could compose a worthy encomium of literacy? For it is by means of writing alone that the dead are brought to the minds of the living, and it is through the written word that people who are spatially very far apart communicate with each other as if they were nearby. As to treaties made in time of war between peoples or kings, the safety *[asphaleia]* provided by the written word is the best guarantee of the survival of the agreement. Generally it is this alone which preserves the finest sayings of wise men and the oracles of the gods, as well as philosophy and all of culture *[paideia]*, and hands them on to succeeding generations for all time. Therefore, while it is true that nature is the cause of life, the cause of the *good* life is education based on the written word.[2]

This is a suggestive account of some of the more grandly positive functions which Greek writing fulfilled. Of course it is far indeed from being exhaustive. In the chapters which follow we shall examine the functions of literacy in each period, under the general headings of economic and legal functions (the world of work), civic functions, religious functions, commemoration of various kinds, the transmission of literature, and letter-writing. The functions of writing in the process of schooling itself will also require some attention.

Writing was used for the following purposes, though some of them could be achieved without it. In almost every case there are two sides to the coin, usefulness to the writer and to the reader:

to indicate ownership
to maintain accounts
to make offers of sale by means of signs
to provide receipts
to label commodities or products
to indicate weights or measures
to make contracts

1. *Pol.* viii.3.1338a15–17: χρήσιμον—ὥσπερ τὰ γράμματα πρὸς χρηματισμὸν καὶ πρὸς οἰκονομίαν καὶ πρὸς μάθησιν καὶ πρὸς πολιτικὰς πράξεις πολλάς.
2. xii.13, here translated freely.

to write letters
to give instructions to a subordinate
to make notes of useful information for oneself
to make wills

to record treaties
to state statute law
to issue an edict
to display political slogans
to put legends on coins
to cast a vote
to record trial proceedings
to record the proceedings of officials
to compile military records
to compile lists of demesmen, citizens, etc.
to record an award of citizenship
to record manumissions
to declare a birth or death
to record the names of magistrates
to apply to or petition authority
to answer petitions
to announce entertainments

to honour a distinguished person
to commemorate one's presence
to memorialize the dead

to dedicate something to a god
to publicize a religious calendar
to record prayers
to circulate prophecies
to record a magic spell
to curse someone
to transmit a sacred story

to transmit works of literature
to transmit compendia of information (textbooks and such)
to perform school exercises

This list is certainly not an exhaustive one either, but it probably covers the great majority of what was written down in antiquity.[3]

3. As far as epigraphical uses are concerned, M. Guarducci, *Epigrafia greca* ii–iv (Rome, 1969–1978), provides an exceptionally full catalogue.

Any list of this kind necessarily has some artificiality about it, and we shall have to counterbalance that by asking at appropriate moments how deeply embedded acts of reading and writing were in people's lives, and how authoritative the written word had become.

By using such examples as votes and treaties, Diodorus shows that he realizes that much more may be involved in the use of a written text than a wish to communicate the surface message across time or space. Other needs, solemnity for example, may lead to the decision to put the message into writing. As we shall see, one purpose of written ballots was in effect *non*-communication—replacing public voting with secret voting. The message communicated may in many circumstances be different from the apparent one, perhaps most obviously when the author is implicitly making some claim to political power or social status. Speculating about the "real" message which a given written text contained has its dangers, but there is also the opposite danger of ignoring powerful motives which gave rise to texts. A written text may have a partly or largely symbolic function, as has recently been argued for the inscriptions recording the acts of the Arval Brothers.[4] It may invoke the prestige which goes with written expression or at least with some forms of it, rather as a painting or relief which shows someone in the act of reading or writing may tap this same prestige. Writing, it has been well said, possesses an "inherent dignity, born of its challenge to time,"[5] and without doubt this was widely felt in antiquity. We shall have to consider this problem with regard to texts as diverse as the fifth-century Athenian tribute lists (a declaration of political power by the Athenian citizens, as well as a public accounting by the responsible officials?), the painted electoral propaganda of first-century Pompeii (in some cases it was curious propaganda—for there could be no competitors), and Roman epitaphs whose authors seem in general eager to emphasize social distinctions.

We shall be asking what lay behind such acts of writing, what the purpose of the writer was, or of the person or persons who commissioned the writer. Since the twentieth century is among other things the century of organized lying and the organized misuse of both written and spoken language, we ought perhaps to be skilled at analysing the functions of the written word. The two generations of in-

4. M. Beard, *PBSR* liii (1985), 114–162.
5. R. Pattison, *On Literacy. The Politics of the Word from Homer to the Age of Rock* (Oxford, 1982), 37.

tense philosophizing about language which started with Wittgenstein might have helped. But in the event historians and anthropologists seem not to have written much about the symbolic use of written language.[6] We shall be moving across imperfectly charted waters.

The written word could be employed by a person who wished to practise magic, and we may feel a temptation to attribute to the Greeks and Romans a feeling that magical or quasi-magical force sometimes attached to other uses of the written word.[7] However it would be far-fetched to see anything magical in most uses of writing, and here again we shall be faced with the recurrent problem of giving the correct weight to a factor which has never been fully investigated.[8]

It is a commonplace in some scholarly circles that the Greek and Roman worlds always remained highly dependent, by modern standards, on oral communication; this was true not only in the archaic periods of Greece and Rome but even in the cities of classical and Hellenistic Greece and even in the most advanced cities of the high Roman Empire. For clear and vivid illustration we need only compare ancient forms of political persuasion, which involved above all the political speech, with the heavy use of written propaganda in the era just before we were invaded by electronic methods of influencing opinion. The diffusion of literature is another important example; as we shall see, it always remained more oral than is generally realized. And the vast majority of the population made its living with little or no use, even indirect use, of pieces of writing.

Thus the written word always remained less vital to the individual than in practically any early-modern culture—not to mention the modern world. Even though literacy was always, from early in Greek and Roman history, virtually universal among the men who made up

6. The most interesting single study of such matters by a historian is M. T. Clanchy, *From Memory to Written Record: England, 1066–1307* (Cambridge, Mass., 1979); cf. also B. V. Street, *Literacy in Theory and Practice* (Cambridge, 1984), 84–86. One claim which is plainly *not* true is that "writing is always a kind of imitation talking" (W. J. Ong, *Orality and Literacy. The Technologizing of the Word* [London, 1982], 102): this ceases to be valid as soon as people begin to take advantage of the durability of the written word.

7. Unusually explicit, but all the same suggestive, is a text of about 675–650 B.C. which is scratched on an aryballos from Cumae: ὸς δ'ὰν με κλεφσει θυφλος ἐσται, "whoever steals me will be blind" (*IG* xiv.865 = L. H. Jeffery, *The Local Scripts of Archaic Greece* [Oxford, 1961], 240 no. 3).

8. For an account of the magical use of writing in ancient cultures other than those of Greece and Rome see G. van der Leeuw, *Phänomenologie der Religion* (2 ed., Tübingen, 1956), 494–503.

the political and social elite, most people could live out their lives, if they were content to do so, without the use of reading or writing.

It may be symptomatic of this state of affairs that literacy and illiteracy often go unnoticed or unemphasized in Greek and Roman contexts in which we might expect one or the other to be mentioned. The democratic politicians of classical Athens showed no interest in mass education, as far as we know. A rustic such as the one who appears in Theophrastus' *Characters* would commonly have been illiterate, but the detail is not added.[9] In Lucretius' account of the invention of culture, little attention is given to the art of writing.[10] The occasions when Greek and Roman writers refer to the disadvantages or demerits of illiteracy are, it may be thought, surprisingly rare. Even when Diodorus does refer to its disadvantages, he says that the illiterate are cut off from "the noblest pursuits"[11]—not from enjoying their rights or making their livings.

Several facts about the Graeco-Roman world mitigated the need for personal reading and writing. One was the *strength of ancient memories*.[12] For the "Egyptian" myth which Plato makes Socrates tell to Phaedrus is generally thought to correspond to the truth: writing brings not improved memory but forgetfulness, by providing the literate with an external device to rely on.[13] Caesar agreed with the Platonic Socrates: in his ethnographic remarks about Gaul he says in effect that literacy tends to weaken memory.[14] What suggested to Plato that writing has this effect we unfortunately do not know, and the claim was a polemical one; but living in (or having lived in) a period when the use of writing was expanding, he may have had some

9. Theophr. *Char.* 4.

10. He simply says "nec multo priu' sunt elementa reperta," v.1445. There were numerous opinions about who the inventor had been: see F. Dornseiff, *Das Alphabet in Mystik und Magie* (2 ed., Leipzig & Berlin, 1925), 5–9; L. H. Jeffery in *Europa. Festschrift für Ernst Grumach* (Berlin, 1967), 152–166; and we can add that several aretalogies of Isis claim part of the honour for her: see Y. Grandjean, *Une nouvelle arétalogie d'Isis à Maronée* (Leiden, 1975), 75.

11. Diod.Sic. xii.12.4.

12. On this topic cf. J. A. Notopoulos, *TAPhA* lxix (1938), 465–493 (not always convincing).

13. Pl. *Phaedr.* 274c–275b. On the importance of memory in Plato's thought see M. Bretone, *Quaderni di storia* xx (1984), 223–231. Plato's criticisms of writing go beyond this factor, as we shall see.

14. Caes. *BG* vi.14.4: "quod fere plerisque accidit ut praesidio litterarum diligentiam in perdiscendo ac memoriam remittant"; but perhaps he simply took this from Plato.

real information. It is not, incidentally, clear whether he had specific memory functions in mind (the main memory feat discussed in the *Phaedrus* is the literate Phaedrus' attempt to learn by heart an essay written by Lysias).

There is after all a very great difference in practice, whatever the psychological foundations of the fact may be, between the ability to learn a continuous text by heart and the ability to recall needed information.[15] Dramatic memory feats tend, for obvious reasons, to concern the memorization of texts or lists. That the kind of information recall which does *not* depend on the remembering of a continuous text is as a rule stronger in non-literate cultures is an assumption which is in need of some empirical testing. Some recent work suggests that the acquisition of literacy does not, in the short term anyway, impair this kind of memory.[16] But the assertion made by Socrates and Caesar is not to be discarded lightly; and, as we shall shortly see, there is other evidence in its favour.

At all events there is reason to believe that non-literate cultures are characterized by people with remarkably capacious and tenacious memories for continuous texts. Tahiti provides a clear instance: the language was not written down until 1805, and some of the earliest Tahitians who learned to read and write are said, for example, to have known by heart entire books of the New Testament.[17]

The topic of memory feats is naturally obscured by exaggerations. We can believe without much difficulty that the sophist Hippias could repeat fifty names after hearing them only once.[18] But when Pliny asserts that L. Scipio (presumably the consul of 190) knew the names of the entire Roman people—which would have meant nearly a quarter

15. Cf. Marrou, *Histoire* 99. On the psychology of memory see esp. M. M. Gruneberg, P. E. Morris & R. N. Sykes (eds.), *Practical Aspects of Memory* (London, 1978), and the journal *Memory and Cognition*.

16. S. Scribner & M. Cole, *The Psychology of Literacy* (Cambridge, Mass., 1981), 124–126, 221–233.

17. G. Duverdier, *Revue française d'histoire du livre* xlii (1971), 43–44, taking the fact from the missionary William Ellis (*Polynesian Researches, during a Residence of Nearly Six Years in the South Sea Islands* [London, 1829], ii.20), who, however, does not provide circumstantial detail. Prodigious powers of recall became something of a commonplace in ethnographic literature; cf. S. Gandz, *Osiris* vii (1939), 305–306. Concerning the supposedly accurate oral transmission of the Vedas see Ong, *Orality and Literacy* 65–66; Street, *Literacy in Theory and Practice* 98. Powerful memories among the sixteenth-century Incas: A. Seppilli, *La memoria e l'assenza. Tradizione orale e civiltà della scrittura nell'America dei Conquistadores* (Bologna, 1979), 57–63.

18. Pl. *Hipp.Mai.* 285e.

of a million names—and that Charmadas recited by heart any book in "the libraries,"[19] something has gone wrong. He also lists Cyrus (who knew the names of all his soldiers); Cineas, the representative of Pyrrhus (who knew the names of all the senators and knights of Rome within a day of arriving there); and Mithridates (who addressed his subjects in their twenty-two different languages). It is apparent, and significant, that Pliny knew of many other memory feats besides those he describes,[20] and significant too that he regarded memory as a serious field of endeavour worth including in his anthropology.[21]

What day-to-day reality lay behind all this is hard to tell. It is likely that during most of antiquity one was considered to know a text by heart even if, by modern standards, one's memory of it was inexact; so much we might infer from the inexactness of ancient methods of quotation.[22] But respect for memory was deeply entrenched in Greek culture, as Hesiod illustrates by making Mnemosyne one of the daughters of the primaeval union between Heaven and Earth; she in turn united with Zeus and gave birth to the Muses.[23] Greek and Roman education laid heavy stress on learning things by heart.[24] The schoolchildren of some Hellenistic cities competed for memorization prizes,[25] and the elder Seneca boasts that as a schoolboy he had been able to repeat in order a list of 2,000 names which had been read to him and

19. Plin. *NH* vii.88–89. Other sources on memory feats: Xen. *Symp.* iii.5–6 (Niceratus could recite the entire *Iliad* and *Odyssey*); Pl. *Menex.* 236bc; Cic. *Tusc. Disp.* i.59; Sen. *Contr.* i praef. 18–19; etc. Cf. E. Wüst in *RE* (1932) s.v. "Mnemnonik," cols. 2264–65.

20. "Memoria necessarium maxime vitae bonum cui praecipua fuerit haud facile dictu est tam multis eius gloriam adeptis": vii.88.

21. For feats of text memorization attributed to early Christians see below, p. 301.

22. On methods of quotation see provisionally W. C. Helmbold & E. N. O'Neil, *Plutarch's Quotations* (Baltimore, 1959), viii–ix. That modern exactness was not required fits the fact that the illiterate Yugoslav epic singer Demo Zogić told an informant that he had repeated "the same song, word for word" when in a literal sense he had done nothing of the kind; A. B. Lord, *The Singer of Tales* (Cambridge, Mass., 1960), 27; cf. 119. In oral cultures memory tends to lack verbal exactness, according to Ong, *Orality and Literacy* 60–66.

23. *Theog.* 135, 53–54. In Hesiod and Homer invocations of the Muses commonly occur when the poet requires a quantity of "catalogue" material: W. W. Minton, *TAPhA* xci (1960), 293.

24. Cf. Pl. *Protag.* 325e, *Laws* vii.809–811 ("learning whole poets by heart"), Ps.-Plu. *De lib.educ.* 13 = *Mor.* 9ef.

25. Cf. Marrou, *Histoire* 252.

to repeat in reverse order more than 200 single lines of poetry.[26] A Greek writer under the Roman Empire could see the training of memory as the main aim of early education.[27] In particular it was always important for an orator to be able to commit his oration to memory, and as is well known a set of specialized techniques was devised—initially, so it was believed, by Simonides of Ceos—which enabled him to do this.[28] There is something too to be learned from the famous story of how the Athenians won favours or freedom from their Syracusan captors by reciting passages from Euripides; presumably they had to manage more than a phrase or two. Plutarch adds to this a similar story about how some men from Caunus gained entry to the harbour of Syracuse.[29] (It is the fame of Euripides at Syracuse and Caunus which is really remarkable here.)

However all the memory champions just mentioned were literate, and what matters more in the present context is the memory of the illiterate and of the semi-literate. There is at least some reason to suppose that such people were better than the literate at making written records superfluous. Plato says so, and comparative evidence supports him. Clearly there were limits to the retentive powers of illiterate memories, and a recent study has argued that when a pre-literate population learns reading and writing, one of the advantages which it reaps is that people find it much easier to make lists and tables.[30] It is evident that there is some truth in this, but on the other hand the taste for catalogues of information which is visible in some of the Greek writers who without much doubt come closest to reflecting a pre-literate world—Hesiod, Homer and Herodotus—should warn us not to underestimate the ability of the illiterate to list things and to remember lists.[31]

The individual's need to know how to read and write was also diminished by the fact that illiterates and semi-literates were often

26. Sen. *Contr.* i praef. 2.

27. Ps.-Plu. l.c.

28. See F. A. Yates, *The Art of Memory* (London, 1966), 1–49.

29. Satyrus *Vita Eur.* 39.xix (p. 75 Arrighetti), Plu. *Nic.* 29.

30. J. Goody, *The Domestication of the Savage Mind* (Cambridge, 1977), esp. 82–111, thinking primarily of pre-Greek literacy in the Near East. I. M. Lonie, in F. Lasserre & P. Mudry (eds.), *Formes de pensée dans la collection hippocratique* (Geneva, 1983), 150–152, extends to the Hippocratic writings the theory that lists are especially characteristic of literate culture.

31. For other lists put together in the earliest period of Greek writing see W. Schmid & O. Stählin, *Geschichte der griechischen Literatur* i.1 (Munich, 1929), 661.

able to make use of or benefit from the written word *through inter-mediaries*. This was an utterly commonplace occurrence among the Greeks and Romans, as indeed in many other societies with low levels of literacy.[32]

It could happen in many different ways, from having legal and business documents written or read by others on one's behalf, to asking a bystander to read or explain an inscription, to listening to a speech or recitation given by someone who was himself relying on a written text. The papyri offer plentiful examples of the first of these three situations, and we can sometimes follow in considerable detail the documentary lives of illiterate individuals. Aurelius Sakaon of Theadelphia, for instance (who will make an appearance in Chapter 8), a well-to-do villager explicitly attested as illiterate, was well acquainted with ways of exploiting paperwork. An illiterate individual might easily be involved with several different pieces of writing in the same transaction, as for instance in a case in which an illiterate policeman in Roman Egypt declared in writing that he had posted up an edict of the Prefect of Egypt at a certain place.[33]

The inhabitants of Graeco-Roman Egypt who were compelled, or who wished, to produce documents even though they were illiterate were studied in some detail by H. C. Youtie, who was so struck by their ability to lead full and untroubled lives that he perhaps somewhat underestimated the risks and disadvantages of illiteracy.[34] It did after all compel people to depend, in their written transactions, on the honesty of others. Youtie showed that in Egypt they preferred on the whole to find surrogates among their close relatives, and that they turned to public scribes when literate relatives or friends were not available. No doubt the same happened elsewhere. Of course none of this means that very large numbers of people made use of documents through intermediaries; the practice was simply a mitigation.

"What does it say?" A person who asked this question about a public inscription in an ancient town could expect to find someone who would answer. This may be what is happening in the genre painting

32. E.g., Clanchy, *From Memory to Written Record* 2, observes of mediaeval England that "those who used writing participated in literacy, even if they had not mastered the skills of a clerk." Charlemagne and William of Normandy are simply the most famous of the early-mediaeval rulers who were illiterate or semi-literate. By the second half of the thirteenth century, peasants made at least some use of charters for conveying property to each other (Clanchy 34).

33. *P.Fayum* 24.

34. H. C. Youtie, *ZPE* xvii (1975), 201–221.

from the house of Iulia Felix at Pompeii in which men are reading a text displayed in the forum while others stand by (see Figure 7). In any case this must have been a commonplace scene in Mediterranean cities, where men spent a lot of time in outdoor public spaces. Here there would be discussion among both the literate and the illiterate about the import of inscribed or posted texts; here there were scribes plying their trade for the benefit of those who could not write properly for themselves. Even in private, there could be intermediaries: a schooled family member could help one who was unschooled (papyrus texts confirm that it was not unusual for literacy and illiteracy to exist side by side in the same family).

Most of this "second-hand" literacy depended on the honesty, but also on the helpfulness or the didacticism, of other humans; sometimes it simply depended on their doing their jobs. Almost needless to say, society did practically nothing to protect the ignorant from the consequences of being illiterate (Roman law eventually did give a little protection).[35] And although the wish to understand something written and the will to make use of documents can come to a person who is illiterate, they do not come automatically to those who live in a semi-literate culture. So there were palliatives for illiteracy, but their effectiveness was limited.

Meanwhile speeches and recitations, like performances of plays, transferred thoughts from the written page to the listener. In a Greek city there was plenty to listen to, and a Roman city normally had a theatre as well as a forum and other public and private spaces which could be used for talk. But there were severe limitations of space and time:[36] if you did not see *Oedipus Tyrannus* on its first day, you would wait a long time to see it again. If you lived in Capua, it was not easy to attend a *contio* in Rome. Furthermore, and very important, the majority of Greeks and Romans lived in villages or otherwise in the countryside.

The Greek and Roman elites always, after the archaic periods, made extensive use of writing, and indeed their world was defined by

35. *Dig.* xxii.6, "De iuris et facti ignorantia," still offers little comfort to those suffering from ignorance of the law. Cf. T. Mommsen, *Römisches Strafrecht* (Leipzig, 1899), 92–94. In the nature of things there is little testimony about frauds perpetrated on the illiterate (*P.Oxy.* i.71 is a petition to the Prefect of Egypt which complains of such a fraud).

36. As M. Stubbs remarks (*Language and Literacy. The Sociolinguistics of Reading and Writing* [London, 1980], 13), listeners, unlike readers, "have to understand in real time."

it. It is nonetheless also true that they retained a strong element of orality in their lives.[37] By this I do not mean that they relied heavily on the spoken word in their daily lives—for how could they avoid doing so, or how could we?[38] I mean that they relied on the spoken word for purposes which in some other cultures have been served by the written word. They frequently dictated letters instead of writing them for themselves; they listened to political news rather than reading it; they attended recitations and performances, or heard slaves reading, without having to read literary texts for themselves; and so on. Did this have any effect on the semi-literate and illiterate? The fact that politics, for instance, were carried on so extensively through the spoken word may have been an additional palliative of illiteracy.

It may appear from my earlier reference to those who have given high estimates of ancient literacy as "optimistic" that I have already judged the effects of literacy and illiteracy. The term is used partly for convenience, but it does indeed reflect my opinion about the overall effects of literacy on the Greeks and Romans. The effects and implications of literacy are, however, a very controversial matter.

Literacy is not idolized or idealized in this book, and it will emerge in considerable detail in the following chapters that writing was often an instrument of power (which does not automatically make it evil). It sometimes resulted in forms of lying, obfuscation and conservatism unknown to pre-literate cultures. By helping to undermine a traditional culture of an essentially oral kind, literacy may undeniably lead towards a relatively "modern" world which contains its own forms of exploitation.[39] On the levels of social, political and economic organization, it is fairly plain, literacy has its victims as well as its beneficiaries. But there are beneficiaries, and for the individual Greek and Roman, in spite of all that has been said in this chapter, it was an important positive accomplishment. Yet the belief that literacy is beneficial is very far from universal among contemporary scholars—indeed, it is under assault. The origins of this negative view are worth investigating.

37. The practice of reading out loud was one manifestation of this. For differing views of how extensive this was see esp. J. Balogh, *Philologus* lxxxii (1927), 84–109, 202–240; B. M. W. Knox, *GRBS* ix (1968), 421–435 (even the latter agrees that books were normally read aloud).

38. The error of supposing that the spoken word somehow loses importance in a literate world is nicely satirized by Pattison, *On Literacy* 24–25, in a chapter which puts forward a definition of literacy which is not a definition at all.

39. Cf. Clanchy, *From Memory to Written Record* 264, summarizing his work on Norman England.

The first mention of writing in European literature, in the *Iliad*, represents it as doing harm by bringing about the death of Bellerophon, and writing continued to have sinister associations.[40] The classic critique of literacy itself is the one in the *Phaedrus*, though this did not prevent Plato from showing a quite conventional attitude towards literacy in the educational programme set forth in the *Laws*.[41] In any case the notion that the spread of literacy might have negative effects on an individual or a community, or that the lack of it was a matter of indifference, had only very slight circulation among writers who survive from antiquity. It apparently gained some strength with modern interest in and idealization of primitive cultures. The earliest text known to me in which illiteracy has positive associations is Gonzalo's idealistic speech in *The Tempest* (1611):

> I´ th´ commonwealth I would by contraries
> execute all things: for no kind of traffic
> would I admit; no name of magistrate;
> letters should not be known; riches, poverty,
> and use of service, none . . .[42]

In *Gulliver's Travels* (1726) Swift describes a race more civilized than man, the Houyhnhnms, and the fact that—being horses—they are necessarily illiterate does no harm.[43]

But even the "natural" education of Emile led to his being able to read and write "perfectly" by the age of ten, however reluctant Rousseau was to let his charge have anything to do with books.[44] And until the twentieth century most of the not inconsiderable hostility to the mass diffusion of literacy came from those who thought that its diffusion would hurt their interests by causing expense or social unrest.[45] Conservative opponents of mass education believed that they

40. See below, p. 48.

41. Cf. Pl. *Laws* vii.809e–810b.

42. II.i.143–147. Perhaps Verg. *Georg.* ii.502, where it is specified that the blessed country-dweller has not seen the "insanum . . . forum aut populi tabularia," lies behind this.

43. *Gulliver's Travels,* part IV, chaps. iii and ix. The fact that mass education might be a threat to property and to religious orthodoxy had already been noticed before this date: cf. L. Stone, *P & P* xlii (1969), 84–85.

44. J.-J. Rousseau, *Emile,* trans. A. Bloom (New York, 1979), 117: "I am almost certain that Emile will know how to read and write perfectly before the age of ten, precisely because it makes very little difference to me that he knows how before fifteen."

45. Cf. Stone 88–89.

were withholding something which was in itself useful or desirable. With the advent of the Malinowski-Mead period of anthropology, however, admiration for what was tribal, primitive, remote, began to take on more extreme forms among intellectuals. From this point of view D. H. Lawrence denounced the dissemination of the written word:

> "we really can prevent [our children's] eating much more of the tissues of leprosy, newspapers and books . . . The great mass of humanity should never learn to read and write—never." [46]

Such were the words of one of the most humane men of his age.

Some thirty years later, in *Tristes Tropiques,* Lévi-Strauss described the use made of writing by an illiterate petty chief among the Nambikwara in the Mato Grosso. [47] He also took the opportunity to reflect more generally about the functions of literacy in the history of civilization:

> The only phenomenon with which writing has always been concomitant is the creation of cities and empires, that is the integration of large numbers of individuals into a political system, and their grading into castes or classes . . . it seems to have favoured the exploitation of human beings rather than their enlightenment. . . . My hypothesis, if correct, would oblige us to recognize the fact that the primary function of written communication is to facilitate slavery. [48]

The validity of the brilliant passage from which this is taken will require further discussion; for the moment it is enough to point out that it contains a degree of confusion between societal conditions in which a few use writing (or, as in the case of the Nambikwara, pseudo-writing) to impose their will on the majority, and conditions of mass literacy, in which the masses may indeed be manipulated via the written word, [49] but in which the ordinary human has at least a chance of exercising some mental, economic, and even political independence.

In recent times a number of writers have maintained that literacy in itself does not necessarily bring any benefits to those who possess it

46. *Fantasia of the Unconscious* (New York, 1922), 116.

47. C. Lévi-Strauss, *Tristes Tropiques,* trans. J. & D. Weightman (London, 1973), 296–297, 300.

48. Ibid. 299.

49. For Lévi-Strauss (300) the things that come with mass education are conscription and proletarianization.

(and it will readily be agreed that there is nothing automatic about its benefit to the individual). Two main lines of argument are involved which have relevance for antiquity. The first, which is closely related to Lévi-Strauss's view, claims that literacy serves as an instrument of "social and cultural control and hegemony."[50] The use of writing as a means of exercising power has been widely noticed. Written laws and administrative paperwork can in various ways assist men of power who know how to make use of them. Another facet of the subject is the religious one: since early in the history of writing the gods have been imagined as expressing their authority by means of the written word.[51] Over and over again "divine" ordinances have assumed written form; Moses is simply the most famous "intermediary." Zeus acquired writing-tablets soon after the Greeks. What this means is that men who claimed religious authority employed the reality or the image of the written word to enhance their authority.

It could be argued, furthermore, that writing encourages a sort of canonization of discourse. When the *Iliad* and the *Odyssey* took on written form, they became among other things a training ground where one generation of Greeks formed the character of the next until the end of antiquity; the *Aeneid* eventually filled the same role for the Romans. Here, it could certainly be said, were written texts which became instruments of cultural hegemony (a Greek who did not know Homer to some degree would undoubtedly have been regarded as uncouth by some of his fellow-citizens). But were these not rather mild "instruments of hegemony"?

That in fact is just the weakness of this kind of argument: what is hegemonic or exploitative merges imperceptibly into what is an instrument of social discipline, and that in turn into what is benign. Writing makes empires possible, indeed; only the Incas are known to have created one without it, and they could hardly have maintained their dominion without an elaborate form of mnemonic device, the *quipu*.[52] Writing was also vital to the development of the city; but are we to say that the city has been mainly a source of exploitation? There is also complexity in the notion of cultural hegemony: a canon of

50. H. J. Graff in Graff (ed.), *Literacy and Social Development in the West: A Reader* (Cambridge, 1981), 4.

51. Cf. J. Goody in D. Tannen (ed.), *Spoken and Written Language: Exploring Orality and Literacy* (Norwood, N.J., 1982), 211.

52. J. V. Murra, *Formaciones económicas y políticas del mundo andino* (Lima, 1975), 243–254; M. & R. Ascher, *Code of the Quipu: A Study in Media, Mathematics, and Culture* (Ann Arbor, 1981).

texts may do good as well as harm, at least if the canon is not too impermeable and the texts are not too inaccessible. To these matters we shall return.

The second main line of argument is that literacy contributes far less than has often been supposed to the development of advanced culture in general and in particular to the development of logical, critical and historical modes of thinking, whether on the part of previously non-literate cultures or on the part of illiterate individuals within literate cultures. There is a marked polarity between those scholars who have argued that literacy was responsible for vast changes in Greek intellectual culture—most conspicuously E. A. Havelock and J. Goody[53]—and those who have denied that it had any such effects. This problem will be discussed in Chapters 3 and 4, and again at the end of the book (to deal with it in full would require an entire new intellectual history of the classical world). On the one side it has been maintained that writing made it possible for the Greeks to organize city-states; furthermore, that it enabled them, perhaps even led them, to develop a critical attitude by allowing them to set assertions and theories side by side for comparison. Philosophical and scientific advance followed. Writing also enabled the laws to be posted in public, and by this and other means encouraged the spread of democracy. A critical attitude, coupled with an accumulation of facts about the past embodied in written records, led to the development of historiography. Literacy, in other words,

> made it possible to scrutinise discourse . . . this scrutiny favoured the increase in scope of critical activity, and hence of rationality, scepticism, and logic . . . It increased the potentialities of criticism because writing laid out discourse before one's eyes in a different kind of way; at the same time [it] increased the potentiality for cumulative knowledge . . . No longer did the problem of memory storage dominate man's intellectual life.[54]

53. See esp. E. A. Havelock, *Preface to Plato* (Cambridge, Mass., 1963), *The Origins of Western Literacy* (Toronto, 1976), *The Literate Revolution in Greece and Its Cultural Consequences* (Princeton, 1982) (mainly a reprint of his earlier work); J. Goody & I. Watt, *CSSH* v (1962–63), 304–345, reprinted in J. Goody (ed.), *Literacy in Traditional Societies* (Cambridge, 1968), 27–68; Goody, *Domestication* (cf. *The Logic of Writing and the Organization of Society* [Cambridge, 1986]). The response of classicists has consisted mainly of justifiably severe reviews of Havelock's work (e.g., F. Solmsen, *AJPh* lxxxvii [1966], 99–105; F. D. Harvey, *CR* xxviii [1978], 130–131).

54. Goody, *Domestication* 37.

Such woolly and grandiose thoughts have led to the charge of "technological determinism" and other negative reactions. According to one recent writer, "writing did not make the Greek mind skeptical, logical, historical, or democratic. Instead it furnished an opportunity for these predispositions to flourish."[55] This author then turns to the necessarily difficult task of showing that these predispositions were already flourishing in Greece when people began to write. Did the Homeric Odysseus scrutinize language in a critical fashion? And, if so, what does that mean? Another critic, observing the great importance which some discussions of the effects of literacy have attributed to the case of classical Greece, has challenged Havelock and Goody in somewhat more detail,[56] maintaining that literacy had little effect on the Greeks. Unfortunately, the argument is conducted in such an amateurish fashion that its force is lost.[57]

The reaction of a historian faced with claims such as those of Havelock and Goody is likely to be a desire for detail. If the Greeks became more rational, sceptical and logical under the influence of literacy, how did this tendency manifest itself? What exactly was the role that writing played in the emergence of the *polis?* What were the "democratic" practices or beliefs which supposedly resulted from the spread of literacy? Furthermore, we want to know who was involved: which social groups or social classes took part in these momentous changes? These are complex questions, and the role of other historical causes besides the spread of literacy obviously has to be considered carefully. One writer has pleasingly observed that the acquisition of literacy is like drinking a bottle of wine:[58] the effects may be dramatic or insignificant, according to circumstances and the physiology and psychology of the individual. Anyway bottles of wine do sometimes have effects.

What little is known about the cognitive effects of literacy does not support any facile conclusions. The effects of literacy on individuals are not easy to judge, essentially because of what has been called

55. Pattison, *On Literacy* 45.
56. Street, *Literacy in Theory and Practice* 49–56, 62–63; cf. 103–125. "Technological determinism": 51.
57. Street argues, for instance, that Greek historiography represented practically no advance over what came before, since it was "imbued with . . . ideology" (54), which entirely misses the point that the great historians attempted with some success to do something that had not been done before, namely to use critical methods to construct a narrative and to explain the logic of political events.
58. Pattison 41.

the "covariation of literacy with other major changes in life experience";[59] in other words, we may not be able to tell whether a person shows such-and-such mental characteristics because he or she is literate, or whether those same characteristics led the subject to become literate in the first place. The most systematic attempt so far undertaken to test the effects of literacy in a contemporary setting led its authors to remark that the population in question (in Liberia) did not experience any rapid intellectual or social change as a result of literacy;[60] but this literacy was of such a special kind, and the setting was so vastly different from that of the ancient Mediterranean, that nothing clear emerges for the study of the Greeks and Romans.

There is in fact nothing to predict for us the likely long-term effects of literacy on a population which, having previously had no writing at all, devises an alphabetic script for itself and slowly—by modern standards—puts it to use for a growing variety of purposes. This problem is beyond the limits of comparative history, and it is the Greeks themselves who provide most of the evidence. Furthermore, we shall be asking not just about the effects of basic literacy but about the effects of real facility with reading and writing, a system of reading and writing which within the limits of the class structure and the economic system was accessible to everyone. To describe the effects of literacy on Greek and Roman culture (in the wider or the narrower sense of that term) would in fact be an extremely difficult task.

The following chapters do not attempt to perform this task in full. There are vital things to do first; the most elementary facts about Greek and Roman literacy need to be brought out. We shall try to establish the volume and social range of ancient literacy, using the methods outlined in Chapter 1, and to determine both the importance and the unimportance of reading and writing in ancient lives by sketching the manifold uses which the Greeks and Romans made of their literacy.

59. Scribner & Cole, *The Psychology of Literacy* 10; cf. 13, 55. On this difficult subject see also C. R. Hallpike, *The Foundations of Primitive Thought* (Oxford, 1979), 126–131.
60. Scribner & Cole 234–260.

PART TWO

The Literacy and Illiteracy
of the Greeks

3 The Spread of Literacy in Archaic Times

Fully alphabetic writing was invented by Greeks in or shortly before the eighth century B.C., probably well before 750.[1] A person or persons unknown adapted the Phoenician script to Greek use, with the crucial addition of five signs, themselves drawn from Phoenician script, to represent vowels.[2] We do not know why. That is to say, we do not know what kind of message or record the very earliest users of the Greek alphabet wanted to put into writing. It is likely that the Greeks in question were involved in maritime trade but there is no certainty about this, still less about the exact purpose for which such men would have found writing useful.[3]

1. For conspectuses of opinion on the date see A. Heubeck, *Schrift* (*Archaeologia Homerica* iii.X) (Göttingen, 1979), 75–76; and B. S. J. Isserlin, *Kadmos* xxii (1983), 151–163. On the earliest inscriptions see A. Johnston in R. Hägg (ed.), *The Greek Renaissance of the Eighth Century B.C.: Tradition and Innovation* (Stockholm, 1983), 63–68.

2. See L. H. Jeffery, *The Local Scripts of Archaic Greece* (Oxford, 1961), 1–40; G. Pfohl (ed.), *Das Alphabet. Entstehung und Entwicklung der griechischen Schrift* (Darmstadt, 1968).

3. G. Glotz suggested the keeping of accounts, *Ancient Greece at Work*, trans. M. R. Dobie (London, 1926), 116; inventory control is an obvious possibility, perhaps soon followed by rudimentary commercial correspondence. Johnston's observation (67) that "numerals are not found for sure in extant Greek material before 600 B.C." carries little weight, given the types of text that survive. He emphasizes "proprietorial concern." The recurrent notion that writing was devised specifically as a vehicle for what had been oral poetry (H. T. Wade-Gery, *The Poet of the Iliad* [Cambridge, 1952], 13–14; K. Robb in E. A. Havelock & J. P. Hershbell [eds.], *Communication Arts in the Ancient World* [New York, 1978], 23–36) was already known in antiquity (Diod.Sic. iii.67.1: Linus invented the Greek alphabet), but it is suspiciously romantic and is sometimes based (as with A. Schnapp-Gourbeillon, *Annales E.S.C.* xxvii [1982], 717) on the fallacy that early texts were not utilitarian because the earliest surviving texts are not (presumably they were written on perishable materials). The fact that the innovation occurred in a period of drastically increased contact with the Phoenicians favours the view that commercial uses were the earliest.

The event was in any case revolutionary, notwithstanding the fact that Phoenician script had already given vocalic value to certain letters.[4] It is true that a mass public can, in spite of what has sometimes been suggested, become literate in a script more difficult to read than the Greek or the Roman. Modern experience in various countries, above all in Japan, has demonstrated that it is not necessary to have a simple script such as ours as a basis for mass literacy. Most Israelis are used to dealing with unpointed Hebrew. But in the more arduous conditions of ancient teaching, with no elementary textbooks, the simplicity and virtual comprehensiveness of the Greek alphabet helped its diffusion greatly in the long run. In this chapter we shall consider how far this diffusion went, in social terms, in the period down to about 480 B.C., a date which forms a convenient limit because it is shortly before then that we encounter the first pieces of evidence that literacy had reached a remarkably large segment of the Greek population.

In the short run the invention was not heavily used, though the contrary is often asserted.[5] The relatively slight volume of surviving epigraphical evidence form the first 250 years of Greek literacy might, it is true, give a false impression, for texts written on potsherds had poor chances of survival, and those written on papyrus, leather (used by the Delphic oracle), or wood (used by Athens for laws) were certain to perish. Nevertheless the sheer shortage and brevity of surviving inscriptions indicate that writing was still rare in the experience of most Greeks. And for many generations, written texts were employed for a very limited range of purposes and by a very limited number of people. In the inscriptions of the eighth and seventh centuries, of which L. H. Jeffery registered about 100, the largest group of surviving texts served to identify the owners of ceramic vessels;[6] a few inscribed tombstones are known, a few religious dedications and a few draftsmen's signatures. Some of the earliest Athenian inscriptions on ceramics create the impression, by their insistence on the verb

4. Jeffery 22.

5. Murray, *Early Greece;* J. N. Coldstream, *Geometric Greece* (London, 1977), 301, writes of the "rapid spread of literacy"; cf. also A. Burns, *JHI* xlii (1981), 374, B. M. W. Knox, in *Cambridge History of Classical Literature* i (Cambridge, 1985), 5.

6. The oldest Greek inscription published was until recently (see the Preface) the one scratched on the Dipylon *oinochoe* (*IG* i².919), which indicates that it was a prize in a dancing competition; G. Annibaldis & O. Vox, *Glotta* liv (1976), 223–228. For a drawing see Heubeck, *Schrift* 116.

graphein and by their repetition of the first few letters of the alphabet, that writing was still a most impressive achievement.[7]

Meanwhile papyrus must have been, for almost everyone, expensive and hard to obtain.[8] As for organized instruction in reading and writing, we do not know when it began, but in the eighth century it was probably still several generations in the future.

At Dreros, in eastern Crete, laws of no great length were inscribed on stone in the middle or late seventh century,[9] and the Athenians later believed that in the 620s, in Draco's time, they had first had written laws[10]—a plausible belief, at least as far as a homicide law is concerned. Other states may also have been writing down their laws by the end of the seventh century. In the same period writing may have extended its functions in long-distance diplomacy and commerce. At a date that is much disputed, perhaps as early as 730–700, certainly by 600, poetry began to be written down; and in the course of the sixth century the Ionian philosophers also used writing. These were all, in varying degrees, radical changes, but the volume of use is small by comparison with what came into being after the middle of the sixth century.

Who, then, was literate in very early Greece? Some people in many different places: Rhodes, Thera, Crete, Naxos, Athens, Aegina, Cor-

---

7. Cf. R. S. Young, *AJA* xliv (1940), 8. On the insistent use of *graphein* see M. K. Langdon, *A Sanctuary of Zeus on Mount Hymettos* (Hesperia Suppl. xvi) (Princeton, 1976), 18–21, 46–47 (she concludes fantastically that in Attica by about 600 there were "as many literate citizens as illiterate"). Other early Attic *abecedaria*: C. W. Blegen, *AJA* xxxviii (1934), 15–16; E. Brann, *Hesperia* xxx (1961), 146. A summary guide to the archaic Greek *abecedaria* now known: M. Lejeune, *RPh* lvii (1983), 8. For trademarks on vases, which start in Ionia and Corinth before 600, see A. W. Johnston, *Trademarks on Greek Vases* (Warminster, 1979).

8. Cf. Hdt. v.58.2.

9. Dreros: Jeffery, *Local Scripts* 311 no. la; Meiggs & Lewis, *GHI* no. 2. The chronological problems concerning particular inscriptions are numerous but need not be discussed here. It is significant that no eighth- or seventh-century Greek colony can be said, on the evidence that survives, to have had a foundation document; *SEG* ix.3 (Cyrene) can hardly go back to the seventh century in anything like its present form (the inscription itself is of the fourth century), in spite of A. J. Graham, *JHS* lxxx (1960), 94–111. The treaty of the Locrians with their colonists in Italy mentioned in Polyb. xii.9.3 may well have been inauthentic (see F. W. Walbank's commentary), even though Polybius' argumentation to this effect is not strong.

10. [Aristot.] *Ath.Pol.* 41.2. *Ath.Pol.* 3.4, where the pre-Draconian *thesmothetai* ("decision-recorders"?) are said to have written down *ta thesmia*, is a much-disputed text.

inth, Sicyon, the Argolid, Laconia, Aetolia, Corcyra, Pithecusae and Cumae, among others. With regard to social level, however, almost everything is conjecture. To speak of mass literacy is plainly mistaken, but might it not be correct in a sense to say that "ordinary people could and did learn to write"?[11] Early epitaphs are unhelpful in this respect, religious dedications likewise. A certain number of masons, bronzeworkers and potters of the seventh century evidently found the skill useful; and, having learned to write, they presumably passed the knowledge on to their sons.[12] The skill was certainly not confined to aristocrats or to a class of specialists. But it is likely that only those who were exceptionally enterprising or fortunate became properly literate.

As to women's ability to read and write in this period we lack concrete information, but we must suppose that they were largely excluded. The illustrious case of Sappho, who presumably learned to read and write well either in Lesbos or in Sicily during the last quarter of the seventh century, should be regarded as exceptional though not unique, her family having been a privileged one.[13]

Perhaps the first truly striking texts, from the point of view of social class, because it is clear that neither aristocrats nor merchants nor craftsmen were involved, are the graffiti which Greek mercenaries left at Abu Simbel in 593/592.[14] Nine writers were involved, it seems, including two from Ialysus (Rhodes) and one each from Teos and Colophon.[15] One text runs to thirty-six words, another to thirteen; the rest are very simple. The writers were probably something more than rank-and-file soldiers,[16] though there is no proof of this.

Nothing in the texts of Homer or Hesiod suggests that writing was at all important in the everyday world in which the poets lived. In fact the well-known reference in *Iliad* vi.168 to *semata lugra*, "baneful signs," which describes a letter written by the Argive prince Proetus "in a folded tablet,"[17] is the only reference by either poet to the art of

11. Jeffery 63. She refers to "casual graffiti," but their casualness may be deceptive.

12. Cf. ibid. 62.

13. W. Aly, *RE* (1920) s.v. "Sappho," col. 2361, gives references.

14. See A. Bernand & O. Masson, *REG* lxx (1957), 1–46; Meiggs & Lewis, *GHI* no. 7.

15. All these men may have been connected with the commercial settlement of Naucratis (see Hdt. ii.178.2 for the cities which participated).

16. Bernand & Masson 20.

17. Did the poet hold that writing was an activity for a prince with a special purpose in mind? Perhaps he even saw writing itself as sinister. He certainly insists on the

writing. And while the act of writing down the poems themselves was of enormous significance, it did not imply the expectation of a large readership. The experience of poetry continued to be aural for almost everyone. The only early poem which might at first sight seem to presuppose a sizeable audience of actual readers is the *Works and Days*, but it is to be seen not as a didactic poem for farmers but rather as an example of wisdom literature,[18] and hence it no more presupposes a numerous readership than do its ancient Near Eastern predecessors in the same genre.[19] The fact that Semonides and Alcaeus knew this poem[20] is of interest, especially as they were not Boeotians; but this fact tells us nothing about general literacy. There was clearly an "international" circuit for rhapsodes, and it had existed before any poetry was written down.

There is thus no epigraphical or literary evidence to suggest that more than a very small percentage of Greeks were literate before 600.

Writing undoubtedly proliferated in sixth-century Greece. The number of surviving inscriptions makes this clear; Jeffery, for example, lists some 450 texts (including coins) in a selective catalogue. Their geographical range spreads, and to some extent this probably reflects a spread in literacy itself. The functions of writing, however, remain similar. It has been claimed that these inscriptions indicate the existence of a large audience of readers,[21] and it is true of course that there must have been a relative growth in the number of literate people. There must have been an audience of hundreds in the most cultivated cities, such as Athens, Corinth, and Miletus, and a nucleus of dozens of fully literate men in many Greek cities. Nothing implies a wider readership, at least until late in the sixth century. It is remarkable, however, that many small city-states were involved. It may even

---

evilness of Proetus' letter (θυμοφθόρα πολλά, 169; σῆμα κακόν, 178). For a certain sinister quality attaching to writing at a slightly later date see Archilochus fr. 224 Lasserre = 185 West (ἀχνυμένη σκυτάλη), with the comments of B. Gentili, *Poesia e pubblico nella Grecia antica* (Bari, 1984), 26 n.77. It remains possible, but unlikely, that σήματα λυγρά refers entirely to Linear B (see, e.g., L. A. Stella, *Tradizione micenea e poesia dell'Iliade* [Rome, 1978], 166–167). For an exhaustive analysis see Heubeck, *Schrift* 128–146.

18. F. Dornseiff, *Philologus* lxxxix (1934), 397–415; M. L. West, *Hesiod, Works and Days* (Oxford, 1978), 25–30.

19. West (60) underlines this point by transcribing the first few lines in the way in which they were originally written.

20. West 61.

21. Burns, *JHI* xlii (1981), 374.

be symptomatic that one of the first known prose writers, Pherecydes, active in or just before the middle of the sixth century, was from Syros, though he certainly spent a lot of time away from his native island.[22] And the fact that Pherecydes chose to write his cosmogony in prose, dispensing with the mnemonic assistance which verse would normally have offered to his hearers and readers, plainly marks an important step in the acceptance of written texts.

In the course of the sixth century, however, writing began to be used much more widely for purposes which it had previously served seldom or only in a handful of places. Thus it probably began to be used much more in public and semi-public life, as we may infer from the existence of the first known official secretaries at Athens, who appear to date from before 550.[23]

Three new uses of literacy, with various implications, can be illustrated from the epigraphical material. Most familiar is the fact that during the sixth century the inscribing and public display of laws, a practice which before 600 had probably been confined to a very few states, became notably more common. The well-known evidence we possess concerning Athens and Chios is in a loose sense accidental,[24] and it suggests that other cities will have been doing similar things. Legal texts of one kind or another survive from Paros (600–550?), Eretria (550–525?), Ozolian Locris (525–500?), Elis (525–500?),

22. The evidence about him is in D–K i.43–51. The Suda (Suidas s.v., iv.713 Adler) reports that "some say" he was the first to publish prose (cf. G. S. Kirk & J. E. Raven, *The Presocratic Philosophers* [Cambridge, 1957], 49–50). Who really did so is not at all certain: H. Thesleff, *Arctos* n.s. iv (1966), 90. Anaximander probably wrote in prose (cf. F. Solmsen, *AJPh* lxxxvii [1966], 104) and before Pherecydes.

23. Our knowledge of these *grammateis* seems to be limited to two dedications: A. E. Raubitschek, *Dedications from the Athenian Akropolis* (Cambridge, Mass., 1949), nos. 327, 328. Not long afterwards we know that Polycrates of Samos had a *grammatistes* (Hdt. iii.123), who (not coincidentally) became very powerful. For a parallel to this in fifth-century Etruria see below, p. 150. The high status of Athenian *grammateis* at some date in the last third of the sixth century is suggested by the three statues illustrated by H. Payne, *Archaic Marble Sculpture from the Acropolis* (2 ed., Oxford, 1950), pl. 118 (commented on misleadingly by E. A. Havelock, *New Literary History* viii [1976–77], 384–385 = *The Literate Revolution in Greece and Its Cultural Consequences* [Princeton, 1982], 200–201).

24. Athens: about Draco I make no judgement, but it would be hard to deny that Solon's laws were written down soon after they were passed (see the evidence collected by E. Ruschenbusch, ΣΟΛΩΝΟΣ ΝΟΜΟΙ [Wiesbaden, 1969], 62–69; in fr. 24 Diehl = 36 West he says that he wrote down his *thesmoi*). The most likely date is 594. The earliest extant law text from Athens is *IG* i³.1 (= Meiggs & Lewis, *GHI* no. 14), a "sacral law" of approximately 510–500 B.C. Chios: the law text is in Meiggs & Lewis as no. 8.

and a number of small cities in Crete.[25] Even in their original forms these texts were probably not long, and in any case it goes almost without saying that the public display of a text or two did not presuppose that a city's entire population, or even a large proportion of it, could be reached directly by means of the written word. However, such texts strongly suggest a change of attitude; it was now assumed that a substantial number of citizens in the cities in question had the right to know the law and could benefit from a written text, and that the law had a fixed content. The limitations of all this should be plain: we are not dealing with full-scale codifications, and many citizens may still have had to depend on having the law revealed to them by word of mouth. Furthermore, neither legislation nor litigation is likely to have been important in the daily lives of the Greeks of this or any other period. In the case of sacral laws, of which a few survive from the sixth century,[26] it is even less likely that a mass readership was assumed; the important point is rather that a written regulation was now assumed to be authoritative. The same applies to treaties. What is probably the earliest surviving one (twenty-six words in all) was set up at Olympia and with the guarantee of the gods, most likely in the second quarter of the sixth century. It was meant to last "for eternity," and its written form was presumably meant to assist this aim.[27] Another kind of public text which was meant to be authoritative appeared in Athens by about 500, in the shape of inscribed public weights and measures.[28]

A second development of some significance is that by the end of the sixth century nearly forty Greek states had minted coins with their own names, normally abbreviated, and more were soon to do so.[29] This fact does not imply that a majority of the citizens of these states

25. Paros: *IG* xii.5.105 (Jeffery, *Local Scripts* 305, no. 26). Eretria: E. Vanderpool & W. P. Wallace, *Hesperia* xxxiii (1964), 381–391 (= Jeffery 87, no. 9). Ozolian Locris: Jeffery 108, no. 2. Elis: Jeffery 220, nos. 2, 4, 5. The Cretan texts are listed by Jeffery 315–316. I leave aside texts of very uncertain interpretation.

26. E.g., from Cleonae (Jeffery 150, no. 6), Tiryns (ibid. no. 8 = F. Sokolowski, *Lois sacrées des cités grecques. Supplément* [Paris, 1962], no. 26), and Argos (Jeffery 168 no. 8 = Sokolowski no. 27).

27. No doubt there were some written treaties before this. The treaty between Sybaris and the Serdaioi: Meiggs & Lewis, *GHI* no. 10. For other early cases see M. Guarducci, *Epigrafia greca* ii (Rome, 1969), 536–542.

28. For the evidence see M. Lang in Lang & M. Crosby, *Weights, Measures, and Tokens* (= *The Athenian Agora* x) (Princeton, 1964), 25–26, 61–62.

29. Based on Jeffery, *Local Scripts*. See also the map in C. Renfrew & M. Wagstaff (eds.), *An Island Polity. The Archaeology of Exploitation in Melos* (Cambridge,

were even semi-literate, but it shows that all over the Greek world, from the Black Sea to southern Italy, city officials now regularly labelled with letters an object which was mass-produced. And although the coin issues in question must have been of quite limited size, and passed many people by altogether, they helped to make the written word more familiar.

A third revealing set of facts concerns the inscriptions on Athenian black-figure vases. In the first quarter of the sixth century they are rare. Then, about 575, comes the spectacular François Vase, a crater with no fewer than 129 inscriptions (signatures and names), an exuberant display which suggests that in the milieu in question writing was still a novel toy.[30] Other black-figure vases illustrate the same attitude on a smaller scale.[31] More significant still are the nonsense inscriptions which occasionally appear on later black-figure vases (the majority have no inscriptions at all),[32] for these imply both that writing in itself enjoyed prestige among the purchasers—prosperous men, obviously—and that for many of them illiteracy was no cause for shame (guests would not be shocked by mumbo-jumbo). It is probably as a result of a higher level of literacy in the early fifth century that nonsense inscriptions became rarer.[33]

Literacy had clearly been increasing in Athens in the second half of the sixth century. This is suggested by the attempts of the Peisistratids, no doubt paralleled by those of ambitious politicians in some other states, to make use of inscriptions as well as monuments for propaganda. A pseudo-Platonic text concerning the cultural policy of Peisistratus' son Hipparchus describes how he brought poets to Athens, "wishing to educate the citizens"; when he had educated

---

1982), 5: some seventy-five city-states, even with the western cities omitted, were issuing coinage about 500.

30. For the inscriptions see M. Cristofani in *Materiali per servire alla storia del Vaso François = Bollettino d'arte*, Serie speciale i (1981), 177–178. It is possible that this vase, which was found at Chiusi, was made for a non-Greek market. On the painter's attitude towards writing cf. Havelock, *The Literate Revolution* 37 n.42.

31. E.g., two cups in Boston (Museum of Fine Arts): 99.518 (Painter of the Boston Polyphemus) (J. D. Beazley, *Athenian Black-Figure Vase-Painters* [Oxford, 1956], 198, though he does not describe the writing), 61.1073 (Neandros) (Beazley, *Paralipomena* [Oxford, 1971], 69–70).

32. On this topic cf. J. Boardman, *Athenian Black Figure Vases* (London, 1974), 200–201. For a Corinthian crater of 575–550 with nonsense words see *CVA Sweden* fasc. 2 (Stockholm, 1983), fig. 164.

33. J. Boardman, *Athenian Red Figure Vases. The Archaic Period* (London, 1975), 213.

those in the city, he set about educating the country-dwellers. What he did was to erect Herms along the roads between the city and the demes, each with the words "This is a monument of Hipparchus," followed by a pithy piece of instruction such as "Do not deceive a friend."[34] An inscription from such a Herm survives.[35] The point is not that Hipparchus systematically attempted to have the citizens taught to read, still less that he thought all countrymen in Attica could already read. Rather, he knew that in each district there were men who could read short simple texts, and he put this fact to political use. It is also reasonable to suppose that the inscriptions, paternalistic in tone and ubiquitous, were an effective indication of the tyrant's power.[36]

That the sons of Peisistratus attached importance to the written word also emerges from the fact that Hippias had been in possession of a notable collection of oracles before his expulsion (Cleomenes took them off to Sparta). The Peisistratids may have been helped in the making of this collection by Hipparchus' associate Onomacritus, whom Herodotus describes as "oracle-collector and compiler of the oracles of Musaeus." Onomacritus was out of favour with the Peisistratid family for a time, having been caught in the act of making an interpolation in one of Musaeus' prophecies (whether Hipparchus objected to the interpolation on principle or for political reasons—the latter seems more likely—is regrettably unclear). The implications are in any event considerable: not only was a written collection thought valuable by a tyrant, the written text had a high enough status in itself to be worth tampering with.[37]

Within a decade of Hipparchus' propaganda in the demes of Attica the Athenians invented or adopted the practice of ostracism (510–

34. Ps.-Pl. *Hipparch.* 228b–229d. The author's interpretation (228e4–7) implics that Hipparchus was aiming at those with the leisure to visit the city regularly. For background and speculations see most recently B. M. Lavelle, *Echos du monde classique* xxix (1985), 411–420.

35. *IG* i².837 (cf. *SEG* x.345 = Jeffery, *Local Scripts* 78, no. 35). It comes from Koropi, across Mt. Hymettus from the city. Other inscribed Peisistratid monuments: Jeffery 78, nos. 37, 38.

36. It is possible that tyrants sometimes sought to enlist the prestige or mystique of the written word in other ways: the alleged Peisistratan redaction of Homer and the large libraries ascribed to Peisistratus and to Polycrates of Samos (Athen. i.3a) would be relevant here.

37. Hippias' collection: Hdt. v.90. Onomacritus: ἄνδρα Ἀθηναῖον χρησμολόγον τε καὶ διαθέτην χρησμῶν τῶν Μουσαίου (Hdt. vii.6). The interpolation was to the effect that the islands near Lemnos would disappear into the sea.

508), which has been regarded as proof that most male citizens could write.[38] An ostracism was valid only if at least 6,000 votes in total were cast against all candidates.[39] Recent scholarship has tended towards the conclusion that ostracism originally took place in the Council with no more than 201 votes required to condemn,[40] which diminishes its importance for literacy in the time of Cleisthenes. But by the 480s at the latest the quorum of 6,000 voters was required,[41] and they cannot have come into existence overnight. This means that although there were by that time hardly more than 30,000 male Athenian citizens, at least 6,000 were believed to be capable of casting a written ballot, in other words of inscribing a stranger's name on a potsherd.

This is far indeed from being evidence for majority literacy. Furthermore, it was not customary or necessary to write more than the candidate's name.[42] Even those who cast ballots required only semi-literacy—if that. An observant archaeologist, examining a cache of 191 ostraca which were written against Themistocles, noticed that they were the work of merely fourteen hands;[43] in other words they were to some degree mass-produced (see Figure 1). Those who were expected to use such ostraca were not necessarily illiterate, for the prepared ostracon may simply have been a convenience. On the other hand it is highly probable that in reality many other ostraca were mass-produced which have not been detected as such.[44]

38. G. Nieddu, *S & C* vi (1982), 246 ("la maggioranza del corpo sociale"). F. D. Harvey, *REG* lxxix (1966), 590–593, is relatively sceptical about the value of ostracism as evidence for Athenian literacy.

39. R. Thomsen, *The Origin of Ostracism* (Copenhagen, 1972), 66 n.23; P. J. Rhodes, comm. on [Aristot.] *Ath.Pol.* 22.3 (p. 270).

40. C. Pecorella Longo, *Historia* xxix (1980), 257–281. The cause of this trend is the republication of a part of *Vat.Gr.* 1144 by J. J. Keaney & A. E. Raubitschek, *AJPh* xciii (1972), 87–91.

41. Probably by 501/500: Pecorella Longo 270–273.

42. A minute number of voters wrote more than the name, patronymic and deme of the candidate (and the deme is not usual): E. Vanderpool, *Ostracism at Athens* (Cincinnati, 1970), 8–9. On the other hand, the photographs of voting ostraca printed by Vanderpool and others do *not* suggest that many writers had more difficulty in scratching letters than was inevitable in the material circumstances.

43. O. Broneer, *Hesperia* vii (1938), 228–243.

44. The fourteen hands would hardly have been detected if they had not been found in the same cache of unused ostraca. To say that the "psychology" of ostracism was oral (Havelock, *New Literary History* viii [1976–77], 383 = *The Literate Revolution* 199) makes no sense. However, the "optimists" cited above have also gone far astray in their inferences from the introduction of ostracism.

Ostracism does tell us that by the 480s thousands of Athenians reached at least the level of semi-literacy. It does not prove very much about schools, which are not otherwise attested quite as early as Cleisthenes' time, but it certainly suggests that a number of elementary schools existed, and taught writing, by about the turn of the century.[45] And it is important to notice that Athens was not the only, and perhaps not the first, city to practise ostracism: Argos, Syracuse, Megara and Miletus did so at one time or another.[46]

Ostracism also seems to show that writing had gained greatly in public esteem: one of its most important implications is that the Athenians judged it appropriate to carry out such a solemn business by means of written texts.

Cleisthenic Athens also recognized the civic usefulness of writing in other ways. In particular it is likely to have been at this date that the demes of Attica began to keep registers of their members.[47]

The collections of written oracles put together in late sixth-century Athens raise the apparently unanswerable question of when writing was first used in Greek oracular practice. The Delphic oracle normally spoke. Those who had been sent to consult her might write down the answer,[48] and this may have happened more and more in the late archaic period; but on the other hand writing was clearly not an integral part of the oracle's own practice, here or elsewhere. As for other religious uses of the written word, it is now established that written curse-tablets had already come into use in some places in the sixth century.[49]

Writing had thus broadened its literary, civic, political, and religious functions to a very notable degree by the end of the sixth century. Though we scarcely have enough evidence in this period to draw up the orderly account of the functions of writing which will be possible for the classical era, we must take stock of some of the other functions which writing fulfilled in the decades just before 480.

One area of uncertainty is the use of writing in legal procedures.

45. Marrou, *Histoire* 83.

46. Argos: Aristot. *Pol.* v.3.1302b18 (listing Argos before Athens). Syracuse: Diod.Sic. xi. 86–87 (where ostracism was called *petalismos* because the votes were written on leaves). Megara and Miletus: Schol. Ar. *Eq.* 855.

47. C. Hignett, *A History of the Athenian Constitution* (Oxford, 1952), 136.

48. Hdt. i.48 (the Lydians at Delphi) may reflect long-standing practice; so too may Eur. fr. 627 Nauck (oracles of Apollo on leather). It is unlikely that the questions were submitted in writing.

49. See below, p. 83 n.83.

Eventually the Athenians devised a procedure called *graphe,* writing, and made fairly extensive use of documents for certain legal purposes. But when did documents start to play a part in legal transactions? It is tempting to think that the *horoi,* boundary markers, which marked debt-encumbered land in Attica until Solon removed them, were inscribed, but they may well not have been. As for *graphai,* it is sometimes said that Solon created them when he gave every citizen the right of "obtaining redress on behalf of injured persons";[50] but no Greek writer says so, and the first mentions of them do not occur until the 420s.[51] There is practically no evidence that Athenians used written wills or contracts in the sixth century, and even in the fourth century the role of writing in the testamentary and contractual practice of Athens was limited. These arguments from silence are not overwhelming, but we must suspect that at least down to the period of the Persian Wars private legal matters did not involve the Athenians to any significant extent with written material.

Letters are another problem. The world of far-flung colonies and trade which the Greeks created in the eighth and seventh centuries seems to be a natural setting for correspondence. The silence of the sources, apart from the case of Proetus, may be fortuitous. The fact remains that the first known historical letters are those of Polycrates of Samos and King Amasis, in the early 520s.[52] But the most remarkable early letter is one which actually survives, a private letter written on lead about 500, which was found at Berezan on the north coast of the Black Sea.[53] The ineptitude of both composer and scribe is of interest, but most important of all is the simple fact that an ordinary Greek knew that writing could be used for long-distance messages. It should also be noted that the author wrote because he was in acute distress (he was in danger of enslavement),[54] and that the message was apparently travelling to or from the colony of Olbia, daughter city of Miletus. This could all be characteristic: a message of desperation could be written down by this date, but the author might have to rely

50. [Aristot.] *Ath.Pol.* 9.1; A. R. W. Harrison, *The Law of Athens* ii (Oxford, 1971), 76.

51. G. M. Calhoun, *TAPhA* l (1919), 180.

52. Hdt. iii.40–43.

53. Y. G. Vinogradov, *VDI* cxviii (1971), 74–100; J. Chadwick, *PCPhS* xix (1973), 35–37; B. Bravo, *Dialogues d'histoire ancienne* i (1974), 111–187; J. & L. Robert, *Bull.Ep.* 1976, 251–252, etc. I take the date from L. H. Jeffery, cited by Chadwick 35.

54. It is also relevant that the letter refers to itself as τὸ μολίβδιον: the author probably knew no word for "letter."

on inconvenient material and might barely know how to express himself.[55]

It is, in short, extremely difficult to know how much importance the written word had assumed by this date. It was in constant use by a small number of specialists, while for the mass of country-people it was of little or no concern. For a considerable number of men living in cities, however, written texts were periodically of interest or even of vital importance.

What then of the earliest Greek schools?[56]

There must already have been some in the sixth century. If Charondas of Catana was really responsible for the enlightened school law described earlier, he would stand at the beginning of historical Greek education; but it is much more likely that the law belongs to the 440s or is a later invention.[57] Our earliest explicit evidence concerns Chios in 496, Astypalaea (the southeastern Aegean again) in the 490s, and, very questionably, Troezen in 480.[58] It is also tempting to refer a story which Aelian tells about Mytilene, a story which implies that both the Mytilenaeans and their subject allies had schools where "letters" were taught, to this same period or even earlier.[59] In any case these are all incidental allusions containing no hint that schools were an innovation. As to Solon's supposed law about schools, it is plainly a fiction,[60] but nonetheless we can be virtually certain that at Athens there was some schooling in "letters" by the time of the Persian Wars.[61]

55. For another commercial letter on lead, found at Emporion in Spain and perhaps written by a Phocaean, see E. Sanmartí & R. A. Santiago, *ZPE* lxviii (1987), 119–127. The date seems to be in the first quarter of the fifth century.

56. We need scarcely stress that a good proportion of the Greeks who learned to read and write must have done so without schooling even at the end of this period. Yet in the classical age the principal function of schooling was held to be teaching letters (Xen. *Cyr.* i.2.6).

57. See below, p. 98.

58. Chios: Hdt. vi.27.2. Astypalaea: Paus. vi.9.6–7. Troezen: Plu. *Them.* 10.5.

59. Aelian, *VH* vii.15: "when the Mytilenaeans ruled the sea" they punished some rebellious allies by forbidding them to teach their children letters or *mousike*. The story is of little worth, according to E. Ziebarth, *Aus dem griechischen Schulwesen* (2 ed., Leipzig & Berlin, 1914), 32 n.6.

60. Cf. Ruschenbusch, ΣΟΛΩΝΟΣ NOMOI 110; P. Schmitter, *Die hellenistische Erziehung im Spiegel der* Νέα Κωμῳδία *und der Fabula Palliata* (Bonn, 1972), 112–115.

61. In spite of Havelock, who claims that "organized instruction in reading at the primary level . . . cannot have been introduced into the Athenian schools much earlier than about 430 B.C." (*New Literary History* viii [1976–77], 371 = *The Literate Revolution* 187). On the evidence of the vase paintings see below.

The most striking aspect of the events recounted at Chios and Astypalaea is the large number of children involved. At Chios 120 boys were "learning letters" when a roof collapsed and killed all but one of them. If we were to assume, for the sake of argument, that five annual age cohorts were present, the interesting corollary would seem to follow that a free population of more than 2,000 was sending its sons to this institution.[62] At Astypalaea the Olympic boxer Cleomedes caused the roof of what Pausanias specifically calls the school to fall in, killing about 60 boys.[63] These figures may lead us to believe that practically all prosperous Greeks, and some who were not, sent their sons to school by the 490s. Much less reliable, however, is Plutarch's story that the city of Troezen paid for teachers for the evacuated sons of the Athenians in 480.[64] Both of the authentic cases, be it noted, are from the area of the southeastern Aegean just described. Mytilene is near.

The organized teaching of large numbers of boys (we have no evidence that girls were included, although in some places they may have been) was a remarkable innovation, about which no Greek writer offers any information. This schooling is most likely to have grown out of organized choral training for religious festivals, but we have no way of knowing when the transition took place. There is of course some temptation to think that the early schools were less interested in teaching reading and writing than in giving training in music and athletics. Such seems to be the fantasy of Aristophanes,[65] as it was that of Havelock, who claimed that Athenian schools did not give organized writing instruction much before 430.[66] But although Herodotus cannot perhaps be entirely trusted to have known what was going on in

62. The *paides* must all have been boys. For the percentage of the population which is likely to have made up the five-year cohorts at the age in question see B. W. Frier, *HSCPh* lxxxvi (1982), esp. 245.

63. This is *paides* again. This story is perhaps less trustworthy than Herodotus', and Pausanias goes on to give a legendary account of how Cleomedes came to be worshipped as a hero at Astypalaea. The island is small (in 1951 it had a population of 1,789).

64. The circumstantial detail that the decree was proposed by one Nicagoras favours the story. Its implication would be that many Athenian and Troezenian boys were normally at school, but not necessarily those of all social classes; cf. A. R. Hands, *Charities and Social Aid in Greece and Rome* (London, 1968), 125. In truth the story has a decidedly apocryphal look (Ziebarth, *Aus dem griechischen Schulwesen* 32–33; C. Habicht, *Hermes* lxxxix [1961], 20–21).

65. Ar. *Nub.* 963–976; cf. *Eq.* 987–996.

66. Above, n.61.

the school at Chios in 496, he probably did know what sort of instruction was being given in a city so similar to his own. And the early fifth-century Athenian vases depicting school scenes make it certain that the teaching of letters was part, though only part, of the Athenian curriculum.[67] What Aristophanes says is no more to be trusted than his other fantasies about the past.

This account still leaves unexplained the decision of archaic Greek families to send their sons to school and have them taught, among other things, how to read and write. The decision may have been based on material advantage (which, however, for most people would not have been great), on the hope for social prestige, on a sense of the civic value of writing, possibly on a desire to bring boys into still closer contact with the Homeric epics (the texts which came to be most used in schools), or on any combination of these motives. To solve this problem would require a far better knowledge of the mentality of the archaic Greeks than the sources allow us. Which is to say that we are unable to account in a definitive way for the rise in Greece of that level of literacy diffusion which I call craftsman's literacy.

We can now attempt to summarize what can be known (and it is not very much) about the number of Greeks able to read and write in the archaic period. The context established in Chapter 1, the absence, in other words, of social, economic and technological conditions favourable to the spread of literacy, will compel us to scrutinize carefully any philhellenic claim that the level of literacy was high. Yet by 480 the Greeks of some cities probably had attained something close to craftsman's literacy.

Of the evidence cited above, that which concerns ostracism (not only at Athens) and schools is particularly impressive. It indicates that in a number of Greek cities there existed by the end of the archaic era not only a few people who were thoroughly at home with writing but also a solid minority, at least, among the male citizens who possessed limited skill at both reading and writing. It does not mean more than that.

An item of evidence which seems to suggest that literacy had made very great progress by about 480 is the story told by Herodotus—in a general context where his accuracy is in serious doubt—about Themistocles after the Battle of Artemisium. Allegedly he sailed around the watering places where the Persian fleet could be expected to call, and wrote up a patriotic appeal directed to Xerxes' Ionian sailors. Herodotus gives the text, a composition of his own which is

67. See below, p. 97.

eighty-seven words long; Themistocles' purpose, he says, was either to win the Ionians over or to make Xerxes distrust his Greek allies.[68] On the first score, the results were meagre.[69] Herodotus may not in any case have envisaged every Ionian sailor as having been able to read for himself, even though the Ionians were more likely to be literate than most other Greeks. Any expectation that the ordinary sailors would all have been able to read, in Themistocles' day or for that matter in Herodotus', was certainly deluded.

The special nature of the southeastern Aegean—that region which stretches from Chios down to Rhodes—with respect to literacy is hinted at in the Abu Simbel graffiti and thereafter practically throughout antiquity. Perhaps we should include Lesbos, especially if it is true that schools grew up there at an early date. There is no single item of evidence which demonstrates conclusively that the cities of this region were more literate than the rest of Greece, but it seems likely that even before the strong evidence which we shall encounter in the Hellenistic and Roman periods—evidence for a relatively well-developed school system—both the Ionian and the Dorian inhabitants fostered a tradition of ensuring that many of their children learned to read and write. Perhaps this is why Ionic script shows the influence, from the period 575–550 onwards, of cursive script, as if the masons were used to writing with pens.[70] Furthermore, this hypothetical Ionian preeminence in literacy may have been responsible for a phenomenon which is otherwise unexplained—the spread, visible in epigraphic writing, of the Ionic alphabet into other parts of Greece.

In addition to general considerations which tell against the wide diffusion of literacy in archaic Greece, there are some specific indications. Some, such as the nonsense inscriptions on sixth-century Athenian vases, have already been mentioned; others will appear in the next chapter. As an indication of how scarce truly literate men were in Crete about 500, we may mention the contract made by a city, unfortunately unidentified, with a certain Spensithios to be its public scribe (*poinikastas,* "Phoenicizer") and archivist, a contract made on extraordinarily generous terms.[71]

68. Hdt. viii.22. Apart from other considerations, the text is too long to be credible; it also adds to Herodotus' description of Themistocles by demonstrating his unusual resourcefulness (S. West, CQ xxxv [1985], 286). Cf. further R. W. Macan's commentary.

69. Hdt. viii.85.2.

70. For the facts see Jeffery, *Local Scripts* 57, 327. Havelock, *The Literate Revolution* 22, suggests that the earliest schools were in Ionia.

71. For the contract see L. H. Jeffery & A. Morpurgo-Davies, *Kadmos* ix (1970),

The conclusion which should be drawn from all this is that archaic Greece reached no more than a rather low level of craftsman's literacy. It would be astonishing if as much as 10% of the population as a whole was literate in the sense defined earlier. Yet *any* level of craftsman's literacy was also a great achievement. Its foundation was the alphabet itself, but the invention might have remained inert had it not been for certain other developments.

A common theory of what converted scribal literacy into craftsman's literacy in the late Middle Ages puts heavy emphasis on administrative and business documents and the desire to make use of them.[72] The suggestion that a similar desire might have had a considerable effect in Greece, especially from the sixth century on, may be repellent to those who take an idyllic view of early Greek history; nonetheless it is plausible. The *polis,* trade over long distances, and the hoplite form of warfare had already produced profound changes in Greek life, and by the sixth century a powerful civic consciousness had arisen. When, therefore, it became more and more obvious that writing could be extremely useful in civic life (for writing down laws, for record-keeping, for propaganda, for ostracism), those who could afford to do so would naturally want their sons to learn at least the rudiments of reading and writing. Those who could afford to do so were above all the members of the hoplite class, and the ability to deal with the complexity of written texts may well have added to the political self-confidence of this class. We have met no reliable evidence that the notion was already circulating in the archaic period that a respectable Greek citizen was obliged to know letters, but the roots of the notion were there.

The results of the new education were complex; they included, for instance, the paradoxical entrenchment in the minds of many ordinary Greeks of the heroic, militaristic and religious ideals of the *Iliad* and the *Odyssey.*

As for the wider effects of the emergence of a literate, or rather, semi-literate culture, one at least was glimpsed by Herodotus. For he asserts that it was Hesiod and Homer who "made a theogony for the

---

118–154; H. van Effenterre, *BCH* xcvii (1973), 31–46; etc. The contract, which was to be hereditary, seems to have given him among other things many or all of the privileges of the *kosmoi* (magistrates).

72. H. Lülfing, *Johannes Gutenberg und das Buchwesen des 14. und 15. Jahrhunderts* (Munich, 1969), 12–24; M. T. Clanchy, *From Memory to Written Record: England, 1066–1307* (Cambridge, Mass., 1979); E. Eisenstein, *The Printing Press as an Agent of Change* (Cambridge, 1979), i.62.

Greeks," gave the gods their titles, distinguished their honours and their skills, and indicated their forms.[73] Though he does not say so, the reason the words of Hesiod and Homer rather than those of any earlier thinkers became authoritative on religious subjects—as many texts, most notoriously Plato's *Republic,* show that they did—is that these poets *wrote* (or at least were written down). What they had to say on religious subjects gradually became the oldest knowledge available. There could hardly be a clearer instance of the way in which writing itself tends to canonize knowledge.

But we think of archaic Greece as an era of innovation; hence the question arises how far literacy and the diffusion of literacy were responsible for the great changes. Once the growth of literacy has been noticed, there is some temptation to suppose that it led to vast consequences, including not only literature (which does not, strictly speaking, depend on alphabetic literacy) but also the city-state, democracy, philosophy, historiography, and an increase in rationality. Nothing more than some brief remarks about this will be possible in the present context.

The writing ability of a handful of eighth-century Greeks did not give rise to or even provide an essential precondition for the rise of the city-state. The hard question is whether the growth of the *polis* mentality preceded the rise of craftsman's literacy (as has already been suggested above), or whether events occurred in the reverse order. Both events are gradual and difficult to date. No doubt the relatively complex forms of economic life that the city required (such as large and orderly markets) were made easier by the existence of a minimum of literacy, and in a sense the *polis* and literacy had reciprocal effects. However, if we take the earliest written laws and the earliest evidence for popular assemblies as signs that the classical *polis* and its characteristic attitudes had come into being, we are several generations ahead of the late sixth- and early fifth-century evidence which suggests that literacy had made remarkable growth.

How did the rise of literacy affect the distribution of political power in the archaic period? The question is all the more difficult to answer because Athens is the only "democracy"—of course it was never a democracy in any ideal sense—whose early development can be traced in detail, and even there central elements, such as the Cleisthenic reforms, are highly problematical. Literacy was never a popular cause or a subject which interested democratic politicians. They

73. Hdt. ii.53.

did not see mass literacy as a sign of, or a necessity of, democratic government or think that a democratic government ought to foster literacy. The genesis of citizen government in Greece is clearly connected with, or part of, a growth in the non-aristocratic citizen's belief in his own worth and his own rights and duties. Such beliefs encouraged men to learn letters and have their sons taught letters, and thus led to the widespread semi-literacy presupposed by the institution of ostracism. Writing could work for democracy, in various senses of that term, or—as in the case of Hipparchus—against it. But there was a connection between literacy and democracy. We may presume that the self-confidence and particularly the ability to deal with complex governmental affairs which literacy generated in much of the free male population of Athens made it far more difficult than it would otherwise have been to restrict their political rights. This, however, was a development of the 480s and later. The same general trend took place in most other Greek cities, but the uncertainty of the causal connection is emphasized by the frequent difficulties which democratic government experienced in cities such as Chios and Miletus, which probably had relatively large numbers of literate citizens.

The connection between the rise of literacy and the early development of philosophy is still more elusive, but again there is a connection. At the very least, the desire of the early Ionian philosophers to perpetuate and diffuse their opinions by writing them down inevitably created a sort of rudimentary dialectic, since all ambitious thinkers were increasingly compelled to confront the ideas of their best-regarded predecessors. From this it should not be concluded that literacy by itself leads to critical inquiry about the nature of the universe, for it would have been possible to treat written works as simply authoritative (although the extreme difficulty of some of the problems discussed told against that).

Histories of Greek philosophy never discuss this issue in full.[74] Anaximander and Anaximenes of Miletus (not Thales) were the earliest philosophers whose ideas survived in writing,[75] but it turns out to be most unclear what effects this had. No one before Aristotle refers

74. There are some useful comments on the problem in G. E. R. Lloyd, *Magic, Reason and Experience* (Cambridge, 1979), 239–240.

75. Themistius *Or.* xxvi.317 says that Anaximander, out of rivalry with Thales, was "the first of the Greeks we know who dared to publish a *logos* about nature" (the earliest possible date would have been about 580). It may have been very brief (Diog. Laert. ii.2). The confused statement about Anaxagoras in Clem.Alex. *Strom.* i.78 possibly refers to this feat of Anaximander's.

to these men, still less to their writings.[76] In fact the earliest philosopher whose writings are known to have had reverberations in and soon after his own time was Xenophanes of Colophon,[77] who significantly wrote not in prose treatises but in accepted poetic forms. His chronology is disputed, but he is unlikely to have written much before the last quarter of the sixth century. That writing was still a quite subsidiary part of being a philosopher in the next generation (again there are chronological problems) is suggested by the fact that Heraclitus, whose book was in Aristotle's opinion very difficult to read,[78] nonetheless obtained relatively extensive circulation for his ideas.[79]

We should like to know how far ideas circulated *in written form* among the pre-sophistic philosophers just mentioned. Did they react to written reports of each other's views? But examining the influence of literacy on early Greek philosophy is outside the scope of this book.[80]

What can be established about the literacy of archaic Greece is from one perspective not very much. The quantity of literacy and semi-literacy attained in Ionia and Athens, not to speak of other places, remains unclear within a fairly broad range. On the other hand, it is clear that very many places achieved something more than scribal literacy, without, however, remotely approaching anything which could be called mass literacy. At all events enough Greeks learned to read and write to permit a steady growth in the functions of literacy, most notably in the public realm; and this growth of functions encouraged yet more people to see to it that their sons—and probably a few of their daughters—joined the ranks of the literate.

76. W. K. C. Guthrie, *A History of Greek Philosophy* i (Cambridge, 1962), 72.

77. Guthrie 368. Though born in Colophon, he probably spent much of his life in the western colonies.

78. On Heraclitus' anxieties about finding the best means of communication cf. Havelock, *BICS* xiii (1966), 57 = *The Literate Revolution* 245–246. It could well be true that Heraclitus' idea of publication was to deposit a single copy of his magnum opus, the three-part φυσικὸς λόγος, his discourse about the physical world, in the temple of Artemis at Ephesus (his home town) (cf. Diog.Laert. ix.6); cf. M. L. West, *Early Greek Philosophy and the Orient* (Oxford, 1971), 5.

79. It seems characteristic of archaic Greece that of the Seven Wise Men who appear on the earliest known list, Plato's (*Prot.* 343a), only one was known to have written for the public, and that was Solon, who did so mainly for political reasons. But the list itself gained a degree of permanence when it was written down.

80. A parallel problem is raised by Hecataeus, *FGrH* 1 F1: "I write these things as they seem to me; for the stories [*logoi*] of the Greeks are, in my opinion, many and ridiculous." F. Jacoby assumes (2 ed., p. 535) that what Hecataeus was reacting against was *written*, but that is quite uncertain.

4 The Classical Growth of Literacy and Its Limits

Down to the end of the sixth century, the available evidence about Greek literacy and illiteracy is extremely limited. In the fifth century we are still badly off, but at least we have some direct allusions to illiteracy and a more solid sense of everyday life, at least in Athens.

The fifth- and fourth-century evidence about literacy is disproportionately Athenian. Whether in this period the Athenians were typical among the Greeks with respect to literacy is extremely dubious; in fact they probably were not. Beginning in the 480s Athens became the wealthiest city, and later on it learned to claim that it was "the education of Greece." It was relatively democratic, and any man who did not take part in politics was regarded, so at least the Funeral Oration claims, as "useless."[1] Although this ideal democratic vision never came near to fulfilment, it was not merely Pericles' idiosyncrasy. Athens was probably a great deal more literate than such regions as Thessaly, Phocis and Elis. Classical Sparta probably had very little literacy indeed.

Athens differed from much of Greece in another respect, namely the great extent of its territory; and this factor must have worked against the level of literacy. The whole difficult question of the degree of Greek urbanization becomes relevant here. It would be instructive to know what proportion of the population lived in towns or near enough to them to benefit from schools and from the other encouragements to literacy which they offered. The heavily agrarian character of the Greek economy requires emphasis. However, as we saw in Chapter 1, towns do not necessarily have to be large to encourage literacy; and in Greece a smallish place might maintain a schoolmaster, as we have seen at Astypalaea and shall see at Mycalessus. We should also keep in mind the partial indistinctness of town-dwellers and country-people—some *poleis* had territories so small that a high proportion of the farmers could have lived in town, at least for most of

1. Thuc. ii.41.1, 40.2.

the year. The majority of Athenians, it is true, lived in the country even when the imperial city was at its height in 431; Thucydides specifically remarks on this fact.[2] But he thereby differentiates Athens from other cities to some extent, and so leaves the general question open.[3] Nor do other writers help much. We can do no more here than notice the problem.

The Functions of Literacy

Before we can consider the extent of literacy in the classical Greek world, we must trace the gradual increase in the functions of the written word during the years 479 to 323.

Several dramatic texts of this period praise writing. The sentiments they express were in some respects controversial, but it is important to see what the poets concerned chose to identify in public as the benefits of the written word. In the *Prometheus Vinctus* the hero, who is depicted as the inventor of writing, describes it as an all-purpose aid to memory and as "Muse-mothering worker," without further detail.[4] The hero of Euripides' lost play *Palamedes,* who was also supposed to have been the inventor of writing, delivers a longer encomium: it permits one to know everything that is going on overseas (presumably the author is thinking of letters), it assists the bequeathing of inheritances (by making inventories possible), and it settles disputes; this may not have been the end of his list. In Euripides' *Supplices* Theseus praises written laws.[5] Thus it is unlikely that any of the four useful purposes which Aristotle says that writing serves—moneymaking, household management, learning things, and civic affairs[6]—would

2. Thuc. ii.14.2 On the relationship between the city and the rural demes see still B. Haussoullier, *La vie municipale en Attique* (Paris, 1884), 178–200; and now D. Whitehead, *The Demes of Attica 508/7–ca. 250 B.C.* (Princeton, 1986).

3. According to A. W. Gomme (n. on 15.1), he is only distinguishing Athens from other highly developed cities such as Corinth and Miletus. On the general problem of rural settlements in classical Greece cf. E. Ruschenbusch, *ASNSP* ser.3 xiii (1983), 171–194; R. Osborne, *ABSA* lxxx (1985), 119–128; and the latter's *Classical Landscape with Figures* (London, 1987), 53–74.

4. Aesch. *PV* 460–1 (ἐξηῦρον αὐτοῖς γραμμάτων τε συνθέσεις, / μνήμην ἁπάντων, μουσομήτορ' ἐργάνην). Gorgias described letters as μνήμης ὄργανον (82 B11a.30 D–K).

5. Eur. *Palam.* 582 Nauck, *Suppl.* 433–437 (quoted below, p. 76). On a different track Democritus had claimed (68 B179 D–K) that learning letters helped to instil modesty *(aidos)* in boys.

6. *Pol.* viii.3.1338a15–17.

have come as any surprise to the more alert among those who attended the dramatic festivals of late fifth-century Athens.

We can begin a more detailed investigation with the first two of Aristotle's categories. What were the functions of writing in the world of work, money and trade? The running of a large estate in Attica would by this time naturally involve some writing. The main text on this subject is Xenophon's *Oeconomicus,* where both the landowner Ischomachus and his long-suffering wife are assumed to be somewhat literate and to use writing in the administration of their household; he gives her his lists.[7] This family, however, is practically at the economic pinnacle of fifth-century Athenian society, quite apart from the element of idealization; Ischomachus at one time possessed property worth more than seventy talents, it was thought.[8] It is certainly of interest that Xenophon can advertise Ischomachus as using documents, and no doubt Xenophon did so himself. At all events, the writer's assumption that a husband in a wealthy family could and would write lists, and that his wife could read them, is casual and therefore probably realistic. At the same social level, a wealthy guardian with a background of diverse investments, whose activities are described in a speech written by Lysias about 400, is said to have kept written accounts of his guardianship; the speaker describes them to the jurors, though without technical detail.[9]

There is, however, not the slightest reason to suppose that the ordinary Greek farmer made use of writing. In some regions farmers may possibly have been literate, but if so it was not from economic necessity. A somewhat ingenuous argument has brought Strepsiades out of the *Clouds* into this matter. Aristophanes represents him as keeping accounts of some kind.[10] Thus some proportion of the Athenian audience was by 423 familiar with the idea of written accounts. On the other hand, this scene does not show that an "uneducated old fellow

7. Xen. *Oec.* ix.10.

8. For biographical details see J. K. Davies, *Athenian Propertied Families, 600–300 B.C.* (Oxford, 1971), 265–268.

9. Lys. xxxii.19–22. For the family of Diogeiton and Diodotus see Davies 151–154.

10. Ar. *Nub.* 18–24: κἄκφερε τὸ γραμματεῖον, which is probably to be thought of as a wooden tablet with a waxed surface. Notice how easily this *grammateion,* just a written thing, becomes a "ledger" or "books" in a modern account: F. D. Harvey, *REG* lxxix (1966), 612 (in this chapter much will be said against Harvey's conclusions, but his article was an important advance on what had been written about Greek literacy before and remains indispensable reading).

living in the country" could commonly keep accounts and was therefore literate,[11] if by that it is meant that an ordinary farmer could do
so. Strepsiades is seen, some of the time at least, as being well-to-do—
he is not a peasant but a country landowner.[12] One may also keep
accounts of a kind without being more than semi-literate, and when
Strepsiades disputes with his creditors, no reference is made to documents.[13] It is also desirable to make some allowance for the fact that
the *Clouds* is a comedy. In Jonson's play *Every Man Out of His
Humour* (1599), the country bumpkin Sordido, "a wretched hob-
nailed chuff," spends most of his time reading almanacks. That tells
us something about the audience, but extremely little about English
peasants. In a comedy it is also appropriate that the father of a spend-
thrift should have some written records to grieve over.

The natural assumption might be that written lists, inventories, and
accounts were commonly used by well-to-do Greeks in the fifth and
fourth centuries, especially if they were engaged in banking, trade, or
manufacturing. At lower social levels, however, the evidence is slight.
Obviously an argument from silence will not carry us far; but on the
other hand nothing tells us that artisans, even in Athens, made much
use of such texts. As for selling things, when the Greeks wanted to
advertise, they made little or no use of the written word.[14]

None of the documentary practices mentioned so far is likely to
have been completely new, and in general new practices can hardly
ever be identified as such. Apprenticeship contracts are a possible
instance. It has been inferred from a passage of Xenophon that "when

11. Harvey 611–613, whose whole account of the functions of documents in classical Athens is undermined by inattention to social distinctions. For discussion of
Strepsiades' social status see K. J. Dover's comm., pp. xxvii–xxviii.

12. See *Nub.* 41–47, etc.

13. *Nub.* 1214–1302.

14. Harvey 613 cites a fourth-century ostracon with a list of household vessels,
guessing that "it is some potter's list, a list of articles sold or for sale." This is now B 12
in M. Lang, *Graffiti and Dipinti* (= *The Athenian Agora* xxi) (Princeton, 1976), and
dated to the late fourth or early third century; B 13 and 14 are shorter but similar lists.
Lang's suggestion that these are shopping lists is entirely implausible. But she seems to
recognize that they must be inventories. Beginning in the fifth century, a few of the
many surviving Greek loom-weights have letters or even occasionally words inscribed
on them: see M. Guarducci, *Epigrafia greca* iii (Rome, 1974), 539–540; F. Ferrandini
Troisi, in *Decima miscellanea greca e romana* (Rome, 1986), 91–114. About advertising see G. Raskin, *Handelsreclame en soortgelijke praktijken bij Grieken en
Romeinen* (Louvain, 1936), 41.

a young man became an apprentice, his terms were embodied in a *sungraphe*," a written agreement.[15] Isocrates refers to *sumbolaia* which concerned training;[16] these, too, must be written agreements. Once again, however, we are in the upper levels of society. Xenophon's remark simply shows that when a Greek of the cavalry class wanted his son to learn a skill *(techne)*, he often made a contract with the instructor. Likewise there is fourth-century evidence for written contracts made with men who worked for hire, but the cases are very untypical of the labour market, and we have no reason to suppose that a hired labourer would commonly see his conditions of work put into written form.[17]

There were other kinds of written contracts in fourth-century Athens. The maritime loans which appear so often in surviving speeches were normally written down,[18] partly (we may suppose) because of their size and complexity, but also for the special reason that the borrower might disappear overseas.[19] By about 340, Athenian commercial law recognized the usefulness of written evidence by stipulating that certain lawsuits could be brought only on the basis of written contracts.[20] Here is a clear case of innovation. Some large-scale leases were also recorded in documents in the fourth century; so were some loans, but these too were large, in the few cases in which figures are known.[21] The loans secured by parcels of land which were marked

15. Xen. *De eq.* 2.2; Harvey 607.

16. Isocr. xiii.6.

17. Harvey 607 cites four texts. Aeschin. i.160–165 (346 B.C.), which concerns male prostitution under contract, suggests, though Aeschines himself resists the notion (165), that *hetairos* relationships were often put into writing in this period. However this is clearly a special type of case, with risks and class connotations which made a written contract appropriate. Lys. iii.22 (about 390) concerns a similar relationship (and, incidentally, the smallest sum known to have been the subject of a written contract in classical Greece, 300 drachmas). The other two texts concern agreements with a painter (Ps.-Andoc. iv.17) and a sculptor (Dem. xviii.102) and are even less likely to be typical of work agreements.

18. Harvey 606.

19. Cf. M. I. Finley, *Studies in Land and Credit in Ancient Athens, 500–200 B.C.* (New Brunswick, N.J., 1952), 22.

20. Ps.-Dem. xxxii.1, concerning *dikai emporikai*, mercantile suits (cf. L. Gernet, *REG* li [1938], 21–26 = *Droit et société dans la Grèce ancienne* [Paris, 1955], 186–189; but the text does not justify his claim that the *sungraphe* was now the standard instrument of all Athenian commerce).

21. Leases: Harvey 606–607; but *IG* i².377 (= Meiggs & Lewis, *GHI* no. 62)

with inscribed stone *horoi* seem, from the size of the loans, to have been transactions among the well-to-do; they definitely did not concern small-scale peasant farmers.[22]

Knowledge of how to use written contracts may in the fourth century have extended further down the social scale than these instances suggest. Orators sometimes refer to written contracts, *sungraphai*, as part of the normal furniture of life,[23] and jurors who are not well-to-do presumably understand at least something of what is involved. And when Xenophon recommends that a horse-owner should make a written contract with the man who is to break the horse in,[24] he assumes that the party of the second part, who is not at all likely to be a member of the social elite, will know what is involved.

Aristotle takes it for granted that there should be in every state an official with whom private contracts could be registered (as there was not in fact at Athens, where they could be deposited with private citizens). This practice demonstrates the normality and the importance of written documents for a small and influential section of the Greek population of the third quarter of the fourth century.[25]

We have moved gradually from the subject of business practices to the subject of legal procedure. Other legal practices fill out the story of an expansion in the functions of the written word. From Isaeus, for instance, we learn that testamentary adoption—the principal way in which an Athenian could determine who received his property after his death, and not standard practice, since it was unavailable to a man who had legitimate sons—now involved writing.[26] Allegations of tes-

---

belongs to another category, being a public document. Loans: 4,000 drachmas in Ps.-Dem. xxxiii.12, 1,000 in liii.9–10. Concerning the kinds of documents used and not used in fourth-century banking see J. Hasebroek, *Hermes* lv (1920), 113–173.

22. Finley 79–87; P. Millett, *Opus* i (1982), 223. Of those *horoi* that are dated, the earliest belongs to 363–362.

23. Ps.-Andoc. iv.17 (390s or 380s, but not delivered). In the 340s or later: Aeschin. i.161; Dem. xlvi.28; Ps.-Dem. xxxiii.36. Cf., decades later still, [Aristot.] *Rhet.* i.15.22.1376b11–14.

24. Xen. *De eq.* 2.2 again.

25. Aristot. *Pol.* vi.8.1321b34–38: "Another office [*arche*] is the one with which you have to have registered [*anagraphesthai*] private contracts and the verdicts of the law courts; the same official must have the keeping of legal indictments and the introductory documents. In some places they divide this office." Cf. W. Lambrinudakis & M. Wörrle, *Chiron* xiii (1983), 336–337. For the sources on fourth-century Athenian practice see G. M. Calhoun, *CPh* ix (1914), 142.

26. It is likely that writing had long played a part in property transmission by per-

tamentary fraud seem to be so common,[27] however, that they tend to suggest that documents as such generally inspired little trust in the Athenian mind.

The manumission of slaves was a procedure for which writing was well suited, since an inscribed text imparted some durability to a condition which the former slave-owner might wish to revoke. Such a text is first known about 425 B.C., and from the fourth to second century manumission inscriptions, normally associated with a religious cult, are commonplace in the Greek world.[28] There could hardly be a clearer example of written texts which went beyond the transcription of oral utterances and served to guarantee the continuing validity of their message.

Closely connected with the growth in the legal functions of the written word is the belief of many Greeks in the value of written laws. This belief was already well established in a number of places in the sixth century, but it gained further ground thereafter.

Written pleadings were in use at Athens in both public and private actions by the last quarter of the fifth century; they are attested from 425 and 424, respectively. The actual writing was done by the clerk of court.[29] By Demosthenes' time, however, litigants generally seem to have written the pleadings for themselves, or at least it was their responsibility to get the writing done. This change has been dated to the 370s.[30] By Demosthenes' time, in addition, a remarkable Athenian law required that in some types of cases all the evidence of witnesses should be presented in written form,[31] and though there can be

mitting inventories (cf. Eur. *Palam.* 578 Nauck). The earliest allusions to a written disposition (the word *will* would be somewhat misleading) seem to be Soph. *Trach.* 157 and Ar. *Vesp.* 583–586 (on which cf. Gernet, *REG* xxxiii [1920], 255–256 = *Droit et société* 146). For references in Isaeus see esp. iv.13, vi.7, vii.2, ix.2, xi.8. For an account of Athenian inheritance practices see W. E. Thompson, *Prudentia* xiii (1981), 13–23. No doubt Harvey, *REG* lxxix (1966), 617, is correct to see written dispositions as the preserve of those who were "at least moderately well off."

27. Isaeus i.41, iv.12–14, vii.2, etc. See Calhoun, *CPh* ix (1914), 134–44.

28. See Guarducci, *Epigrafia greca* iii.263–294.

29. G. M. Calhoun, *TAPhA* l (1919), 180–182.

30. Calhoun 183–193. In the earlier orators references to pleadings are in the form "this is what he swore"; now they say "this is what he wrote" (190). But Calhoun was perhaps too dogmatic in excluding some earlier instances: Andoc. i.43, 47 (399 B.C.) and Ar. *Plut.* 480–481 (388 B.C.) deserve reconsideration.

31. Dem. xlv.44: ὁ νόμος μαρτυρεῖν ἐν γραμματείῳ κελεύει, ἵνα μήτ' ἀφελεῖν ἐξῇ μήτε προσθεῖναι τοῖς γεγραμμένοις μηδέν. See further E. Leisi, *Der Zeuge im*

no presumption at all that the document had to be autograph, the growth in the importance of writing is evident. The change dates from roughly the period between 380 and 364. Written evidence was said to have the advantage that nothing could afterwards be subtracted from or added to it; in other words, it became fixed and solemn through being written. And turning from formal procedure to the practices that litigants freely chose to follow, we happen to hear that Pericles was the first to speak in a law-court from a written text, a practice which may be alluded to a little later by Aristophanes and was to become a subject of intense controversy in the fourth century.[32]

In later times Theophrastus expected a litigious man to carry a document-jar *(echinos)* in his clothing and sheaves of papers in his hands.[33] This would certainly not have been so in the mid-fifth century. It was the greatly increased use of writing in the fourth century, for contracts and for evidence especially, which led to this mass of paperwork.

However, in spite of the developments described above, legal practice, like the administration of large-scale business, remained to a considerable extent oral and independent of documents.[34] The law of sale set little store by documents; live witnesses to oral contracts were what counted.[35] Receipts were still unknown.[36] While documents gained authority, they remained subject to a lot of oral control: when an Athenian witness's evidence was read, he had to be there consenting.[37] The reason for all this was not that Greek writing was inher-

---

attischen Recht (Frauenfeld, 1908), 75–77. The date: R. J. Bonner & G. Smith, *The Administration of Justice from Homer to Aristotle* i (Chicago, 1930), 353–362. They are puzzled by the innovation, not observing that it was assisted by the higher status now attributed to documents. The earliest reference to written testimony is in Isaeus v.3 (392–387 B.C.) (Bonner & Smith i.358); at that time it was still a voluntary procedure.

32. Suidas iv.1179 Adler (but for doubts about this see M. Lavency, *LEC* xxvii [1959], 354); Ar. *Vesp.* 960–961.

33. Theophr. *Char.* 6.8, describing the man who is without shame. Theophrastus' *Characters* is itself characteristic of an age in which orators used books to assist their preparations; see D. J. Furley, *Symb.Osl.* xxx (1953), 56–60.

34. Cf. G. Pasquali, *SIFC* vii (1929), 243–249.

35. F. Pringsheim, *The Greek Law of Sale* (Weimar, 1950), 43. Unwitnessed written contracts seem to have been acceptable at Athens by about 330: F. Pringsheim in *Aequitas und Bona Fides. Festgabe zum 70. Geburtstag von August Simonius* (Basel, 1955), 290–291.

36. J. Hasebroek, *Hermes* lviii (1923), 393–395.

37. Cf. Dem. xlvi.6, etc.

ently inappropriate for signature-writing.[38] Rather, the oral way of doing things was established and universally understood, while letters and some other types of document had a certain reputation as a source of fraud, a reputation which was periodically reinforced by the discovery of forgeries. Even we, with our great trust in signatures, require that for certain purposes they shall be multiple or shall be witnessed. The Greeks had ways of authenticating documents—they did it with seal rings[39] and with witnesses. During the late fifth and fourth centuries these mechanisms helped them to increase their use of documents considerably, but to a certain degree the old attitude also persisted.

The difficulties of constructing a detailed chronological account of the growing use of the written word in economic and legal life during this period are plain enough (see the chronological table at the end of this section). There must also have been notable divergences between developments in different cities. At Athens, a period of quite rapid expansion in such functions might be hypothesized for the 430s and 420s. Less uncertainly, there was another period of expansion roughly between the speeches of Lysias and Isaeus on the one hand and those of Demosthenes on the other. One view has it that the growing use of written contracts in this period was connected with a growth in investment capital;[40] part of the explanation, however, is certainly a growing belief in the authority of the written word.

Leaving aside for the moment Aristotle's remark that writing was useful for *mathesis,* learning, we should next consider its usefulness for *politikai praxeis,* civic affairs. Here again there is a great increase in the use of the written word during the classical period. Some cities

---

38. As Pasquali claimed, 246. But his argument that it was impossible to sign distinctively in classical Greek handwriting (accepted by Harvey, *REG* lxxix [1966], 610–611; and by R. Bogaert, *Banques et banquiers dans les cités grecques* [Leiden, 1968], 337) is unpersuasive on various counts. It was known in fourth-century Athens that an individual's handwriting was distinctive: Dem. xxix.21 (a passage which is misinterpreted by E. Berneker in *RE* Suppl. x (1965) s.v. χειρόγραφον, col. 126); Ps.-Dem. xxxiii.17. Cf. Hyperid. *Lycophr.* fr. IVa, from Pollux ii.152. In favour of the strong probability that a cursive hand was known in fourth-century Athens see E. G. Turner, *Athenian Books in the Fifth and Fourth Centuries B.C.* (London, 1952), 8; however the development of cursive writing was gradual and apparently not complete by 323; cf. G. Cavallo, *Scriptorium* xxii (1968), 291–292, commenting on R. Seider, *Paläographie der griechischen Papyri* i, plates vol. l, (Stuttgart, 1967).

39. See, e.g., Dem. xxxvii.42. Detailed discussion: R. J. Bonner, *CPh* iii (1908), 399–407.

40. L. Gernet, *REG* li (1938), 29–32 = *Droit et société* 191–193.

had officials called *mnemones,* "rememberers," and in the mid-fifth century at least some of the *mnemones* truly relied on memory.[41] By Aristotle's time, however, they were normally concerned with documents.[42] And by now civic institutions in many Greek states had long depended on there being numerous citizens who were at least semi-literate. At Athens one can see in outline how the role of writing in civic life increased during the fifth and fourth centuries. It is obvious that by the fifth century anyone who wanted to play a leading part in the public affairs of Athens or of practically any other Greek city, with the possible exception of Sparta, had to be literate and able to make use of the written word. To what extent this was true for those who simply wanted to exercise their rights as citizens remains to be seen. First we must consider what writing was and was not used for in the affairs of the cities.

Once again the question of the typicality of Athens is bound to arise. Athenian epigraphy gives the impression that from the mid-fifth century public life there was full of documents, and though in other cities too laws and treaties were more and more on display, the number of civic inscriptions is far smaller than at Athens. This is probably to some extent a difference based on money: Athens was the imperial city, awash with money by classical Greek standards, and it was Athens which saw the great proliferation of public inscriptions.[43] But a democratic attitude, sometimes expressed in the phrase *skopein toi boulomenoi,* "for whoever wishes to inspect,"[44] also seems to have contributed,[45] and this attitude was not peculiar to Athens.

In the previous chapter we took note of the increasing role of writing in the public life of Athens, especially from the time of Cleisthenes. These changes implied a certain degree of literacy on the part of men of the *zeugites* class, broadly speaking the hoplites. Ostracism, which required 6,000 votes to be cast, is the clearest instance of this, and the

41. Thus in *SIG*[3] 45 (Halicarnassus, about 460) = Meiggs & Lewis, *GHI* no. 32, lines 20–22, jurors are required to swear that "what the *mnemones* know shall be binding." Cf. G. Busolt, *Griechische Staatskunde* i (Munich, 1920), 488. See also the problematic text of the 460s or 450s from Teos published by P. Herrmann, *Chiron* xi (1981), 1–30, line d18.

42. Aristot. *Pol.* vi.8.1321b38–40.

43. Cf. M. I. Finley, *Annales E.S.C.* xxxvii (1982), 705. Athens' unusually good supply of marble probably had some effect here.

44. On this see W. Larfeld, *Handbuch der griechischen Epigraphik* ii (Leipzig, 1902), 720; B. D. Meritt, *Epigraphica Attica* (Cambridge, Mass., 1940), 90.

45. Cf. P. A. Cartledge, *JHS* xcviii (1978), 36.

procedure was successfully put to use in the 480s and on a few later occasions; seven individuals are known to have been ostracized from Themistocles (about 470) to Hyperbolus (in 417) inclusively.[46] The functions of writing in Greek public life seem gradually to increase in the decades after 480. Honorary decrees in favour of foreigners begin to be known from about 460.[47] State decrees, treaties and public dedications had been inscribed in earlier times. More novel, probably, are the honorific casualty lists set up in Athens, the famous codification of law at Gortyn, and various kinds of public financial accounts, most of these also from Athens.[48] Public officials with financial responsibilities now kept written accounts, like well-off private individuals. Yet all or most of these documents must have developed out of types of documents which already existed in earlier periods.

The relationship between writing and the Athenian Empire of the fifth century raises complex questions. How much use did Athens make of writing in exercising power over its allies? Could it have exercised that power without written messages and records? It is clear in any case that the mass of epigraphical documents gathered in *The Athenian Tribute Lists* represents only a fraction of the writing which the empire entailed, and that many of these documents had vital functions in the empire's administration and in expressing the authority of the Athenians. In the early history of the Delian League the Athenians were already "very exacting in their management," Thucydides remarks,[49] and the collection of tribute and ships was a demanding administrative task. Athens could not have carried out this task without possessing a sizeable body of literate citizens, and in the 470s that was a fairly new phenomenon.

Meanwhile the belief in the value of written laws certainly grew stronger. It would be interesting to know when widespread legends about the law-*writing* activities of the early lawgivers—not only Solon but also Zaleucus of Locri, Charondas of Catana and the others— really began to flourish. We are on firmer ground with Gorgias, who asserted that written laws were the guardians of justice,[50] a senti-

46. See P. J. Rhodes, comm. on [Aristot.] *Ath.Pol.*, p. 271.

47. I. Calabi Limentani, *QUCC* xvi (1984), 91.

48. See, respectively, D. W. Bradeen, *The Funerary Inscriptions* (= *The Athenian Agora* xvii) (Princeton, 1974), nos. 1–16; R. F. Willetts, *The Law Code of Gortyn* = *Kadmos* Suppl. i (1967); B. D. Meritt, *Athenian Financial Documents of the Fifth Century* (Ann Arbor, 1932).

49. i.99.1.

50. 82 B11a.30 D–K.

ment which was presumably shared by considerable numbers of "democratic"-minded Greeks. Theseus' statement in Euripides' *Supplices* was undoubtedly meant by the poet to be authoritative, and it must have reflected the feelings of much of the audience. Contrasting tyranny with a city which has an accepted body of laws, the king goes on:

> But when the laws are written the weak man and the wealthy man have an equal suit [*dike*], and the weaker if he is defamed may sue the more fortunate, and the lesser man, should he be in the right, defeats the big man.[51]

An increase in the civic and political uses of the written word may well have occurred during the Peloponnesian War (raising an unanswerable question about the role of war as a catalyst in this social change). One new type of text is the political pamphlet, represented for us by the pseudo-Xenophontic *Constitution of Athens* (the "Old Oligarch"), written by an Athenian, probably in the early years of the war. On a more practical level, it may be symptomatic that by the late fifth century the official indication that an Athenian age-class was required for military service came in a written announcement.[52] Lists of names were apparently posted on the base of the statues of the ten eponymous tribal heroes in the Agora, and this began to be used as a kind of public notice-board for other purposes, too; the texts of proposed new laws had to be posted there, for instance, and later on it was for a time the place where lists of ephebes were put up.[53] It is certainly significant that in the political crisis of 411–410 great importance was attached to written texts of supposed early laws, with

51. Eur. *Supp.* 433–437. Stobaeus' version of these lines (49) is in effect bowdlerized, suggesting that such sentiments were felt at some point to be politically charged—unless, that is, the received text is actually Hellenistic.

52. [Aristot.] *Ath.Pol.* 53.7; cf. Ar. *Av.* 448–450, *Pax* 1179–84; Dem. liv.3.

53. The monument is believed to date from just after 430: see T. L. Shear, *Hesperia* xxxix (1970), esp. 209–212 (but it might not be the earliest one; cf. Rhodes on [Aristot.] *Ath.Pol.* 21.6). Its notice-board function is first attested in Ar. *Pax* 1179–84 (those who suffer, he says, are the countrymen); then in Andoc. i.83, where it is said that a decree of 403/402 required that the *nomothetai* should post the texts of proposed laws "in front of the Eponymous Ones" *en sanisin*, on boards, and also required that laws which were confirmed should be inscribed "on the wall where they were previously written up." Later allusions include Isaeus v.38; Dem. xx.94 (which shows that the proposed laws had to be read out in the Assembly), xxi.103, xxiv.18, 25. Ephebe lists: [Aristot.] *Ath.Pol.* 53.4. See further R. E. Wycherley, *Literary and Epigraphical Testimonia* (= *The Athenian Agora* iii) (Princeton, 1957), 85–90.

the eventual result that *anagrapheis,* "inscribers," were appointed to produce definitive texts of the laws of Solon and Draco.[54] In 403/402 a law was passed that "an unwritten law must not be applied by the magistrates in any case."[55] Meanwhile, after a period of some disorder in public record-keeping, the Athenians created a state archive, apparently some time between 409 and 405.[56] And without overestimating the importance of an argument from silence, we may see it as natural that it is in Aristophanes' *Frogs,* in 405, that we first hear of a class of junior public clerks *(hupogrammateis).*[57]

The fourth-century democracy at Athens made heavy use of writing for some purposes. Between 403 and 321 we have epigraphical evidence of no fewer than 482 decrees passed by the Assembly.[58] The Council presidents not only put up notices of the Council's agenda; they also gave written notice of meetings of the Assembly[59] (which emphatically does not show that all its members could read). The names of those who owed money to the city were written up on boards, as were those of convicted criminals.[60] In the fourth century each Athenian citizen who was willing to undertake jury service had a bronze (later, wooden) ticket with his name and deme written on it[61]—which suggests that he would normally at least be able to read it for himself. An intriguing passage in a forensic speech of the 360s claims that the speaker would have written up an explanatory list of the defendant's relatives on a *pinax* had it not been for the fact that those sitting furthest away would have been unable to see it.[62] How-

54. Nicomachus became the most famous of these. For a summary account see D. M. MacDowell, *The Law in Classical Athens* (London, 1978), 46–47.

55. Andoc. i.85. This naturally did not prevent men from invoking *agraphoi nomoi;* cf. E. Weiss, *Griechisches Privatrecht* (Leipzig, 1923), 75 n.140.

56. A. L. Boegehold, *AJA* lxxvi (1972), 23–30.

57. Ar. *Ran.* 1084; cf. Lys. xxx.28; Dem. xix.237.

58. M. H. Hansen, *GRBS* xix (1978), 317 n.6 = *The Athenian Ecclesia* (Copenhagen, 1983), 163 n.6.

59. [Aristot.] *Ath.Pol.* 43.3–4; again, we have no information as to when these practices started. Written notice of Assembly meetings is referred to in Aeschin. ii.60–61 (343 B.C.).

60. Dem. xxv.70; Isocr. xv.237.

61. On these *pinakia* see [Aristot.] *Ath.Pol.* 63.4; Harvey, *REG* lxxix (1966), 595; J. H. Kroll, *Athenian Bronze Allotment Plates* (Cambridge, Mass., 1972). For the complex system by which jurors were assigned to courts see *Ath.Pol.* 63–65.

62. Ps.-Dem. xliii.18. Harvey 596–597 overestimates the clarity of this passage and its importance as evidence for the level of Athenian literacy, even though he cites A. H. M. Jones, *The Athenian Democracy* (Oxford, 1957), 36–37, on the disproportionate presence of the comfortably off in the juries of Demosthenes' time.

ever, it may be significant that the voting in large jury trials at Athens was organized in such a way that the jurors did not have to read or write.[63]

Some of the other functions which writing did *not* fulfil in public life deserve attention. On the level of popular politics, the scrawling of political slogans seems to be practically unattested. On the governmental level, it is of interest that no classical Greek state seems to have put together an effective property census which might have served as a basis for tax-gathering (no doubt the liturgy method of raising revenue suited the Athenian democracy quite well). Athenian commanders when they were on campaign rarely wrote letters home to the Council or the Assembly. When Nicias did so from Sicily in 414, it was worthy of remark.[64] In fact Thucydides explains in copious detail why Nicias chose to write: not only was his situation extremely dangerous, but also he feared that oral messengers might fail to convey that situation, either through lack of speaking ability or through poor memory (notice that it is assumed that they would rely on memory rather than memoranda) or through wishing to please popular opinion. A letter would reveal the truth. We may gain the impression here that both Nicias and Thucydides had made a discovery, and that the latter was explaining it to his public. In any case Nicias wrote, and, if Thucydides is to be trusted, at some length. Nonetheless, when the messengers reached Athens, they delivered their oral message before they handed over the letter; the clerk of the Assembly then read this out to the Assembly.[65]

Heralds naturally still played a highly visible part in the public life of Greek cities in the late fifth century. They were not only the officials who summoned and dismissed assemblies, who proclaimed honours and the victors of competitions; they were also the normal means by which public announcements were made. One reason why Aristotle

63. For the fact see [Aristot.] *Ath.Pol.* 68.2–4.

64. Thuc. vii.8.2 (and he had probably not written often if at all before, in spite of 11.1, where ἐπιστολή probably means "message": see Gomme's commentary ad loc.; he can hardly have sent many letters before, as is supposed by O. Longo in *Studi in onore di Anthos Ardizzoni* [Rome, 1978], i.540 n.7). The only earlier instance is the letter which Cleon may have written from Pylos (Eupolis 308 Kock, but the letter element depends on later Greek interpretation of the passage). Subsequent cases, also on exceptionally important occasions: Xen. *Hell.* i.1.23, 7.4. Cf. R. Weil in *Le monde grec. Hommages à Claire Préaux* (Brussels, 1975), 163–164; Longo 517–524.

65. vii.8.2–16.1.

will not permit a city to exceed a certain size is that no *kerux* would be able to address it.[66]

The ambiguity of the relationship between literacy and democracy has already been mentioned: although proponents of democracy favoured written laws, tyrants as well as democracies could make use of writing.[67] And it was never essential for the functioning of the Athenian democracy—or, we may assume, of most other Greek democracies—that practically every male citizen should be literate or even semi-literate.[68] Standing on the tragic stage in Athens in the 420s, Theseus proclaimed the equality before the law of the rich and the weak in a city which has written laws—such as Athens. A fine theory. It was also a fine theory, enunciated as we have noticed in the Funeral Oration, that Athens was a democracy of mass participation. This it was not, and the fact must be appreciated if the functioning of the written word and the limits of literacy are to be understood. In the first place there were legal restrictions: a member of the thetic class, the lowest of the four property classes, was excluded from office and even from the Council.[69] A recent study shows in detail how restricted active participation in political life was in relation to the conventional image of classical Athens.[70] Politics and even jury service in the famous popular juries of democratic Athens left most farmers and artisans toiling at their banausic and necessary means of making a living. How much this obtained in other democracies with smaller territories and hence better access to the city for country-dwellers is a matter for speculation—as indeed it is partly a matter of speculation how much such cities paralleled Athens in the increased use of the written word. At all events the limited participation of the Athenians in civic life makes a number of things easier to understand: the increase in documentation (the illiterate mass was only marginally involved—and was

66. See, e.g., Andoc. i.40; Thuc. ii.2.4; and E. Saglio in C. Daremberg & Saglio (eds.), s.v. "praeco," *Dictionnaire des antiquités grecques et romaines* (1907) 607–609 (a new study is needed). Cf. Aristot. *Pol.* vii.4 1326b6–7.

67. Cf. Pl. *Leg.* ix.859a.

68. Contrary to what is often asserted, for example by H. R. Immerwahr, in *Classical, Mediaeval and Renaissance Studies in Honor of Berthold Louis Ullman* (Rome, 1964), i.17; and by S. Flory, *AJPh* ci (1980), 19 ("virtually every male citizen needed . . . name-signing literacy").

69. [Aristot.] *Ath.Pol.* 7.4, 26.2 (it is true that the curious phrasing of the former of these passages shows that by the mid-fourth century some people evaded the rule).

70. L. B. Carter, *The Quiet Athenian* (Oxford, 1986), esp. 76–98.

less and less likely to cause trouble by seeking involvement as civic life became more technical); the end of ostracism (there were simply not enough politically active and at least partially literate citizens after the Sicilian Expedition); and the almost total lack of interest in popular education, even in democratic states (those who really participated had sufficient resources to ensure that their sons acquired at least a smattering of literacy).

Before leaving the civic functions of writing, we must at least glance at a new use of writing which began to condition the Athenians' and others' views of their political past, namely historiography. Oral performance and tradition, and texts too, already gave the Greeks extensive information about the past—highly unreliable information.[71] After shadowy beginnings, history-writing makes its appearance, and with a work of extraordinary size.[72] Herodotus consulted some books while preparing his history, and to a certain extent he appreciated the usefulness of epigraphic texts for one who is reconstructing the past.[73] However, documentary research was not a major part of his undertaking (admittedly this was in part a result of his choice of subject), and he freely invents texts—not only speeches but even texts which had in fact been written down in their original forms.[74] Herodotus himself wrote, and in prose, and then proceeded to give oral performances of parts of what he had written.

This work was probably completed in the 420s.[75] Writing twenty or thirty years later, Thucydides treated documents with somewhat greater respect. He still preferred oral testimony to written, and "it could never occur to him that written records were the primary source

71. On the latter point see esp. M. I. Finley, *The Use and Abuse of History* (London, 1975), 13–30. J. Vansina, *Oral Tradition as History* (Madison, Wis., 1985), is the most useful single item in the growing literature on this subject.

72. The size of Herodotus' work by the standards of the time is well emphasized by Flory 13–16.

73. On the latter point see S. West, *CQ* xxxv (1985), 278–305, who concludes *inter alia* that Herodotus was "just as happy with texts whose meaning he had to take on trust as with those which he might himself verify" (302), and that for his main subject "he gives the impression of setting relatively little store by inscriptions" (303).

74. E.g., i.124, viii.22. Verse he is more likely to preserve accurately. There seems to be no fully adequate discussion of Herodotus' place in the transition from oral culture to partly literate culture (but see F. Hartog, *Le miroir d'Hérodote* [Paris, 1980], 282–297); even the basic question about his variation between the verbs *graphein* and *legein* needs further investigation.

75. This is not the place for an elaborate statement of views about the dates at which Herodotus and Thucydides wrote.

for history."[76] But besides seeking a much higher level of general reliability than Herodotus had achieved, he was prepared to include transcriptions of key texts.[77] At least so it is normally supposed (precise transcription can never, as far as I know, be proved, and there often had to be a transposition from one dialect to another). The difference hardly stems from a greater degree of honesty; rather, the written word is belatedly imposing its own logic. The change could be compared to the invention of photography; even without it there could be artistic realism, but with it realism was dramatically increased.

The crisis of 411 revealed symptoms of the change that was going on, with appeals to old written *nomoi* playing an important role. Writing was now felt to have the vital function of being the most reliable source of information about the political past. This did not of course produce a complete change: fourth-century orators and politicians frequently invented historical facts in a most abandoned fashion, and historians avoided documentary research. But by 342, when Isocrates is commenting on Spartan illiteracy, he can single out as the virtue of *grammata* that "they have so much power that those who understand and use them become expert not only on what has been done in their own time, but on what has ever happened," where he is plainly alluding to historical knowledge as Greeks now understood it.[78]

The ambivalent force of written records of the past emerges clearly at the end of this period from the fact that when Alexander of Macedon set out on his conquests he took a historian with him—Callisthenes, the nephew of Aristotle—plainly for purposes of propaganda rather than science.

History was perhaps one of the subjects which Aristotle had in mind when he said that writing was useful for "learning." Since he

76. A. Momigliano, *Secondo contributo alla storia degli studi classici* (Rome, 1960), 37 = *Studies in Historiography* (London, 1966), 135; cf. *RSI* lxxxvii (1975), 21 = *Sesto contributo alla storia degli studi classici e del mondo antico* (Rome, 1980), 38. It is entirely anachronistic of J. Goody, *The Domestication of the Savage Mind* (Cambridge, 1977), 91, to suppose that archives were necessary for history-writing.

77. Concerning the problems raised by the documents in Thucydides see above all C. Meyer, *Die Urkunden im Geschichtswerk des Thukydides* (Munich, 1955); O. Luschnat in *RE* Suppl. xii (1971), cols. 1124–32. Their importance plainly decreases if they are really a sign of the work's incompleteness. *IG* i².86 is part of an epigraphical copy of the treaty recorded in Thuc. v.47; the texts correspond closely but are not identical.

78. Isocr. *Panath.* 209.

was concerned with useful learning we may, however, conjecture that what was uppermost in his mind was handbook literature. A good deal of this certainly existed at least from the fifth century onwards,[79] practically all of it later superseded and therefore known to us only by allusions. Medicine was probably the field most written about. The reading of such works would not necessarily in Greek conditions have been confined to the professionals concerned, and Thucydides seems to have had some close contact with medical writings.[80] The earlier rhetorical handbooks, those written by the Syracusans Corax and Tisias some time after 466,[81] began another important genre. The readership of all technical works must have remained minute in relation to the population at large, and a lot of technical teaching probably continued to be conducted without the intense use of books. Nonetheless, most Greeks doctors probably read, and in some other occupations the use of some technical literature must have been commonplace by Xenophon's time. The occupations that came to his mind in this context, besides doctoring, were those of engineer, surveyor, *astrologos* (whatever that meant exactly) and rhapsode.[82] As for the effects of all this compilation of technical works, we may say—without underestimating the capacity of ancient memories—that they are likely to have been very great within some of the fields concerned: really large quantities of precise information could now be transmitted to minds that were by no means exceptional.

Writing had many other functions in classical Greece besides those which Aristotle listed as "useful." Important among these were religious and commemorative functions, and such functions probably widened during the fifth and fourth centuries. The evidence is admittedly very fragmentary, and once again it is hard to know what is new. With regard to inscribed curses, for example, many of which survive on small sheets of lead (see Figure 2), it seemed until recently that the earliest ones dated from the fifth century; but it was always possible

---

79. Cf. Turner, *Athenian Books* 18; H. Thesleff, *Arctos* n.s. iv (1966), 105–107. See also M. Fuhrmann, *Das systematische Lehrbuch* (Göttingen, 1960), esp. 122–144.

80. Ar. *Nub.* 332 (*iatrotechnas*) suggests that the Athenian theatre public was aware of medical writers. See also Pl. *Phaedr.* 268c; Xen. *Mem.* iv.2.10 On Thucydides cf. D. L. Page, *CQ* iii (1953), 97–110 (but he might have acquired his knowledge orally).

81. Cic. *Brut.* 46.

82. In Xen. *Mem.* iv.2.10 Socrates first suggests to Euthydemus that the latter may have accumulated books in order to become a doctor (πολλὰ γὰρ καὶ ἰατρῶν ἐστι συγγράμματα)—or an engineer (ἀρχιτέκτων)? or a surveyor (γνωμονικός)? or an *astrologos*? or a rhapsode?

that the practice was older, and now one or two sixth-century instances are known from Selinus.[83] It seems to have been the "inscribers" of the years 410–404 who were responsible for putting up the first systematic religious calendar at Athens; but the writer who reveals this shows that, not surprisingly, there was already written information about the prescribed sacrifices.[84] Written oracles had had some circulation in archaic times—yet when Aristophanes makes mock of an oracle-book, or, better, oracle-sheet *(biblion)*, it may be suspected that he is attacking something that was in some way novel in 414.[85] In the fourth century a successful soothsayer might own esoteric and valuable books *(bibloi),*[86] which with the spread of specialized literature of many kinds is scarcely surprising. In the fourth and third centuries an exceptional Greek grave might contain a small gold tablet with an esoteric text concerning the afterlife.[87] It is likely, however, that the religious practices of most ordinary Greeks were touched by the written word lightly or not at all.

It could easily be assumed that Greeks of widely divergent social classes used writing for commemoration by commissioning funerary inscriptions. An informed scholar says that in Attica, when private funerary monuments came into use again after about 430, there emerged "monuments commemorating the domestic virtues of the ordinary citizen."[88] Yet even in this period it may be doubted that the democratization of epitaphs went very far. The labours of Greek epigraphists have not yet extended to any thorough sociological investi-

83. Recent literature on this topic, which gives guidance to earlier works: D. R. Jordan, *GRBS* xxvi (1985), 151–197; C. A. Faraone, *JHS* cv (1985), 150–154 (on the early chronology: Faraone 153). The earliest texts known at that time were collected by L. H. Jeffery, *ABSA* l (1955), 69–76. The sixth-century texts: A. Brugnone, in *Studi di storia antica offerti dagli allievi a Eugenio Manni* (Rome, 1976), 67–90, nos. 1–3, whence *SEG* xxvi (1976–77), nos. 1112–14. For inscribed public imprecations of fifth-century date from Teos see *SIG*³ 37 and 38 = Meiggs & Lewis, *GHI* no. 30, P. Herrmann, *Chiron* xi (1981), 1–30.

84. Lys. xxx.17–21; some of the background is discussed by S. Dow, *Historia* ix (1960), 270–293.

85. *Av.* 974–991, where the refrain is λαβὲ τὸ βιβλίον, as the Oracle-monger tries to deceive Pisthetairus with a spurious prediction. In Eur. *Hipp.* 953–954 Theseus had derided Hippolytus for his devotion to Orphic *grammata*.

86. Isocr. xix.5. It is noteworthy, however, that the superstitious man (Theophr. *Char.* 16) is not shown consulting prophetic books for himself.

87. Such texts have been much written about; cf. S. G. Cole, *GRBS* xxi (1980), 223–238; R. Janko, *CQ* xxxiv (1984), 89–100.

88. S. C. Humphreys, *JHS* c (1980), 123 = *The Family, Women and Death. Comparative Studies* (London, 1983), 121.

gation of funerary inscriptions. However neither the absolute number of surviving epitaphs from the classical period nor the funerary monuments to which they are commonly attached suggest that the mass of the population was involved.

Epitaphs, more than most other forms of ancient writing, had functions that went beyond the straightforward transcription or recording of some spoken message. The desire to perpetuate the memory of the deceased is only one of the possible purposes of such texts, which may also include claims of social standing as well as the natural wish of the survivors to assuage their grief.[89]

We turn to the circulation of literary compositions. While the Homeric poems continued to be the dominant works of literature, it would scarcely be an exaggeration to say that during the four generations which extended from the mid-fifth century to the death of Aristotle in 322 the minds of men were to a considerable extent remade by contemporary books. Both the writing and the personal reading of literary works increased in volume and significance.

The completion of a literary work as vast in its demands on the author as Herodotus' history—twice as long as a Homeric poem and more carefully structured—was a remarkable feat. Because of the practical limits of recitations, Herodotus also begins an era in which private reading had much more point than previously. Tragedy too, and perhaps in the first place the outstanding and continuing popularity of Aeschylus, contributed to the popularity (relatively speaking) of reading.[90] Works in these and other genres proliferated in the late fifth century, and new genres appeared. Forensic speeches are an important instance; it is a credible story that Antiphon, who died in 411, was the first to make such a work available to the public.[91]

A trade in books, of some kind, is first mentioned by Eupolis in the

89. Closely related to epitaphs are inscribed names of the deceased placed *inside* their graves; on this phenomenon see Guarducci, *Epigrafia greca* iii.141–142.

90. It so happens that the first reader of a literary work whom we meet in a Greek text is reading Euripides: this is Dionysus himself in Ar. *Ran.* 52–54. A solitary reader appears at about the same date on the famous Grottaferrata funerary relief (from Asia Minor): see T. Birt, *Die Buchrolle in der Kunst* (Leipzig, 1907), 15, fig. 90; E. Pfuhl & H. Möbius, *Die ostgriechischen Grabreliefs* 1 (Mainz, 1977), 25–26, no. 56. Of course there must have been solitary readers before (and a youth is shown reading on a red-figure *lekythos* of about 470: J. D. Beazley, *Attic Red-Figure Vase-Painters* [2 ed., Oxford, 1963], 452; F. A. G. Beck, *Album of Greek Education* [Sydney, 1975], 14, 20 no. 77).

91. For Antiphon's being first see Diod.Sic. in Clem.Alex *Strom.* i.79.3 (cf. A.

420s or 410s. In the *Apology* Plato refers with apparent casualness to the ease with which texts by Anaxagoras could be purchased. And by the 370s an inter-city trade in books had become rather commonplace.[92] It is in 405 that we first hear of a personal collection of books, that of Euripides.[93] All this fits well with the growing civic functions of the written word: the written mode of communicating was more and more accepted and exploited. Still, it is striking that even now it remained strange for an individual who was not a rhapsode to own the complete works of the most famous of all poets.[94] Who in fact was the first truly bookish individual among the Greeks? Hardly Socrates, though he is depicted by Xenophon reading with his friends the books of "the wise men of long ago."[95] Some might say Euripides; but by the standards of later Greek intelligentsias, the best answer is Aristotle,[96] for he is the first extant writer who makes it plain that he has consulted a large number of written works for himself.

More important for present purposes, however, is the limited audience for literary works; in default of any evidence to the contrary—in

---

Andrewes in A. W. Gomme, A. Andrewes & K. J. Dover, *A Historical Commentary on Thucydides* v.173).

92. Eupolis 304.3 Kock: there is no strict necessity to see the βυβλίον mentioned here as more than sheets of papyrus, but the joke depends on their having certain pretensions. Aristophanes' silence about booksellers may be significant. Both the comic dramatists Aristomenes (fr. 9 Kock) and Nicophon (fr. 19 Kock) refer to book-selling and may date from before or after 400. The next clear reference to a trade in books is in Pl. *Apol.* 26, where it is said that anyone can buy the βιβλία of Anaxagoras for a drachma "in the orchestra" (presumably in the market). These works must have been brief (a few sheets only?), in view of the low price; and perhaps they were second-hand; cf. R. Pfeiffer, *History of Classical Scholarship* i (Oxford, 1968), 27–28. Xen. *Anab.* vii.5.14, written in the 370s but set twenty years earlier, includes βίβλοι γεγραμμέναι (probably meaning to refer to literary or technical works, in spite of Flory, *AJPh* ci [1980], 20 n.33) among the kinds of goods which sea-borne merchants often carry. On these texts cf. G. F. Nieddu, *S & C* viii (1984), 246–249. Mobile booksellers: Dion.Hal. *Isocr.* 18.

93. Euripides' books: Ar. *Ran.* 1407–10; cf. 943. It has often (since Athenaeus i.3a, at least) been inferred that Euripides possessed a library. E. A. Havelock, *QUCC* xxxv (1980), 86–87 = *The Literate Revolution in Greece and Its Cultural Consequences* (Princeton, 1982), 286–287, attacks this notion, which obviously does have anachronistic connotations. The fact remains that Euripides is portrayed as possessing an impressive quantity of literature, presumably on papyrus rolls. Whether he actually owned them himself is of secondary importance.

94. Xen. *Mem.* iv.2.10.

95. Xen. *Mem.* i.6.14; cf. Pl. *Phaed.* 98b.

96. Cf. Strabo xiii.608, with Pfeiffer 67.

the shape of information about accessible libraries or organized book-copying workshops—we must suppose that the circulation of written literary works remained very small, even in Athens, throughout this period, and minuscule in Greece as a whole. The main way people got to know literary texts was still oral, as the author of the *Rhetorica ad Alexandrum* shows when he picks out two poets who are *anagnostikoi,* suitable for reading rather than for performance; they are the secondary figures Chaeremon and Licymnius, and they are exceptions.[97] The dissemination of prose works could also be partially oral: Protagoras read his works aloud at Athens, or had them read out for him; Anaxagoras was read out loud; and in the fourth century, though these habits may well have changed somewhat, we are told that Isocrates sometimes read out his productions.[98] Of Isocrates Aristotle says that "very numerous bundles of his forensic speeches" were carried around by booksellers; but although this has a certain value as an indication of what could occur, the statement is not only highly dubious but also in any case very relative (how many bundles?).[99] As for historians, we hardly know how the classical successors of Herodotus reached their audiences.[100] The point is in any case that in the main the authors of prose literature could not and did not have to depend heavily on individual reading for the diffusion of their works.

Many assume that literary references in the dramatists presuppose a large number of book-readers in the audience. This assumption, it seems to me, is misguided. If understanding a joke in Euripides' *Electra,* produced about 415, depended—as it did—on knowing Aeschylus' *Choephori,* produced in 458,[101] and on knowing it well, we should not conclude that there was a large public for written literature.[102] This is so for three reasons. First, it is plain that Euripides

97. [Aristot.] *Rhet.* iii.12.2.1413b.

98. Protagoras: Diog.Laert. ix.54. Anaxagoras: Pl. *Phaed.* 97b–c. For fifth-century parallels see Nieddu, *S & C* viii (1984), 250–251. Isocrates: see xv.1 and the comments of Turner, *Athenian Books* 19. Isocrates assumes that a written discourse will be read out to the recipient (v.26); see further H. L. Hudson-Williams, *CQ* xliii (1949), 65–69.

99. Dion.Hal. *Isocr.* 18 (cf. Dover, *Lysias and the Corpus Lysiacum* 25).

100. Cf. A. Momigliano, *ASNSP* ser.3 viii (1978), 62–63 = *Sesto contributo* 364–365.

101. G. Roux, *REG* lxxxvii (1974), 42–56. The texts are *Choeph.* 164–224 and Eur. *El.* 524–579.

102. Contrary to the opinion of Weil in *Le monde grec* 165.

was satisfied if the highest level of understanding of a scene in one of his plays was reserved for a small proportion of the audience.[103] Second, Aeschylus was still popular in the last decades of the fifth century, and some knew his plays from revivals;[104] in fact the *Oresteia* was probably his best-known work. Third, oral tradition and memory made some difference; some rather ordinary Athenians and Caunians benefited from their ability to recite Euripides,[105] and it is clear that tragic poetry had a large oral public. In short, Euripides' use of the *Choephori* does not come near to showing that the average member of the audience in 415 was in the habit of reading tragedies. We should suppose that Aristophanes was similarly content to have some of his best lines pass over the heads of most of the audience—and this should not cause us the slightest qualm, since the Elizabethan dramatists sometimes show this same attitude.

A well-known line in Aristophanes' *Frogs* might be thought to show that this interpretation is mistaken. As the contest between Aeschylus and Euripides is about to begin, the chorus tells them not to fear that the audience may fail to understand: "for each one has a *biblion* ["piece of writing on papyrus" rather than "book"] in his hand and learns the subtle points."[106] This comment does not provide us with any precise facts about cultural history (and we have no reason to suppose that the audience was made up of a cross-section of the Attic population), but the function of the remark is clear enough. The forthcoming contest sounds as if it may be something of a strain for the audience, and the playwright offers an excuse. The excuse is an exaggeration at least, indeed a rather fantastic one, but it makes sense since books are a growing phenomenon in contemporary Athens; as the poet interestingly says, conditions are "no longer" what they were.[107]

None of this, however, will make us underestimate the effects of the growth in the written transmission of literature, which encouraged the growth of a canon of texts, with all that that entailed. This process was vividly exemplified about 330 by the copying and archiving, on

103. Aristotle even claims (*Poetics* 9.1451b25–26) that the established tragic myths were known only to a few.

104. Popularity: Ar. *Ach.* 10, etc. For the revivals see *Vita Aeschyli* 12, Philostr. *V.Ap.* vi.11; but it is not clear how long they continued.

105. See above, p. 33.

106. Ar. *Ran.* 1114. On the ironical tone of this line: Nieddu, *S & C* viii (1984), 260.

107. *Ran.* 1112.

the initiative of the politician Lycurgus, of an official text of Aeschylus, Sophocles and Euripides.[108]

A final function we must discuss is the use of writing in correspondence. What could be more natural in this polycentric and inquisitive culture than exchanges of letters, if the population was as literate as is usually believed? Yet letters did not develop into commonplace objects of daily use, as far as we can tell from surviving evidence. Literary sources seem to suggest that they were largely reserved for grave occasions or for sensitive secret communications, at least until the fourth century and perhaps even then. When letters are mentioned by fifth-century writers, they often have a surprisingly sinister import, like Proetus' letter in the *Iliad*: they are authoritative and deceptive at the same time, and so bring death to a powerful satrap,[109] and (unjustly) to Hippolytus and to Palamedes; important Medizers write them to the Great King.[110] It is remarkable how much the letters in Thucydides—political of course—are instruments of death, betrayal, and deceit.[111] According to Antiphon, messages are sent in writing only to keep them secret from the bearer or when they are very long.[112]

By the last decades of the fifth century a specific word was needed for "letter," and *epistolai*, "instructions," took on this new meaning.[113] Without doubt there was an increasing amount of mundane correspondence which dealt with long-distance business affairs. By Demosthenes' time it was unremarkable for a merchant in Athens to write about business matters to a slave who was looking after his

108. Ps.-Plu. *Vitae Decem Orat.* 7 = *Mor.* 841f (he also set up bronze statues of them).

109. Darius' emissary Bagaeus brings about the death of the satrap Oroetes by giving the latter's guardsmen a succession of letters purporting to be from Darius, the last of which tells them to kill Oroetes, which they promptly do (but the procedure is still partly oral: Bagaeus sees that the guards respect his βυβλία καὶ τὰ λεγόμενα ἐκ τῶν βυβλίων ἔτι μεζόνως (Hdt. iii.128). See also i.124–125, where Harpagus plots with Cyrus by letter, and the latter forges a letter from Astyages (which he then reads out). Euripidean cases: *Hipp.* 1311–12, *Palam.* 578 Nauck (where ὑπὲρ πλακὸς probably refers to letters, and not—as Turner, *Athenian Books* 16–17, supposes—to scientific books).

110. Hdt. viii.120; Thuc. i.128, 129, 137.

111. Concerning the letters in book viii see Longo in *Studi in onore di Anthos Ardizzoni* i.530–531; cf. also Longo, *Tecniche della comunicazione nella Grecia antica* (Naples, 1981), 68–69.

112. v.53–56.

113. The earliest instances appear to be in Thucydides (i.129, etc.) and Eur. *IT* 589. The word is not in Herodotus in this sense.

affairs at the Bosporus.[114] "What is a man not capable of who, like the defendant, accepted letters but did not properly and justly deliver them?"[115] The orator's question implies a standard and well-known procedure. Nonetheless, long-distance trading was something of a specialized milieu. The editor of the ostraca from the Agora of Athens was perhaps somewhat too ready to recognize letters among the texts of classical date from that source. All four of the alleged cases are of dubious function or extremely short.[116] A letter on an ostracon can hardly fail to be short, and we have to make allowances for the heavy odds against the survival of everyday correspondence. Our impression of the amount of letter-writing that took place in the classical period might possibly be very different if we had the types of evidence we have from Egypt later on—masses of papyri and ostraca. But in fact the argument from silence, or near-silence, is impressive, when we consider the volume of forensic speeches that survives from fourth-century Athens. References to and remains of letters among the pre-Hellenistic Greeks are largely confined to special circumstances, and it is likely that other correspondence was quite rudimentary.

However, if we consider the totality of the functions of the written word which have been mentioned in this section, it is clear that they expanded very greatly during the classical age. Outside Athens, it is true, the indications available to us are sketchy; but there is enough evidence to show that the same trend was at work in most Greek cities (though perhaps not at Sparta). The written word had by 323 taken a much stronger hold as a means of bolstering or supplanting memory and as a means of conveying messages, sometimes highly complex messages, from one human being or collective of human beings to another. Some men now spent large amounts of time in the company of written texts, and very large numbers of people—many of them illiterate—were now affected to some degree by operations carried on in writing.

114. Ps.-Dem. xxxiv.8, 28 (327/326 B.C.).

115. xxxiv.29.

116. Lang, *Graffiti and Dipinti* B 1 (of the sixth century—an enigmatic text, as H. A. Thompson remarked, *Hesperia* xvii [1948], 160), B 2 (a seven-word text dated to the beginning of the fifth century; it is hardly a credible message as normally restored), B 7 (a five-word message dated to the second quarter of the fifth century), B 9 (six words: last quarter of the fifth century). *SIG*³ 1259 is a fourth-century Attic letter on lead (and for a parallel see J. and L. Robert, *Bull.Ep.* 1944 no. 90). For other epigraphically recorded private letters of the classical period (they are very few) see Guarducci, *Epigrafia greca* iii.317–321.

The written word had other functions which are harder to define. It is an obvious fact that writing often made an implicit claim to be authoritative, all the more so because it was not completely commonplace or at the disposal of everyone (indeed, it was at the ready disposal of no more than a small minority of the population). The stories of Proetus, of Herodotus' Oroetes, and of Euripides' Hippolytus are elements in the psychological background. In the present are, among other things, ostracism, inscribed laws, written treaties and legal testimony which has to be in writing. Any publicly displayed text may aim in part at gathering prestige; this is likely to have been one of the motives behind the great array of public inscriptions, including the tribute lists, put up in imperial Athens from the 450s.[117] Both citizens and foreigners could learn to appreciate Athens' strength.

For much of the fifth century, and even later, writing seems to have had a remarkably ambivalent reputation at Athens, and presumably elsewhere too. This in itself suggests that writing was invading new functional territory. The positive side we have already seen, as well as fragments of the negative side. There is, however, a good deal more in the way of hostile comment. Aeschylus contrasts a written decision with one which is clear—what is written, it is implied, may be unnecessarily obscure.[118] Both Herodotus and Thucydides seem to be fully aware of the deceptive possibilities of written texts. The moral code continues to require obedience to *un*written laws, so the *Antigone* teaches.[119] Aristophanes in the *Birds* brings in fraudulent oracles with emphasis on the fact that they are in writing, and a little later shows a citizen's resentment about the number of documents that nowadays come into public affairs.[120] There are other, milder texts too: it may be that in the Funeral Oration Pericles is represented as comparing epigraphical commemoration with *agraphos mneme,* "unwritten memory," to the detriment of the former.[121]

117. Hence they are fragile evidence for widespread literacy, contrary to the view of Turner, *Athenian Books* 9.

118. Aesch. *Supp.* 944–949.

119. Esp. Soph. *Ant.* 450–455; cf. Thuc. ii.37.3 (the Funeral Oration), with Gomme's n. On the role of unwritten laws in classical Greece see esp. J. W. Jones, *The Law and Legal Theory of the Greeks* (Oxford, 1956), 62–64; J. de Romilly, *La loi dans la pensée grecque* (Paris, 1971), 27–38.

120. Ar. *Av.* 974–991, 1024, 1036.

121. Thuc. ii.43.3. Longo, in *Studi in onore di Anthos Ardizzoni* i.535–539, offers an interesting discussion of this passage but exaggerates the degree to which Thucydides contrasts written and unwritten communication (the advantage of the latter, in this context, is that it maintains the memory of the dead even outside their own land).

It also seems natural to suppose that on that dramatic occasion when the Athenians collected all the *biblia* of Protagoras and burned them in the Agora because of his impiety,[122] the papyrus-sheets or books themselves were thought to be especially hateful. But unfortunately for us, the story may be apocryphal.[123]

There is a current of more explicit disapproval. Socrates' real attitude is unknown,[124] but some of his followers certainly saw reading as harmful to memory and therefore as a bad thing[125]—a tradition which culminates in the description Plato offers in the *Phaedrus* of the results of the invention of writing. Plato's critique, or rather the one which Plato puts into the mouth of Socrates, is wide-ranging. Thamous predicts to Theuth, in a story attributed to Socrates, that the use of writing will weaken memory, for it is a *pharmakon* (medicine or magical potion) for reminding, not for remembering. Socrates continues by saying that writing will convey only the appearance of wisdom instead of the truth, and that those who rely on reading will be not wise but "opinion-wise," *doxosophoi*. What is written is not clear *(saphes)* or fixed *(bebaion)*. Like paintings, written texts cannot answer questions.[126] When once a *logos* is written down, it is tossed about among those who understand and those who have nothing to do with the matter. It does not know who it ought and ought not to speak to, and it cannot defend itself. The philosopher may write for the sake of amusement, but for his serious teaching he will use the dialectical method.[127]

In this discussion Socrates moves quite rapidly to the plane of philosophy and leaves mundane considerations aside. Eventually, however, he returns to a more general discussion; and it is fairly clear that Plato is in a sense continuing a debate which had ranged beyond philosophy. When he comes back to *bebaiotes* (fixedness) and *sapheneia* (clarity), it is to say that anyone who has written, or will write, a political document *(sungramma politikon)* in the belief that it has

122. Cic. *ND* i.63; Diog.Laert. ix.8.52; etc. There is no way to date the event closely, but the Archidamian War is the likely period.

123. M. I. Finley maintained (*Belfagor* xxxii [1977], 613) that Plato did not know of it when he wrote *Meno* 91e.

124. Contrast Xen. *Mem.* i.6.14 and iv.2.1–10.

125. Oinopides 41 A4 D–K, Antisthenes in Diog.Laert. vi.1.5; but these are very mild remarks.

126. Cf. Pl. *Protag.* 329a.

127. Pl. *Phaedr.* 274c–277a; cf. what follows down to 278e. The passage seems to be feebly echoed in *Ep.* vii.344c–e.

some sort of great fixedness and clarity should be ashamed.[128] In saying this, he is denying what were probably two of the virtues which were held by others to be inherent in written texts.

In the same period the rhetorical expert Alcidamas, follower of the sophist Gorgias, fervently urged the superiority of skillfully improvised speeches to written ones; the contrary point of view was put by another of Gorgias' pupils, Isocrates.[129] Yet Isocrates himself says that "all men trust the spoken word more than the written word" and echoes—or possibly foreshadows—the Platonic argument that the written word cannot clarify or defend itself.[130] In a later work he explains in some detail why a written *logos* is less persuasive than a spoken one, starting from the assertion that all men assume that a written one is composed "for display and for personal gain."[131] This hostility towards writing, or rather towards certain uses of writing, on the part of Plato, Alcidamas and Isocrates was no doubt shared by many other educated Greeks of the fourth century. It was more than some vestige of lost ages past, for it was evidently based on a strongly held belief that writing was having some negative results in the contemporary world. But such men were needless to say creatures of a partly literate culture and heavily dependent on writing. Their eventual acceptance of the written word was inevitable. In the end Plato came to recommend universal education,[132] not without some effects.

Chronology of the use of written texts at Athens

460s?	Earliest preserved praise of writing (Aesch. *PV* 460–461)
just after 430	Monument of the Ten Eponymous Heroes, the place for public notices
420s?	Earliest reference to a written will (Soph. *Trach.* 157)

---

128. 277d–e. The strangeness of this sentiment in a work by Plato has often been commented on; part of the explanation is probably that Plato is telling us what Socrates used to say at the dramatic date of the dialogue, some forty years earlier. For the intriguing implication that clarity and certainty were the qualities lacking in a written proof (a view attributed to the Spartan ephors of Pausanias' time) cf. Thuc. i.132–133, with Longo, *Tecniche* 63.

129. Alcidamas *Soph.* (found in Antiphon, ed. F. Blass) passim. Isocrates as a writer of speeches: xv.2, etc. This controversy is discussed in detail by S. Gastaldi, *Quaderni di storia* xiv (1981), 189–225.

130. Isocr. *Ep.* 1.2–3 (dating from the period 371–367).

131. Isocr. v.25–27 (346 B.C.). Cf. Pl. *Ep.* vii.344e.

132. Pl. *Leg.* vii.809e–810b.

early 420s	"Old Oligarch": earliest political pamphlet
425	Earliest attested written pleading
423	Accounts mentioned in Ar. *Nub.* 18–24
420s or 410s	Earliest reference to book trade (Eupolis 304.3K)
411	Appeals to old written laws
410–404	The *anagrapheis* (including Nicomachus) work on the texts of Solon's and Draco's laws
409–405	Creation of state archive at Athens
405	Aristophanes' *Frogs*
400	Jury is assumed to understand written accounts (Lys. xxxii. 19–22)
c. 390	Written service contract (Lys. iii.22)
c. 380	Apprenticeship contracts mentioned (Xen. *De eq.* 2.2)
380–364	Written testimony begins to be required
370s	Litigants begin to write their own pleas
363/362	Earliest dated loan *horos*
360s?	Plato's *Phaedrus*
c. 340	Written contracts required for *dikai emporikai*
c. 330	Archiving of the texts of the tragedians

The Extent of Literacy

It was argued in the previous chapter that Greek literacy was spreading in the last years of the sixth century and in the era of the Persian Wars. Confirmation of this can be seen in the fact that at the beginning of the fifth century we begin to encounter rather frequent representations on Athenian vases both of book-rolls and of writing-tablets.[133] Such images are open to diverse interpretations: they may have seemed novel and fascinating to contemporaries, or somewhat commonplace. What in any case was the audience for representations on high-quality red-figure vases? It would be great mistake to use such material as an argument for mass literacy, but on the other hand it does suggest that the written word was now, in some circles, an everyday phenomenon.

Writing was now used for more and more purposes, and this change no doubt resulted in part from the spread of literacy and also encouraged literacy to spread still further. But there is apparently wide room

133. On book-rolls see Immerwahr in *Classical Studies Ullman* and in *Antike Kunst* xvi (1973), 143–147. Representations of writing-tablets and cases can be found through the index entry "tablets and writing-cases" in Beck, *Album of Greek Education* 65.

for disagreement about the degree of literacy which was reached in classical Greece.

The prevailing view of the extent of Athenian literacy is, as we have already noted, that a very high level was achieved. The Greeks in general are sometimes said to have shared this achievement. When scholars speak of "universal" primary education or say that "literacy . . . seems to have been general,"[134] they should not complain if we take them at their word. The exceptions to this idealizing trend are few.[135]

As a preliminary, we need to consider briefly the question of materials, since we need to know whether the price or unavailability of suitable writing materials was any impediment to the use or diffusion of writing in classical Greece. The whole matter is very murky, since the relevant prices are unknown or poorly known, and since people's subjective reactions to writing materials and their costs are practically never attested. Potsherds, which must have been readily available, seem to us highly inconvenient, but they were perhaps as readily used by the Greeks as sheets of paper are now. Yet with the best will in the world they could not be used for lengthy texts if these were to be portable.[136]

The most convenient material for many purposes was papyrus,

---

134. F. A. G. Beck, *Greek Education. 450–350 B.C.* (London, 1964), 314 (in all Greece or only in Athens?); B. M. W. Knox in *Cambridge History of Classical Litterature* i (Cambridge, 1985), 11 ("at varying levels it is true"; he is referring to Athens in the final decades of the fifth century). For other similar views (their authors might not all endorse the expressions quoted above): Turner, *Athenian Books* 8; Harvey, *REG* lxxix (1966), 628 (quoted above); G. Ryle, *Plato's Progress* (Cambridge, 1966), 22 ("we know that literacy was almost universal in Athens"); Weil in *Le monde grec* 165 (everyone in Athens tried to have some notion of reading and writing); A. Burns, *JHI* xlii (1981), 371 ("from the end of the sixth century the vast majority of Athenian citizens were literate"); G. F. Nieddu, *S & C* vi (1982), 235, 246.

135. It is interesting that an economic historian reached the conclusion, definitely correct in my view, that the majority of the inhabitants of classical Attica and of Greece in general were illiterate: H. Michell, *The Economics of Ancient Greece* (2d ed., Cambridge, 1957), 363. Havelock, having forced the evidence somewhat in the cause of showing that literacy was rare before about 430, joins the majority with respect to the period after 430: see esp. *New Literary History* viii (1976–77), 369–372 = *The Literate Revolution* 185–188.

136. The lengthy record of transactions (22 lines) preserved on a fourth-century Athenian ostracon and published by A. W. Johnston, *Ath.Mitt.* c (1985), 293–307, is unique. However it was not impossible to archive ostraca: E. Seidl, *Ptolemäische Rechtsgeschichte* (Glückstadt, 1962), 43, commenting on *BGU* vii.1560–1562.

which is known to have been used in Athens by 490 and must indeed have been used there and in most other cities much earlier.[137] But for most people it was probably expensive. The evidence about this is admittedly thin. Our only reliable prices for papyrus in this period are the sixteen obols paid for two rolls in the Erechtheum accounts of 408–407 and the twenty-one obols (apparently this is the figure) paid for one roll in some other early fourth-century accounts.[138] This variation is uncomfortable, though it should not surprise us in classical trading conditions. In any case these prices show that although the well-to-do could easily afford paper, a man living on a subsistence wage of three obols a day, or living like a countryman with little cash in his life, would have found purchasing even a small quantity of papyrus a serious expense.

Wood was the other important writing surface—wooden tablets *(deltoi)* for portable communications, wooden boards *(sanides)* for fixed public notices. Since such objects were in principle reusable, they may have been inexpensive. Writing-tablets are often mentioned by the tragic dramatists,[139] and they had evidently become quite commonplace objects. That does not demonstrate that they were easily accessible to everyone. However it seems best to conclude that the limitations of the materials seldom acted as a direct constraint, for it was not difficult to come into possession of materials which were adequate for learning to read and write—but that the expensiveness of papyrus, the only material which could conveniently be used for long private messages, limited the usefulness of writing and so indirectly put a brake on literacy.

137. For surveys of Greek writing materials cf. R. Devréesse, *Introduction à l'étude des manuscripts grecs* (Paris, 1954), 1–5; Guarducci, *Epigrafia greca* i.429–442. Papyrus is mentioned in Hdt. v.58 (cf. Turner, *Athenian Books* 13). In the comic fragment Hermippus 63.13 Kock, probably of the 420s, it is said to have been imported from Egypt.

138. Erechtheum accounts: *IG* i².374, lines 279–281 = i³.476, lines 289–291. Papyrologists seem to agree that the word χάρτης, which is used here, means a roll of some twenty sheets, and not a single sheet (N. Lewis, *Papyrus in Classical Antiquity* [Oxford, 1974], 70–78). The other accounts cited: *IG* ii².1655, lines 1–2. Harvey, *REG* lxxix (1966), 615, cites Ps.-Dem. lvi.1: for two copper coins (one-fourth of an obol) you could buy enough to write a contract; this is rhetoric.

139. Also by Pind. *Ol.* x.1–3. The passages of tragedy include Aesch. *PV* 789, *Supp.* 179, *Choeph.* 450, *Eum.* 275, fr. 530 Mette = *P.Oxy.* xx.2256; Soph. fr. 597 Radt, *Trach.* 683, *Phil.* 1325, *Ant.* 709; Eur. *Troad.* 662. See further Pfeiffer, *History of Classical Scholarship* i.26.

It is time to consider classical Greek schooling. How, in organizational terms, did the Greeks learn to read and write? Did they perhaps, in many cases, teach their children to read and write at home? The question is particularly important for the literacy of Greek women, for there is no evidence at all that in the classical period girls attended schools,[140] and it is entirely consistent with what we know about the seclusion of women in Athens that Athenian girls did not do so (some other cities may have been less benighted in this respect). Some Athenian women were indeed literate, but it is probable that most of the literate ones were either the daughters of well-to-do families (with the teaching done by a slave or employee in the home) or *hetairai*. There is in fact no textual evidence for parental teaching in the classical period, and the ordinary Greek family may well have regarded even elementary teaching as the task of a schoolmaster.[141] Xenophon assumes that it is in order to learn *grammata* that Greeks go to school;[142] and elsewhere he distinguishes between the *paidagogos* stage of education, which begins when a boy can understand what is said to him, and the stage for learning *grammata*, *mousike* and athletics, which is in the charge of teachers outside the home.[143] Furthermore, while schools undoubtedly continued to pay plenty of attention to subjects other than reading and writing, the claim that Athenian schools did not give organized writing instruction much before 430 is, as we saw in the previous chapter,[144] nothing better than special pleading. The Attic red-figure cups of the fifth century which show letters being taught or some closely related activity (see Table 2) are clear evidence that such things happened in real life. However they may well refer to a specific social stratum.

140. See. S. G. Cole in H. P. Foley (ed.), *Reflections of Women in Antiquity* (New York, 1981), 226, against Beck, *Album of Greek Education* (cf. also the latter's paper in *Classicum* [Sydney] ix [1978], 1–9). The female figure carrying writing tablets on the red-figure cup Metropolitan Museum 06.1021.167 is intriguing (she is being led reluctantly), but she is an adult or nearly so.

141. However a red-figure cup of about 460 (Beazley, *Attic Red-Figure Vase-Painters* 838/27) showing a boy reciting to a woman who is carrying a book-roll (cf. H. R. Immerwahr, *Antike Kunst* xvi [1973], 144–145) may indicate that at this time some teaching was done at home.

142. *Cyr.* i.2.6.

143. Xen. *Lac.Pol.* 2.1. He is speaking of the Greeks other than the Spartans; admittedly he is also speaking of those who "claim to be educating their sons as finely as possible," which has a class connotation.

144. Above, p. 58.

Table 2.   Attic red-figure vases representing schools where letters were taught

Vase number	Painter	Date	References
Munich 2607	—	530–500	Beazley 104/4, Beck 22 no. 7 (h)
East Berlin F 2322 (a *kyathos*)	Onesimus	c. 490	Beazley 329/134, Beck 20 no. 75a–b.
Oxford G 138	Onesimus	c. 480	Beazley 326/93, Beck 26 no. 119; cf. Immerwahr in *Classical Studies Ullman* i. 19–20
Ferrara 45 C VP	Adria Painter	500–475	Beazley 349/1, Beck 22 no. 7 (i)
West Berlin 2285	Douris	c. 490–480	Beazley 431/48, Beck 18 nos. 53–54; cf. Immerwahr 18–19. See Figure 3.
Tarquinia RC 1121	Tarquinia Painter	475–450	Beazley 866/1, Beck 22 no. 7 (d)
Washington 136373	Akestorides Painter	c. 460	Beazley 781/4, Beck 19 no. 61; cf. Immerwahr 22
Metropolitan Museum 17.230.10	Painter of Munich 2660	c. 460	Beazley 784/25, Beck 19 nos. 58–60; cf. Immerwahr 21
Würzburg 488	Splanchnopt Painter	c. 450	Beazley 893/25, Beck 19 no. 62; cf. Dunedin E 39.107 by the same painter (Beazley 893/24, Beck 19 no. II/43)
Athens 12462	Painter of London D 12	c. 450	Beazley 959/2, Beck 22 no. 7 (e)

Sources: J. D. Beazley, *Attic Red-Figure Vase-Painters* (2d ed., Oxford, 1963); F. A. G. Beck, *Album of Greek Education* (Sydney, 1975) (the list in T. B. L. Webster, *Potter and Patron in Classical Athens* [London, 1972], 244, should not be relied on).

Note: These are the most probable cases I have encountered in the literature (but it is never absolutely certain that the painter intended to represent a regular school).

Individual schoolmasters begin to appear in the sources in the mid-fifth century, and in the fourth we begin to see that their calling is despised by the social elite and perhaps by a wider segment of the citizens, as it was to be throughout antiquity.[145] This attitude possibly derives from some feeling among the educated that part of their birthright was being sold in sordid circumstances. It also hints that the well-to-do saw very little, if any, social utility in the imparting of basic education.

One classical Greek law requiring that all the sons of the citizens should "learn letters" is attested, and it also supposedly provided that the city would pay the wages of the teachers. This is the law attributed by Diodorus Siculus to the legislator Charondas of Catana (no previous lawgiver, he says, had thought of such a law), whom he mistakenly transplants from the sixth century to the colony of Thurii, founded in 443.[146] This strange chronological error raises the question whether Diodorus knew anything reliable at all about the laws of fifth-century Thurii, and this particular law could well be a Hellenistic invention. It is not impossible that Diodorus had authentic information from Ephorus, or indeed from some other source,[147] about the laws of Thurii, and that someone assumed that all the laws of Magna Graecia derived from Charondas.[148] But the lack of fifth-century parallels, above all for city-paid schoolmasters, tells heavily against the authenticity of the law, as does the general unreliability of stories about lawgivers, not least Charondas.[149] The most likely solution is that the whole story is a concoction of the fourth century or a little

145. Epicurus' assertion that Protagoras was once a village schoolmaster (Athen. viii.354c and Diog.Laert. x.8 = Protag. 68 A9 D–K = Epicur. *Epist.* fr. 172 Usener) is unlikely to be true; whether it would even have made plausible invective in Protagoras' time is uncertain. But for an anonymous teacher at Eretria or Erythrae in 440 see Ion of Chios, *FGrH* 392 F6. Contempt for schoolmastering: Dem. xviii.129, 265, xix.249; and on this topic see further A. D. Booth, *Florilegium* iii (1981), 1–20.

146. The source is Diod.Sic. xii.12.4, 13.3–4.

147. There is no way of identifying Diodorus' own source here. It would be interesting to know whether the encomium on writing which he adds (13.1–3) was based on Ephorus or some other fourth-century writer. It may be that Ephorus, a pupil of Isocrates, was influenced by his master in this respect.

148. Plato says that Charondas was the general lawgiver of Italy and Sicily (*Resp.* x.599e); Aristotle limits this to the Chalcidic cities there (*Pol.* ii.12.1274a23–25).

149. It is evident from a comparison of this passage with Aristot. *Pol.* ii.12. 1274b5–6 (Charondas' only novel law concerned perjury) that in the fourth century there was already controversy about the contents of Charondas' legislation. Diodorus' account of Charondas was dealt with fully and sceptically by Richard Bentley, *A Dis-*

later, when notions about the universal education of male citizens were in fairly wide circulation. If this is correct, it provides some evidence of the fervour felt by the partisans of this idea.

The first person to have argued in favour of universal education among citizens was probably the extremely shadowy figure Phaleas of Chalcedon; at least it is with his name that Aristotle associates the view that education should be "equal."[150] We shall come shortly to Plato's *Laws,* which was perhaps the first work to bring the notion of universal education before a sizeable public.

No classical city is in fact known to have required all free-born boys, let alone girls, to attend school or to learn to read or write; nor is any city of this era known to have subsidized elementary education in any way. Certain texts have occasionally been interpreted as evidence that there was indeed compulsory education in fourth-century Athens and also in Crete. In the *Crito* Plato makes Socrates conduct a little dialogue with the *nomoi* of Athens, in which they say that the *nomoi* had told Socrates' father to educate him in music (which would include reading and writing) and athletics.[151] It is obvious, however, that here, as often elsewhere, the *nomoi* are not statutes but social customs, and Plato is writing of a social custom which at his and Socrates' social level was extremely strong.[152] The difficulty, from our

---

sertation upon the Epistles of Phalaris (London, 1699), 258–273. He pointed out among other things that according to Heracl.Pont. in Diog.Laert. ix.50 the lawgiver of Thurii was Protagoras. R. van Compernolle, in *Recueils de la Société Jean Bodin* xxxix (= *L'enfant* v) (1975), 98, regards our law as a fourth-century invention; for Marrou, *Histoire* 175, it is Hellenistic.

150. *Pol.* ii.7.1266b32–33. H. Diels included him among the Pre-Socratics, but even that is a guess.

151. *Crito* 50d: οὐ καλῶς προσέταττον ἡμῶν οἱ ἐπὶ τούτῳ τεταγμένοι νόμοι, παραγγέλλοντες τῷ πατρὶ τῷ σῷ σε ἐν μουσικῇ καὶ γυμναστικῇ παιδεύειν;

152. Cf. K. J. Freeman, *Schools of Hellas* (London, 1907), 57–58; Marrou, *Histoire* 538. As P. Schmitter observes (*AJPh* xcvi [1975], 281), this interpretation is confirmed by the fact that both Plato and Aristotle assume (in passages cited below) that there was no such statute at Athens. Harvey, *REG* lxxix (1966), 589 n.10, prefers to think that "Plato was just carried away by his own eloquence, and made an inaccurate statement." Incidentally Aeschines i.9 provides no evidence for compulsory schooling at Athens: the teachers to whom we consign our sons ἐξ ἀνάγκης are those to whom we—men of Aeschines' kind who want our sons to be educated—*have* to entrust them because there is no alternative. But this passage does show that by 345 Athens had some legislation as to how schools should be conducted; cf. P. Schmitter, *Die hellenistische Erziehung im Spiegel der* Νέα Κωμῳδία *und der Fabula Palliata* (Bonn, 1972), 111.

point of view, is to know how widespread the *nomos* of teaching reading and writing really was.

As for the Cretans, Ephorus apparently said that they made boys learn letters, though unfortunately the verb of compelling seems to have dropped out of the text.[153] The point of his statement in any case is not that *all* the boys learned letters, but that those who learned also had to learn the songs prescribed in the *nomoi* and certain forms of music. It is not impossible that some Cretan cities did encourage their citizens to make their sons "learn letters"—though it is not very likely in default of other evidence. The claim that "the Cretan constitution" required that all boys should learn is misleading.[154] One may properly doubt whether any Cretan law required anything so unrealistic. Yet Ephorus' evidence has some value: there may have been a relatively strong tradition in Crete that boys should learn to read and write, and this may even have extended beyond the literate population of the well-to-do and the specialized craftsmen. The text also provides further evidence that in mid-fourth-century Greece the idea of really widespread education was receiving consideration.

The earliest surviving text which explicitly recommends universal education is Book VII of Plato's *Laws*—which while marking a vital step in the development of written culture insists at the same time on the importance of unwritten rules. At all events Plato now envisages that the ideal city will contain buildings for communal schools, and that it will make schooling compulsory for every boy *and girl*.[155] Children of ten, he says, should have about three years to learn *grammata*: "the children must work hard at their letters until they can read and write, but as far as reaching a high level of speed or calligraphy is concerned, those whom nature has not helped along in the prescribed number of years should be released."[156] Thus nothing less than the universal literacy of the free population is being sought. The question of how to put such a doctrine into practice is not of course considered. Aristotle also recommends compulsory education,[157] hesitantly

153. Strabo x.482 = *FGrH* 70 F149 (p. 88, lines 18–19); the Greek can be translated as it stands ("the boys learn letters . . ."), but the sentence conspicuously lacks an indicative. Heraclides Ponticus (*FHG* ii.211) said that Cretan education did not *go beyond letters*, and information to this effect may be what lies behind Strabo's comment.

154. The claim is made by Nieddu, *S & C* vi (1982), 242 n.31.

155. Pl. *Leg.* vii.804c–e.

156. vii.809e–810b.

157. Aristot. *Pol.* viii.2.1337a33–34 (παιδεία must be made κοινή, which

suggesting that it should begin not at seven years of age but at five;[158] and he also ignores the practical implications of his own advice.

Other fourth-century texts make it certain that parents had to pay for schooling;[159] hence it was beyond the reach of many, and assertions to the contrary arise from unawareness of Greek economic conditions.[160] Plato in fact observes that it is the very wealthy, the *plousiotatoi,* who send their sons to school at the earliest age and take them away latest,[161] clearly implying that everyone other than the *plousiotatoi,* a minute proportion of the citizen population, is to a greater or lesser extent influenced by the cost of education. And for cases of subsidized elementary education in Greek cities we have to wait for the Hellenistic age.

What other evidence is there about the proportion of free-born Greek boys who went to school? In the first place, it is clear that some moderately out-of-the-way places had schools: Astypalaea has already been mentioned, and Thucydides recounts that when Thracian mercenaries attacked Boeotian Mycalessus in 413 they fell upon a school "which was the largest one there" and killed all the boys in it.[162] Mycalessus was a small city, as Thucydides remarks,[163] and the existence of several schools there may suggest that a surprisingly high proportion of the boys attended them. The schools may all have been small, and there is no assurance here that as many as, say, half or a quarter of the sons of the citizens went to school. However this text makes it seem likely that by this date almost every Greek *polis,* except in truly backward regions, possessed at least one school.

Villages were another matter, and it must have been very common, and may simply have been normal, for country children to go without schooling. The typical country existence is thought of as being

seems to mean universal among the citizens). On female education see also *Pol.* i.13.1260b16–20.

158. *Pol.* vii.17.1336a23–24, b35–37. For seven as a normal age to begin see Ps.-Pl. *Axioch.* 366d.

159. Xen. *Mem.* ii.2.6; Dem. xviii.265; cf. Theophr. *Char.* 30.14.

160. S. Flory, e.g., contends (*AJPh* ci [1980], 19) that evidence about the education of children shows that "almost all" adult male Athenian citizens must have been to school for a while.

161. Pl. *Protag.* 326c. There are textual difficulties in this passage, but they do not affect the point being made here.

162. Thuc. vii.29.5.

163. vii.29.3. Calling it a "peasant community" (Harvey, *REG* lxxix [1966], 620) misses the ambitions which a Greek city would normally have.

untouched by education; so an allusion in a pseudo-Lysian speech implies.[164] The figure of the village schoolmaster is not absolutely unknown; a passage of fourth-century abuse makes Protagoras into one.[165] But the very fact that among the educated the role was despised reinforces the conjecture that most villages did without.

There is little sense of social or economic reality in modern discussions of Greek schooling. Most Greeks were small farmers or artisans with little or no surplus to spend, but with a powerful incentive to make their sons work from an early age. It is implicit in what has already been said about the extent of literacy, as well as in the evidence we have cited about schools, that the number of boys who went to school was, in historical terms, surprisingly large. However the probability is strong, given the lack of educational subsidies and given the rural settlement patterns that persisted in the world of the *polis,* that the majority of free Greeks did not go to school for any substantial period.

The procedure which scholars have mostly relied upon to ascertain the level of classical Greek literacy has been to cite texts and occasionally artifacts which show more or less ordinary Greeks reading or writing. This sounds quite unobjectionable. It leads, however, to the complete neglect of historical probability and of the factors (surveyed in Chapter 1) which are likely to have determined the extent of literacy. As if that were not enough, the subject has usually been seen from only one social angle: that of the prosperous male citizen living in the city. It is essential, therefore, to approach the subject differently. We have already to some extent considered the determining factors, including the nascent ideology of citizen literacy, which begins to gain some undeniable strength in the mid-fourth century.

In social terms, the most likely hypothesis is that in the classical period literacy at Athens was confined to males of the hoplite class and above, together with a certain number of craftsmen in occupations in which writing was especially useful, a small percentage of slaves, and a very few women (the greatest uncertainty is perhaps whether female literacy was on the order of 1% or 10%). Semi-literacy adds a complication, and as has already been suggested, this may have

164. Ps.-Lys. xx.11: Phrynichus was poor and looked after flocks in the country, while in the city my father ἐπαιδεύετο. The date of the speech is 409–404 (Dover, *Lysias and the Corpus Lysiacum* 44).

165. Epicurus said that Protagoras had taught letters ἐν κώνη τινι (see above, p. 98 n.145); though the allegation is probably false, such teachers must have been known by Epicurus' time.

been the condition of some of those who participated in the procedure of ostracism. Some other cities were no doubt on a similar level of literacy, others considerably lower.

The social and psychological differences between the classical Greeks on the one hand and most pre-modern populations on the other in some instances favoured Greek, or at least Athenian, literacy. One of these differences was simply the presence of plentiful slave labour. Since the fifth-century Athenians in particular possessed many slaves, they must have had some extra degree of leisure and resources available for, among other things, education. In other words, the hierarchical social structure is likely to have helped the education of its beneficiaries: their young sons did not have to work all year round for a living and could be sent to school. But the average Athenian household contained few slaves and had little indeed in the way of surplus, especially in cash. Slavery did not turn the ordinary citizen into a gentleman of leisure.

Against this background we can consider in more detail the literacy of the free population. Among the well-to-do, practically all males must have been literate,[166] though this literacy may have become more fluent during the fifth and fourth centuries. In this social class it is women who are problematical. We have met the wife of Ischomachus, imagined by Xenophon as possessing at least basic reading ability. It may be that in this wealthy upper stratum some attention was paid to the education of daughters, but the complete absence of evidence that girls attended schools, combined with the early age at marriage and the tendency—powerful at Athens but also present in many other cities—to aim for the seclusion of women of good family, must make us somewhat pessimistic.

We must be alert to the social position of all ancient writers who comment on literacy. Plato mentions an expression, supposedly famous, which was a way of describing an ignoramus: he "does not understand letters or know how to swim." [167] There was a social per-

---

166. E. A. Havelock suggests that "the governing classes" were the last to become literate at Athens (apparently in the fifth century), but he can cite no evidence for this (*New Literary History* viii [1976–77], 372 = *The Literate Revolution* 188). Whatever may have been the case in the eighth or seventh century, there is no reason at all to think that the upper-class Athenian contemporaries of Themistocles looked down upon the skill of writing. However, in my view they are not likely to have made much use of their knowledge by comparison with their counterparts in, say, the mid-fourth century.

167. Pl. *Leg.* iii.689d: τὸ λεγόμενον μήτε γράμματα μήτε νεῖν ἐπίστωνται.

spective at Athens from which illiteracy seemed disgraceful, and the arch-elitist naturally shared it; whether it was shared by the bulk of citizens is part of the question we are investigating. Selective social vision is to be expected in the ancient as in the modern world. When Demosthenes says that Athens has one law on each subject so that "all may read and learn the law in a simple and clear form,"[168] he is expressing an important democratic aspiration, but his words do not mean that he believed that literally all male citizens could do the reading part for themselves, still less that he had any evidence to this effect; he simply takes it for granted that only those who can read will read and that everyone who matters can do so. In fourth-century Athens there were thousands of literates and semi-literates. There is, however, no good reason at all to suppose that they were in a majority even within the free male population.

It is hardly to be expected that the great philosophers and orators of the fourth century will tell us much about the real-life education of the common man, but, as we have already seen, Plato hints that it was sparse. A speaker before an Athenian jury contrasts the world of the *demiourgos*, the more or less skilled free worker, with that of the banker. "If this slave had been bought by a cook or some other kind of *demiourgos*, he would have learned his master's skill . . . But our father, who was a banker, acquired him, educated him in letters, taught him his profession."[169] Countrymen had an especially poor chance of learning to read and write. The illiterate citizen who asked Aristides to write "Aristides" on an ostracon was of course a rustic. This story of Plutarch's is almost certainly apocryphal, but it may be early enough in origin to be applicable to classical conditions.[170]

The civic functions of writing sketched in the previous section have suggested to some scholars that a very high proportion of the Athenian citizen body was literate. There is no need to repeat what was said there about the class limitations of Athenian democracy, and about the "quiet Athenians" who participated in public life seldom or not at all. These considerations, together with sarcasm or irony, provide sufficient explanation of Socrates', or rather Plato's, question to

---

Mediaeval repetitions of this contribute nothing, contrary to the impression given by Harvey, *REG* lxxix (1966), 628 n.5.

168. Dem. xx.93.

169. Dem. xlv.72 (the exact meaning of γράμματα ἐπαίδευσεν is admittedly not clear). For the illiteracy of cooks cf. Damoxenus fr. 2.12 Kock (*CAF* iii.349).

170. Plu. *Mor.* 186a; *Arist.* 7.7–8. It is told without the illiteracy element in Nepos *Arist.* 1.

Meletus, "Do you think that these jurors are so unskilled in letters that they do not know that the *biblia* of Anaxagoras of Clazomenae are full of such remarks?"[171] Being a juror involved, as we have seen, a certain very minimal use of reading ability; but even at Athens, notorious for its litigation, most citizens were not jurors.[172]

The Athenians, however, chose *by lot* those who were to hold certain public offices which practically required the holders to read and write. This included (by the fourth century anyway) some official secretaryships.[173] Yet we never hear even the most reactionary Athenian arguing against such a system on the grounds that it inevitably gave responsibility to illiterates. The reason is presumably that a man's name did not even come up for sortition unless he indicated his willingness or at least his competence.[174]

The case of the Council is somewhat less clear. From the 450s, if not earlier, random selection by lot played a part in determining who was to be one of the 500 members (service was for a year),[175] and one might think that the members had to have some ability to understand documents. We do not know with certainty whether the members of the lowest property class, the *thetes*, were eligible.[176] It seems obvious in any case that only the willing were chosen, and we should suppose that many of the illiterate poor and illiterate countrymen did not come into consideration.[177] The fact that a man was permitted to serve in the Council twice in his lifetime (this regulation is attested in the 320s but may be much older) might imply that each year the city

171. Pl. *Apol.* 26d. It is plainly true, as F. Solmsen remarked (*AJPh* lxxxvii [1966], 104), that these jurors were not the intelligentsia, but that does not mean that they were selected quite at random.

172. In the *Wasps* it is assumed that the jurors are regulars.

173. [Aristot.] *Ath.Pol.* 47–54 lists some 250 officials chosen by lot in his time; 54.3–4 includes in these the Prytany Secretary ("the principal secretary of the Athenian state"; P. J. Rhodes ad loc.) and the Secretary for the Laws (also a vital position).

174. Cf. Harvey, *REG* lxxix (1966), 598.

175. P. J. Rhodes, *The Athenian Boule* (Oxford, 1972), 3.

176. On this controversy see E. Ruschenbusch, *ZPE* xli (1981), 103–105, etc.

177. P. J. Rhodes, *ZPE* xxxviii (1980), 193, argues on other grounds that citizens were not automatically candidates. One may wonder whether the Arbitrators *(diaitetai)*, who were also selected by lot, apparently from among those who were in their sixtieth year ([Aristot.] *Ath.Pol.* 53.4), could do without reading ability. In recent years it has become increasingly clear that they were sometimes quite numerous (±225 men in 371 B.C.: Ruschenbusch, *ZPE* liv [1984], 252), and increasingly likely that they included a number of men who were of the thetic class (cf. Ruschenbusch, *ZPE* xlix [1982], 275) and at best semi-literate. For a board of *diaitetai* praising their secretary and assistant secretary see A. M. Woodward, *ABSA* l (1955), 274.

could expect to have a new cohort of at least 250 competent men available.[178] On any reasonable demographic assumptions, this means that the overall population included many thousands of men who were at least semi-literate. However the firmness of this conclusion is limited by the probability that Council members could in practice function without being able to read or write for themselves.

Athenian inscriptions scarcely help us to specify the extent of literacy. We may be impressed to observe that from 353/352 onwards some honorary decrees state that they are being published "so that everyone may know."[179] But this formula aimed at pleasing benefactors, and there is not the least supposition that every Athenian citizen would gain his knowledge directly from a single copy of a decree. Nor do graffiti help to any great degree over the extent of literacy. The four mostly rather dubious letter-like messages written on ostraca from the classical period of the Agora (referred to in the previous section) have been used as support for a general claim that writing was widely used in classical Athens,[180] a point which they are far from establishing in any literal sense. They have to be set in the context of decades of excavation in the very centre of the city. Nor are the more than 3,000 other graffiti and painted inscriptions of the Agora excavation[181] as much use as might be anticipated. They cover a very long period, and whether the total is large or small is a matter of subjective judgment. What kind of person wrote them practically always remains obscure.

With regard to free Greek women, even optimists recognize that the majority must have been illiterate,[182] and this could easily have extended to 95% of them or more. It may be that in cities other than Athens girls sometimes attended schools, but there is no evidence to

178. The regulation: [Aristot.] *Ath.Pol.* 62.3. The bearing of the *boule* on Athenian population figures is well discussed by M. H. Hansen, *Demography and Democracy. The Number of Athenian Citizens in the Fourth Century B.C.* (Herning, 1986), 51–64, but even he seems too optimistic about our ability to tell how many Athenians there were in this period.

179. Meritt, *Epigraphica Attica* 90.

180. Nieddu, *S & C* vi (1982), 241–242 ("diffusa conoscenza e pratica della scrittura").

181. Lang, *Graffiti and Dipinti* 1.

182. According to Harvey, *REG* lxxix (1966), 621, there was "a high rate of illiteracy" among Athenian women; but he goes on to say that "more, perhaps, were only just literate than were completely illiterate"—and immediately cites the wife of Ischomachus, one of the richest men in the city. The conclusion reached by Cole in her thorough discussion (Foley, *Reflections* 219–245) is that in fifth-century Athens "a literate woman must have been the exception and not the rule" (225), and in the fourth century the number of literate women was "probably still small" (227).

that effect. And in addition to the well-known facts about their exclusion and seclusion, it is worth recalling the connection which we have hypothesized between writing and the exercise of citizenship; if, in other words, civic consciousne·s was one of the reasons for the diffusion of literacy among Greek males, we should be prepared for a very low level of female literacy.

Is there any contrary evidence? On fifth-century Athenian vases women, like men, sometimes make use of or carry book-rolls or writing-tablets.[183] Such scenes are reasonably common, though not startlingly so in comparison with other subjects. The setting is often domestic, the clientele favoured a certain limited degree of realism, and it is a reasonable inference that in propertied families a certain number of women became literate. A certain caution is required, however, for the identifiable female characters who appear on vases are mainly the Muses and Sappho,[184] personalities rather different from the average Athenian matron. To extrapolate from later Greek evidence, it is also evident that to some tastes there was something attractively piquant about scenes of women with books.[185] It may have been an accomplishment of a *hetaira* to be thoroughly literate.

In the fourth century there must have been upper-class Greek males who, agreeing with Plato and Aristotle, believed in a high degree of female education. Their radical proposals cannot after all have been completely unsupported by contemporary opinion.[186] To some extent we should see the philosophers as representatives of an educational

183. For women, including Muses, reading or holding book-rolls, see Immerwahr in *Classical Studies Ullman* nos. 12–35, and in *Antike Kunst* xvi (1973), 143–147 (five more examples); Cole 223. Writing-tablets in association with women: Beck, *Album of Greek Education* 17–18 (nos. II/11, 20, 22, 23), 56–60 (nos. 350, 353, X/11, 364, 399a).

184. Immerwahr nos. 18–35, etc.

185. See in particular Lucian *Eikones* 9. A piquant note is struck by the Attic white-ground lekythos in Boston (00.359) by the Thanatos Painter, which shows a naked woman carrying writing-tablets (450–420: Beazley, *Attic Red-Figure Vase-Painters* 1229/23; Beck 18 no. II/22); by a red-figure pyxis in Athens (1241, of about 430 B.C.) (Immerwahr no. 23; Beck 58 no. 368); and by a seal-stone of about 460 which shows a sphinx *reading* a riddle from a book-roll (for which see R. Lullies, in *Festschrift zum sechzigsten Geburtstag von Bernhard Schweitzer* [Stuttgart, 1954], 140–146; Beck 18 no. 52; etc.).

186. For these proposals see above, p. 100, and other references given by Harvey, *REG* lxxix (1966), 622. For Theophrastus' ambivalence see Stobaeus ii p. 207 no. 31 Wachsmuth (cf. Cole 227): women should be educated in letters as far as is useful for household management, but refining their education generally makes them lazy, talkative, and meddlesome.

point of view, from which some practical effects resulted; but no more than a tiny minority can have been affected.

It seems likely that an Athenian woman (and the same applies to most other cities) had to be exceptionally fortunate or an unusually strong personality with unusual pretensions if she were not to remain illiterate. Stories such as those told by Herodotus about the mother of Scyles the Scythian or by others about Eurydice the mother of Philip II of Macedon, essentially stories about women who were literate and made sure that their sons were too, were recognized as stories about admirable but not at all ordinary women.[187] In both stories the emphasis is on the woman's services to the male. And there were undoubtedly men who specifically preferred women to be illiterate, agreeing perhaps with the character in Menander who says that whoever teaches a woman letters "supplies a fearful serpent with poison."[188] The fifth-century tragic theatre had from time to time shown women making use of writing for purposes of intrigue, and this may well have encouraged hostility to women's education.[189]

But what are we to make of the texts from Attic drama, in both tragedy and comedy, which seem to have some relevance for the extent of literacy? Before returning to women, we shall consider the passages which bear on men's literacy, without forgetting Jonson's character Sordido. This material raises complex questions about the attitudes of both audiences and playwrights to what was said on the stage.

In the *Prometheus Vinctus* and in Euripides' *Supplices* the respective poets praise the written word, and it would be strange if they were doing so to a mainly illiterate audience. Palamedes praised writing too

---

187. The mother of Scyles: Hdt. iv.78.1 (cf. Cole 226–227). She was a Greek who married the king of Scythia and taught her son "the Greek tongue and letters," a detail in a complex Herodotean fable. Eurydice: the story is known to us from a confused version in Ps.-Plutarch, *De lib.educ.* 20 = *Mor.* 14bc, where it is said that she was an Illyrian and "thrice-barbarous" and that she learned letters as an adult for the sake of her children's education. The author records a dedication she made to the Muses mentioning this achievement. The search for texts actually inscribed by women (Cole 230) is not vital, but it should be noted that *IG* iii App. 100, an Attic curse tablet of the fourth century, falls into this category only if we accept an improbable conjecture by R. Wuensch (τὴν in line 13).

188. Men. fr. 702 Kock (emended): γυναῖχ' ὁ διδάσκων γράμματ' οὐ καλῶς ποιεῖ, / ἀσπίδι δὲ φοβερᾷ προσπορίζει φάρμακον.

189. As C. P. Segal remarks (in *Mnemai: Classical Studies in Memory of Karl K. Hulley* [Chico, Calif., 1984], 56), the *Trachiniae*, the *Hippolytus* and Euripides' *Stheneboea* "associate writing, trickery, concealed love, female desire as all related distortions of truth."

in the lost Euripidean play in which he was the hero, a play which also vividly illustrated the sinister quality of writing, since the hero dies because of a letter forged by the malice of Odysseus. Yet these encomia also raise questions: no one would praise writing in a modern literary work, and as far as I can discover no one is known to have done so on the Elizabethan stage. It is likely that the audience in Athens did not, as a whole, have a strong and long-established hold on literacy.

The tragic poets seem to assume that their audiences are familiar with the process of writing, and it has been claimed that the tragedians', and especially Aeschylus', use of the metaphor of the mind as a writing-tablet is evidence for widespread Athenian literacy.[190] Certainly a significant part of the audience must have felt some interest in writing as an aid to memory.[191] Euripides' lost *Theseus* contained a scene which assumes that some or all of the audience knows the alphabet (which is not how we are defining literacy): an illiterate herdsman is made to describe, one by one, the letters which make up the hero's name, which he can see on a ship.[192] But again the text has implications beyond the obvious. The thirteen lines of the herdsman's description seem laboured, and they may have been expected to appeal to an audience which felt some elementary satisfaction in being able to recognize the letters.[193] (Since the scene was a dramatic success and was imitated at least twice by other poets, it particularly requires our attention.)[194] The speaker, being a herdsman (in Theodectes' version, simply a countryman), is differentiated from much of the audience, but that does not mean that everyone in the audience was expected to be fully literate.

An often-quoted text from the *Knights* refers directly to illiteracy: the Sausage-seller says that he does not understand *mousike,* the arts, except for writing, and that very badly, which is supposed to make

190. Nieddu, *S & C* vi (1982), 248.

191. The reflection that a written text is an aid to memory is illustrated by an Athenian lekythos of the second quarter of the fifth century on which Mnemosyne is depicted with an open book-roll (Beazley, *Attic Red-figure Vase-Painters* 624/75; Beck, *Album of Greek Education* 58 no. 369) (cf. Nieddu 260).

192. Eur. *Thes.* 382 Nauck. Beck, *Greek Education* 84, takes this as "proof of the universality of the knowledge of letters."

193. The tragic poet Callias' τραγῳδία γραμματικὴ may have provided similar entertainment; cf. Weil in *Le monde grec* 165–166. The epitaph of Thrasymachus (85 A8 D–K) also plays with the alphabet.

194. Athen. x.454d–e (Agathon fr. 4 Snell; Theodectes fr. 6 Snell). The scene was not, it seems, a joke at the herdsman's expense; it would have been clumsy and un-Euripidean to mock a man at length for what was a common condition.

him good demagogue material.[195] All that these lines require, however, is that Aristophanes and some of his audience must have looked with disdain on semi-literacy when it was manifested by men with political ambitions; and we must suppose that a sizeable section of the audience rose above this level. But this vague supposition does not prevent us from supposing that many of the citizens in the audience, men who did not aspire to political power, knew letters badly or not at all.[196] The *Knights* itself shows that Aristophanes could afford to ignore some of the sensibilities of the mass of the audience, for Demos is treated without sympathy until he reforms in the last eighty lines or so of the play. And when comic poets assert that popular leaders were illiterate or barely literate,[197] the invective simply confirms the unsurprising truths that illiteracy was a familiar phenomenon, and that some Athenians thought that it disqualified a man from political leadership. As for the allusion in the *Frogs* to Dionysus as a reader of Euripides, it tells us practically nothing about popular literacy.[198]

Apart from the shepherd in the *Theseus,* none of the male characters put on the stage by the great tragic poets is pictured as unable to read or write. On the other hand, the women of noble families who appear on the tragic stage are sometimes literate, sometimes not. In fact only Phaedra in the *Hippolytus* is definitely literate, and there it is vital to the plot that she should write a letter herself.[199] (In Menander's *The Sicyonian,* shortly after our period, an Athenian woman can write, and this is not held to be remarkable—but it also happens to be convenient for the plot of the play.)[200] By contrast Iphigeneia in the *Iphigeneia in Tauris,* when she had seen the need for a letter, had had it written for her.[201]

195. Ar. *Eq.* 188–189.

196. Is the audience expected to be familiar at first hand with schools? The answer is unclear: an obscure passage in *P.Oxy.* xxxv.2741 col. i, lines 14–19, a commentary on Eupolis (whence Eupolis fr. 192 Kassel-Austin), may suggest so.

197. Ar. *Eq.* 190–192 implies that they were often illiterate. Eupolis fr. 193 Kock (from Quint. *Inst.* i.10.18) said that Hyperbolus was barely literate. On the other hand, the illiterate who spoke fr. 122 Kock in Cratinus' *Laws* was probably not a demagogue but a respectable character—of what social level the text does not reveal—to judge from the words μνημονεύω γὰρ καλῶς. Longo, *Tecniche della comunicazione* 59–60, takes him to be an average Athenian, but this is far from sure.

198. In spite of Havelock (*New Literary History* viii [1976–77], 338 = *The Literate Revolution* 204), who infers from this passage that Athens "had become literate in our sense, that is, was becoming a society of readers." A monstrous non sequitur.

199. Eur. *Hipp.* 856–81.

200. Men. *Sic.* 131.

201. Eur. *IT* 584–585. In Eur. *IA* 115–123, 891, it is not clear that Clytemnestra

However the social context of all these dramatic references needs to be borne constantly in mind. While the audience was large,[202] it was made up of the relatively sophisticated—a fairly far cry from Boeotian or Euboean peasants who were more typical Greeks—and it was in addition predominantly if not exclusively male.

The literacy of slaves is a special problem which has so far received only intermittent attention. Some literate slaves have been mentioned, in each case trusted agents of well-to-do masters;[203] and other pieces of evidence can be added.[204] Such was the fate of a small number. By the fourth century, well-to-do Greek slave-owners would as a matter of course have possessed some literate slaves. Thus it was natural for Plato to show a slave reading out a lengthy and important text, and for Demosthenes to show one writing down a deposition and another writing out an arbitration agreement.[205] There were also public slaves, a few at least, to keep records in fourth-century Athens.[206] All this, however, has little to do with the ways in which most slaves lived, as farm-workers or household servants. With regard to the great majority of slaves, their masters would plainly have had scant reason to want to teach them to read and write.[207]

What we know of literacy outside Athens is even more heavily dependant on conjecture. The wealth of Athens during the life of the Delian League is a relevant difference, but on the other hand there existed a community of political culture, of economic practice and also of literature which embraced many other states. The difference in literacy between Athens and, say, Corinth, Miletus or Syracuse is not likely to have been great. Miletus, Syracuse and Argos, besides Athens,

---

can read (cf. Cole in Foley, *Reflections* 224, against Harvey, *REG* lxxix [1966], 622). In Soph. *Trach.* 155–163 Deianeira may be seen as unable to read, but this is not certain (cf. Cole, ibid.) (she writes things in her memory: 684).

202. In reality we have very little knowledge indeed of how many people could attend a performance in the theatre of Dionysus before the reconstruction by Lycurgus.

203. See Ps.-Dem. xxxvi.8, 28; Dem. xlv.72.

204. Dem. xxix.11 (cf. 21), for instance, which shows that while the run-of-the-mill slave in Athens did not "understand letters," some were skilled clerks.

205. Pl. *Theaet.* 143b–c; Dem. xxix.11, 21; Dem. xxxiii.17.

206. Cf. [Aristot.] *Ath.Pol.* 47.5, etc.

207. To show that it sometimes happened, Harvey, *REG* lxxix (1966), 623, cites the fourth-century comic poet Theophilus. But what the text in question (fr. 1 Kock = ii p. 473) implies is rather that learning letters from one's master was a privilege for a slave, next down from being initiated into the Mysteries. The assumption in Dio Chrys. xv.15, a story which may well have a classical source, is that the ordinary Athenian slave is illiterate.

were the cities of ostracism. The schools of Chios, Astypalaea and Mycalessus will be recalled. It is even relevant that so many of the most influential minds of this era, though many of them gravitated to Athens, came from elsewhere: Pindar, Hippodamus, Herodotus, Hippocrates, Protagoras, Hippias, Prodicus, Gorgias, Aristotle, Theopompus, Theophrastus, just to take prominent examples. The culture was not entirely Athenocentric. Some regions, however, as was noted earlier, are likely to have had much less literacy. One extreme case was probably Sparta.

An Athenian who undoubtedly knew a lot about Sparta, Isocrates, wrote in about 340 that the Lacedaemonians "are so far behind our common culture [he is referring to Greece in general] that they do not even learn to read and write."[208] The context is admittedly hostile, and it is a risk to base any important historical assertion on the exactness of Isocrates. But when he relents in his anti-Spartan attitude later in the same speech he nonetheless assumes that even an intelligent Spartan could learn its contents only if someone read the speech to him, which implies that virtually all Spartans read with difficulty or not at all.[209] Other, vaguer sources, both hostile and friendly, point in the same direction,[210] and it is likely that very few Spartiates were fully literate in the fifth and fourth centuries.

Recent writers will have none of this, and in effect have claimed more literacy for the Spartiates than can have been possessed even by the Athenians. They allege, fantastically, that every Spartiate was literate at least to some degree,[211] or that many were.

Some were, that is certain. There is good, and in some cases con-

---

208. Isocr. *Panath.* 209.

209. Ibid. 250–251. This passage is ruthlessly mistranslated by T. A. Boring, *Literacy in Ancient Sparta* (Leiden, 1979), 45–46, who takes τὸν ἀναγνωσόμενον to mean someone who will *explain* the speeches instead of someone who will read them out. He offers no parallels.

210. The Spartans were hostile to teaching letters, according to *Dissoi Logoi* ii.10 (D–K ii.408). (However Pl. *Protag.* 342 makes no such assertion, contrary to the view of Cartledge, *JHS* xcviii [1978], 27.) The friendly version was that the Spartans learned letters ἕνεκα τῆς χρείας, "as far as was necessary" (Plu. *Lyc.* 16.10, *Mor.* 237a), which sounds like a euphemism.

211. Harvey's claim (625) that the kings and other leading figures of classical Sparta must have had the same education as every rank-and-file Spartiate is mere idealization. Cartledge 28 claims that no Spartiate male was entirely illiterate. Boring 96 tends in the same direction, but hedges by concluding that the Spartans [i.e., Spartiates] "did learn their letters if they wished to do so" and were "literate to a degree"; he gives no idea of what proportion of them he means.

temporary, evidence about the literacy of some Spartan kings and about army commanders who corresponded with the government.[212] Those involved must have known how to send and read messages on the *skutale,* the Spartan code-stick, which involved conventional writing.[213] It was probably assumed that all who held, or would one day hold, the highest offices would be able to make use of this device unaided. The ephors also knew how to make use of the *skutale* at least as early as the 470s and are attested as having done so on a number of later occasions.[214] Thus it is clear that a certain degree of literacy was common among the kind of man who held the ephorate. It is possible in theory that all this governmental writing was really done by clerks on behalf of illiterate masters, but it seems unlikely.[215] In the 390s King Pausanias and the commander Thibron even seem to have written political statements; no doubt these were rudimentary, and it is perhaps more characteristic that Lysander relied on a foreigner for the written exposition of his political ideas.[216] At all events the literacy of office-holders tells us practically nothing about the ordinary Spartiate, for the small world of the Spartiates was decidedly stratified.[217] This is not to say that literacy was entirely confined to a small aristocracy.[218] Some of the modest number of graffito dedications from Laconian sanctuaries of this period were written by Spartiates, and a few funerary inscriptions are also known.[219] But the literate were probably a small minority.

Literary education certainly received much less attention at Sparta

212. Kings: Hdt. vi.50.3, vii.239.3; Thuc. i.128.6–7, 132.5 (the reliability of the text Thucydides offers is a separate question), etc. Hdt. vii.239.4 implies that Gorgo, daughter of Cleomenes, was familiar with writing-tablets. Army commanders: Thuc. viii.33, 38; Xen. *Hell.* i.1.23; etc. See further Cartledge 29.

213. On this device see T. Kelly in *The Craft of the Ancient Historian: Essays in Honor of Chester G. Starr* (Lanham, Md., 1985), 141–169.

214. See Thuc. i.131.1 and, e.g., Plu. *Lys.* 19.7; Xen. *Hell.* iii.3.8. On the literacy of ephors: Cartledge 28–29.

215. A royal "writer" is attested under King Agesilaus, but see Cartledge 29.

216. Pausanias: Ephorus *FGrH* 70 F118. Thibron: Aristot. *Pol.* vii.14.1333b18. Lysander: the foreigner was Cleon of Halicarnassus; see the sources gathered by Boring, *Literacy* 50–52.

217. See, e.g., P. A. Cartledge, *CQ* xxxi (1981), 96.

218. Both Cinadon, the rebel who was not a full member of the community, and those who were deputed to arrest him were able to write, according to Xen. *Hell.* iii.3.8 and 10.

219. Dedications: Cartledge, *JHS* xcviii (1978), 32 n.46; Boring 8–16; the social rank, when it can be judged, was high. Epitaphs: Cartledge 31, 35.

than in most Greek cities, and writing played a much smaller part in Spartan life.[220] A Spartan tradition disdained the written word.[221] And literacy is likely to have been restricted, among the Spartiates, to a small number of men and a still smaller number of women.[222]

In summary, the notion that every citizen male should know how to read and write made its appearance during the classical period of Greek culture, but came nowhere near to realization even at Athens. We have no reason to suppose that literacy overcame the social barriers which impeded it from spreading to the entire citizen population. The classical Greeks attained the level of literacy which their political economy (based on slavery and on a limited body of rights shared by the citizens of the *polis*), their economic life and their extraordinary psychic energy implied. This level was in a sense remarkably high, for literacy ceased to be scribal and also went far far beyond the circle of the wealthy. Ostracism remains the most important evidence, and it implies that for most of the fifth century the number of literates and semi-literates among the citizens of Athens comfortably exceeded 6,000 (comfortably, because not all the competent men can possibly have appeared for any single ballot).[223] Also important as evidence, within the limits outlined above, are the assumptions of the Athenian dramatists and orators. But for most of the period in question there were probably in excess of 10,000 Athenian hoplites and the total citizen population of Attica was usually over 100,000; for much of the fifth century the total must have been far above that figure. Thus in percentage terms the level of literacy, while still to be considered impressive in view of the obstacles to popular education, was not especially dramatic. For the population of Attica as a whole, it should probably be set in the range between 5% and 10%.

We have too little information to be able to construct a clear diachronic account of the growth in the functions of literacy and in the number of literates in classical Greece. But some suggestions can be offered. The period from about 520 to 480 may have been one of relatively rapid advance, as was suggested in the previous chapter.[224]

220. See Cartledge 35–36 on these points.

221. Plu. *Lyc.* 13.

222. On literacy among Spartan women cf. Cartledge 31.

223. But perhaps the reason ostracism went out of use after 417 was just that there were fewer citizens and not enough literate or semi-literate ones to make the old procedure work.

224. J. M. Camp, *AJA* lxxxvii (1983), 115, hypothesizes that the decline in spelling variation visible in the Athenian ostraca after the 450s resulted from an increase in literacy at that time; this is not impossible.

At Athens another period of rapid development in the functions of writing seems to have occurred during the Peloponnesian War, and several scholars have supposed that literacy also advanced in a significant way about 430.[225] The evidence for this is in reality quite thin, and if we had more literature from the 440s and 430s a different view might prevail. The notion of a major extension of literacy cannot in my view be either established or disproved for any date in the period from 430 to 400. Another possible period of rapid expansion could be situated in the 370s and 360s, with the changes in legal procedure referred to above and with the formation, itself difficult to date with precision but in any case well befcre Plato's death in 347, of theories of universal citizen education.

We have seen that both the functions and the diffusion of literacy in classical Greece were probably more limited than is generally supposed, and it should be plain from the foregoing account what impeded faster growth. What were the factors which pulled in the other direction, that is, which helped to diffuse the use of writing? The answer goes beyond the easiness of the Greek alphabet and beyond the economic success, based largely on colonization and on slavery, which gave some leisure to part of the free population in many cities. The uses of writing accumulated, and we have attempted to describe this process. But there was something still further: in spite of the continuing ambivalence of its reputation, writing gained general prestige and gradually came to be associated with the rights of the citizens, their right to exile politicians, their right to know the laws and the proposed laws, and their right to use the law-courts, whether as litigants or as jurors. Thus its use became, at least in Athens, a mark in theory of a proper citizen and in practice of the urban citizen with property. Such men now found literacy indispensable.

225. For Havelock's view that there was very rapid growth in Greek literacy about 430 see above, p. 94 n.135; according to Nieddu, *S & C* vi (1982), 235, most scholars think there was a notable increase in (Greek or Athenian?) literacy at the end of the fifth century.

5   The Hellenistic State and Elementary Education

In the year 248 B.C. Petosiris, son of Petenouris, an Egyptian pig-keeper in a village in the Fayum, paid seventeen piglets to one Heracleides as the year's rent for ten sows. Heracleides gave him a receipt, fifty-seven words written in Greek on papyrus.[1]

As far as the written word is concerned, we are clearly in a new era.[2] But a text such as this receipt throws into relief several acute problems of method which face anyone who wishes to give an account of Hellenistic literacy. In particular we may ask: was Petosiris literate in Greek? In demotic Egyptian? (Probably in neither.) Did Heracleides, an agent of the rich and powerful Zeno, write the receipt himself? (Probably, but there is no certainty at all.) Was it in fact a novelty of this period that such relatively minor rustic transactions generated receipts? (Probably, but there is no definite proof.) Would there have been a written receipt if the proprietor in the background had not been a wealthy and document-loving man such as Zeno? (Probably not, but there is no certainty about this, either.) In Petosiris' time, did pig-keepers in other parts of the Greek world outside the Ptolemaic domains receive such texts? (It is hard to tell, but on balance it seems unlikely.) Finally, why was such a document deemed necessary?

Heracleides and Zeno were, of course, Greeks. But with the conquests, settlements, and cultural diffusion which took place under Alexander of Macedon and his successors, the connotation of the term *Greeks* changes radically. For the historian the problem of keeping a specific population well in focus thus becomes more severe. In general the subject here will be the speakers of the Greek language wherever they lived. Some at least of the Greeks themselves held that language

1. *PSI* iv.379 = *Sel.Pap.* i.72 (with a longer, outer, text and a shorter inner one).
2. This chapter runs down to roughly the 70s B.C., by which date Rome's influence on the social order was being felt over most of the Greek world; such periodization is undeniably somewhat arbitrary.

or culture, rather than descent, was the best criterion of nationality,[3] and our subject here is in any case cultural history, not ethnic history. The restriction of subject matter to those who spoke Greek will not prevent us from paying some attention to non-Greek-speaking people, such as Petosiris, who were in contact with Greeks. Understanding the social structures of many parts of the Hellenistic world requires us to do this. And in some areas indigenous cultures and traditions certainly influenced the quality and type of literacy to be found among Hellenized "barbarians" and even among Greeks of Greek descent. There were in addition many families, as well as communities, in which two or more languages overlapped.[4]

The most difficult problem of all is to know how much uniformity there was in the uses of writing, in educational practice, and in literacy between diverse Greek communities. The source material is so sporadic: papyrus documents which for climatic reasons come almost exclusively from Egypt and indeed from Egypt outside Alexandria, very limited literary sources which do not always have a single specific geographical frame of reference (Herodas and Theocritus), inscriptions and monuments which may have no significance beyond the single city to which they belong. For many places, for example most of the cities in the Seleucid Empire, we can hardly go beyond a few elementary conjectures.

434 Rolls of Papyrus

Rather than reviewing again all the spheres of life in which writing was used, we shall concentrate in this section on what was most definitely novel. The Greek city did not change fundamentally after Alexander's conquests,[5] and in many respects the role of writing changed slowly or remained much the same. For Greeks to be in charge of large and more or less centralized kingdoms, however, that was some-

---

3. Cf. Thuc. i.3.4; Isocr. *Paneg.* 50; Strabo i.41 end *(dialekton)* (= Poseidonius, FGrH F105a).

4. For some examples see W. Peremans in E. Van't Dack et al. (eds.), *Egypt and the Hellenistic World. Proceedings of the International Colloquium, Leuven, 24–26 May 1982* (Louvain, 1983), 276–277.

5. It is worth recalling M. I. Rostovtzeff's judgement that "the Greek city-state underwent no important changes in its political, economic, and social structure in Hellenistic times" (*The Social and Economic History of the Hellenistic World* [Oxford, 1941], ii.1304).

thing new. And in fact most of the new or newly diffused uses of the written word belong to the kingdom of the Ptolemies.

Even before 323, as we have already seen, the contractual aspect of economic life was more and more being expressed in documents. This is a strong trend, visible in fair detail in the Athenian orators. In some types of transaction, the sale of real estate for instance, it is not completely clear that there were ever straightforward contracts of sale in the fourth century; but certainly some documentation could be involved. In the case of marriage arrangements, it so happens that there is no evidence that they were ever in writing before 323, the earliest evidence being a contract of 310 from Elephantine in Upper Egypt.[6] But again it is unlikely that this was a Ptolemaic innovation.

Some of the transactions committed to writing in the early Hellenistic period were of modest size. A slave girl whose sale was incorporated in a written contract in 259/258 B.C. fetched a price of fifty drachmas.[7] But the persons involved were far from being typical Greeks: a group of cavalrymen and, more to the point, Zeno, an agent of Apollonius, the finance minister of King Ptolemy Philadelphus. In normal circumstances when a slave or some other commodity changed hands at a price of this kind, no written contract is likely to have been made (and in fact the document just referred to is one of only two surviving contracts for the sale of a slave which are of Ptolemaic date).[8] A loan contract of 273 concerns the sum of thirty-four drachmas; the principals were both military men.[9]

When catalogues of private Greek financial documents of various kinds from Graeco-Roman Egypt were compiled a generation ago by Montevecchi, the fact stood out very clearly that early Ptolemaic documents—those earlier than, say, the 130s—are rare; and indeed most of the survivals are of Roman date.[10] It is true that some extra-

6. *P.Eleph.* 1 (partly in *Sel.Pap.* i.1). The interconnectedness of the third-century Greek world is underlined by the fact that the bridegroom was from Temnos, the bride from Cos, and the witnesses from Gela, Temnos, Cyrene and Cos.

7. *P.Cair.Zen.* i.59003, lines 11–22 = *Sel.Pap.* i.31 = *SB* iii.6709 = *CPIud* i.1. Those involved in this transaction, besides Zeno from Caunos, came from Cnidos, Macedon, Miletus, Athens, Colophon, and Aspendos. The slave was Babylonian, and the contract was made at Birta, in Transjordan.

8. The other is *P.Köln* iv.187 of 146 B.C.

9. *P.Cair.Zen.* i.59001, lines 26–56 = *Sel.Pap.* i.66. For other small-scale transactions recorded in writing see H. J. Wolff, *Das Recht der griechischen Papyri Aegyptens* ii (Munich, 1978), 4 n.6.

10. Among the documents known to her, the following proportions are pre-

neous factors contributed to the shortage of private documents from the early Ptolemaic period: we would not expect many documents attesting private land transactions at a time when a high proportion of Egyptian land belonged to the king. Nonetheless, the number of business papers unconnected with the government which survive from this time is remarkably small—smaller perhaps than the fourth-century Athenian orators might have led one to expect—and even after the increase which began in the 130s the number remains small in most categories.

Most of the Greeks in Ptolemaic Egypt carried on their private economic lives without any greater degree of paperwork than the fourth-century Athenians, in some respects perhaps with less.[11] Not one apprenticeship contract survives from this period (in the Roman period they are quite numerous, though even then most of the contracting parties were illiterate).[12] Nor is there any reason to think that in the rest of the Hellenistic world the business functions of writing increased dramatically.[13] The ordinary work of most Greeks did not itself generate much in the way of private records, contracts, correspondence or anything else in writing.

The great exception to this is represented for us by the files of the minister Apollonius and his ubiquitous agent Zeno. These documents of the 250s and 240s deal, as we have already seen in two instances, with their private financial affairs as well as with official matters.[14] Indeed, because of the power which Apollonius and Zeno exercised and the great range of their activities, the distinction is somewhat unreal. It may well be, however, that the impetus to extend paperwork came in the Hellenistic age mainly from governments and

---

Roman: 1 out of 43 slave sales (O. Montevecchi, *Aegyptus* xix [1939], 16) (the text mentioned above); 2 of the 84 animal sales (ibid. 49–50); 15 of the 155 building sales, though only one of the 15 is earlier than 113 B.C. (*Aegyptus* xxi [1941], 94); 76 of 226 land sales—though only 3 of these are earlier than 139 (*Aegyptus* xxiii [1943], 12). In the category "oggetti vari," 12 of 49 documents are Ptolemaic (ibid. 244–261), but only 2 of these are definitely earlier than 146 (ibid. 258).

11. Concerning unwritten contracts in Ptolemaic Egypt see R. Taubenschlag, *The Law of Greco-Roman Egypt in the Light of the Papyri* (New York, 1944), 228–229.

12. Cf. A. Zambon, *Aegyptus* xv (1935), 3–66. To the best of my knowledge this remains true.

13. For the increased use of writing in Hellenistic banking practice see R. Bogaert, *Banques et banquiers dans les cités grecques* (Leiden, 1968), 337–340.

14. P. W. Pestman, *A Guide to the Zenon Archive* (Leiden, 1981), 171–194, provides a typological survey of these documents.

from senior government officials pursuing their own interests. The effect was that documents began to impinge more on the economic lives of ordinary people.

Before we come to the governmental use of documents, it is worth remarking on the changing legal status of private contracts in written form. The status of the written contract was already on the rise in the time of Demosthenes and Aristotle, and the trend seems to have continued. At least, official facilities for registering private contracts gradually spread, and this presumably indicates some recognition that the custody of such documents was of vital importance. The evidence for this development, which took place in different forms in each city, is sporadic (much of it is epigraphical), and no overall account can be given.[15] We happen to possess evidence that this kind of city archive was in existence by the third century at Chios, Cos, Clazomenae, Seleuceia on the Tigris and other places.[16] It may be no accident that most of these attestations come from the southern and eastern Aegean, but the institution was probably by this time a good deal more widespread. Reasonably plain evidence shows that this procedure was being followed in Egypt by the 220s.[17] However no clear evidence seems to exist that registration of a written contract was essential to the validity of a contract anywhere in the Hellenistic world.

The detailed typology of Hellenistic legal documents we can leave aside here.[18] The value of a document as legal proof is, however, of concern to us. It is said that the probative value of documents con-

---

15. Cf. E. Weiss, *Griechisches Privatrecht* i (Leipzig, 1923), 391–425; E. Bikerman, *Institutions des Séleucides* (Paris, 1938), 209; W. Lambrinudakis & M. Wörrle, *Chiron* xiii (1983), 283–368, esp. 336–352. M. Bianchini cannot be right to say (in A. Biscardi et al. [eds.], ΣΥΜΠΟΣΙΟΝ *1974* [Athens, 1978], 249) that the public registration of *sungraphai* began in the second century.

16. Chios: [Aristot.] *Oecon.* ii.2.12 (registration of private debts, a system which on one occasion was exploited by the city). Cos: W. R. Paton & E. L. Hicks, *The Inscriptions of Cos* (Oxford, 1891), no. 368 VI.36–38 (καθ᾽ ὑοθεσίαν δὲ τὰν ἐπὶ χρεωφυλάκων) and VII.39–41 (debt registration again). Clazomenae: *Die Inschriften von Erythrai und Klazomenai* ii (*IGSK* ii), 510, line 10. Seleuceia: R. H. McDowell, *Stamped and Inscribed Objects from Seleucia on Tigris* (Ann Arbor, 1935), 40–41 (reign of Antiochus I).

17. See *P.Tebt.* iii.815 and *P.Petr.* ii.47, with the discussions of C. Préaux in *Recueils de la Société Jean Bodin* xvi (= *La preuve* i) (1964), 185–186; Wolff, *Das Recht* ii.69–70 (who shows decisively that the former document relates to an official archive). The contracts were summarized for the archives by officials. For the summarizing of documents at Paros in the second century see Lambrinudakis & Wörrle, esp. 344.

18. Cf. Wolff ii.57–135.

tinued to increase in relation to that of living witnesses.[19] This may well be true. Yet the conclusion depends quite heavily on a report of a single case in which witnesses were supposedly called upon only because of the loss of the relevant documents.[20] This text does not, however, say that oral testimony was of value in the case *only* because of the destruction of documents,[21] and in the Hellenistic world in general documentary proof may not have gained much or indeed any ground at the expense of direct testimony.

However it was more and more thought to be the responsibility of governments to maintain written records. Already when Theophrastus wrote his *Laws* towards the end of the fourth century, there was an Athenian rule that the officials had to receive written notice of a sale of real estate at least sixty days before the sale could take effect; and in some other cities the magistrates were supposed to keep up-to-date property registers.[22] This represents a growth of governmental power, but also a stronger belief that the most vital facts (who owns this piece of land?) needed to be recorded in writing.

But the truly dramatic increase in the governmental use of writing occurred, as is well known, not in the cities but in the monarchic states, above all in the empire of the Ptolemies. The Seleucid and Attalid kingdoms were no doubt also affected. We do not know how or exactly when some royal courts decided that efficient control required masses of paperwork. By the 250s, however, a sizeable bureaucracy was managing the royal economy of the Ptolemies. The classic piece of evidence dates from 258/257 and shows that the accounting offices of the finance minister Apollonius received 434 rolls of papyrus in thirty-three days.[23] No officials in any pre-Hellenistic Greek state could have had anything like this appetite for paper.

---

19. Most recently by J. Mélèze-Modrzejewski, in *Atti del XVII Congresso internazionale di papirologia* (Naples, 1984), iii.1186, who does not claim to extend the conclusion beyond Egypt.

20. The report is *P.Amh.* ii.30 = *W.Chr.* 9 (169–164 B.C.).

21. Cf. W. Hellebrand, *Das Prozesszeugnis im Rechte der gräko-ägyptischen Papyri* (Munich, 1934), 174.

22. Stobaeus iv.2.20 = Theophr. fr. 97.1–2 = A. Szegedy-Maszak, *The Nomoi of Theophrastus* (New York, 1981), fr. 21.1–2. In earlier times heralds had provided all the needed publicity about such sales (cf. fr. 97.1). For the registration of land- and house-ownership at Mende see [Aristot.] *Oecon.* ii.2.21; the author seems to regard it as unremarkable. Cf. also Préaux in *Recueils Jean Bodin* 194–198. For the official registration of real-estate purchases in Egypt under Ptolemy Philadelphus see *P.Hal.* 1, lines 242–257 (with the commentary of Préaux 198–202).

23. *P.Col.Zen.* iii.4, plus *P.Cair.Zen.* iv.59687.

The Ptolemaic bureaucracy evidently inherited some of its practices from earlier Egyptian administrations;[24] for example, the execution of cadastral surveys followed Egyptian precedents, not Greek ones.[25] But Greek ideas also, as we have seen, prepared the way for the proliferation of paperwork. At all events, the Ptolemies used paperwork on a scale unprecedented in classical Greece to superintend revenue-gathering. Unfortunately, we have no clear information about the size of the clerical staff which operated this system; even the 434 papyrus rolls can only suggest a minimum figure for one section of the bureaucracy.[26]

Full bureaucratization, as far as it could be achieved in the ancient world, was to come only later. It was more characteristic of Roman than of Ptolemaic Egypt to require the population to make all manner of periodic declarations to the government.[27] But in Hellenistic Egypt documents called into being by the government or its agents, such as Zeno, had already intruded much further than governmental paperwork had ever done before. Under Apollonius begins the stream of documents attesting the activities of the "village clerks," *komogrammateis*, who were of course agents of the central government; these begin in 258/257.[28] At the same period the government began to employ "crop controllers," *genematophulakes*, to assist with the gathering of taxes; the first document of this kind dates from 257. We must begin to suspect that Apollonius and Philadelphus deliberately created the new bureaucracy within a very limited time-span.[29]

24. On the difficult question of parallels between dynastic and Ptolemaic Egypt with respect to administrative and documentary practices see U. Wilcken in *Papyri und Altertumswissenschaft. Vorträge des 3. Internationalen Papyrologentages* [1933] (Munich, 1935), 42–61; J. D. Thomas in H. Maehler & V. M. Strocka (eds.), *Das ptolemäische Aegypten* (Mainz, 1978), 188 (the agnosticism of the latter is significant).

25. See D. J. Crawford, *Kerkeosiris. An Egyptian Village in the Ptolemaic Period* (Cambridge, 1971), 5–6. On the other hand E. Grier, *Accounting in the Zenon Papyri* (New York, 1934), 56–57, concluded that the accounting methods she investigated were independent of Egyptian precedents.

26. W. L. Westermann & E. S. Hasenoehrl, *Zenon Papyri* i (= *P.Col.Zen.* iii) (New York, 1934), 17, conjectured that Demetrius, one of Apollonius' subordinates who received 223 rolls, may have had "ten or more" underclerks.

27. Cf. the types of declaration listed by E. G. Turner, *Greek Papyri. An Introduction* (Oxford, 1968), 140.

28. L. Criscuolo, *Aegyptus* lviii (1978), 11. *SB* iii.7202 might date from 265/264. Starting with *P.Petr.* iii.37a (258/257) these documents are very numerous.

29. The documents relating to the *genematophulakes* have been collected and analysed by H. Cuvigny, *Cd'E* lix (1984), 123–135. As it happens, the earliest document, *P.Mich.* i.73, concerns the estates of Apollonius.

The inroads of bureaucracy can be observed in numerous texts. The receipt given to the pig-keeper Petosiris has been mentioned. A house-painter making an estimate for Zeno—for a major piece of work, it is true—puts it, or has it put, in writing.[30] Many kinds of retail business now require the tradesman (who may or may not be literate) to subscribe to official documents; examples are beer-selling, selling roast lentils, keeping a bath-house.[31] In classical Greece there had been police forces, but there is no sign or likelihood that citizens made written complaints to them; under the Ptolemies, however, this becomes a standard procedure.[32] Once again the earliest surviving document dates from the 250s.[33] Such are the symptoms of the spread of administrative efficiency and of bureaucratic control, which incidentally caused many illiterate as well as literate people to become involved with documents.

Every Hellenistic state generated governmental and administrative documents, and in a centralized system the burden of paperwork might strike those in power as heavy. Seleucus I is already supposed to have complained that if people knew what hard work it was to write and read so many letters, they would not consent to pick up a crown if it had been thrown away.[34] The writing of official letters for political purposes certainly increased greatly after Alexander of Macedon's time.[35] What went on in the Ptolemaic kingdom was exceptional, however. The ordinary Greek cities had their magistrates and their public finances, which could grow complex; they had their archives and their inscriptions.[36] But nothing suggests they underwent the profound bureaucratization that took place in Egypt.

It can be conjectured that while writing extended its political and administrative functions in the Hellenistic period, it lost some of its

30. *P.Cair.Zen.* iii.59445 = *Sel.Pap.* i.171 (c. 255 B.C.).

31. See M. I. Rostovtzeff, *A Large Estate in Egypt in the Third Century B.C.* (Madison, Wis., 1922), 118–122.

32. On these προσαγγέλματα see M. Hombert & C. Préaux, *Cd'E* xvii (1942), 259–286; M. Parca, *Cd'E* lx (1985), 240–247.

33. *P.Mich.Zen.* 34 of 254 B.C.

34. Plu. *An seni* 11 = *Mor.* 790ab.

35. See C. B. Welles, *Royal Correspondence in the Hellenistic Period* (London, 1934), esp. xxxvii–xli, on the activities of the royal chanceries. Seleucid royal letters: Bikerman, *Institutions* 190–197. Josephus' claim (*AJ* xii.145) that Antiochus III sent a πρόγραμμα concerning Jerusalem "throughout his entire kingdom" is suspect.

36. On archives for public documents in the Hellenistic cities see G. Klaffenbach, *Bemerkungen zum griechischen Urkundenwesen* (= *SB Berlin* 1960, no. 6), 5–34; cf. E. Posner, *Archives in the Ancient World* (Cambridge, Mass., 1972), 114–117.

awe-inspiring quality. Every city-dweller, whether literate or not, was commonly in the presence of the written word. Yet writing must have retained a certain authoritative quality in the eyes of many people, for it was still associated with the wishes and power of the government.

To what extent the written word was held to have authority or power in the realm of religion is, for the classical period, debatable. It perhaps gathers some authority in the fourth century. In the records of the famous temple of Asclepius at Epidaurus, which seem to have been inscribed in the last quarter of the century,[37] the priests make some appeal to written testimony in order to combat incredulity about Asclepius' cures.[38] But the question whether one should believe in the curative powers of a particular god can hardly be said to have been central to Greek religion even in the Hellenistic period, and the beliefs and practices of most Greeks hardly involved the written word much more than before. There now came into being the genre of so-called aretalogies, descriptions of the earthly feats of a god or hero; but not surprisingly the *aretalogos,* the man who told such tales, was in general an oral performer.[39] There can be little doubt that elaborate magical spells were now in circulation in written form,[40] quite apart from the curse-tablets (such as the one illustrated in Figure 2) which were mentioned in the previous chapter; but these were the professional equipment of specialists.

At one social level, namely among the highly educated, religious ideas did now depend more on the written word. The founding fathers of Hellenistic philosophy, even Diogenes, wrote numerous tracts; and while they obviously did not win followers by this means alone, their long-term influence depended heavily on their writings.[41] The written transmission of ideas made it easier for them to be passed on in an exact form, so that the Epicureans were able to go on saying much what Epicurus himself had said. A great deal remains obscure, however, about the extent to which a Hellenistic intellectual read and

37. Cf. M. P. Nilsson, *Geschichte der griechischen Religion* ii (3d ed., Munich, 1974), 225; M. Guarducci, *Epigrafia greca* iv (Rome, 1978), 148.

38. See esp. *SIG*³ 1168 = E. J. & L. Edelstein, *Asclepius: A Collection of the Testimonies* (Baltimore, 1945), i no. 423.

39. Nilsson 228–229.

40. Cf. M. Smith in *Atti del XVII Congresso internazionale di papirologia* (Naples, 1984), ii.683–693.

41. A. D. Nock, *Conversion* (Oxford, 1933), 167, asked why the philosophical schools occupied "so dominant a place in the spiritual history of the succeeding centuries," but in his answer (167–179) gave too little weight to the existence of texts (though see 179).

was influenced by the writings of Plato or by the other classics of religious thinking; the answer would presumably vary according to the religious temperament of the individual. The pursuit of this question would take us far from the present line of inquiry.

During the fourth century the most cultivated of the Greeks became more interested in books, and in some Hellenistic cities this trend intensified. The literary and philological scholarship which developed at Alexandria is normally considered the centre-piece of this new culture. It was sustained not only by the financial patronage of the Ptolemies but by the library of completely unprecedented dimensions which they collected.[42] The library was to be comprehensive, and therefore in a sense a giant retrospective exhibition of all Greek thinking—and of barbarian thinking too, which could be accepted, if not absorbed, since it could now be put into the unthreatening form of written Greek translations.

There is some temptation to juxtapose the written culture of the Hellenistic elite and the oral culture of the masses.[43] But this dichotomy is altogether too sharp. The culture of the elite continued to have a strong oral component, with oratory and performance retaining their important roles. Poets, expert lecturers, and musicians circulated from city to city.[44] In any case it is often both difficult and pointless to distinguish between elite and mass culture in Hellenistic cities. Which was involved, for instance, when the well-known flute-player Satyrus of Samos sustained the part of Dionysus in a performance of selections from the *Bacchae* in the stadium at Delphi?[45] The point here, however, is whether the public for works of literature now made a greater use of books than in earlier times. Almost any genre of writing might be presented in oral form,[46] and some genres of composition, mimes for instance, were perhaps not read very much in pri-

---

42. On the foundation and scope of the library see esp. R. Pfeiffer, *A History of Classical Scholarship* i (Oxford, 1968), 98–102 (and on the library of Pergamum, founded by Eumenes II, see 235–236); P. M. Fraser, *Ptolemaic Alexandria* (Oxford, 1972), i.320–335.

43. B. Gentili, in *Studi in onore di Aristide Colonna* (Perugia, 1982), 128–130 (virtually repeated in *Poesia e pubblico nella Grecia antica* [Rome & Bari, 1984], 228–231), tends in this direction.

44. See M. Guarducci, *Mem.Acc.Linc.* ser.6 ii (1929), 629–665.

45. *SIG*³ 648B (about the turn of the third to second centuries, perhaps in 194 B.C.).

46. For readings of histories in the Hellenistic era cf. A. Momigliano, *ASNSP* ser.3 viii (1978), 63 = *Sesto contributo alla storia degli studi classici e del mondo antico* (Rome, 1980), 365. Historians themselves were more eager for written sources, to judge from Polyb. xii.25e1.

vate.[47] Even in this period there is still no evidence for any organized publishing industry,[48] and precious little for private libraries of considerable size. On the other hand, the production of works of scholarly learning was quite extensive, and these must have been intended exclusively for the use of the individual reader—in fact exclusivity, the creation of a private, or nearly private, mental world, was presumably a large part of the aim of such authors.

Any assumption that the intellectually less demanding genres of Hellenistic literature aimed at, or reached, a truly popular audience of readers should be resisted.[49] The papyri show conclusively that popular literature did not exist in any ordinary sense of that expression: the literary texts which were most copied were the classics, Homer and Euripides. And if we look at genres of writing which might strike scholars as being undemanding, we do not find works which were intended for mass consumption. The mimiambs of Herodas were written not in contemporary *koine* Greek, but in an imperfect imitation of language current in the sixth century;[50] therefore, the public for this kind of production was a fairly sophisticated one. Some literary papyri of Hellenistic date which could only have appealed to readers of some discrimination have been found on village sites, but quite apart from the problem of cartonnage (the use of papyrus as mummy-wrapping, which could take the material away from its proper location), such texts may in each case have belonged to the single well-to-do inhabitant.[51] Popular culture had little to do with reading.

A type of literature which flourished greatly in the Hellenistic age consisted of technical manuals, and presumably these were intended for individual reading. The variety was enormous, going well beyond the medical, rhetorical and other handbooks of the classical age; in

47. I. C. Cunningham, in his ed. of Herodas, pp. 8 (where he lists the three Ptolemaic papyri which contain mime-like texts), 10. On possible recitations of Herodas' mimiambs: Cunningham 15–16.

48. Cf. P. E. Easterling in *Cambridge History of Classical Literature* i (Cambridge, 1985), 19–20.

49. This notion is found in W. W. Tarn, *Hellenistic Civilisation* (3d ed., London, 1952), 268, who writes of a small highly educated public and of another larger one "which had enough education to read greedily but not to read seriously," this being the audience for "popular literature." All this is a projection of Tarn's view of the modern world around him.

50. See Cunningham 14. This was not "how common people talked" (Tarn 279).

51. Cf. Turner, *Greek Papyri* 81; but no one has written a full account of this matter.

addition to works of literary and philological scholarship, one could by the middle of the second century read works on such subjects as military tactics, mining machinery, dyeing (the *Baphica* of Bolus, a third- or second-century Egyptian pharmacologist and magician), agriculture and bee-keeping. The functions of such books may have differed somewhat; while some were of a truly practical nature, others, at least so it has been argued,[52] had a theoretical or quasi-philosophical purpose. The readership of any given work of this kind was obviously small; surviving papyri strongly suggest that even medical texts were less widely distributed than we might have expected,[53] and that the total circulation of technical works remained small by comparison with the most favoured works of literature.[54] This will naturally not have prevented technical manuals from having the double effect, which we have noted before, of helping knowledge to accumulate and of making it canonical.

In the classical period the writing of letters was probably quite a special activity and by no means a part of everyday life, except possibly for the few men who had far-flung business interests. Various facts suggest that in the Hellenistic era letter-writing became commonplace at certain social levels. The role of letters in administration has already been mentioned. In private life there was also a change. When a man who had left some unspecified Greek city for Egypt did not write to his wife or mistress (her status is unclear) even once in ten months, it could be suggested that he had forgotten her[55]—not that Metriche, the neglected one in Herodas' story, accepts this suggestion. By the 270s, therefore, an educated audience assumed that in such circumstances of separation a man would commonly be expected to

---

52. Rostovtzeff, *Hellenistic World* ii.1203. What little is known of books about metals (Rostovtzeff 1212), for instance, supports this view.

53. From M.-H. Marganne, *Inventaire analytique des papyrus grecs de médecine* (Geneva, 1981), it emerges that some thirteen papyrus texts of medical content (including prescriptions) are unequivocally of Ptolemaic date (nos. 8, 27, 31, 70, 82, 89, 93, 94, 115, 120, 155, 156, and 186; 32, 95, and 187 are simply dated to the first century B.C.).

54. R. A. Pack, *The Greek and Latin Literary Texts from Greco-Roman Egypt* (2d ed., Ann Arbor, 1965), registers two fragments of agricultural texts (nos. 1985, 1986), three mathematical fragments (2315, 2322, 2337; but notice also six ostraca listed under 2323), and two or three from musical treatises (2443–45). There are some four Hellenistic fragments of astronomical or astrological content (2011, 2025, 2029, 2036).

55. Her. i.24: κοὐδὲ γράμμα σοι πέμπει.

write. A certain number of truly private letters survive on papyri, some even written by women; in some instances, however, it is plain that the letter was not an everyday affair but was inspired by some emergency.⁵⁶ Given the difficulties of getting long-distance letters delivered,⁵⁷ we would not expect to have more evidence about them than we do; what is worthy of remark is that letters were not, as far as we know, used for private local communication.

The more or less reasoned opposition to the use of writing which had persisted into the fourth century seems not to have reverberated much at later dates. But certain uses of writing could still arouse hostility or suspicion. When a democratic revolution broke out at Dyme in Achaea in the 110s, the revolutionaries wrote new laws but burned the city archives and the public documents *(demosia grammata)*.⁵⁸ This was certainly not a unique event.⁵⁹ In addition, the sinister quality which attaches to letters in Herodotus and Thucydides seems to continue in Polybius.⁶⁰ No doubt stories of this kind helped to maintain the personal and oral character of most Hellenistic diplomacy.

At all events, while the Ptolemaic bureaucracy presided over a dramatic increase in the functions of the written word, an increase which

56. Examples: *P.Petr.* ii.13.19 (= *Sel.Pap.* i.94) (about 255–250 B.C.) (adult son to father, Alexandria to the Fayum; the father is a high-level employee of the government) ; *P. Lond.* i.42 (= *UPZ* i.59 = *Sel.Pap.* i.97) (168 B.C.) (wife to husband; from a *polis*, probably Alexandria, to Memphis; a special complaint); *P.Paris* 43 (= *UPZ* i.66 = *Sel.Pap.* i.99) (153 B.C.) (announcement of marriage); *P.Paris* 47 (= *UPZ* i.70 = *Sel.Pap.* i.100) (about 152 B.C.) (a bitter complaint); *W.Chr.* 10 (= *Sel.Pap.* i.101) (130 B.C.) (adult son to parents: "I often write to you"; a long distance is involved); *P.Tebt.* i.56 (= *Sel.Pap.* i.102) (late second century) (an emergency message, between men with Egyptian names); *P.Grenf.* ii.36 (= *Sel.Pap.* i.103) (95 B.C.) (an Egyptian to a group of Egyptians).

57. Another long-distance letter (Lemnos to Athens): Ter. *Phorm.* 149–150. Plaut. *Pseud.* 20–73 concerns a love letter written by a slave girl to a boy next door, but this too is an emergency message. It is probably significant that letters do not play a larger part than they do in New Comedy; the *Pseudolus*, discussed in the next chapter, is somewhat exceptional.

58. *SIG³* 684 = R. K. Sherk (ed.), *Roman Documents from the Greek East* (Baltimore, 1969), no. 43, lines 18–22 (admittedly a hostile source). One implication of this is that the discontented poor had been involved in documentary procedures.

59. For the burning of *sungraphai* in Egypt in the 160s see *P.Amh.* ii.30, lines 33–36, with the comments of Rostovtzeff, *Hellenistic World* ii.722.

60. See, e.g., Polyb. v.43.5–6 (forged letters), 50.11–12 (another forged letter), 57.5 (a usurper's letters), 61.3 (a traitor's letter). Cf. Plu. *Mul.virt.* 15 = *Mor.* 252a (deceptive letters which did not get written; a Hellenistic story), 17 = *Mor.* 254d (a treacherous letter written by a Naxian woman, probably a Hellenistic tale).

seems to have been particularly rapid in the 250s, the ordinary Hellenistic city experienced a gradual and much milder change in the same direction. Some cities also experienced changes in their educational arrangements. How extensive these changes were is our next question.

Elementary Education

We have already had to consider the difficult question of the transmission of literacy outside the framework of schools. It seems to be the assumption of Hellenistic, as of both earlier and later literary sources, that school and not home is the place for learning letters. But this does not mean that the amount of literacy which was imparted outside the system of schools was negligible, for several reasons: "learning letters" could involve far more than learning to read and write, and it is possible that the barest elements of reading and writing were often taught separately and at home; and the newly diffused population of Hellenistic Greeks must sometimes have found it impossible to obtain a schoolmaster. In a village in Upper Egypt such as Pathyris-Aphroditopolis, where Greeks were few,[61] they must have had to pass Greek literacy on within the family. This, however, was a fairly extreme situation, and for most parts of the Greek world the school system's vigour, or lack of it, provides a vital indication of the state of literacy.

Greek elementary education in the mid-fourth century was in a superficially anomalous condition, with some of the leading minds of the age recommending that it should be universal, even for girls—a recommendation which clearly harmonized, at least as far as boys were concerned, with the views of many educated Greeks about the importance of the written word—while at the same time nothing was being done to put such a programme into effect. No city is known to have taken any official step to encourage, let alone maintain, any school. However, the anomaly is only apparent: the cities were not as the philosophers wished them to be, and the nature of their educational systems was determined not by such aspirations but by class and economic structures and by the real-life functions of reading and writing.

Changed attitudes towards basic education certainly made schooling more readily available in some Hellenistic cities than it had been

---

61. *P.Lugd.Bat.* xix.4, lines 18–21 (126 B.C.).

in the classical city, but it is not altogether easy to say how far the change went. Marrou presented without hesitation an extraordinary tableau of educational diffusion. "In truly Greek territory," he claimed, all children other than slaves normally went to school.[62] And he was deliberately speaking of children and not simply of boys, for he held that in Hellenistic schools the sexes were generally treated alike.[63] Furthermore, he believed not only that Greek schools grew up all over the Hellenistic world, which in a sense is plainly true, but that in Egypt they could be found "even in the smallest rural centres."[64]

The recommendations of Plato and Aristotle in favour of quasi-universal education must have won a certain amount of assent. Such a point of view may have been advanced in some of the now fairly numerous monographs which philosophers wrote about education,[65] though the fact is not attested. Some such text is likely to lie behind Diodorus Siculus' praise of universal education for boys.[66] It seems certain at least that some of these monographic writers wished to increase the amount of primary education, for Chrysippus suggested that it should begin at the age of three.[67] And the educational foundations of the third and second centuries which subsidized ordinary teachers presumably coincided with expressly formulated theories.

These foundations belong to four cities of "old" Greece, Teos (on the coast to the north of Ephesus), Miletus, Delphi, and Rhodes. In the late third century, Polythrous, a citizen of Teos, gave his city 34,000 drachmas, the income from which, 3,900 a year, was to be used to pay teachers.[68] Similarly, at Miletus in 200 or 199 a citizen named Eudemus presented to the city a sum which was to produce 480 drachmas a year for each of four teachers (*grammatodidaskaloi*) in addition to some money for athletic trainers (*paidotribai*).[69] Forty years later Attalus II of Pergamum came to the assistance of the city of Delphi by giving it 18,000 drachmas, which was to produce 1,260

---

62. Marrou, *Histoire* 221. His argument is that the Teos and Miletus donations, discussed in the text, presume this. They do not, even for Teos or Miletus.

63. *Histoire* 162, 329; ibid. 174 seems more cautious on this point.

64. *Histoire* 221.

65. On these works cf. Marrou, *Histoire* 158.

66. Diod.Sic. xii.12.4.

67. Quint. *Inst.* i.i.16 = *SVF* iii.733.

68. *SIG*³ 578.

69. *SIG*³ 577. Note the edition and commentary by E. Ziebarth, *Aus dem griechischen Schulwesen* (2 ed., Leipzig & Berlin, 1914), 2–29.

drachmas a year for the payment of teachers of children.[70] Lastly, Polybius tells us that Eumenes II, Attalus' brother, had during the previous year given the city of Rhodes 280,000 bushels of grain to create a fund for the payment of teachers.[71] Though we cannot tell what price the Rhodians were able to realize for this grain, it is practically certain that this was much the most valuable of the attested benefactions, with the consequence that Rhodes may for some time have been the city with the nearest thing to universal public education for boys ever seen in antiquity.[72]

There are likely to have been other such benefactions in this timespan,[73] at least in other cities which lay on or near the Asia Minor coast between Pergamum and Rhodes, or were of political interest to the Attalids. The cities did not live in cultural isolation from each other, and since Eumenes and Attalus between them ruled for nearly sixty years they had plenty of opportunity to make such gifts. While they were subsidizing education at Delphi and Rhodes, it is probable that the Attalids helped others in the same way, perhaps including the citizens of Pergamum itself. The Delphians may have learned from the case of Rhodes or from similar incidents that they could ask for a benefaction in this department and be understood.

Polybius in fact criticizes Rhodes for accepting Eumenes' gift, on the grounds that it was undignified, possibly implying (he does not make the point clearly) that any notably prosperous Greek city would want to take care of such matters for itself.[74] It may also be significant that these donations were all made to the cities as such,[75] which implies that elementary education was held to be a matter of civic concern.

An inscription from a small town in Caria which is probably to be identified as Eriza honours one Chares because of his "perseverance"

70. *SIG*³ 672.

71. Polyb. xxxi.31.1.

72. A possible hint of Rhodian education: the Hellenistic amphorae from Rhodes are the ones which are most frequently stamped with letters (Y. Garlan in P. Garnsey et al. [eds.], *Trade in the Ancient Economy* [London, 1983], 28).

73. Marrou, *Histoire* 177, seems, paradoxically, to underestimate this likelihood.

74. In the comparison he makes with what a private citizen would do (xxxi.31.2), he assumes that the prosperous man pays for education. Does it not almost follow that a prosperous state, such as Rhodes (31.3), would normally do so too? And Polybius does not imagine the Rhodians defending themselves by saying that otherwise they would have been unable to pay for education. But all this is very tenuous.

75. Cf. Marrou, *Histoire* 177, remarking that there were no Anglo-Saxon trustees.

in the matter of the *didaskaloi*. The presence of teachers in such a place is in itself interesting, but the hint of philanthropy is still more so.[76] Other Hellenistic inscriptions commemorate public expenditure and private benefaction for the support of advanced teachers in various fields and in favour of *paideutai*.[77] The latter term is to be taken to refer on all or almost all occasions to something more advanced and pretentious than an ordinary teacher of letters. As we shall see in more detail later, there is hardly anything paradoxical, in the Graeco-Roman world, in the fact that state and individuals provided funds for higher education while much remained to be done for elementary education.

On a pair of occasions governments are known to have given up revenue in order to encourage basic education. From the 250s the Ptolemaic government exempted teachers of letters and their descendants, together with athletic trainers and others, from the payment of salt tax.[78] And at Lampsacus at some early Hellenistic date teachers from other cities were apparently (the whole case is quite obscure) given immunity from some form of taxation.[79] In other words, there was in a few places a certain very limited official and public desire to favour teachers.

The Teos donation has two truly remarkable features. One is Polythrous' declared intention, clearly acceptable to the city, that *all* the free boys of the place should receive education.[80] The second feature is that the three teachers are also to teach girls,[81] though not specifically *all* the free girls of Teos. No other Hellenistic text indicates that any city aimed at universal education of its boys. The practical obstacles in the path of any such ideal were, of course, immense, and the generosity of such men as Polythrous of Teos was not by itself sufficient to overcome them. The three teachers of letters which his gift was to support cannot, even with very large classes, have taught all the children

---

76. For the text see G. Cousin & C. Diehl, *BCH* xiii (1889), 334–340 no. 4; the date is 115 or 114.

77. See Ziebarth, *Aus dem griechischen Schulwesen* 59–60. A case in which the pupils may have been young is that of Protogenes of Thespiae, who was honoured by the city for his expenditures εἰς τοὺς παιδευτὰς τῶν παίδων, *IG* vii.1861 (first century B.C.).

78. *P.Hal.* 1, lines 260–264.

79. The inscription: A. Wilhelm, *Neue Beiträge zur griechischen Inschriftenkunde* i (= *SBAW Wien* clxvi.1) (1910), 46–48.

80. *SIG*³ 578, lines 3–4: ἵνα δὲ πάντες οἱ ἐλεύθεροι παῖδες παιδεύωνται.

81. οἵτινες διδάξουσιν τοὺς παῖδας καὶ τὰς παρθένους (lines 9–10).

of a city and territory with many thousands of inhabitants. Four teachers could not by themselves have educated all the sons of the free inhabitants of Miletus. The inclusion of girls in the Teos donation was also, in the surviving record for this period, unique (in reality there were probably some other instances).

No philanthropic schemes in favour of teachers' salaries are known to have been started after 159, and it is to be presumed that the steadily encroaching power of Rome and the end of the Attalid monarchy in 134/133 dried up most of the available resources. It is also unlikely that any of the foundations in the Aegean region survived the financial troubles brought on by the Mithridatic War of 88 to 83.

Every city in old Greece except perhaps the very smallest, which in demographic terms were not cities at all, and also with the possible exception of Sparta, must normally have had some sort of school in operation. There was often public regulation even when there was no subsidy. The inscription which records the donation to Miletus shows that the city already had an education law *(paidonomikos nomos);* this apparently regulated "displays" on the part of the teachers and pupils, which means that the city was concerned, in how effective a way we cannot tell, with the results of such schooling as was already available.[82] The epigraphical record contains a sprinkling of other references to such laws, and more numerous ones to the office of *paidonomos,* "boy-regulator," itself.[83] This should not be taken as evidence that the cities in question were concerned to educate all the citizens' sons or to ensure that schools were efficient. On the other hand, a text from Astypalaea refers to the care which the city expended on the education of some boys from Ephesus who were set free at Astyalaea after being taken prisoner, and it clearly reveals the interest of both cities in *paideia.*[84] Literary evidence also makes it plain that at least in the more populous kind of city a school was a commonplace phenomenon.[85] By the first century an informed Sicilian writer can appear to make the assumption that all Greeks ensure that their sons are taught

82. *SIG*[3] 577, lines 53–54; cf. 578, lines 32–33.

83. A law about displays is mentioned in *I.v.Priene* 113. On Hellenistic *paidonomoi* see M. P. Nilsson, *Die hellenistische Schule* (Munich, 1955), 57–59.

84. *IG* xii.3.171 and Suppl. 1286.

85. For Herodas iii, see below. It may be thought that the New Comedy poets are too Athenocentric to be very informative about social conditions in other, more typical, cities; but their references to schools have some value: see Men. fr. 430a Koerte, Ter. *Eun.* 476, and the passages of Plautus which will be discussed in the next chapter.

letters.[86] His vision was restricted by social class, but he was no doubt correct in implying that throughout the Greek world all substantial citizens shared a common attitude.[87]

But what of the schools which are supposed to have existed "even in the smallest rural centres" in Hellenistic Egypt? The texts by means of which Marrou claimed to establish their existence are in fact uniformly irrelevant.[88] Most of these are "school papyri," written by teachers or pupils, but the only one cited which is of Hellenistic date[89] lacks a specific provenance and is not known to have had anything to do with a small village. A few other Hellenistic papyri which Marrou does not cite do show or suggest the existence of schools,[90] but none of those published so far comes from a small rural centre.[91] In fact his assertion obscures one of the most vital distinctions between city and country in antiquity: the city had education, and the country generally did not.

The Hellenistic *gumnasion,* particularly in Egypt, presents a delicate historical problem. What in fact was the purpose of the physical plant which Greeks put up under this name not only in every city but even in some semi-Greek villages?[92] It has always been an easy assump-

86. Diod.Sic. i.81.7: of the Egyptians he says that they give their sons a small amount of education in letters, "not all of them, but especially those engaged in *technai.*"

87. For a similar perspective see Easterling, in *Cambridge History of Classical Literature* i (1985), 23, who argues, reasonably enough up to a point, that there was "a uniform educational system" in the Hellenistic world, on the grounds that intellectuals sometimes hailed from insignificant places.

88. Listed in *Histoire* 555 n.5.

89. O. Guéraud & P. Jouguet, *Un livre d'écolier du IIIe siècle avant J.-C.* (Cairo, 1938) = *Publ.Soc.Fouad* ii. All that is known is that it came from the Fayum (p. XI).

90. Only one other text which is regarded by B. Boyaval, *Rev.arch.* 1977, 223, as a *cahier scolaire* has a pre-Roman date: *P.Freib.* i.1 (provenance unknown). G. Zalateo, *Aegyptus* xli (1961), 170–173, numbers 38 texts under the heading "primi elementi dello scrivere," and 2 of these are Ptolemaic: *O.Mich.* iii.1099 (an *abecedarium* from Karanis) and *UPZ* i.147. Of 225 documents listed by J. Debut (*ZPE* lxiii [1986], 251–278) under the heading "acquisitions des rudiments," about 32 are Ptolemaic.

91. An apparent but not real exception: a certain Hermias who appears in *P.Tebt.* i.112 (112 B.C.), introduction, and who probably resided in the village of Kerkeosiris is described there by the abbreviation παιδα, which the editors resolved as παιδα-γωγοῦ, meaning in effect "family boy-custodian"; Crawford, *Kerkeosiris* 123 n.1, gives "schoolmaster (?)." But παιδαγωγός does not mean "schoolmaster," and the resolution should in any case probably be παιδαρίου, a far commoner word in documentary papyri.

92. For their distribution in the Hellenistic world see J. Delorme, *Gymnasion. Etude sur les monuments consacrés à l'éducation en Grèce* (Paris, 1960), esp. figs.

tion for scholars that these were in the main academic institutions.[93] This is a mistake: the evidence for what went on in *gumnasia* concerns athletic, social and to some extent religious life.[94] Of course the Greeks who founded *gumnasia* must have been literate, and the existence of a *gumnasion* in a particular place may serve as a hint that a schoolmaster teaching Greek letters was active in the vicinity. But the presence of a *gumnasion* is not in itself proof that systematic education at any level was under way.

In any case it is probable that in the great majority of Greek cities, throughout the Hellenistic period, parents had to pay for their children's education.[95] This alone would be enough to invalidate Marrou's claim that "in truly Greek territory" all children normally went to school. Schooling was obviously not restricted to the children of the rich and privileged,[96] but it is not legitimate to suggest that Greek schools in Egypt had a wide social range because the fictional Metrotime, the schoolboy's mother in Herodas, complains about the schoolmaster's fees.[97] We have no way of knowing whether poor Greek parents who truly scrimped to pay school fees were numerous or not.

There was certainly no great improvement in the social standing of Hellenistic schoolmasters. They still suffered the contempt of the upper class.[98] Whether they were badly paid[99] is a relative question,

---

61–64; and, for Egypt, H. Maehler in Van't Dack et al., *Egypt and the Hellenistic World* 195.

93. A classic instance of this is Nilsson, *Die hellenistische Schule*. Even Delorme (451) lapses into saying that from the fourth century the *gumnasion* became a university.

94. This remains as true as when U. Wilcken noted the lack of evidence for intellectual instruction in the Egyptian *gumnasia* (*Grundzüge und Chrestomathie der Papyruskunde* i.1 [Leipzig & Berlin, 1912], 138).

95. This is assumed in, e.g., Theophr. *Char.* 30.14; Her. iii.9–10.

96. Maehler 203.

97. Her. iii.9–10.

98. For earlier attitudes see p. 98. Herodas iii does not leave the schoolmaster with much dignity. For the stories about Epicurus and his father, who were accused of schoolmastering, see Diog.Laert. x.2–4. No doubt Hellenistic writers preserved and embellished, if they did not invent, the story of Dionysius' descent from tyranny in Syracuse to schoolmastering in Corinth, for which see Cic. *Disp.Tusc.* iii.12.27; Justin xxi.5. See further *FCG* iv.698 Meineke (ἤτοι τέθνηκεν ἢ διδάσκει γράμματα); *Anth.Pal.* xi.437 = Aratus 2 Gow–Page. Marrou, *Histoire* 224, claims that the main reason for the disdain for schoolmasters was their lack of a professional qualification; but this is a thoroughly modern atittude.

99. Marrou, *Histoire* 223. This was certainly the opinion of the comfortably off: cf. Diog.Laert. x.4.

about which we have in any case only a minimal amount of evidence. But the low esteem enjoyed by Hellenistic schoolmasters does not make it impossible to think that there was a certain growth in public interest in basic education.

In the classical Greek tradition, girls did not generally attend schools. To Theophrastus, it is still sons who go.[100] For reasons which are unclear, this custom changed to some extent in at least a few Hellenistic cities.[101] The Teos donation includes girls among the beneficiaries.[102] At Pergamum itself, some girls received a degree of education, probably in part at school, and were able to compete in calligraphy.[103] Marrou, however, went far beyond probability and indeed possibility in claiming that the sexes were for the most part treated alike in Hellenistic schools. Even the more limited claim that in the fourth century schooling was usually available to girls goes beyond the evidence;[104] it relies on an improbable interpretation of a single scene from a painted tomb of roughly 300 B.C. from Cyrene—a scene which probably does not represent teaching at all, and certainly does not represent a school.[105]

There remain the terracottas from various parts of the Greek world which represent women or girls with writing-tablets[106]—important evidence that, as in fifth-century Athens, some people found the conjunction of women and writing attractive. These figurines could not have been devised in a culture which never permitted women or girls

100. *Char.* 30.14. For his attitude to women's education, see above, p. 107 n.186.

101. It is formally possible that in the cities we are about to consider girls were educated even in the classical period; but it is more likely that there really was a change, consonant with the mild degree of emancipation visible in other respects.

102. *SIG³* 578, lines 9–10.

103. L. Robert, *Etudes anatoliennes* (Paris, 1937), 58–59.

104. S. B. Pomeroy, *Women in Hellenistic Egypt* (New York, 1984), 48.

105. For the material see L. Bacchielli, *Quaderni di archeologia della Libia* viii (1976), 355–383 (the teaching interpretation: 365; the date: 378). To mention only four objections: the supposed pupil is at least as full-grown as the teacher, she is naked from the waist up, the scene takes place in the country, and none of the usual paraphernalia of learning are depicted.

106. See Marrou, *Histoire* 555 n.7; S. B. Pomeroy, *AJAH* ii (1977), 52 and n.9; both offer some bibliography. For a list of provenances see P. Bruneau, *BCH* xciv (1970), 472: he lists Tanagra, Olympia, Argos (the gender of this specimen is uncertain), Attica (gender uncertain), Myrina (a secondary city on the coast south of Pergamum), Cyprus, Tarsus, Alexandria and Cyrene. Except in the case of Myrina, these are isolated finds. The type in question must of course have been in circulation in many other places.

to take writing-tablets in their hands; but they do nothing at all to show that education for girls was the norm.[107]

It is obvious that in practically every city girls of a certain social class could obtain some education. There was now some sense of obligation on the part of Greek fathers, a certain proportion of them at least, to provide their daughters with *paideia*.[108] On the other hand, it is not established that in most cities girls were able to receive such education in an institutional framework; a high proportion of the instruction girls received may have been at home—which does not mean that it was necessarily ineffective.[109]

For those who did attend them, Greek and Roman schools had their own deficiencies. A regime which combined corporal punishment with a narrow selection of literary classics may not have been wholly ineffective. Even in the Hellenistic age, however, if we may judge from a third-century Greek collection of school-texts from Egypt, there were still apparently no readings for children between single words on the one hand and Homer on the other.[110] Papyri of Roman date suggest that learning to write was, by modern standards, a slow business, for some children were engaged in doing so who were ten and even thirteen years of age.[111] But one extremely useful educational innovation which seems to belong to the Hellenistic era should be mentioned: examinations.[112]

In the end, however, it is reasonably clear that there was more elementary education in the cities of Hellenistic Greece than there had been in the classical period, and that this improvement resulted from a widespread change of attitude. What was the cause of this change? Any answer is bound to be very speculative. We can point to the influence of philosophers, not forgetting those such as Chrysippus whose views can only be glimpsed, and also of Isocrates. But then we must try to explain why their views gained the acceptance of those who were making no specific attempt to live according to Platonic or Aris-

107. Cf. Marrou, *Histoire* 221.

108. Thus in *P.Enteux.* 26 (= *Sel.Pap.* ii.268), of 220 B.C., a petitioner to the king says that he has nurtured, educated, and brought up his daughter (and is therefore entitled to be supported by her); it is not clear what social class is in question.

109. P. Schmitter, *Die hellenistische Erziehung im Spiegel der* Νέα Κωμῳδία *und der Fabula Palliata* (Bonn, 1972), 119, observes that in such texts there is no mention of girls' schooling. For mothers teaching daughters see Ter. *Eun.* 116–117.

110. Guéraud & Jouguet, *Un livre d'écolier.*

111. See below, p. 240.

112. Marrou, *Histoire* 558 n.16.

totelian or Chrysippan precepts. Nor is the relative prosperity of the Hellenistic Greeks much of an explanation, though it certainly has some relevance.

An important factor was the increased contact with "barbarians," together with the self-conscious desire to maintain Greek identity which resulted from this. It is possible that Charondas of Catana's alleged regard for basic education was heightened by the fact that he lived only a few miles from non-Greek populations, more possible still that the Greeks of the southeastern Aegean may have been made more eager to maintain their Greek cultural identity by the nearness of the Carians and other local barbarians. Hence a strong desire to organize the transmission of *paideia* to the next generation. The proximity of the barbarians was not new in the time of Alexander, but it vastly increased, and the whole question of whether all the Greeks were maintaining their Greekness became a matter of concern. Throughout the Hellenistic world there was a powerful assumption on the part of the Greeks, well indicated by their strange abstention from learning foreign languages, that what was Greek was best; in fact the assumption may have applied with especial strength to language.[113] Naturally there were individual exceptions, in Egypt and elsewhere. Marrou somewhat idealized this attachment of the emigrant Greeks to their ancestral culture, and exaggerated its effectiveness in creating educational institutions;[114] but he correctly appreciated that there was a connection between the concept of barbarism and Hellenistic educational practice. It might be objected that most of the evidence for the relative interest of the Hellenistic Greeks in elementary education (the only kind which directly concerns us here) comes not from the semi-barbarian periphery but from solidly Greek cities, and up to a point this is true. Were the Greeks of "old" Greece more conscious of barbarians in the third and second centuries than they had been in the fifth? Hardly so, but they may in fact have been more aware that a

113. Essential on this subject is A. Momigliano, *Alien Wisdom* (Cambridge, 1975). There are pages about Greek attitudes towards barbarians in most standard works about the Hellenistic world, e.g., in Nilsson, *Geschichte der griechischen Religion* ii.20–28. But there could be more investigation of Greek-barbarian relations on the mundane non-intellectual plane. Amid a mass of evidence consider, e.g., *P.Col.Zen.* ii.66 (250s B.C.), where an employee of Zeno laments to him that Greeks "have treated me with scorn because I am a barbarian . . ." See further W. Peremans, *EFH* viii (1962), 138–140 (who claims, 131, that this trend resulted from an increased isolation of Greeks from the barbarians—just the opposite of what really happened); N. Lewis, *Greeks in Ptolemaic Egypt* (Oxford, 1986), 59–60.

114. *Histoire* 157.

Greek could cease to be a Greek. Many of the leading intellectuals came from cities with non-Greek neighbours or, as in the cases of the philosophers Zeno and Chrysippus and the poet Aratus, from cities which were themselves partly barbarian. Something of a question mark could hang over the Alexandrians and the Massiliots—had they maintained their Hellenism intact? [115]

A New Expansion of Literacy?

By contrast with the idealization which influences scholars' estimates of how much literacy there was in the classical age of Greece, there seems to be no accepted modern wisdom to the effect that literacy was truly widespread in the Hellenistic world. [116] Idealization of the classical Greeks still apparently falls off abruptly with the death of Alexander of Macedon. There is also no doubt some general awareness among scholars that from this period onwards papyrus documents demonstrate incontrovertibly that literacy was far indeed from being universal.

Some circumstances certainly favoured a further growth in literacy. The general increase in documentation, particularly in the legal sphere, meant more work for clerks and provided some extra incentive for parents of modest means to ensure that their sons learned to read and write. This will have been particularly true in Egypt. The lack of texts testifying that such an obvious process of reasoning took place should not disturb us. And we have considered other ideas, more and less elevated, which are likely to have encouraged Greek literacy. Among the educated it was inevitably the accepted wisdom that literacy was a good thing: thus the author of the *Rhetorica ad Alexandrum* remarks that those who are illiterate cannot communicate with others, [117] and Menander sententiously pronounced that "those who have learned letters see twice over." [118] However such texts also leave an impression

115. On Alexandria see Polyb. xxxiv.14.5; the controversy about Massilia in Liv. xxxvii.55.22 and xxxviii.17.11–12 must have a Greek origin.

116. Even Marrou, while glorifying Hellenistic education, says somewhat guardedly that in Egypt writing, "without being general" was "widespread even outside the ruling class" (221). He evidently holds that in old Greece it was more widespread still.

117. [Aristot.] *Rhet.* iii.12.1.1413b. This seems to be his meaning, unless *graphein* here means "to know the style of written Greek."

118. διπλῶς ὄρωσιν οἱ μαθόντες γράμματα: Men. *Sent.* 657 Meineke = 180 Jäkel. Cf. also Philemon fr. 11 Kock (*CAF* ii p. 481): γράμματα are the physician of the soul.

that there was still something to argue about, in other words that some of the well-educated knew that plenty of illiterates existed.

The evidence which Greek and Latin writers provide about the extent of literacy is as slight in this period as in any other. One relevant text, however, is Herodas' third mimiamb, "The Schoolmaster," probably written in the 280s or 270s. Its geographical setting is unspecified, but the author's associations are with the Dorian southeastern Aegean as well as with Alexandria. With appropriate caution the conditions Herodas describes can probably be taken as typical of a certain social level in any sizeable Greek city of the time. Unfortunately, we are given no clear idea of the social status of the wayward schoolboy's parents.[119] At all events both parents are envisaged as being able to read, while the son, who is no longer in early childhood, is having serious difficulty in learning to read and write. The boy's grandmother is scarcely able to read at all, but his mother in her anger implies that the only kind of male who has any right to be as illiterate as this boy would be a Phrygian (elementary education is thus almost seen as a requirement for Greekness).[120] The boy's difficulties at school are the central feature of the scene which the poet presents, and we are entitled to infer that simply learning to read and write was commonly regarded as quite a serious hurdle.

Two strong impressions are conveyed by this evidence, though both are somewhat weakened by our uncertainty about the social class from which Herodas was drawing his characters: one is that his small audience of educated urban Greeks found nothing startling in a woman's being literate, the other that at least with some comic exaggeration a boy who is no longer very young can be imagined as still learning to read and write. However the sketch also suggests in an imprecise way that there had been some growth in the public desire for elementary education.[121]

None of the evidence which we have encountered about the expanding functions of the written word in the Hellenistic period could lead us by itself to the conclusion that literacy spread beyond

119. Metrotime's family lives in a συνοικία (47); this does not sound at all grand, but "tenement" (Cunningham) may be unkind. The infirmity of the husband (31–32) complicates the tale.

120. See, respectively, lines 30–31, 17–26, 34–35 (the grandmother is γραμμάτων χήρη, "widowed of letters"), 36.

121. On this point cf. S. G. Cole in H. P. Foley (ed.), *Reflections of Women in Antiquity* (New York, 1981), 231.

the social limits which still restricted it in the late classical period (say, 400–323 B.C.). Developments in education, on the other hand, and above all the charitable foundations, make it very probable indeed that within the communities in question there was for a time a notable change. We have no reliable means of reducing this assertion to numbers. In view of the comparanda mentioned in Chapter 1, we ought to suppose that any community whose male citizens reached a level of 20% to 30% literacy achieved something truly remarkable. This may possibly have happened for a time during the second century in Teos, Rhodes and a few other cities.[122] It is probable that a higher proportion of girls now attended school, and that by this means and others a higher proportion of girls learned to read and write than in the classical era.[123] Since the foundations which assisted elementary education had very few counterparts under the Roman Empire (only one is known), it would be reasonable to conjecture that in quantitative terms the high point of Greek literacy fell in the third or more probably second century B.C.

But we are anticipating an important body of evidence, the first tranche of by far the largest block of direct evidence about ancient literacy. A very large number of Greek papyrus documents, almost all from Egypt, mention the literacy of one or more of those participating in the recorded transaction.[124] Documents are commonly subscribed with formulae of the type "I wrote on his/her behalf because he/she does not know letters" or (less often, and not in the Ptolemaic period) "because he/she is *agrammatos*." Sometimes the subscriber says that he is writing on behalf of a person who "writes slowly." Some of these documents are too slight or too fragmentary to provide us with useful

122. When Hannibal entered Tarentum in the winter of 213/212, he assembled those citizens who favoured his cause and instructed them to write Ταραντίνου on their house doors, as a preliminary to pillaging the houses of the Romans (Polyb. viii.31.4). Thus in this city the ordinary house-owner could either write or quickly find someone to write the necessary word.

123. Cole 229–236 gathers some evidence for the literacy of individual Hellenistic women, without attempting, however, to systematize the results in terms of geography or social class.

124. It is sometimes possible, and very occasionally it is likely, that the person referred to as illiterate was illiterate *in Greek* but literate in Egyptian. H. C. Youtie laid heavy emphasis on this point (*HSCPh* lxxv [1971], 162–163, etc.). However Greek documents did sometimes distinguish between illiteracy in Greek and total illiteracy, e.g., in *SB* i.5117 (55 A.D.) and *P.Tebt.* ii.383 (46 A.D.) . The extent of literacy in the Egyptian-speaking community will remain uncertain until more progress has been made with the editing of the very numerous unpublished demotic texts.

information, but others allow us to see the social condition of the illiterate or slow-writing person and of the literate stand-in. The illiteracy formula is not used in every kind of document but mainly in documents which directly concern money: receipts, leases, sale-contracts and contracts for loans. Of all these texts, which now appear to number more than 1,500, the vast majority are Roman or Byzantine (which does not mean that illiteracy was commoner in those times). It may be estimated that about forty belong to the Ptolemaic period.[125]

For the Roman and Byzantine periods papyrus texts offer a reasonably clear social profile of Greek literacy in Egypt. What happened under the Ptolemies is more speculative, the papyri, which are in any case fewer, being very unevenly distributed with respect to provenance.[126] But at least there are no real surprises: no one of high or highish social position is known to be illiterate—or at least, no such person admits to illiteracy. A man with a Greek name who was "an interpreter of the Troglodytes" in the second century, but was illiterate, is merely a curiosity.[127] Agron, son of Leontiscus, who appears as an illiterate in a document of 227 B.C., seems to have been an agent of the chief minister and was in charge of a very large quantity of wheat.[128] An illiterate military settler who is attested in a document of about 226 once caused some consternation in the scholar who originally published the text, but hardly deserved to do so.[129] More noteworthy is the illiterate ship's master *(naukleros),* by name Herodes, who is attested in a document of 221,[130] for it would be easy to make the mistaken assumption that such a middle-level entrepreneur would normally be able to write.

When the occupation or the social position of the person writing is visible in Hellenistic documents, there are no revelations of lower-class literacy. In fact no artisan and very few who could by any means

---

125. E. Majer-Leonhard, ΑΓΡΑΜΜΑΤΟΙ (Frankfurt-a.-M., 1913), is still a valuable collection. See also R. Calderini, *Aegyptus* xxx (1950), 17–41, who unfortunately did not publish her collection of material. For Ptolemaic documents written on behalf of people who were probably illiterate though *not* said to be such see Calderini 38–39.

126. On the latter point see Turner, *Greek Papyri* 45–46.

127. *UPZ* ii.227.

128. *Archiv für Papyrusforschung* ii (1903), 80 = *W.Chr.* 410.

129. *P.Petr.* ii.25 g (where J. P. Mahaffy wrote, in 1893, that it was "remarkable" that "a man who could not write should have charge of 15 horses and 10 mules"; such were the painful early revelations of papyrology) = iii.61 g.

130. *P.Lille* i.23. For the same man see also i.24, with the comments of Calderini, *Aegyptus* xxx (1950), 38.

be described as farmers are known to have written for themselves. The literate are in the main officials, clerks, bankers, tax-collectors. A military settler can be literate.[131] But to imply that members of the "lower middle class," even male members of it, were commonly literate[132] is seriously misleading as far as Ptolemaic Egypt is concerned. The only literates who might be assigned to that social rank are holders of specialized jobs in which this skill was essential. Alexandria, where the papyrus evidence can help us very little, may perhaps have been somewhat different, and it is tempting to think of it as a place with many schools and plenty of incentives to learn to read and write. However, specific testimony is lacking.

Insofar as there is any direct evidence about the relative literacy of men and women, it suggests the expectable conclusion that literacy was more restricted among women than among men. The archive of Dryton from the village of Pathyris, in Upper Egypt, shows not only that such a place would have had very few men in it who were literate in Greek (the converse would be surprising indeed),[133] but also that a female member of the family of an unquestionably literate Greek cavalryman who lived there had considerable difficulty in writing.[134] In another Ptolemaic text we encounter a son subscribing a contract on behalf of his illiterate mother.[135] There are presumably some fully literate women in Hellenistic papyri, and we might expect to find them well represented among the writers of private letters. However the tacit use of third parties and scribes for the writing of letters makes it difficult, perhaps impossible, to isolate clear cases.[136] When a certain Isias wrote from the city (Alexandria?) to her husband Hephaestion in 168 B.C., there is no hint that she was relying on an intermediary,[137] but even here the possibility cannot be excluded.

What is perhaps most noteworthy about the extent of Greek lit-

131. As in *P.Hibeh* i.94 (258/257 B.C.).

132. Youtie, *HSCPh* lxxv (1971), 173. In fact his attention was probably focussed on the Roman period.

133. *P.Lugd.Bat.* xix.4. Cf. H. C. Youtie, *ZPE* xvii (1975), 204.

134. See *P.Grenf.* i.15. Pomeroy, *Women in Hellenistic Egypt* 118, resists the natural inference from the quality of Senmonthis' handwriting in this document.

135. *P.Rein.* i.16 (109 B.C.).

136. Cf. Cole in Foley, *Reflections* 235, commenting on *P.Oxy.* vii.1067, a letter from a woman with a postscript by her father, all written in one hand, a hand which may belong to either of them or to a third party. The illiteracy formula is never used in private letters (J. L. White in White [ed.], *Studies in Ancient Letter Writing* [= *Semeia* xxii] [Chico, Calif., 1982], 95).

137. *P. Lond.* i.42 (see above, p. 128 n.56). *P.Lond* i.43 also appears to have been

eracy in the Hellenistic papyri is that in the third century it already reached a certain number of Egyptians.[138] But the proportion of the indigenous population which learned to read or write in Greek was certainly minuscule.

The documentary papyri not only tell us something about who was and was not literate in Greek Egypt; they also provide some indications about people's attitudes towards illiteracy. Though most of the evidence belongs to the Roman or Byzantine periods, the problem is so important that we must give it some attention here too. There certainly existed, as we have already seen, diverse mechanisms for helping an illiterate or semi-literate person to deal with the written word. With regard to the Greeks in Egypt, however, Youtie went so far as to claim that they did not mind much whether they were literate or not, and were never embarrassed by illiteracy.[139] In favour of this hypothesis is the fact that when a man was called upon to act as a *kurios* (guardian) for a literate woman, illiteracy on his part was not regarded as disqualifying him; and it was possible to make substantial amounts of money without being able to read or write.

But Youtie overreacted to the discovery that illiteracy was much less of a handicap to the Greeks of Egypt than it is to illiterates living in a modern society. An illiterate man did not always "associate on equal terms with his literate neighbours";[140] much of the time he did, and Egyptian society possessed mechanisms, such as the services of scribes,[141] at least some of whom were on hire to the public, which helped him to do so. Egypt, however, was just the place where the illiterate were most vulnerable, because the Ptolemaic bureaucracy imposed documentation on those who were unable to understand it

---

written by a woman; but see R. Rémondon, *Cd'E* xxxix (1964), 130, for the suggestion that it may have been the work of a scribe.

138. See Majer-Leonhard, ΑΓΡΑΜΜΑΤΟΙ 4, 36, etc. For letters in Greek exchanged between Egyptian-named people see Maehler in Van't Dack et al., *Egypt and the Hellenistic World* 192 n.1. For families which used both languages see Peremans in Van't Dack 276–277. Examples of ways in which Egyptians came to use some Greek documents while holding on to their own writing systems can be found in P. W. Pestman, *L'archivio di Amenothes, figlio di Horos (P.Tor.Amenothes)* (Milan, 1981).

139. In his view literacy was almost a matter of "casual indifference" in Graeco-Roman Egypt: Youtie, *HSCPh* lxxv (1971), 166. Lack of embarrassment: 170–171.

140. Youtie, *ZPE* xvii (1975), 201.

141. For the availability of professional scribes cf. Youtie, *HSCPh* 165. See, e.g., on *monographoi* in the Hellenistic period, *P.Paris* i.49 = *UPZ* i.62 = *Sel.Pap.* i.98.

for themselves. In private affairs, too, both financial and nonfinancial, the vulnerability of the person who is illiterate or semi-literate is fairly obvious. Youtie was right to say that illiteracy was not the stigma which it is in the modern world, but that does not alter the fact that at crucial moments an illiterate Greek might find himself dangerously dependent on the good will or honesty of others. The occasions when we can see this danger becoming reality are extremely rare,[142] but that is a natural consequence of the fact that people seldom document their crimes. Many people who might have found reading and writing, or a greater proficiency in reading and writing, somewhat advantageous allowed themselves to remain illiterate or semi-literate; but that will cause no surprise to anyone who has encountered twentieth-century illiterates.

The same scholar also maintained that for the Greeks of Egypt writing was an accomplishment which had "no implications of social superiority."[143] Now this is perhaps true in the sense that bare literacy did not convey social superiority, but in the upper class the lack of *paideia* which illiteracy indicated was undoubtedly something to be deplored, at least in a man and perhaps in a woman (the attitudes of the poorer Greeks can hardly be discovered). No Hellenistic text can be quoted which shows in a completely clear-cut way the rather obvious fact that most Greeks assumed that a man of property would be literate and a poor farmer illiterate. Relevant texts are not, however, entirely lacking; one instance is the passage in Herodas in which Metrotime imagines illiteracy as a characteristic of the Phrygians. The frequent appearance in Greek funerary reliefs, from the Hellenistic period onwards, of book-rolls and writing-tablets as attributes of the deceased confirm that many Greeks of the propertied class attributed real importance to a certain degree of *paideia*.[144]

An illiterate or semi-literate person can of course make use of documents or take part in a written transaction if there is help available and if he or she knows enough about documents to do so. This occurred in early classical Greece, but not surprisingly the phenomenon remains poorly attested until the papyrus evidence comes into play. It is likely to have been common during the third and second

142. But see above, p. 35 n.35.

143. Youtie, *ZPE* xvii (1975), 220–221.

144. Such motifs are very rare in the previous period. Cf. E. Pfuhl & H. Möbius, *Die ostgriechischen Grabreliefs* i–ii (Mainz, 1977–1979). Most but not all of those who receive these attributes are male.

centuries. The evidence is still thin by the standards of the Roman period, but we may cite receipts required by officials and a marriage contract in which the bridegroom at least was illiterate.[145] The number of written transactions in which the illiterate participated was certainly very great.

The pitfalls of extending conclusions drawn from the Egyptian papyri to other parts of the Hellenistic world are, with regard to the extent of literacy, plain enough. Long-standing indigenous traditions favouring a measure of bureaucratization, the peculiar social structure (which eased the lot of the settlers), and perhaps also the sheer availability of extremely convenient writing material, papyrus, are all factors which may have favoured literacy. On the other hand, and more important in my view, there is not likely to have been any significant degree of philanthropy in favour of elementary education in the Ptolemaic empire, particularly not in Egypt itself. Other possible sources of difference, such as the greater attachment to written Greek culture which may have resulted from being stranded among the barbarians, are still more hypothetical.

It is to be concluded that in the parts of the Greek world furthest from educational enlightenment, levels of literacy remained similar to those of the classical period, with the full possession of the skills of reading and writing being the preserve of a very small minority. In a number of places, however, various factors are likely to have led the proportion upwards, perhaps even far enough to classify their literacy as craftsman's literacy in the sense that was assigned to that expression in Chapter 1. Civic consciousness and local tradition may have helped in some cities. But the most important factor by far is likely to have been financial support for schoolmasters.

The interest of Hellenistic man in subsidizing elementary education was never overpowering, and it apparently faded. It never became a democratic cause, and in any case when the Romans arrived democracy steadily lost ground. With the financial miseries brought on by the spread of Roman power, especially from 148 onwards and even more after 88 B.C., far fewer individuals and cities were in a position to provide large capital sums for educational foundations. The movement towards quasi-universal education ended its relatively brief life without having achieved more than a few local successes.

145. Receipts: *P.Petr.* ii.25 g = iii.61 g; *P.Lille* i.23, *UPZ* ii.214 and 227, *P.Rein.* i.16. The marriage covenant: *P.Tebt.* i.104 (= *Sel.Pap.* i.2).

Figure 1. Ready-made Athenian ostraca. Three sets of ostraca, each inscribed by a single hand, intended to help possibly illiterate or semi-literate citizens vote for the expulsion of Themistocles. Athens, 480s or 470s. Photo courtesy of American School of Classical Studies in Athens, Agora Excavation.

Figure 2. Greek curse-tablet. "Earth, Hermes, Gods of the Underworld, accept Venusta the slave of Rufus." Writing such a text, a common practice, was evidently felt to add strength to the curse. This is a very simple example. Morgantina, Sicily, Hellenistic. Photo courtesy of Malcolm Bell.

Figure 3. Athenian school-room scenes. *Top:* The book-roll which the teacher holds is presumably meant to be a master-copy, not the boy's exercise, and the lesson may be a recitation. Nonetheless the boy has presumably learned to read. See A. D. Booth, *Échos du monde classique* xxix (1985), 276. The pupils are clearly from wealthy families. The text on the roll is an otherwise unknown hexameter. *Bottom* (the other side of the same vase): correcting a writing exercise. Vase painted by Douris, Athens, c. 490–480. Photo courtesy of Antikenmuseum Berlin, Staatliche Museen Preussischer Kulturbesitz.

Figure 4. Roman writing materials. From left to right: a hexagonal inkpot with pen, a papyrus roll, a codex of wax-tablets with pen, a tablet with handle (*tabula ansata*) bearing an inscription. House of Iulia Felix, Pompeii, before 79 A.D.

Figure 5. Writing as a sign of status. As in other examples of such formal portraits, the wife holds a pen to her lips, and writing tablets, while the husband holds a roll of papyrus. The exact social level is hard to define, but the couple belongs to the well-to-do middle class, not the upper elite. Pompeii (VII.ii.6), probably from the reign of Tiberius. Photo courtesy of Alinari/Art Resource, New York.

Figure 6. Official records being burned as an act of imperial beneficence. A relief from the so-called Anaglypha Traiani, erected in the forum to commemorate the destruction, by the emperor's order, of records of debts to the state. The codices embody the government's exactions. Rome, reign of Trajan. Photo courtesy of Fototeca Unione, American Academy in Rome.

Figure 7. Reading a notice in the forum of Pompeii. One of a series of
genre scenes situated in the forum; it was a typical activity in the forum
of an Italian city. The character of the notice cannot be determined. House
of Iulia Felix, Pompeii, before 79 A.D. Photo courtesy of Deutsches Archaeologisches Institut, Rome.

Figure 8. Christ and the authority of a book-roll. Christ, enthroned in heaven between two disciples, holding up a book-roll. Sarcophagus from Rome, c. 350–360 A.D. Vatican. Photo courtesy of Deutsches Archaeologisches Institut, Rome.

PART THREE

Literacy and Illiteracy
in the Roman World

6   Archaic Italy and
       the Middle Republic

800–200 B.C.

Writing probably spread quite quickly from the Greeks in Italy to
some of the native peoples. How and exactly why this happened we
do not know, but since Greeks traded extensively with Etruscans from
the eighth century onwards, some of the latter must soon have learned
about various of the functions which writing could fulfil. The first
indigenous inscriptions in Italy are Etruscan and date from the early
seventh century.[1] Something over a hundred Etruscan inscriptions are
dated to the seventh century as a whole.[2] Before long there were
objects at Praeneste and Rome with short Etruscan texts written
on them.[3] That literacy in Etruria was not merely the possession of
passing Greeks, and not merely a fringe phenomenon, is suggested by
Etruscan variants on the adopted Greek alphabet; these begin to
appear relatively early, by the middle of the seventh century.[4]

Most of the surviving Etruscan texts from this earliest phase are
inscribed on objects buried with their owners as marks of prestige or
for use in the afterlife. Since some of the early texts are *abecedaria*
inscribed on objects of considerable value, it can plausibly be argued

---

1. M. Cristofani, in *Popoli e civiltà dell'Italia antica* vi (Rome, 1978), 403–410,
and in *S & C* ii (1978), 6. The earliest texts are from Tarquinia (about 700 B.C.:
Cristofani, *ASNSP* ser.3 i [1971], 295–299), Caere (several of about 700–675:
G. Colonna, *MEFRA* lxxxii [1970], 637–672), Vulci (several of about 675–650:
Cristofani, *Arch.Class.* xxv–xxvi [1973–74], 155–156).

2. G. Colonna in *Atti del colloquio sul tema L'Etrusco arcaico* (Florence, 1976), 8.

3. A silver cup from the Tomba Bernardini at Praeneste, for which see *Civiltà del
Lazio primitivo* (Rome, 1976), 374, no. 127, seems to date from the early seventh
century. The earliest Etruscan texts at Rome are of the late seventh century: Cristofani
in *Popoli e civiltà* vi.408. The seventh-century sites in central Italy which have produced inscriptions are plotted in Cristofani, *S & C*, figs. 3 and 4.

4. For the date cf. Cristofani in *Popoli e civiltà* vi.408. On the diffusion of the
various alphabets, idem, *S & C* 16–19.

that even a man of wealth might have only a rudimentary acquaintance with writing.[5]

The classical period of Etruscan culture, in the sixth and fifth centuries, was certainly one of expanding literacy, as the inscriptions testify.[6] But the number and the scale of these inscriptions never, even in the richest cities, approach what is found in Athens, and it is probable that Etruscan literacy remained at the level reached by many Greek cities in the decades before and after 600 B.C.: writing was firmly entrenched but played a very limited role in the economic, political and religious spheres; and literacy was still the province of a very small minority of citizens. The few Etruscan monuments which are relevant seem to point in this direction, notably a funerary relief of about 475–450 from Chiusi which shows a scribe in a position of prominence next to a pair of rulers.[7] Such rulers clearly now have writing as part of their systems of power, but the scribe is privileged and his activity is considered remarkable.[8] Writing retained some capacity for instilling respect. Family names are inscribed on the outside of the chamber tombs in the fifth-century Crocefisso del Tufo cemetery at Orvieto, and it has been suggested that the city of Volsinii actually required this.[9] Much more probably the leading families of the city employed this simple use of writing in order to emphasize their social standing.

The entire early history of literacy in Italy is, however, extremely murky until at least the third century, and not only because of the virtual absence of literary texts earlier than Plautus. Even where there is an extensive historical tradition surviving, at Rome, its value for our topic is very limited, and we shall be faced with fragmentary and tangential evidence, and general probabilities.

The inhabitants of Rome and of some other places in Latium had a

---

5. See J. A. Bundgård, *Analecta Romana Instituti Danici* iii (1965), 11–72, discussing in particular the ivory writing-tablet from Marsiliana d'Albegna (often illustrated, e.g., in M. Cristofani [ed.], *Civiltà degli etruschi* [Milan, 1985], 98; M. Michelucci, ibid. 100, comments on the evident prestige which attached to the writing kit buried in this "princely" tomb).

6. On this material see in general Colonna in *Atti del colloquio* 7–24.

7. See G. Colonna in *L'Italie préromaine et la Rome républicaine. Mélanges offerts à Jacques Heurgon* (Rome, 1976), 187–195; cf. Cristofani, *Civiltà* 252–253.

8. Colonna goes somewhat beyond the evidence in supposing (*L'Italie préromaine* 191) that this scene proves the existence of public archives in this period.

9. Colonna in *Atti del colloquio* 21–22. All of the thirty-six tombs in the "new" excavation which had façades intact show such inscriptions.

secure indigenous literacy by the late seventh century and perhaps earlier, for otherwise they could not in turn have developed their own distinctive local variant of the Etruscan alphabet. This is first attested by graffiti, mainly owners' marks on vases;[10] inevitably the social origins of such texts are unclear.[11] However no serious consideration supports the notion that reading ability was widespread by the end of the sixth century,[12] if such an expression means literacy among more than, say, 5% of the male citizens. There may even have been some decrease in the use of writing as Etruscan power and influence declined about 500, but in any case an aristocratically governed city on the outer fringes of the Greek world, such as Rome was in the fifth and fourth centuries, is unlikely to have given wide functions or diffusion to the written word.

The earliest surviving Latin inscriptions other than graffiti are consistent with this view. These are not at all numerous in the sixth, fifth, or even the fourth century.[13] The earliest which have more or less intelligible functions are religious dedications (inscriptions from Tibur and Satricum, perhaps the Duenos Vase) and a set of religious rules (the stele from the forum).[14] All of these are probably sixth-century texts, unless the Satricum inscription belongs to the first half of the fifth.

With the Twelve Tables, however, we come to a text which, from

10. These texts were inventoried by Colonna in C. M. Stibbe et al., *Lapis Satricanus* (Archeologische Studiën van het Nederlands Instituut te Rome, Scripta Minora v) (The Hague, 1980), 53–69. Many of them consist of only a few letters. Two (nos. 29, 34) are dated to the seventh century, some twenty to the sixth, some fifteen more to the fifth.

11. Colonna 69 describes the writers as "gente modesta," but not even this is known.

12. This view was once espoused by E. Fraenkel, *Rome and Greek Culture* (Oxford, 1935), 7 = *Kleine Beiträge zur klassischen Philologie* ii (Rome, 1964), 584, arguing that the archaic cippus in the forum (*ILLRP* 3) was meant to be read by passersby. By contrast F. Leo saw writing as still being, in the age of the Twelve Tables, a science of the few (*Geschichte der römischen Literatur* i [Berlin, 1913], 24; Leo was in general very conscious of the oral character of archaic Roman culture).

13. If it is genuine, the "Manios" fibula (*ILLRP* 1) dates from the seventh century and is the oldest Latin inscription. But its authenticity has often been denied in recent times, most strenuously by M. Guarducci; see esp. *Mem.Acc.Linc.* ser.8 xxiv (1980), 413–574. The inscription of Servius Tullius' reign referred to by Dion.Hal. iv.26.4–5 is very dubious; the one mentioned in x.32.4 (456 B.C.), the Lex Icilia, may have existed. On treaties ascribed to this period see below.

14. These are, respectively, *ILLRP* 5; the *lapis Satricanus* (see Stibbe); *ILLRP* 2; and *ILLRP* 3. *ILLRP* 1271a is the dedication to Castor and Pollux from Lavinium, datable to the late sixth or early fifth century (sixth: M. Torelli, *Lavinio e Roma* [Rome, 1984], 12).

the standpoint of a study of literacy, is more problematical than any of these. Much later on they were regarded by the Romans as a code of laws composed in or about 451–450, and this view has normally been accepted by moderns without demur. Yet there is a great deal of implausibility about supposing that the transmitted "fragments" date from the fifth century; they were certainly modernized later with regard to language if not content. The ancient accounts of the decemvirs' lawgiving are loaded with apocryphal matter,[15] and we may suspect that the date of the Tables was, for standard patriotic reasons, set too early. Further complexity is introduced by the story of Cn. Flavius, the famous aedile of 304, who is said—credibly but obscurely— to have "published the civil law," which had previously been kept secret by the priests.[16] All this might suggest that the origins and original date of the Twelve Tables are in reality irrecoverable.

These questions have been debated at length, and another investigation would be out of place. On the whole it seems reasonable to suppose that there was indeed a great giving of laws at some date in the age before 390. In fact a number of other Latin and Etruscan cities are very likely to have done something similar in the same general period, some of them under more or less direct Greek influence; it would also be reasonable to suppose that Charondas, Zaleucus, and other Greek lawgivers enjoyed some fame in Etruria.[17] However what was written down at Rome is likely to have been even more rudimentary than the developed text of the Twelve Tables which we partly know from evidence concerning the late Republic. We cannot ascertain how much alteration took place before 304 (the concept of pedantic textual fidelity may not have existed at this date, even for laws), though afterwards changes presumably did not go beyond modernization of language. When M. Cicero and his brother were made

15. Including, obviously, the instructions which the decemvirs gave to the *populus:* "ire et legere leges propositas" (Liv. iii.34.2).

16. Liv. ix.46.5: "civile ius, repositum in penetralibus pontificum, evolgavit fastosque circa forum in albo proposuit, ut quando lege agi posset sciretur." Pomponius in *Dig.* i.2.2.7: "subreptum librum [containing the *actiones*] populo tradidit." Cf. Cic. *Mur.* 25, *Att.* vi.1.8, *De or.* i.186; Val.Max. ii.5.2; Plin. *NH* xxxiii.17. The event is very problematical; cf., most recently, F. d'Ippolito, *ZSS* cii (1985), 91–128.

17. The Roman story that Rome sent an embassy to Athens to copy the laws of Solon is a fiction (with all due respect to G. Crifò in *ANRW* i.2 [1972], 124–126 = *Libertà e uguaglianza in Roma antica* [Rome, 1984], 99–101); cf. R. M. Ogilvie on Liv. iii.31.8; P. Siewert, *Chiron* viii (1978), 331–344. On the question of Greek influence on the Twelve Tables cf. F. Wieacker, *EFH* xiii (1966), 330–353.

to learn the Twelve Tables by heart in boyhood,[18] this was useful schooling but also a survival of oral culture; in any case the text which they learned is unlikely to have been a purely fifth-century text.

We must beware of thinking of the Twelve Tables as an elaborate legal code, a temptation to which legal scholars have often surrendered. We should think rather of a very terse set of basic rules about the civil law, which probably did not explain the important details of legal procedure,[19] and which by later Roman standards still left a great deal of discretion to judges.

As to the significance of writing down the laws of the Twelve Tables, the action both reflected and increased the power of those who could easily read them. A similar conclusion has been reached by a scholar who has carefully reconsidered the general political and social context of this event.[20] Prosperous people outside the political class may have enjoyed some benefit, though to a limited degree if the text was not posted.[21] An ordinary citizen who was interested in their contents would usually have to arrange to get them read to him.

Also very obscure from our point of view is the case of the pontifical annals. Most scholars hold that the chief priest of Rome maintained a written record of public events from the earliest years of the Republic.[22] On the other hand, there is no question that, from the second century on, Roman authors elaborated accounts of early republican history, and many of them claimed more of a documentary basis for their work than really existed.[23] Whenever the chief priest began to maintain a record (let it be granted for time being that this was well before 390), the motive was plainly not antiquarian or historical. In addition to his religious reasons for maintaining such rec-

18. *De leg.* ii.59 ("discebamus enim pueri XII ut carmen necessarium, quas iam nemo discit"). *De or.* i.195 says that they were contained in a *libellus*.

19. Cf. A. Watson, *Rome of the XII Tables: Persons and Property* (Princeton, 1975), 185–186.

20. W. Eder, in K. Raaflaub (ed.), *Social Struggles in Archaic Rome* (Berkeley, 1986), 262–300, arguing that the codification was intended "to ensure aristocratic predominance" (263).

21. The later tradition held that the text was posted (Diod.Sic. xii.26.1; Liv. iii.57.10; Pomponius in *Dig.* i.2.2.4); but since this tradition could not agree whether the material used was bronze or wood—the latter is more plausible—the claim is a little suspect even before we attempt to square the story with our information about Cn. Flavius.

22. E.g., B. W. Frier, *Libri Annales Pontificum Maximorum: The Origins of the Annalistic Tradition* (Rome, 1979), 127.

23. Cf. Frier 151.

ords, he no doubt desired to bolster his authority by reference to something impressive and, to most of his countrymen, unintelligible. Down to 304, as we have already noted, the *pontifices* also enjoyed authority through their confidential possession of the procedures for the use of the civil law.

The respect and even awe which religious uses of writing could inspire in antiquity are already familiar to us. In the religion of the Roman state written texts had played a considerable role from a date which is too early to specify. The most important of these texts were the books containing the Sibylline oracles (which at Rome were not so much predictions of the future as instructions about appeasing the gods) and the books in which the *pontifices* and the augurs transmitted their technical knowledge. Books, some said to be "Sibylline," some *fatales* (prophetic), some just *libri,* are a common feature of the state religion throughout the Republic, but tracing their earliest history is an impossibility: no trustworthy sources exist. However, Livy first mentions the Sibylline books by name in 399; and the officials charged with consulting books of this type were apparently converted from a commission of two to a commission of ten *(decemviri sacris faciundis)* in 367.[24] By this period their authority must have been well established. As to the books of the priests and augurs, their earliest development is if anything even more obscure.[25] But the practice of ensuring the verbal precision of prayers and other religious formulae by having them dictated from a written text[26] could well have been very old indeed. All these books were, in varying degrees, inaccessible to the public.[27]

Many of the archaic functions of writing in Rome and Italy resembled its functions in Greece. However this complex of religious uses is something of a distinguishing mark of archaic Roman and Italic culture, just as the preservation of poetic texts is a distinguishing mark of archaic Greece.

In fourth- and third-century Rome the functions of writing must gradually have expanded. The establishment of colonies, some of them far off, required an organizational effort which presumably depended in part on writing; some thirty-three new Roman and Latin colonies were founded between 338 and 218. The case is roughly par-

24. Liv. v.13.5; vi.37.12, 42.2, etc.
25. As is shown, with regard to the latter, by the meticulous account of them by J. Linderski in *ANRW* ii.16.3 (1986), 2241–56.
26. See Varro *LL* vi.61; Plin. *NH* xxviii.11; etc.
27. Cf. J. Linderski, *HSCPh* lxxxix (1985), 207–234, esp. 212.

allel to the archaic colonization of the Greeks, but different in that Rome maintained closer official control over its colonies, which were generally more accessible. Meanwhile the increasing complexity of military affairs, especially after Rome began acquiring large numbers of "allies" all over the peninsula in the late fourth and early third centuries, must also have demanded an increase in the use of the written word. And by the late fourth century the treaties Rome made were in all likelihood normally committed to writing.[28]

As for the strictly internal affairs of the state, they too probably came to depend to a somewhat greater degree on the written word: the list-making of the censors, which involved reading and writing performed by officials and their agents, though not by the citizens themselves, is an obvious instance. Several constitutional practices involving the written word which are clearly attested for the years after 200 B.C., such as the posting of proposed laws, may well have begun long before. In Roman history, as in Greek, we are constantly faced by the difficulty of dating the introduction of new ways of using the written word. Cn. Flavius' publication of the civil law in 304 is at least attested as a novelty.[29] It was very probably symptomatic of the growing importance of written texts, and reflected the fact that men were now mentally more capable of making use of such texts to assert their rights.[30] Flavius' rise from official clerk *(scriba)* to aedile seemed remarkable in later times, in spite of the high status which *scribae* still enjoyed in the late Republic, and it probably resulted in some way from his ability to take advantage of the increasingly central role of the written word.[31]

The earliest Roman coin legends may help to indicate the limited

28. For the famous archaic treaty with Carthage, allegedly made in 509 and probably in fact of very early republican date, see Polyb. iii.22–23 (but some scholars have thought that its true date was 348). The "Foedus Cassianum" between Rome and the Latins, supposedly made in 493, was inscribed on bronze by the early first century (see esp. Cic. *Balb.* 53), but the date of the original text is highly uncertain. Even the second treaty with Carthage (made in 348, in my view) is likely to have been drafted on the Carthaginian side (F. W. Walbank on Polyb. iii.24.3–13). It is somewhat surprising that not a single phrase survives from any treaty made by Rome in Italy, but this must be an accident.

29. It is all too easy to describe this action in anachronistic terms. Even G. de Sanctis (*Storia dei Romani* ii [Turin, 1907], 64) said that Flavius published the rules of procedure in one volume accessible to all the citizens, even those resident far away.

30. This is not to overlook the fact that a good deal else was involved, including loss of power by the *pontifices*.

31. According to Plin. *NH* xxxiii.17, this was a consequence of his making public the days when legal proceedings were permitted.

interest of late fourth-century Romans in the written word. The name of the Romans appears on the earliest issue in Greek, the coins being the work of Neapolitans, and this fact may suggest that Rome lacked not only the means to make coins but also any strong interest in what was written on them. From about 300, however, Latin legends appear.[32] They amount to nothing more than the words "Romano" and "Roma," which is hardly surprising; down to the 210s some issues are entirely without legends.[33] What is perhaps most striking is the appearance of more complicated legends from that date onwards. However the introduction of the earliest Latin coin legends, even though they were doubtless for the convenience of the authorities rather than of the ordinary citizen, already implies that more than a handful of citizens were now able to read.

This growth in literacy is also strongly suggested by the fact that some Latin-speaking people of no apparent distinction were already commissioning simple epitaphs before 300.[34] There is, on the other hand, no reason to think that this custom spread to the mass of the population.

Another significant new use of writing is the inscribing of makers' names on domestic objects. The best-known examples from this period are the black-glaze cups made at Cales, in Campania, and found in that region and elsewhere.[35] These texts say such things as "Retus Gabinio, slave of Gaius, made you at Cales."[36] They must have been made after 334, the foundation date of the Latin colony of Cales, at the very earliest; and they are normally dated somewhat later.[37] Some of the writers were slaves, some free. Behind such texts there seems to have been a continuous artisans' tradition, probably going back to fourth-century Magna Graecia; also part of this tradition are the

32. For the date see A. Burnett, *Schweizerische Numismatische Rundschau* lvi (1977), 116.

33. The last such issues appear to be M. H. Crawford, *Roman Republican Coinage* (Cambridge, 1974), nos. 41, 43/1 and 43/2a, dated to the period 215–212. It is also suggestive that as late as the First Punic War plainly visible control-marks consisting of *Greek* letters, a system imitated from Ptolemaic coinage, appear on a major coin type (ibid. no. 22).

34. For the chronology see A. Degrassi's notes in *ILLRP* ii pp. 211 (concerning Caere), 225 (Tusculum); and F. Coarelli in *Roma Medio Repubblicana* (Rome, 1973), 261 (Praeneste).

35. On the epigraphical aspect of this material see Degrassi, *ILLRP* ii pp. 345–346.

36. *CIL* i².412a = *ILLRP* 1215.

37. Cf. A. Rocco in *EAA* (1959) s.v. "Caleni," 271–272, who knew of about seventy such inscriptions.

artisans' inscriptions, in Greek and Oscan, on strigils from Praeneste.[38] The total number of such texts is small, and they are not to be used as evidence of mass literacy. However they do serve to indicate that at least a limited use of writing had now spread, at the places in question, outside narrow circles of specialized scribes.

We have seen how the functions of the written word were enlarged in Latin Italy of the mid-republican period. But concentrating on the evidence for this may distract us from the continuing strength of oral procedures. The oral culture of the archaic and classical Greeks has received a fair amount of recent scholarly attention, that of the Romans very little. One of the reasons for this is that the poetic part of this culture, concerning which we do possess some indirect information,[39] failed to survive the Hellenization of late third- and second-century Rome. But that does not mean that thereafter poetry met its public in exclusively written form. On the contrary, in the culture of the middle and late Republic oral and written procedures were intermingled, with the former retaining far more importance than in any modern culture while giving up ground from time to time to written forms of communication.

What, then, is the likely social structure of literacy in this epoch? By the end of the fourth century at the very latest, no male member of the senatorial order could possibly have done without the ability to read. Livy's story about the brother of Fabius Rullianus (consul for the first time in 322), who was brought up at Caere and knew Etruscan *litterae*,[40] somewhat confirms that senators now set some value on literary education.

A considerable number of ordinary citizens were literate in Latin-speaking cities of the third century. The steadily increasing complexity of economic life and the spread of commercial interests bestowed practical value on the written word. Civic life gave some impetus in the same direction, though not on the same scale as in fifth-century Athens. In fact, with respect to the uses of writing and the probable diffusion of reading and writing ability, third-century Rome seems to have resembled a fairly advanced Greek city of the middle or later part of the sixth century. But the mass of the population, especially in the

38. On these see Coarelli in *Roma Medio Repubblicana* 282–285.

39. On the lost songs sung in praise of famous men at early Roman banquets see Cic. *Brut.* 75, etc.; cf. W. V. Harris, *War and Imperialism in Republican Rome, 327–70 B.C.* (Oxford, 1979), 25.

40. Liv. ix.36.3.

countryside, must have been very heavily illiterate. Literate women were probably very few (admittedly we have no direct evidence of any value). The economy was agrarian, the school system was weak or nonexistent, slaves were available to fill clerical positions, the masses did not participate in the government. In numerical terms all this means is that the probable range of literacy was minimal, perhaps not more than 1% or 2%, undoubtedly much below 10%.

Plutarch recounts that the first person to open an elementary school (*grammatodidaskaleion*) at Rome for paying pupils was a certain Sp. Carvilius, a freedman of the consul of that name who held office in 234.[41] The story is plausible enough, coinciding with the period in which Livius Andronicus and Naevius were writing what was later regarded as the earliest Latin literature, and of considerable importance. There might have been a school at Rome before the decline of Etruscan influence in the fifth century, but in the period prior to Carvilius such elementary instruction as there was may have taken place inside families. The motives of the fathers who sent their sons to Carvilius' new school were probably down-to-earth ones, leavened by a growing knowledge of the Greek world and its multiple attractions. A consequence of the taste for Greek literary culture was that men such as Livius Andronicus and Ennius who knew both languages now came into demand as teachers.[42]

The limited extent of Roman formal education in the 230s and 220s is hinted at by a remark made by Valerius Maximus about Cato (who was born in 234). This remark cannot be literally true: how late in life came Cato's desire for a Greek education we can judge, says Valerius, from the fact that "he was almost an old man when he learned Latin letters."[43] Now Cato served as a military tribune at the age of twenty, and it defies belief that he was at that time a real illit-

---

41. Plu. *QR* 59 = *Mor.* 278e. The fact that Plutarch possessed other information about Carvilius (cf. *QR* 54 = *Mor.* 277d) lends some extra credibility to this statement. The story about the schoolmaster of Falerii (Liv. v.27, etc.) is hardly to be cited as counterevidence, as it is by, among others, Bundgård, *Analecta Romana Instituti Danici* iii (1965), 29.

42. Cf. Suet. *De gramm.* 1: ". . . semigraeci . . . Livium et Ennium dico quos utraque lingua domi forisque docuisse adnotatum est." See S. F. Bonner, *Education in Ancient Rome* (London, 1977), 20–22; but "foris" probably means "outside Rome," not "in other households."

43. Val.Max. viii.7.1: "idem Graecis litteris erudiri concupivit, quam sero, inde aestimemus, quod etiam Latinas paene iam senex didicit, cumque eloquentia magnam gloriam partam haberet." The passage is not hostile.

erate. It has been suggested that in this text "learning Latin letters" refers to the study of Latin literature[44]—which is possible but not convincing, since "learning letters" naturally refers to acquiring literacy, and the Latin literature available for study was still so slight. Valerius more probably alludes, without fully understanding his source, to a somewhat defective education in Cato's boyhood. That this should be true of the son of a country landowner in these years ought not to cause astonishment, and it is possible that Cato became fully literate only in adolescence.

How partial, even by ancient standards, the transition from oral to written culture had been is suggested for late third-century Rome by the fact that the term *scriba* still applied indiscriminately to clerks and to poets. So at least Festus asserts.[45] Such semantic arguments are admittedly fragile, particularly when they depend on one text. In the classical language a *scriba* is always a clerk, and one in an official or quasi-official position: the Romans were now better aware of different kinds of writers.

At all events we must regard Roman literacy in the period prior to Carvilius' school, and perhaps for some time afterwards, as mainly confined to male members of the aristocracy, a very small proportion of their slaves (some of whom were literate in other languages), and to a very small percentage of ordinary citizens who were led on by ambition or occupational need to acquire a specialized skill.

Literacy and the Written Word in the Second Century B.C.

Did the freedman schoolmaster Carvilius soon have numerous imitators?[46] This is in the first place a question about interpreting Plautus, who might also be expected to be a rich mine of allusions about the use of writing at the beginning of the second century. Unfortunately, Plautus' references to schools must always be assumed to reflect references in the Greek plays which he was adapting for Roman audiences unless specific reasons suggest otherwise.[47] The same applies when his

44. A. E. Astin, *Cato the Censor* (Oxford, 1978), 159.

45. Festus 446 and 448 Lindsay, referring to Livius Andronicus and the Second Punic War.

46. As was claimed by Ogilvie, n. on Liv. iii.44.6, arguing from Plautus; schools "must have become fashionable quickly."

47. The main texts in question are *Asin.* 226; *Bacch.* 129, 427–448; *Curc.* 258; *Merc.* 303; *Pers.* 173.

characters talk about learning letters or failure to learn them.[48] An apparent exception comes in Philolaches' very "Plautine" monologue in the *Mostellaria*,[49] where parents are compared to builders: "They think expenses are not expensive; they finish the job carefully, by teaching letters, justice, and laws."[50] It is the norm to teach letters; but it is the norm for the kind of parent who teaches law as well—that is, for the upper classes. Nor are schools mentioned. Hence even this passage tells us very little about the growth of educational institutions at Rome.

However, there was certainly an increased demand for education in Rome in the first decades of the second century. One person who attempted to meet it was, not surprisingly, Cato; he owned a slave *grammatistes* named Chilon who "taught many boys."[51] Cato's own son was not among them, for Cato decided to teach the boy himself; this is regarded by Plutarch as unusual behaviour.[52] Schools taught by men such as Carvilius and Chilon must have multiplied in second-century Rome, and there was no shortage of slaves and ex-slaves with sufficient educational accomplishments to man them.[53]

The allusions to writing in the plays of Plautus and Terence are normally to be referred to the dramatists' Greek originals too, but that fact does not deprive such passages of all relevance to Roman conditions. For it can be assumed that some at least of the audience was expected to understand scenes which involved the use of written texts (which is not to say that the audience was expected to be literate). For example, two elaborate scenes concerning letters are central to the action of the *Pseudolus*,[54] while in the prologue of the *Rudens* Arcturus describes how he and the other stars discover the good and

48. The texts are *Pers.* 173, *Pseud.* 23, *Truc.* 735. The same goes for Caecilius Statius, *CRF* ii.51, where being *inliteratus* (whatever this means exactly; cf. above, p. 6) is associated with barbarism.

49. On the originality of this passage see, e.g., R. Perna, *L'originalità di Plauto* (Bari, 1955), 219. The lines on military service (129–132) help to indicate that there was no Greek model at this point.

50. *Most.* 125–126: "nec sumptus ibi sumptui ducunt esse; / expoliunt, docent litteras, iura, leges."

51. Plu. *Cat.Mai.* 20.5.

52. Aemilius Paullus' involvement in his sons' education seems to have been limited to attending while they were being instructed by others (Plu. *Aem.* 20.8–10).

53. Another reference to a school for boys at Rome: Cato, *ORF*³ fr. 205.

54. Plaut. *Pseud.* 20–73 and 983–1014 (the letter in question first appears at 647).

the wicked on earth and send their names *in writing* to Jupiter.[55] As in the case of the Athenian dramatists, there is some uncertainty about the social composition of the audience for these plays, which was in any case certainly tolerant of very Hellenic presentations; but the *Pseudolus* cannot possibly have been staged in a city in which only a handful of people understood the procedures of letter-writing.

Plautus' allusions to writing are not in fact all of Greek origin. In the prologue of the *Amphitruo*, to take a clear example, the speaker parodies in some detail the Lex Cornelia Baebia of 181 about electoral corruption.[56] One of the means by which the law forbade the corrupters to communicate was apparently "per scriptas litteras" (by letters, or a letter, in writing),[57] a prohibition which implies that by 181 this had become a fairly common practice. It would have been particularly useful for offering inducements to literate voters who resided far away in country towns. However no great knowledge of the Roman electoral system is needed to save us from the mistake of using this text as an argument for mass literacy.

From the famous letter written by the consuls of 186 B.C. concerning the Bacchanalia we might infer that in this same period the government was seeking to rule Italy partly by issuing written instructions; but the crisis was an unusual one, and no firm conclusion can be drawn. In any case it is evident that the Senate was thoroughly aware that oral communication was what reached a large audience, for the letter had first instructed the Teurani to proclaim *(edicere)* the Senate's orders at a series of public meetings.[58]

The source material concerning Roman literacy in the period of Polybius and the Gracchi, from the 160s to the 120s, makes it possible to go somewhat beyond the sketchy comments with which we have had to make do so far in this chapter, although we are still far

---

55. Plaut. *Rud.* 13–21 ("bonos in aliis tabulis exscriptos habet").

56. See most recently M. McDonnell, *AJPh* cvii (1986), 564–576, who argues that the passage is a slightly later interpolation, probably of the 150s.

57. Plaut. *Amph.* 70.

58. *CIL* i².581 = *ILLRP* 511, etc. According to the letter, the Senate instructed the Teurani to inscribe the text on a bronze tablet "and order it to be fastened up where it can very easily be known" (". . . ubei facilumed gnoscier potisit"; lines 25–27). Proclamation: lines 22–23. For the combination of written and oral technique cf. the senatorial decree about Astypalaea of 105 B.C., *IGRR* iv.1028 = R. K. Sherk, *Roman Documents from the Greek East* (Baltimore, 1969), no. 16, lines 12–15.

from having any body of evidence which a modern historian would regard as useful.

Polybius himself apparently thought that the Romans were negligent in providing for boys' education, and Cicero implicitly admits the charge that there was no common education which Roman citizens aimed at.[59] On the other hand, the standards Polybius set for an educational system were probably quite high.[60] The great increase in the number of inscriptions in second-century Italy suggests that acquaintance with the written word was spreading. What is most impressive is not the use of inscriptions by members of the ruling order, who had long been literate, but rather the relatively modest epitaphs in the country towns, partly in Latin but also in Etruscan and Oscan.[61]

We still at this period have no useful information about the price or availability of writing materials. Even when Cato, for instance, reveals that his record of one of his speeches was kept not conveniently on papyrus, but on a codex of wooden tablets,[62] no clear conclusion follows. It is scarcely remarkable that there were pens present in an army camp or, after the Lex Papiria of 130, in a legislative assembly.[63]

But we must return to the functions of literacy. As far as economic life is concerned, there are signs that more and more was being written down. The earliest Roman amphora "label" is a graffito from Cosa giving the name of one M. Se(stius), a member of a family which was amassing a considerable fortune; the amphora can be dated no later than the 180s.[64] During the decades after the Second Punic War the wealth of the Roman elite increased rapidly, and by the mid-second

59. Cic. *De rep.* iv.3: "disciplinam puerilem ingenuis, de qua Graeci multum frustra laborarunt, et in qua una Polybius noster hospes nostrorum institutorum neglegentiam accusat, nullam certam aut destinatam legibus aut publice expositam aut unam omnium esse voluerunt."

60. For the influx of Greek teachers see Polyb. xxxi.24.7; but he was hardly thinking of the elementary level.

61. The standard works which contain the non-Latin texts are *Corpus Inscriptionum Etruscarum* (in which fourth- and third-century epitaphs are also numerous) and E. Vetter, *Handbuch der italischen Dialekte* (Heidelberg, 1953).

62. *ORF*[3] fr. 173, dated by E. Malcovati to 164.

63. Pens at Numantia: A. Schulten, *Numantia* iv (1929), pls. 22.13, 28.4, 34.10–13. The styli (*grapheia*) at the meeting described in Plu. *CG* 13 were allegedly special large ones destined to be used as weapons; cf. E. E. Best, *Historia* xxiii (1974), 434 n.25.

64. E. L. Will in A. M. McCann (ed.), *The Roman Port and Fishery of Cosa* (Princeton, 1987), 173.

century some of its members had highly complex finances,[65] for the control and manipulation of which they must have relied more and more on documents. There is already some evidence for written accounts early in the second century.[66] In the time of Cicero some Roman accounts still showed receipts with the archaic form "af" (= "ab"),[67] which had by the Gracchan period become the less common form; this suggests that by that time accounting practices were long established. In *De agri cultura* Cato takes it for granted that on a wealthy man's estate there will be accounts *(rationes)* for cash, wheat, wine and olive oil; these are clearly thought of as being in documentary form. He also advises that orders should be left for the overseer in writing.[68]

These circumstances make it rather remarkable that the making of contracts remained throughout this period a largely oral procedure (at least so it seems to be believed; the lack of contemporary evidence makes the whole topic obscure). When Roman citizens obligated themselves, it was very often by means of an oral *stipulatio*.[69] Eventually there came to be a particular form of contractual obligation which Roman law scholars refer to as the *litteris* contract. Apart from one thoroughly dubious instance a little earlier, this is not attested until the first century B.C.[70] Its name obviously implies that other forms of obligation, the great majority, were still not put into writing. But we must be cautious, because oral *stipulationes* might have been accompanied by documents. Furthermore, Cato seems to recommend written contracts in connection with various agricultural operations, including olive-oil and wine production.[71]

Looking at legal proceedings more generally, we see that Cato envisaged tablets *(tabulae)* as possible evidence in lawsuits, and that

65. Cf. J. H. D'Arms, *Commerce and Social Standing in Ancient Rome* (Cambridge, Mass., 1981), 34–37.

66. In moneylending: Liv. xxxv.7.2. In banking: Plaut. *Truc.* 70–72 (apparently not derivative), 749; Plaut. *Most.* 304; Polyb. xxxi.27.7.

67. Cic. *De or.* 158.

68. Cato *RR* ii.5–6.

69. Cf. A. Watson, *The Law of Obligations in the Later Roman Republic* (Oxford, 1965), 1–9.

70. Watson 18–24. A good brief account: Watson, *Roman Private Law around 200 B.C.* (Edinburgh, 1971), 123–124. The dubious case is described in Cic. *De off.* iii.58.

71. Cato: Gellius xiv.2.21 (cf. *ORF³* pp. 83–84). The complex business arrangements alluded to in Plu. *Cat.Mai.* 21.6 would have been difficult without legal documents.

by the 80s of the first century arguing about documents was a standard part of forensic oratory.[72] It remains unclear whether sufficient evidence exists to permit a satisfactory account of the transition from a world in which legal proceedings were carried out with very little use of the written word to the hybrid one which we encounter in the late Republic, with the oral element still strong but with documents in heavy use.[73]

As for public life, some major problems of interpretation arise. An ordinary Roman citizen in the middle Republic could fulfil his duties and enjoy his privileges without reading or writing. Yet it has been asserted that "writing was insistently present" throughout civic life.[74] This claim is seriously misleading, but writing did indeed have some important civic functions. By the third quarter of the second century (a period of fairly rapid cultural change) it could always be assumed that the male members of at least the most prosperous citizen families could read and that they could write at least a little.

We can begin with the Senate. Its decrees had probably been made public in written form from a considerably earlier date, some form of publicity about its decisions being quite necessary because of the secretiveness of its actual proceedings.[75] Nonetheless it is hardly fortuitous that the earliest epigraphically recorded decrees and also the earliest apparently authentic text of a decree preserved by an author go no further back than the second century.[76]

The texts of proposed new laws and the names of electoral candidates were supposedly posted; and it has been implied that these practices were meant to give information directly to the citizens in general.[77] Proposed laws must indeed from early times have been put into written form, as they were in the late Republic.[78] It so happens

72. *Rhet. ad Her.* ii.9.13.

73. This topic requires the efforts of a Louis Gernet. For a Romanist's account of written proof in the late-republican/Augustan period cf. G. Pugliese in *Recueils de la Société Jean Bodin* xvi (= *La preuve* i) (1964), 333–340.

74. C. Nicolet, *Le métier de citoyen dans la Rome républicaine* (Paris, 1976), 517.

75. On the archiving and publication of senatorial decrees see esp. Sherk, *Roman Documents from the Greek East* 5–13.

76. See Sherk for the decrees preserved in Greek. Some of the procedure imposed on the Teurani by the letter to them about the Bacchanalia written by the consuls of 186 may well have reflected what was normally done at Rome by this time. The Senate ordered both a proclamation and the setting up of a bronze inscription (see above). Literary sources: Suet. *De rhet.* 1 quotes a decree of 161 B.C.

77. Nicolet, *Le métier* 517.

78. G. Rotondi, *Leges Publicae Populi Romani* (Milan, 1912), 123–124; M. Cor-

that the earliest occasion when such a text is specifically known to have been put up in public gaze is no earlier than 63 B.C.[79] At all events the way in which the public had traditionally found out about such proposals, insofar as it did so, was by means of a reading out loud (followed by "word of mouth"); and we should assume that this continued to be the case for most citizens even in the late Republic.[80] With regard to elections, though it is official doctrine that by the late Republic candidates' names were published,[81] the fact is doubtful, and publication may have been a one-copy formality.

When laws were passed, there was no requirement either that they should be preserved in any archive or that they should be inscribed for public inspection and use. Apparently the plebeian aediles were meant to keep copies of *plebiscita*,[82] but other laws were not systematically recorded. Cicero in fact criticizes the Roman system on this point, saying that in consequence the laws are what the *apparitores* (magistrates' clerks) want them to be.[83]

What, then, of the surviving bronze tablets of the Gracchan period and later which contain the texts of laws? It is not enough to say that the inscribed laws were the most important ones,[84] for there was evidently a change. Some laws may perhaps have been inscribed earlier on perishable material such as wood, but it seems unlikely to be an accident that whereas we have no text from before the third quarter of the second century, there exist copies of about a dozen laws (many not from Rome itself) dating from between that period and 49.[85]

---

bier in *L'Urbs. Espace urbain et histoire. Actes du colloque (Rome, 8–12 mai 1985)* (Rome, 1987), 40.

79. Cic. *De lege agr.* ii.13. *Sest.* 72 probably refers to such a procedure's being followed in 58. Cic. *De leg.* iii.11 (presiding magistrates are to file proposals in the *aerarium*) is of little help here.

80. For the usual procedure see, e.g., App. *BC* i.11.47. Cf. C. Williamson, *Classical Antiquity* vi (1987), 164, citing Cic. *Rab.Post.* 14 (law proposals were still read out).

81. T. Mommsen, *Römisches Staatsrecht* i (3d ed., Leipzig, 1887), 502 ("aufgestellt"; presumably he meant in writing).

82. Pomponius in *Dig.* i.2.2.21; Zonar. vii.15 end.

83. *De leg.* iii.46: "legum custodiam nullam habemus; itaque eae leges sunt quas apparitores nostri volunt, a librariis petimus, publicis litteris consignatam memoriam publicam nullam habemus. Graeci hoc diligentius." F. von Schwind, *Zur Frage der Publikation in römischen Recht* (Munich, 1940), 30, and others, have tried in vain to evade the sense of this admittedly vague passage.

84. Rotondi, *Leges Publicae* 170.

85. The earliest are probably the fragments *CIL* i².595 and 596 (on which see W. V. Harris, *Rome in Etruria and Umbria* [Oxford, 1971], 173–174), which were

These texts were definitely not meant for popular consumption. They are written in a legalese rendered all the more opaque by the use of technical abbreviations.[86] In any case the masses certainly could not read. But although we clearly are not dealing with the democratization of the legal system, a certain widening of legal and hence political and social power was in operation, just as it had been with the publication of laws in Greece. It seems likely that an innovation in publication practice occurred in the 130s or slightly earlier, closely connected with the limited liberalization which during the 130s gave rise to a series of ballot laws. From the Gracchan period onwards, anyone who could read or find someone to read on his or her behalf could, if they were determined, consult the texts of some at least of the laws which had been enacted in that period or subsequently. Hence there was strong emphasis on the real physical accessibility of the inscribed law: it was to be displayed openly in such a place that anyone who wished might stand and read it from ground level.[87] The conclusion should be that in the course of the second century the use of writing in Roman civic life increased significantly but not dramatically.

Certain procedures followed in the second-century army may also be important here, namely the means used for distributing the password and for inspecting the night guard in the Roman legions, as they are described by Polybius.[88] This evidence has, however, been widely misused, with the password procedure being cited to show the high level of literacy allegedly prevailing among Roman citizens.[89] What Polybius says is that at sunset a soldier from each of the tenth maniples in the legion (five men in all) goes to his commanding tribune to get the password, which is given to him written on a wooden tablet.

---

written on either side of the same sheet of bronze, probably in the third quarter of the second century. Not much later are the Lex Repetundarum (*CIL* i².583) and *CIL* i².597.

86. On the latter point see C. Williamson, "Law-Making in the Comitia of Republican Rome" (Ph.D. diss., London, 1983), 257–264. On the density of the layout in the surviving texts see ibid. 115, and on other difficulties which may have arisen in reading them 176. She emphasizes the monumental quality of the laws inscribed on bronze and the fame which accrued to their named authors (see esp. 183–187).

87. *FIRA* i no. 7, of 123 or 122 B.C.; no. 9 (the "Pirate Law," now known as the Lex de provinciis praetoriis), B 25–26, of 101–100, with the parallels given by M. Hassall, M. Crawford & J. Reynolds, *JRS* lxiv (1974), 213; the *Fragmentum Tarentinum*, of about 100 (R. Bartoccini, *Epigraphica* ix [1947], 10, line 14).

88. vi.34–35.

89. E. E. Best, *Classical Journal* lxii (1966–67), 123, followed by C. Nicolet (comm. on Polyb. vi.34.8, Budé edition).

The soldier takes the tablet to his own maniple commander (a centurion by rank) and hands it over in front of witnesses. The tablet is then passed from one maniple commander to the next until it returns to the tribune. At no point in this procedure is anyone below the rank of centurion required to read. A high level of organization, depending on the written word, is thus attested, and there is no reason to think that it was especially new in Polybius' time; but nothing here suggests an unexpectedly high level of literacy.

Inspecting the night guard also involved writing, but very little, and again not by ordinary soldiers. The soldiers who are to take the first watch, says Polybius, come to the tribune in the company of an *optio,* a junior officer, and receive tiny wooden tablets with signs on them *(echonta charactera),* and then they go to their posts. Later four cavalrymen, selected by an *optio,* collect each of these tablets. These cavalrymen receive written orders, a *graphe,* from the tribune telling them which guard stations to visit on each watch. During the course of the night they collect all the tablets, making sure that the guards are awake at their posts. The cavalrymen must be able to read, but the guards themselves have no reason to do so. The cavalrymen are not to be taken as typical soldiers. First of all, the cavalry still remained to some extent a social elite;[90] second, individuals may well *not* have been chosen at random for this duty;[91] and third, the higher officers had an incentive to use written orders—the wish to maintain strict control—even if it meant that some cavalrymen could not be employed for the task of inspecting the guard. It is likely enough that practically all cavalrymen could read, but this Polybian text must not be cited as evidence that the ordinary infantryman (himself seldom from the most indigent social stratum at this time) could read and write.[92]

With the introduction of written ballots at Rome from 139 onwards

90. C. Nicolet in J.-P. Brisson (ed.), *Problèmes de la guerre à Rome* (Paris & The Hague, 1969), 127–133.

91. Notwithstanding Best 122. In fact προκριθέντες (Polyb. vi.35.11) implies the opposite.

92. On special occasions the republican army seems to have used tesserae to distribute written orders: Liv. xxvii.46.1, xxviii.14.7 (cf. vii.35.1 and ix.32.4, where this is an annalistic embellishment). But xxviii.14.7 contradicts Polyb. xi.22.4 and is therefore highly dubious. Anyway we should not suppose, in spite of Best 125, that such orders went to the ordinary infantryman in written form (the production of enough copies to pass around would in any case have been a cumbersome business). Presumably the purpose of the operation was simply to permit the officers to stay with their men.

we come to some evidence which is somewhat more informative about the level of contemporary literacy. The use of these ballots shows that vital organs of government could rely on some degree of literacy on the part of a substantial number of citizens. But who wrote in this new system, and exactly what was written?

Four laws are in question: the Lex Gabinia of 139, which substituted written ballots for oral voting in elections; the Lex Cassia of 137, which made the same change for judicial votes, except those which concerned *perduellio,* treason; the Lex Papiria of 130, which reformed legislative voting in the same way; and the Lex Coelia of 107, which extended balloting to *perduellio.*

Thus not only the centuriate assembly was involved but also the somewhat more democratically organized tribal assembly. However the amount of writing required under these laws was small indeed. In elections it was enough to write the initials of the preferred candidate or candidates on the waxed wooden voting-tablet.[93] In legislative and judicial votes, no more than a single letter was needed: in the former, V for *uti rogas* (as you propose) or A for *antiquo* (I reject); in the latter, A for *absolvo* or C for *condemno* (but under the Lex Coelia L for *libero* or D for *damno*). In the Gracchan extortion court ready-made A/C tablets were used, on which the citizen had only to perform the undemanding task of obliterating one of the two letters.[94] It looks as if a democratic-minded legislator intended this provision to help those who might have had some difficulty in writing. Officially pre-inscribed ballots also seem to have been used in legislative assemblies,[95] at least by 61 B.C. Cicero describes a vote which took place in that year in which the remarkable thing was not that pre-inscribed little tablets *(tabellae)* were employed, but that thanks to Clodius' supporters only A and not V was available (with the eventual consequence that the assembly was dismissed).[96] As for electoral voting, we

93. Cic. *De domo* 112 seems to be the only clear evidence on this, but it is enough. Cf. Mommsen, *Römisches Staatsrecht* iii.405 n.5. The voter probably wrote the initials of each of his candidates, up to the number of offices to be filled, on the same tablet: U. Hall, *Historia* xiii (1964), 299. Presumably voters who needed to would have the opportunity to read the candidates' names from whitened boards, as later provided in the Tabula Hebana, sec.20; cf. L. R. Taylor, *Roman Voting Assemblies* (Ann Arbor, 1966), 79, 160.

94. *CIL* i².583 (= *FIRA* i no.7), line 51.

95. Cf. Taylor 77.

96. Cic. *Att.* i.14.5: "operae Clodianae pontis occupaverant, tabellae ministrabantur ita ut nulla daretur 'VTI ROGAS.'" The passive "ministrabantur" seems to suggest that the ballots were official. Cf. Taylor 77.

know that by the late Republic ballots were on occasion prepared unofficially for distribution to cooperative voters; however Plutarch, our only source, did not fully understand the incident which he describes,[97] and it remains unclear exactly what was illegal, as well as what was normally done. We cannot therefore be at all sure that the electoral voting system was "a severe test of literacy,"[98] but it did set apart those who possessed and those who lacked the requisite writing ability.

All this ballot legislation poses the following broad dilemma: either the legislators knew that voting would be restricted to a prosperous and literate minority, or literacy was now remarkably widespread among Roman citizens.[99] The former interpretation is much closer to reality.[100] And in fact the ballot legislators of the 130s intended something less than mob rule, notwithstanding Cicero's later huffing and puffing against written ballots in general.[101] The Lex Gabinia passed without causing a great political storm—and as a result made very little impression on ancient writers[102]—presumably because it benefited not the poor but those who, to the very limited degree required, could write and manage simple documents; and they were a small percentage of the population. The same kind of person continued to be elected (which is not to say that the law made no difference at all), and to encourage this the *optimates* managed to inspect a lot of ballots,[103] a practice which Marius' *lex tabellaria* of 119 was designed to

97. Plu. *Cat.Min.* 46.2. But he cannot be right that all the ballots were written in one hand (and for this reason K. Ziegler attempted to emend the text: *RhM* lxxxi [1932], 65).

98. Taylor 80.

99. Nicolet, *Le métier* 517–518. He chose the latter alternative, substantially relying on the painted and graffito inscriptions of Pompeii some 200 years later, evidence which does not establish majority literacy or anything like it even for Pompeii. Best, *Historia* xxiii (1974), 428–438, develops in detail the view that full literacy was very widespread among the poorest citizens by the time of the ballot laws. He bolsters this by the implied argument (437–438) that if some freedmen were literate practically all free-born males must have been; this is based on a serious misunderstanding of the social structure.

100. R. MacMullen, *Athenaeum* lviii (1980), 454–457, showed it to be very likely that the turnout of voters was normally below 2%. In any case a turnout above 10% is extremely improbable.

101. *De leg.* iii.33–39.

102. Best 432 entirely fails to explain why, if the laws involved a "fundamental struggle" and if "the demand . . . for the written ballot . . . may have been stronger than the zeal for land reform," there was so little excitement.

103. On this point see T. P. Wiseman, *New Men in the Roman Senate, 139 B.C.–14 A.D.* (Oxford, 1971), 4–5.

prevent. Even in 139 many voters no doubt felt that their *libertas* had been strengthened;[104] but there is no sign that mass participation was expected.

The Lex Cassia went further in a sense, since it only required the voter to distinguish two letters from each other. But even this was not apparently expected to produce revolutionary consequences. The proposal was backed by, perhaps originated by, Scipio Aemilianus,[105] and its proposer, L. Cassius Longinus Ravilla, went on to become consul in 127 and censor in 125–24—not the fate of a man who had deeply offended the aristocracy. C. Papirius Carbo, the proposer of the third law, is a more complex political figure: though to a great extent a sympathizer of Ti. Gracchus, when he reached the consulship a decade after the tribunate he had held in 130 he defended the arch-representative of conservative violence, L. Opimius. It may be that his ballot law had the effect of facilitating the legislation of C. Gracchus, and perhaps it was intended to help reformist legislation; but it would be quite mistaken to suppose that Carbo assumed that all citizens would be able to use the ballot with which he provided them, even though all that a "Papirian" voter had to do was choose between the pre-inscribed letters *V* and *A*.

The ballot laws represent a significant moment in the cultural history of the Romans, when, as in the case of ostracism at Athens and other cities, important political procedures were entrusted to pieces of writing.[106] In each case several thousand men are in confident possession of the necessary technical skill. But in this case as in the other we should avoid exaggerating the amount of literacy which participation required of the individual (it was somewhat less at Rome than at Athens) and avoid misunderstanding the change as a sign that an entire population was now literate or semi-literate.

In the religious sphere, very closely linked in the case of republican

104. That this was the later view is hinted at in Cic. *De leg. agr.* ii.4. When Cicero put into Laelius' mouth the notion that because of the Gabinian and Cassian laws "multitudinis arbitrio res maximas agi" (*De amic.* 41), it is plain that he was more or less willfully ignoring the complexities of the politics of that period.

105. Cic. *De leg.* iii.37: "quo auctore lata esse dicitur"; cf. A. E. Astin, *Scipio Aemilianus* (Oxford, 1967), 130. It was opposed by the consul M. Lepidus Porcina. The general assertion "dissentiebant principes" can without difficulty be seen as propaganda.

106. The phenomenon probably went beyond the city of Rome itself. At any rate an attempt was made at Arpinum not much later to introduce a ballot law (Cic. *De leg.* iii.36), and presumably some Italian towns did pass such laws.

Rome with the political sphere, the functions of the written word at this time are not altogether clear. Prophetic books of an illicit kind seem sometimes to have circulated, and sometimes to have been suppressed.[107] Such works may or may not have stayed mainly in the hands of specialist soothsayers *(harioli* and *haruspices)*. If written oracles or written spells were in wide use, we get no indication of the fact from the surviving sources; but this is the merest argument from silence. The well-known Roman uses of the written word for religious purposes, for public dedications to deities and for the transmission of the arcane pontifical, augural, and other texts discussed in the previous section, have nothing democratic about them.

The written word could certainly be a powerful religious lever. When in 162 the augur Ti. Sempronius Gracchus caused the resignation of the consuls at whose election he had presided in the previous year, the grounds on which he did so were a fault in the auspices, which he became aware of "when he was reading the books,"[108] evidently the specialized texts pertaining to his office. However sceptical our interpretation of this event may be, considerable authority was being attributed to a written text. But religious *libri* did not often have such serious effects on political life. The written *sortes* (prophetic tablets) of Praeneste were another authoritative kind of text. These were made of wood, and according to the local story had been discovered inside a rock by one Numerius Suffustius after he had received instructions in a dream.[109] By Cicero's time, however, only the *vulgus* was impressed, he says; *sortes* had lost favour with the upper classes. In 181 another attempt had been made to exploit a "found" text—the "books of Numa" found on the Janiculum.[110] The urban praetor's decision to burn them implies that they would otherwise have been accorded some authority.

The roots of Roman literary culture go back to the third century, and perhaps beyond. By the mid-second century a certain section of the upper class was seriously affected by a zeal for literary composition. Many of the main genres of writing known to the Greeks had

107. Cf. Liv. xxxix.16.8 (a consul of 186 speaking): "quotiens hoc patrum avorumque aetate negotium eat magistratibus datum, uti . . . vaticinos libros conquirerent comburerentque." Such an incident had occurred in 213: Liv. xxv.1.6–12 (cf. 12.3).

108. Cic. *ND* ii.11.

109. Cic. *De div.* ii.85–87; cf. W. Speyer, *Bücherfunde in der Glaubenswerbung der Antike* (Göttingen, 1970), 23–24.

110. Speyer 51–55, etc. The sources are listed by T. R. S. Broughton, *The Magistrates of the Roman Republic* i (New York, 1951), 384.

now arrived. Epic and dramatic poetry, histories, and technical handbooks of various kinds had been committed to writing. Speeches began to circulate in written form and show some degree of survival power (quite apart from the special case of the speeches of Cato which the author included in his *Origines*).[111] Not all the authors of these literary works were aristocratic, and naturally some, such as Caecilius Statius and Terence, were privileged slaves, but none on the other hand is known to have been a man of the people.

But although we possess quite numerous fragments of information about the literary history of the period, very little of it concerns the dissemination of literary works. It is to be assumed that this occurred on a relatively small scale and in a relatively simple fashion. Some of those works of archaic Latin literature which never became school texts probably never existed at any date in more than a few score copies. Given the relative scarcity of evidence for private life in the second century, it may not be relevant that we hear practically nothing of accumulations of books even among Roman aristocrats;[112] but it is obvious in any case that literary texts circulated in very limited quantities. Signs of markedly new conditions appear only in the first century: an early indication is the fact that the philosophical writer C. Amafinius, who probably flourished in the first decades of the century, stirred up the *multitudo* by his writings—according to Cicero's account—to such an extent that he and the writers who succeeded him "captured the whole of Italy."[113]

Works of technical literature also began to multiply in second-century Rome. Besides the juristic writings of Sex. Aelius Paetus (consul in 198)[114] and the didactic productions of Cato, which concerned agriculture, military affairs, and religious law (but probably not medi-

---

111. Speeches that still existed in Cicero's time: a Greek one by Ti. Sempronius Gracchus (the consul of 177) (*Brut.* 79), some of those of Ser. Sulpicius Galba (consul in 144), the younger Laelius and Scipio Aemilianus (*Brut.* 82), etc.

112. The only collection of which we hear consisted of the books of King Perseus, which Aemilius Paullus allotted to his sons out of the plunder after the Battle of Pydna (Plu. *Aem.* 28).

113. Cic. *Tusc.Disp.* iv.3.6–7: "C. Amafinius exstitit dicens, cuius libris editis commota multitudo contulit se ad eam potissimum disciplinam [that of the Epicureans] . . . Post Amafinium autem multi eiusdem aemuli rationis multa cum scripsissent, Italiam totam occupaverunt."

114. On this and somewhat later legal works see A. Watson, *Law Making in the Later Roman Republic* (Oxford, 1974), 134–142. It seems very doubtful that Ap. Claudius (consul in 307 and 296) wrote a book *De usurpationibus* (Pomponius in *Dig.* i.2.2.36); a later Claudius may have been responsible.

cine or rhetoric),[115] we know of a number of other works. The pattern in this period is that individual enthusiasts from the upper class, often drawing on Greek sources, committed their knowledge to writing for the benefit of a small social group. Thus, for example, C. Sulpicius Gallus, consul in 166, wrote about astronomy.[116] The real wave of instructional works came only in the first century.

The volume of mid-republican literacy cannot possibly be measured. The ballot laws are the best evidence, and even they do not carry us as far as has sometimes been supposed. Three crucial factors, however, prevent us from thinking that more than, say, 10% of the population as a whole was literate: we have reasons to think that the mid-republican Romans possessed no more than a rudimentary network of schools; no economic or other incentive led the rulers of Rome to attach importance to the education of the ordinary citizen; and no set of beliefs, such as existed in classical Athens and probably in a number of Hellenistic cities, told the citizens at large or a large section of them that they had any duty to acquire enough elementary education to be able to read and write. At the same time it is evident both from the ballot laws and from other evidence that a solid minority of citizens were now literate, without doubt a considerably greater number than in the third century, and a still greater number was in possession of varying degrees of semi-literacy.

The level of women's literacy was probably minimal. Even in the upper class a woman of some education such as Cornelia, "mother of the Gracchi," was probably an exception.[117] Admittedly the argument from silence is not strong in this case, and by the second century actual illiteracy is not likely to have been common among the female members of the upper orders of society. But with the mass of women, it is evident that the traditional ethos effectively discouraged all but the most fortunate and ambitious from learning to read and write.

115. This matter has been clarified by Astin, *Cato the Censor* 182–210, 332–340. In seeking to explain the "disorder and fragmentation" which characterize *De agri cultura*, Astin mentions several hypotheses (193–199), but not the possibility, indeed the probability, that its composition was in effect oral, the work being dictated to a secretary (cf. Plu. *Cat.Mai.* 24.3 for his secretarial staff) and revised little or not at all (though he observes that Cato may sometimes have composed in this fashion, 202 n.43, and envisages the possibility that some of the later sections of this book were written in by a secretary); this would be all the more likely if the story about Cato's education discussed above contained some truth.

116. See M. Schanz & C. Hosius, *Geschichte der lateinischen Literatur* i (4th ed., Munich, 1927), 242–243.

117. Cicero singles her out, *Brut.* 104, 211.

Some apparent novelties appear in the use of writing at the end of the second century and the beginning of the first. One is the political pamphleteering of Gaius Gracchus;[118] about this almost nothing is known (certainly nothing specific about its intended audience), but its existence suggests a certain widening of the audience for written compositions. A second is the use of a list: the consuls of 95 helped to provoke a great war by tightening up on the usurpation of Roman citizenship by citizens of allied states, and the censors' list of citizens abruptly gained in importance.[119] Another novelty is the attempt of Q. Sertorius, to which we shall return in the next chapter, to institute Latin education as a political measure during his period of rule in Spain in the 70s.

118. Plu. *TG* 8.9, *CG* 4.6. It is also worth mentioning graffiti written up in public: Cic. *De or.* ii.240 (perhaps fictional, but in any case realistic), Plu. *CG* 17.9.

119. This must be what is referred to in Diod.Sic. xxxvii.13.1. Very close to this date the use of large codices in drawing up the citizen list happens to be illustrated on the Altar of Domitius Ahenobarbus (photo in M. Torelli, *The Typology and Structure of Roman Historical Reliefs* [Ann Arbor, 1982], pl. I.4a); the procedure itself was very old.

7 The Late Republic and the
High Empire, 100 B.C.−250 A.D.

As Rome step by step enlarged its empire and gradually came to affect the social fabric of every region under its domination in both east and west, a new period in the history of literacy began. Insofar as the extent of literacy in the Roman Empire has been investigated, previous writers have generally concluded that a high degree of literacy was achieved;[1] and it is true that under Roman rule many regions reached higher levels of literacy than before, while some regions which had scarcely known writing at all came to have partly literate populations. The Latin world now came to make wider use of the written word, and in some respects this holds good for the eastern part of the empire as well. But the transition from oral to written culture always remained sporadic (though not by any means random) and incomplete. And, as we shall see, there are strong reasons for giving low estimates of Roman literacy.

Spoken and Written Languages of the Roman World

One reason for giving a low estimate of Greek and Latin literacy is simply that many of the inhabitants of the Roman Empire spoke neither Greek nor Latin. This linguistic diversity is now perhaps more generally acknowledged than before, but its full extent is seldom if ever realized. The users of Greek and Latin are, as in earlier chapters, the main subjects of this investigation, but we must be clear about who among the inhabitants of the Roman Empire made partial or exclusive use of other languages. At least a dozen languages other than Greek and Latin were sometimes used in written form within the Empire, and an indeterminate number of others were spoken without being written. Several languages, such as Etruscan, Oscan and Iberian, went out of written use or died out altogether during the period under

1. There have, however, been some important exceptions. For a survey of opinion see above, pp. 9−10.

consideration and are minor though interesting phenomena from the point of view of Graeco-Roman literacy. Other local languages remained numerically predominant in their own areas throughout this era, and the mass of the population might speak nothing else.[2] In some cases even members of the upper class retained knowledge of the traditional language. In wide areas of the eastern Empire and in some parts of the west the need for written texts was met partly by such local languages.

A study of Roman literacy must consider these "secondary" languages because people who could not speak Greek or Latin would not, for the most part, have been able to read them, and can almost never have had the ability to write them.[3] However we must be alert for bilingualism and multilingualism.[4] Many things might encourage a person whose mother tongue was not Greek or Latin to learn one or the other: cultural prestige, commercial advantage, a wish to communicate with officials, social contact. A slave would commonly find it necessary to communicate in a second language. In many provincial communities different languages served different purposes, and a certain degree of bilingualism may have been common. None of this can be measured, and a provincial community would in general have had no practical need for more than a limited number of people capable of conversing in one of the dominant languages; moreover, in many provincial backwaters it must have been difficult or impossible to learn Greek or Latin properly.[5]

The main evidence for the use of most of the secondary languages

2. J. Herman, in *Etrennes de Septantaine. Travaux de linguistique et de grammaire comparée offerts à Michel Lejeune* (Paris, 1978), 112, infers from the homogeneity of the epigraphical Latin of the provinces that Latin was a "langue de prestige minoritaire."

3. Also because the ways in which some of the subject peoples had used or continued to use writing in their own languages probably influenced the ways in which they used writing in Greek and Latin. This topic is, however, too specialized to be pursued here.

4. And for the possible existence of mixed patois such as the Latin-Celtic which for a time had some existence in Gaul (see the testimonia listed by A. Tovar, *Kratylos* ix [1964], 122 = R. Kontzi [ed.], *Zur Entstehung der romanischen Sprachen* [Darmstadt, 1978], 420, and also W. Meid, *Gallisch oder Lateinisch? Soziolinguistische und andere Bemerkungen zu populären gallo-lateinischen Inschriften* [Innsbruck, 1980]).

5. For these reasons it may be doubted whether Tovar is right to think of "remote villages [in the western provinces] whose dwellers . . . were for many generations bilingual" (129 = 428). For the extraordinariness of bilingualism in the eyes of Greeks see Galen viii.585 Kühn.

consists of inscriptions. But the difficulties of inferring from epigraphical evidence which languages were spoken in given areas at given periods are extreme.[6] We could not have told from the inscriptions of Julio-Claudian Lystra, which are purely Greek and Latin, that many of the townspeople spoke Lycaonian;[7] or from the Greek inscriptions of Tomi that Getic was widely spoken there;[8] or from the inscriptions of North Africa that a large number of people still spoke Punic there in the late Empire. While it is likely, though not provable, that practically all the epigraphical languages were also spoken in the same periods in which they were used for inscriptions, spoken languages often left no epigraphic trace. In other words, the epigraphic remains severely under-record the linguistic heterogeneity of the Roman Empire.

For written languages we can get at least some rough guidance from the inscriptions. It is hard to imagine that any language was used extensively in written form in the Roman Empire without leaving considerable epigraphic traces. On the other hand the inscriptions undeniably fail, at least in some instances, to indicate the extent of the written use of a language: nothing in the Gallic inscriptions of the third century A.D. quite prepares us for the information that the language was sometimes used for preparing legal trusts, or for what that implies in terms of language use. Inscriptions do not prepare us for the range of purposes which demotic Egyptian served in texts written on papyrus and on ostraca.

Thus before we come fully to grips with the problem of Roman literacy, we must briefly consider to what extent other languages remained in use. We can do this most conveniently by examining three geographical milieux which between them cover the entire Empire outside Latium and Greece proper:[9] Italy; the western provincial regions (defined for the sake of convenience as those in which Latin predominated over Greek), extending as far east as Dacia and

6. Cf. F. Millar, *JRS* lviii (1968), 126–127.

7. Acts xiv.11.

8. Cf. Ov. *Trist.* v.7.13–14, 51–58, 12.58; *Ex Pont.* iv.13.19–20. However R. Syme, *History in Ovid* (Oxford, 1978), 17, 164, has poured some cold water on the "native" features of Tomi in Ovid's time.

9. What follows is merely an outline account of a subject which, notwithstanding the valuable volume of G. Neumann & J. Untermann (eds.), *Die Sprachen im römischen Reich der Kaiserzeit* (Bonner Jahrbücher Beiheft xl) (Cologne & Bonn, 1980), needs to be studied anew (with full attention to the problems of multilingualism and of Vulgar Latin).

Lower Moesia;[10] and all those parts of the eastern Empire which were incompletely Hellenized.

Italy itself, in the first decades of the first century B.C., was in a state of cultural as well as political turmoil. The use of Latin was spreading rapidly at the expense of the indigenous languages, but the process would not be complete, at least as far as written languages were concerned, for more than another hundred years. At the time of the Social War (91–89), written Oscan was probably familiar to the leading men of those places in central and southern Italy which had not been colonized by Rome, but many of them could probably speak Latin, and soon after if not before 90 B.C. Latin must have become their first school language. Yet Oscan lived on, and not just in remote backwaters;[11] it is likely that some of the Oscan inscriptions of Pompeii are of the first century A.D.[12] The vast majority of Pompeian texts were by now in Latin, but more remote places probably preserved the old language better, and it was presumably still spoken in many districts. Written Etruscan was driven from the field in the same general period, though it is likely that its retreat both began and ended somewhat later than that of Oscan. At the time of the Social War there must have been many in Etruria who could write Etruscan but not Latin. By the late first century B.C. such persons probably existed only in small numbers or remote places, and the last Etruscan inscriptions date from the second quarter of the first century A.D.[13] In the towns, spoken Etruscan cannot have lasted much longer than this; in the countryside there is no knowing.[14]

10. For the epigraphical dividing line between Latin and Greek in the Balkans see B. Gerov in Neumann & Untermann 149; on the meaning of such lines see A. Mócsy, *Pannonia and Upper Moesia* (London, 1974), 259–260.

11. Cf. Strabo v.233 (a debated passage).

12. Most of the evidence can be found in E. Vetter, *Handbuch der italischen Dialekte* (Heidelberg, 1953), 46–67; P. Poccetti, *Nuovi documenti italici* (Pisa, 1979). Cf. W. V. Harris, *Rome in Etruria and Umbria* (Oxford, 1971), 183, E. C. Polomé in *ANRW* ii.29.2 (1983), 521. However, as John Lenz has pointed out to me, there is considerable implausibility about dating the crucial "eituns" *dipinti* to the last years of the colony, and one of them, Vetter no. 28, is certainly not so late, since a window was sunk through it before 79: see M. della Corte, *Not.Sc.* 1916, 155–158.

13. The last narrowly datable inscriptions (from the Hepennius tomb at Asciano) are Augustan (Harris 179), but some of the Volterran epitaphs are probably a little later: cf. E. Fiumi, *SE* xxv (1957), 413–414; M. Nielsen in P. Bruun (ed.), *Studies in the Romanization of Etruria* (Rome, 1975), 387.

14. On the evidence of Gell. xi.7.4 see Harris 183.

In the regions north of the Apennines the Celtic and Venetic languages were still in limited written use in some areas in the first century B.C.,[15] but even there the population was rapidly being Romanized. From the beginning of the principate on, there is no evidence for the written use of any language other than Latin except in secluded Alpine Valleys. Complete Latinization of the spoken word in northern Italy presumably took somewhat longer. From the time of Augustus, however, and in part because of the military recruitment and the resettlement for which he was responsible, it is reasonable to judge that all or almost all regions of Italy were primarily Latin-speaking.

In the Punic- and Libyan-speaking provinces of North Africa the local languages survived throughout antiquity, while Latin came in with settlers and at the same time gradually converted the social elite. The colonizations carried out under Caesar and Augustus probably had an important effect on the linguistic pattern, here as elsewhere. Punic inscriptions which date from after the conquest are known from sites all along the north African coast from Tripolitania westwards,[16] powerfully suggesting that it was not only the illiterate poor who continued to use the old language. Until the time of Tiberius coins were minted with partially Punic legends at Leptis Magna and Oea,[17] and a dedication on a public building in Leptis Magna was written partly in Punic as late as about 180.[18] In about 160 it could still be alleged with some plausibility that a young ne'er-do-well of good equestrian family spoke Punic and a little Greek.[19] Septimius Severus from Leptis, roughly a contemporary, is said to have spoken Punic fluently, and his sister could scarcely speak Latin.[20] All this shows that even now Punic was far from being confined to backwoodsmen. Ulpian gives the opinion that trusts *(fideicommissa)* could be established in Punic or Gallic or any other national language as well as in

15. Cf. Polomé 519–520.

16. See the map provided by W. Röllig in Neumann & Untermann, *Die Sprachen im römischen Reich* 287. Not all of these sites have inscriptions from all periods. Cf. also M. Bénabou, *La résistance africaine à la romanisation* (Paris, 1975), 483–487.

17. C. T. Falbe, J. C. Lindberg, & L. Müller, *Numismatique de l'ancienne Afrique* ii (Copenhagen, 1860), 6–7, 16.

18. *KAI* 130 seems to be the last of the series (the Latin part of the text is in *IRT* 599).

19. So says Apuleius of his stepson Sicinius Pudens (*Apol.* 98: "enim Latine loqui neque vult neque potest"); this was perhaps quite untrue.

20. *Epit. de Caes.* 20.8, SHA *Sept.Sev.* 15.7.

Latin or Greek.[21] Presumably the question was or had recently been a live one, much the most likely reason being that Caracalla's extension of Roman citizenship had for the first time created a substantial number of citizens with a thorough ignorance of both Latin and Greek.[22] This text suggests that written Punic possessed a quite wide range of functions, with some men of property using it for legal affairs. In many places Punic continued to be used at least until the fifth century A.D.;[23] notoriously it was still being spoken in Augustine's time.[24]

The Libyan language, too, was widely used, as the total of 1,123 inscriptions in a now somewhat outdated corpus indicates.[25] Like the Punic inscriptions, they range from Tripolitania to Mauretania. Most of them date from the Roman period, and they continue at least until the third century.[26] The overwhelming majority are epitaphs, and they leave unsettled the question whether written Libyan ever had much wider functions. There is no specific evidence that the language was still spoken under Roman rule, but it is extremely probable. The conclusion that "knowledge of Latin was general throughout the whole area covered by the African provinces"[27] can be admitted only if it is understood to refer to the town bourgeoisie, and even for them the accomplishment came only step by step.

21. Ulp. in *Dig.* xxxii.1.11 pr.: "Fideicommissa quocumque sermone relinqui possunt, non solum Latina vel Graeca, sed etiam Punica vel Gallicana vel alterius cuiuscumque gentis." This represented a new tolerance of provincial languages, according to R. MacMullen, *AJPh* lxxxvii (1966), 2–3.

22. We should see this text as an indication of the spread of Roman law rather than of a reversion to Punic by people who had previously used Latin.

23. The last surviving Punic inscriptions were written in the Latin alphabet in the fourth and fifth centuries, according to Röllig in Neumann & Untermann, *Die Sprachen im römischen Reich* 295.

24. Spoken Punic: August. *Epist.* 66.2, 84.2, 108.14, 209.2 (a presbyter who was "et Punica lingua . . . instructus"); cf. also August. *Serm.* 167.4 and *Ep. ad Rom. Inch.Exp.* 12 (= *PL* xxxv.2096). That is was also being written is confirmed by *In Psalm.* 118.32.8 (acrostic psalms: they must have been a visual phenomenon). See further W. M. Green in *Semitic and Oriental Studies: A Volume Presented to William Popper* (U. of Calif. Publications in Semitic Philology xi) (Berkeley, 1951), 179–190; Röllig 297–298.

25. J.-B. Chabot, *Recueil des inscriptions libyques* i (Paris, 1940–41). There are additional texts in L. Galland et al., *Inscriptions antiques du Maroc* (Paris, 1966). For further bibliography see O. Rössler in Neumann & Untermann 267–284.

26. Millar, *JRS* lviii (1968), 129.

27. Millar 133, referring to the more than 30,000 known Latin inscriptions of the region.

In Spain the language history of the third to first centuries B.C. is complicated by the presence of Celtiberian, Lusitanian and South Lusitanian as well as Iberian, Punic, Greek and Latin.[28] Of the four epigraphically attested languages that were indigenous to the peninsula, three at least were in written use under the Romans (the South Lusitanian inscriptions all appear to be pre-Roman).[29] In fact Lusitanian and perhaps Celtiberian began to be used for inscriptions only after the Romans arrived. As for how long these two languages and Iberian went on being written under Roman power, clear facts are few. It appears that Celtiberian continued to be written down to Augustus' time,[30] and the same has been suggested for Iberian.[31] In none of these languages, however, are the surviving inscriptions at all numerous, and with the usual reservations we may suppose that none of the indigenous languages had ever been the vehicle of an extensive written culture. It is significant that the Lusitanian inscriptions are all in the Latin alphabet. In any case writing in all these indigenous languages put together was at no time in epigraphical use in more than one-third of the Iberian peninsula.

It was very probably the indigenous Spanish elites which led the movement away from the local languages to bilingualism and to the exclusive use of Latin. The conversion to the mass use of spoken Latin had only taken place in a few areas by the time Strabo wrote, to judge from what he says about the Turdetanians.[32] The colonization sponsored by Caesar and Augustus, coming on top of other Romanizing influences, must have driven the indigenous languages out of a number of areas. Not surprisingly, however, a countryman from the

28. For the areas in which the first four of these languages were used see J. Untermann in Neumann & Untermann, figs. 3 and 4, or in *ANRW* ii.29.2 (1983), map opposite 808.

29. U. Schmoll, *Die südlusitanischen Inschriften* (Wiesbaden, 1961); Untermann in Neumann & Untermann 6–7.

30. At any rate a group of Celtiberian inscriptions from Villastar (near Teruel) includes a graffito of Verg. *Aen.* ii.268–269 in an identical or very similar hand: see M. Gómez-Moreno, *Misceláneas* (Madrid, 1949), 207, 326–330; A. Tovar, *Emerita* xxvii (1959), 349–65; Untermann 10–11.

31. Cf. Untermann 7. Scholars have sometimes relied on insufficient evidence in their desire to show the persistence of the local languages. None of the inscriptions cited by A. García y Bellido in *ANRW* i.1 (1972), 485, can be shown to be as late as the second half of the second century A.D.

32. iii.151: the Turdetanians, and "especially those near the Baetis," have been Romanized and do not even remember their own language (διάλεκτος). However it is possible that Strabo, like Velleius in the case of Pannonia, was ignoring the lower orders.

region of Celtiberian Termes still, during the reign of Tiberius, spoke the local language.[33] After this we hear no more from the literary sources about local languages in those regions which Rome had conquered in the second century B.C., and they may well have died out in the late first or second century A.D.[34] The far north probably took longer. A reference by the younger Seneca to Cantabrian words[35] may mean less here than the fact that under Vespasian a town on the north coast was founded with an old Celtic termination: Flaviobriga.[36] And in this general region dwelt the one Spanish people, the Vascones, who throughout antiquity remained mainly speakers of their indigenous language.

The chronology of the demise of Gallic is also difficult. Written Gallic had some, but apparently not much, currency prior to the Roman conquest;[37] most of the surviving Gallic inscriptions were written afterwards. They are not numerous: according to a recent estimate, there exist about sixty from Narbonensis and twenty from Comata, apart from coin legends.[38] Latin must have made some headway in Gallia Comata from Caesar's time onwards,[39] but in the late Republic

33. At least while being tortured by the Roman authorities: Tac. *Ann.* iv.45 (25 A.D.).

34. Fronto's reference to the "Hiberos" who speak in their own language (i.303 Haines) is no help; it probably refers to the Iberians of the Caucasus, as the word normally does in prose. García y Bellido, in *ANRW* i.1 (1972), 489–490, also cites the fifth-century tract *De similitudine carnis peccati* (*PL* Suppl. i.55), but there is no need to identify the barbarous languages which it alludes to with those of Spain; they were probably Gothic dialects.

35. *Ad Helviam* 7.9.

36. Cf. García y Bellido 478.

37. The earliest text, written, as the Celtic inscriptions of Narbonensis always were, in the Greek alphabet, may go back to the third century B.C.; J. Whatmough, *The Dialects of Ancient Gaul* (Cambridge, Mass., 1970), no. 76.

38. K. H. Schmidt in Neumann & Untermann, *Die Sprachen im römischen Reich* 24. For some new Celtic graffiti from La Graufesenque see R. Marichal, *CRAI* 1981, 244–272. There is also a new *Recueil des inscriptions gauloises*, ed. P.-M. Duval et al. (= *Gallia* Suppl. xlv) (1985). The longest Celtic inscription now known is the curse-tablet of about 100 A.D. from near La Graufesenque published by M. Lejeune et al., *Etudes celtiques* xxii (1985), 95–177 (some 160 words are preserved). In Gaul it is especially clear, because of mixed Celtic-Latin inscriptions (see above, p. 176 n.4), that some who could write Gallic were also at least partially literate in Latin. For the continued use of Iberian down to the time of Augustus in the region between Montpellier and the Pyrenees see G. Barruol in D. M. Pippidi (ed.), *Assimilation et résistance à la culture gréco-romaine dans le monde ancien* (Paris & Bucharest, 1976), 403.

39. Indeed even earlier. Caesar used Greek as a code to keep a letter secret from

Gallic apparently survived even in as cosmopolitan a city as Massilia.[40] It was probably to the survival of the independent language that Irenaeus of Lyons referred, towards the end of the second century, when he wrote that, living among the Gauls, he was generally busy with a "barbarous dialect."[41] That it was not simply the language of peasants is confirmed by the text of Ulpian which has already been cited concerning the documents needed to establish trusts. There is some epigraphical evidence throughout the principate, the last item being a vase inscription which may be as late as the fourth century. There can be no doubt that Gallic continued to be spoken fairly widely, especially among poor people in the countryside, until late antiquity.[42]

No written word of the Celtic language has survived from Roman Britain, and those of its inhabitants who spoke only Celtic must have been profoundly illiterate. Latin quickly made some advances into the native upper class and among other town-dwellers. It is likely, however, that the great majority of the population continued to speak Celtic dialects, perhaps until the spread of Christianity.[43] It is certainly hard to think that many indigenous country-dwellers can have learned more than a smattering of Latin at any time under the Roman Empire.

All or most of the other provinces of the western Empire were, like Britain, without writing before Roman influence began to be felt, and their populations never came to make much written use of their local languages. How much the inhabitants continued to speak these languages is in every case hard to tell. The quantity of Latin inscriptions emanating from Dalmatia and even from Pannonia is impressive,[44]

---

the relatively remote Nervii (*BG* v.48.4), evidently because he thought that some of them knew or might know how to read Latin.

40. Varro, cited by Jerome *Comm. in Gal.* ii praef. (*PL* xxvi.380b); Isid. *Etym.* xv.1.63.

41. *Contra haeres.* i praef.3. In the view of A. Momigliano (*ASNSP* ser.3 xii [1982], 1107 n.3 = *Settimo contributo alla storia degli studi classici e del mondo antico* [Rome, 1984], 465 n.3), he may have been referring to the local variety of Latin; but the word διάλεκτος seems normally to refer to a distinct language (cf., e.g., Strabo iii.151, xiv.662) or to a major dialect of Greek.

42. Cf. J. Whatmough, *HSCPh* lv (1944), 71 = *The Dialects of Ancient Gaul* 71; Schmidt in Neumann & Untermann, *Die Sprachen im römischen Reich* 37; J. Herman in *ANRW* ii.29.2 (1983), 1045–48 (emphasizing the limitations of our knowledge). The Treveri spoke Gallic, according to Jerome *Comm. in Gal.* ii praef. (*PL* xxvi.382c).

43. Cf. C. C. Smith in *ANRW* ii.29.2 (1983), 945–946.

44. Cf. below, p. 268.

but they result in part from the military occupation, and in general they are inherently uninformative about the mass of the population. Velleius Paterculus wrote that as early as 6 A.D. all the Pannonians knew Latin and many of them were literate. (He does not say that they had forgotten their own language.)[45] He himself had served in Pannonia, but nonetheless his comments are not to be taken literally—he must be referring to the kind of Pannonian with whom a Roman officer of senatorial rank might deal, and whom Roman officials sometimes had brought up in a Roman fashion.[46] The judgement of a linguist is that practically all the Alpine and Danubian provinces had speakers of the indigenous languages in them throughout antiquity,[47] and in Pannonia, Dalmatia, and Moesia they were probably in the majority. Specific indications are few indeed,[48] but a careful study of Moesia Superior has shown that knowledge of Latin was limited in the main to specific social groups: municipal notables, the legions, and administrative personnel.[49]

As for Dacia, after the Roman conquest it was heavily settled by people from outside the province. The native language has left practically no epigraphical traces,[50] as might be expected, but something is known of it through a series of glosses in classical writers.[51] Presumably many of those Dacians who survived the conquest went on speaking it[52] in a province where a great deal of Latin was also spoken.

We can summarize the linguistic pattern of the western provinces as

45. ii.110.5: "in omnibus autem Pannoniis non disciplinae tantummodo, sed linguae quoque notitia Romanae, plerisque etiam litterarum usus." Presumably he is thinking of *litterarum usus* in Latin.

46. Cf. A. Mócsy in *Rome and Her Northern Provinces. Papers Presented to Sheppard Frere* (Gloucester, 1983), 171–172. It is no doubt true that Velleius made the rebellion which he was describing seem more formidable by exaggerating the abilities of the Pannonians (Mócsy 169).

47. Cf. Untermann in Neumann & Untermann 57.

48. "The extremely large number of personal names epigraphically recorded . . . give a clear indication" that Celtic continued to be understood everywhere in Noricum, according to G. Alföldy, *Noricum* (London, 1974), 134. But the inscriptions are of course in Latin, and the inference is not at all certain.

49. A. Mócsy, *Gesellschaft und Romanisation in der römischen Provinz Moesia Superior* (Amsterdam, 1970), 231–232.

50. A single obscure inscription is cited: V. I. Georgiev in *ANRW* ii.29.2 (1983), 1181.

51. Georgiev 1179–80.

52. Whether there is really a Dacian substratum in Rumanian (cf. Georgiev 1180–81) I cannot judge.

follows: practically everywhere the men of property soon learned Latin, and indeed came to participate in the shared culture of the Latin world; many others, including artisans (we shall encounter some further evidence later on), eventually learned Latin. Some regions became Latinized throughout their social hierarchies. However, on most occasions when we get any indication of the language habits of the mass of the population, we see the indigenous tongues persisting even many centuries after the establishment of Roman power.

We are generally somewhat better informed about language use in the huge semi-Hellenized areas of the eastern Empire, which included all or part of the following provinces: Moesia, Thrace, the provinces of Asia Minor—that is, Asia, Bithynia-Pontus, Galatia, Lycia-Pamphylia, Cappadocia, Cilicia—Syria, Judaea, Arabia and Egypt. The linguistic fragmentation of this region is illustrated in the passage of the Acts of the Apostles in which a miracle is necessary for Jews from all over the world to be able to understand the Galilaeans.[53] The catalogue of the different groups runs as follows: Parthians, Medes, Elamites, those who live in Mesopotamia, Judaea, Cappadocia, Pontus, Asia, Phrygia, Pamphylia, Egypt and the parts of Africa near Cyrene, Romans, Cretans and Arabs. These are the populations which the writer believes to speak divers languages other than Aramaic.[54]

The main language spoken in the Balkan region of the eastern provinces, besides Latin and Greek, was Thracian.[55] The handful of its surviving inscriptions date from the fifth or fourth centuries B.C.,[56] and it is very unlikely that it was a written language in the Roman period. However, though the specific evidence is slight,[57] it is probable that it survived as a quite widely spoken language in the Roman province.

With regard to Asia Minor, Strabo seems to say that Mysia and

53. Acts ii.5–11.

54. Unfortunately, it is not a catalogue of languages. The basic bibliography concerning the epigraphical remains of the languages of the eastern Empire is now listed in F. Bérard et al., *Guide de l'épigraphiste* (Paris, 1986).

55. There are unsolved problems here. What language, for instance, was spoken by the Paeonians in Macedonia? Cf. R. Katičić in Neumann & Untermann, *Die Sprachen im römischen Reich* 108.

56. Georgiev in *ANRW* ii.29.2 (1983), 1159–63.

57. Greg.Nyss. *Contra Eunom.* ii.406 (i.344 Jaeger) is not quite as rhetorical or useless on this point as John Chrys. in *PG* lxiii.501. The survival of Thracian is discussed in detail by A. Besevliev, *Untersuchungen über die Personennamen bei den Thrakern* (Amsterdam, 1970), 72–77.

perhaps other parts of the northwest had become Greek-speaking by his time,[58] and that there was now no trace of Lydian,[59] remarks which are open to the usual suspicions of class bias. On the other hand he appears to speak of Carian as a living language.[60] Elsewhere many of the descendants of the non-Greek population retained their own languages. Under the Romans people sometimes wrote Phrygian, Pisidian, and Galatian Celtic, as well as speaking these languages; and others sometimes spoke Lycaonian, Cappadocian, and probably other languages too. Whether such populations also knew Greek is sometimes unclear. Phrygian, for example, is known from some 110 inscriptions of the second to fourth centuries—but they are written in Greek script.[61] Their geographical range is very considerable.[62] Some people probably went on speaking Phrygian as their main and even exclusive language throughout antiquity.[63] For the language of the Pisidians, immediately to the south, the evidence of survival is even more slender: it consists of 16 inscriptions, written in Greek script, from a single minor site.[64] But even this group of texts, minuscule in relation to the corpus of Greek inscriptions of Pisidia, suggests that Pisidian was a living spoken language at least in a small area.

Galatian Celtic is also attested as a written language, for Lucian claims that written questions in Celtic were put to the prophet Alexander of Abonuteichos in the latter's home town in Pontus.[65] It probably continued to be a spoken language in Galatia itself. Lycaonian

58. xii.565. For some possible counterevidence (concerning Mysia in the fifth century A.D.) see K. Holl, *Hermes* xliii (1908), 241–242.

59. xiii.631.

60. xiii.663 beginning (but some of the discussion at 662 is antiquarian and irrelevant to real conditions).

61. See O. Haas, *Die phrygischen Sprachdenkmäler* (Sofia, 1966); and for the longest and possibly earliest (first century A.D.?) neo-Phrygian text see C. Brixhe & G. Neumann, *Kadmos* xxiv (1985), 161–184.

62. The area can be described as a pentagonal one bound by Dorylaeum, the Salt Lake (Tuz Gölü), Iconium, the Pisidian Lakes, and Cotyaeium (G. Neumann in Neumann & Untermann, *Die Sprachen im römischen Reich* 174).

63. It is still a spoken language in Socrates *Hist.Eccl.* v.23.

64. They are dated by means of the Greek script. See W. M. Ramsay, *Revue des Universités du Midi* i (1895), 353–362; also J. Friedrich, *Kleinasiatische Sprachdenkmäler* (Berlin, 1932), 142–143; L. Zgusta, *Archiv Orientální* xxxi (1963), 470–482; Neumann 176. Pisidian had formerly been among the languages used further southwest, at Cibyra: Strabo xiii.631.

65. Luc. *Alex.* 51; cf. Paus. x.36.1; Jerome *Comm. in Gal.* ii praef. (*PL* xxvi.382c) (with J. Sofer, *Wiener Studien* lv [1937], 148–158).

is mentioned in Acts, and the allusion is all the more striking since it concerns the Augustan colony of Lystra; nor is it to be explained away as a reference to a local dialect of Greek.[66] This evidence concerns the town population, and in the countryside the local language must have lasted longer still.[67] Many of the Cappadocians too probably continued to be ignorant of Greek, especially as their cities were widely scattered; though not until a sermon of Basil of Caesarea in the 370s do we find Cappadocian mentioned as a living language.[68]

Other regions of Asia Minor where the evidence is even more uncertain may have continued to harbour spoken local languages without leaving any positive sign in the literary or epigraphical sources. It is very unlikely that the northern territories of Bithynia, Paphlagonia and Pontus, which were not heavily urbanized, ever came near to completing the transition to Greek. And in Commagene, whatever we may think of Lucian of Samosata's remark that as a youth he spoke with a "barbarian voice,"[69] very many must have spoken only a dialect of Aramaic.

In Syria, Judaea and Arabia we encounter an extremely variegated linguistic situation, in which, however, Greek occupies a fairly definable place. It is one of the languages of provincial and city government. It is the language of immigrants and their descendants, and of partially Hellenized social and commercial elites, whose members, together with their dependents, may have a stronger or weaker grasp of it while they simultaneously hold on to one or more local languages. It is not the language of the streets except in a few places, and it is not the language of the ordinary villager. Nonetheless the degree of linguistic Hellenization is often hard to judge. The inscriptions, for instance, here as elsewhere, can sometimes give an exaggerated

---

66. Neumann 179 attempts to interpret Acts xiv.11 in this manner, on the a priori grounds that Lystra was fully Hellenized. He cites no parallel for such a use of an adverb like λυκαονιστί. For the late-antique survival of Lycaonian see Holl, *Hermes* xliii (1908), 243–246.

67. Cf. A. H. M. Jones, *The Greek City from Alexander to Justinian* (Oxford, 1940), 289. For the survival of Isaurian see Holl 243.

68. Even he is not explicit: Basil *De spiritu sancto* 74 (*PG* xxxii.208). Cf. Greg. Nyss. *Contra Eunom.* ii.406 (i.344 Jaeger); also Holl 247.

69. *Bis Acc.* 27. This is taken by R. Schmitt, in Neumann & Untermann, *Die Sprachen im römischen Reich* 200, to refer to Aramaic. However *De merc.cond.* 24 and *Pseudolog.* 1 tell somewhat against this interpretation. C. P. Jones, *Culture and Society in Lucian* (Cambridge, Mass., 1986), 7, holds that his barbaric voice was probably a matter of accent and vocabulary.

impression: the city inscriptions from southeastern Syria (Batanaea, Trachonitis, and Auranitis) are Greek, but the local procurators who were used to doing business in Greek apparently still needed an interpreter.[70] The other main languages to be encountered in these provinces were Aramaic, Phoenician, Syriac, Palmyrene, Safaitic, Hebrew, and Nabataean.

In a large area of the eventual provinces of Syria and Judaea, Greek was commonly to be heard. No great fuss is made in the New Testament about the transition backwards and forwards between Aramaic and Greek, because the latter, besides being the language of the texts themselves, is a standard feature of Judaean life. This is also evident from Josephus.[71] However Aramaic was the language of ordinary speech for the mass of the population. Hence when one of the inhabitants asks a Roman officer a question, the latter replies in surprise, "Do you know Greek?"[72] He expected to hear Aramaic around him most of the time. As to how many Aramaic-speakers there were who knew little or no Greek, there can of course be no precision; one might guess that prolonged periods of Seleucid, Ptolemaic and Roman power had the effect of making Greek widely known in the towns and not much in the countryside; but that is conjecture.

There were other, more localized languages. Phoenician still lived on in some of the coastal cities, with inscriptions down to the first century B.C. and literary allusions until the second century A.D.[73] It may be that most Phoenician-speakers also knew some Greek.

That was almost certainly not the case with Syriac, an offshoot of Aramaic, which first emerged as a written language around Edessa, east of the Euphrates, and came into written use on the other side of the river only to a very limited extent during the period under con-

---

70. A. H. M. Jones, *The Greek City from Alexander to Justinian* (Oxford, 1940), 290, arguing from *IGRR* iii.1191 (from Saccaeae).

71. When he remarks (*AJ* xx.264), seeking to excuse his own Greek, that "our people do not approve those who have learned thoroughly the languages of many nations . . . because they consider that it is a skill commonplace among the free-born and possessed even by those slaves who wish to do so." For a more detailed discussion see E. Schürer, *The History of the Jewish People in the Age of Christ* rev. ed. G. Vermes et al., ii (Edinburgh, 1979), 74–80.

72. Acts xxi.37.

73. The last literary references are Orig. *Contra Cels.* 3.6, Lucian *Alex.* 13; but neither is evidence for a living language. Coin legends continue until the last decade of the second century A.D. Cf. Schmitt in Neumann & Untermann, *Die Sprachen im römischen Reich* 200–201.

sideration here.[74] One papyrus and three inscriptions survive from the second and third centuries,[75] while numerous Greek texts were being produced. Nevertheless the predominant oral language was undoubtedly the indigenous one, especially but not exclusively in the countryside.

The district of Palmyra also had its own written form of Aramaic, attested in more than 2,000 inscriptions—a remarkable concentration which indicates the city's wealth as well as its relative cultural independence. The dates of these inscriptions extend from 44/43 B.C. to 274/275 A.D. The Palmyrene dialect must have been the numerically dominant spoken language of the city and its immediate region.[76] However the unusual number of bilingual inscriptions in the local language and in Greek points to a high degree of bilingualism at least in the more prosperous stratum of the population; and in the bilingual texts from after 100 A.D. Greek seems to gain importance at the expense of Palmyrene.[77]

The most extraordinary epigraphical corpus of this entire area of the Roman Empire is, however, made up of the Safaitic inscriptions of southwestern Syria (Syria as it is defined now) and northern Jordan. Out of the desert have come over 12,000 rock-cut Safaitic graffiti, more than have been read at Pompeii. They were apparently the work of a nomadic population on the fringe of Roman power; though a precise chronology is lacking, their general period appears to be from the first to the fourth century A.D.[78] Their number is so large that it raises important questions about ancient literacy in general.[79] At all

74. See H. J. W. Drijvers, *Old-Syriac (Edessean) Inscriptions* (Leiden, 1972), XI; Schmitt 201–202.

75. Drijvers XI.

76. On Palmyrene see Schmitt 202–203, with bibliography. The inscriptions are collected in J. Cantineau et al. (eds.), *Inventaire des inscriptions de Palmyre* (Beirut & Damascus, 1930–1975).

77. J. Cantineau, *Grammaire du palmyrénien épigraphique* (Cairo, 1935), 5; Schmitt 203.

78. See esp. F. V. Winnett, *Safaitic Inscriptions from Jordan* (Toronto, 1957); F. V. Winnett & G. L. Harding, *Inscriptions from Fifty Safaitic Cairns* (Toronto, 1978); cf. also Schmitt 204–205.

79. This material is to be compared with the 13,000 Thamudic inscriptions known from the desert area further south, most of them from northwestern Arabia (see E. Littmann, *Thamūd und Ṣafā. Studien zur altnordarabischen Inschriftenkunde* [Leipzig, 1940], 1–92; A. van den Branden, *Les inscriptions thamoudéennes* [Louvain, 1950]; etc.). It also appears that precisely because of the nomadic character of the peoples in question, graffiti acquired among them a surprisingly wide range of

events, here is another provincial population which probably had no more than weak linguistic contact with the dominant culture.

Naturally the Nabataeans retained their own language after they became Roman provincials in 106,[80] though there is in fact some evidence for their use of both Aramaic and Greek.[81]

In Egypt Greek had long been the language of the government and of its complex administrative machine as well as that of most of the immigrants. In spite of the mass of documentary papyri, there is no way of measuring how far a speaking knowledge of Greek had penetrated to the Egyptian population itself. Spoken demotic carried over from the Ptolemaic to the Roman period without the slightest difficulty, and at least in the villages most Egyptians spoke their own language and had little or no reason to learn any Greek.[82] The cultural abyss between Greek and non-Greek was as large as it was anywhere in the Empire. On the other hand it is commonplace under the principate for people with Egyptian names to be involved in transactions with Greeks. In other words, while the majority of Egyptians were probably unable to understand Greek, a considerable number had some opportunity and motive to acquire the rudiments.

Thus in the eastern Empire too, while the common language of the elite had thoroughly conquered some whole regions and was to be heard in every city, the local languages showed great survival power throughout the period, so that in many regions Greek was not the predominant language of the streets or fields. In a number of provinces knowledge of it is likely to have been confined to a minority of the population.

City and Country

In the romance *Daphnis and Chloe* the hero and heroine are foundlings who grow up in the countryside as the children of a goatherd

---

functions. Circumstances encouraged them to leave written messages in order to maintain contact with each other and to establish rights to wells and camping sites.

80. On Nabataean see J. Cantineau, *Le nabatéen* i–ii (Paris, 1930–1932) (who points out, i.12, that bilingual Nabataean-Greek inscriptions are few—by contrast with Palmyrene-Greek bilinguals—and infers that Greek was not much understood by Nabataeans); Schmitt in Neumann & Untermann, *Die Sprachen im römischen Reich* 205–208.

81. On the "archive" of the Jewish woman Babatha, which contained documents in all three languages, see now G. W. Bowersock, *Roman Arabia* (Cambridge, Mass., 1983), 75–79, 85–89.

82. Cf. H. C. Youtie, *ZPE* xvii (1975), 204.

and a shepherd. In the ordinary way such children, even in Greece, do not learn letters, as the author implicitly recognizes. But since they are really of distinguished birth and their foster-fathers Lamon and Dryas suspect the fact, these two "educated them in letters," and the children "were brought up in a more delicate manner."[83] An educated Greek such as Longus cannot easily make his hero or even heroine illiterate.

The literary association of illiteracy with rusticity was old and trite,[84] but certainly based on fact. It would help us greatly if we knew what proportion of the Roman population lived within reach of the amenities of towns, since those who did not were usually without schools and in the main without much occasion to use the written word. What requires attention here is the degree to which the population lived in or near places large and prosperous enough to afford teachers. There is some realistic possibility that one day we may be able to answer this question more clearly,[85] but at present we still know quite little. Widely differing opinions have been expressed. Beloch, whose judgement still demands consideration, held that as far as Greece was concerned, the inhabitants were generally concentrated in the towns; he compared it with Sicily as it is described in the census of 1871, according to which 83% of the population lived in centres with 2,000 inhabitants or more (though most of them remained illiterate).[86] More recent writers tend to see the overall pattern of Roman settlement as very much more rural.[87]

Classical Greece and Italy were full of cities, in the sense of *poleis,* and the Romans notoriously brought urbanization of this kind to those conquered provincial lands in the west which had not already

83. i.8.

84. See above, p. 17.

85. The distribution of the population of the Roman Empire between towns, the immediate periphery of towns, villages and outlying countryside will eventually require a new study of a synthetic character. With regard to most regions it will be based largely on surface-survey archaeology, a kind of study which has at last gained widespread popularity but, as usually put into effect, still involves very high levels of conjecture (for an important warning see R. Hope-Simpson, *JFA* xi [1984], 115–117).

86. J. Beloch, *Die Bevölkerung der griechisch-römischen Welt* (Leipzig, 1886), 476.

87. Such now-conventional views may need some modification in view of recent work on towns in the Celtic and Iberian regions, but the central fact about the Roman Empire is not in doubt. See in general R. P. Duncan-Jones, *The Economy of the Roman Empire: Quantitative Studies* (Cambridge, 1974), 260. To what extent the peasants in Roman Italy lived on their land, in villages or in towns is discussed by P. D. A. Garnsey, *PCPhS* n.s. xxv (1979), 1–25. See also M. W. Frederiksen in P. Zanker (ed.), *Hellenismus in Mittelitalien* (Göttingen, 1976), 342–343.

come under Greek or Phoenician and Punic influence. Furthermore, in many areas a fundamental need, security, made it sensible to live in a town or a substantial village rather than in the open countryside, and the countryside did not necessarily grow safe when wars became rare.[88] The considerable distances which separated towns in large areas of the western provinces[89] do not by themselves establish that most people lived outside towns, for many outlying areas may have been very sparsely populated.

There is on the other hand some clear evidence that in some regions, at least, the pattern was radically different from that of Sicily in 1871. Centuriation (establishment of standardized rectangular land-divisions) often extended large distances from the towns, and while it is conceivable that the outer reaches of centuriated land were sometimes populated thinly or not at all, the system must in the main have been applied to land on which people were expected to live. Now at Parma, for example, land was centuriated up to at least twenty kilometres away from the city, and some 55% of the centuriated land lay more than eight kilometres from the centre;[90] at Emerita some of it lay as much as forty kilometres from the city.[91] Furthermore, as has been pointed out for region after region, in Italy and elsewhere, a very common pattern of settlement was by small villages or *vici*, which tended to leave a large part of the population far from any city.[92]

Prolonged peace under Roman rule may gradually have led people away from towns, in both west and east. In the eastern half of the Empire there is no detectable regularity about the proportion of the inhabitants who lived away from the towns, or rather none has yet been detected and described.[93] Elis, for instance, possessed a large territory containing numerous small settlements. The cities of the

88. On the dangers of country life cf. B. D. Shaw, *P & P* cv (1984), 3–52.

89. For Gaul, T. Bekker-Nielsen, *Bydannelse i det romerske Gallien* (Arhus, 1984), 89–90; for Britain see I. Hodder in W. Rodwell & T. Rowley (eds.), *The "Small Towns" of Roman Britain* (Oxford, 1975), 67–74. G. C. Picard, in *ANRW* ii.3 (1975), 98–111, shows indirectly how little is still known about the balance of population between town and country in the Gallic and African provinces.

90. I follow P. L. Tozzi, *Saggi di topografia antica* (Florence, 1974), pl. XVa, and treat the centuriated area as 450 sq kms (cf. Tozzi 46). Cf. Garnsey 13–14.

91. See the map given by J. G. Gorges in P. A. Fevrier & P. Leveau (eds.), *Villes et campagnes dans l'Empire romain* (Aix-en-Provence, 1982), 106.

92. For this pattern in Italy see Garnsey 7.

93. For the classical period of Greece see above, pp. 65–66.

Argolid, on the other hand, were close together; the same was true in some coastal areas of western Asia Minor. The epigraphy and topography of the colonies of Pisidia suggest that plenty of the inhabitants of their *territoria* lived fifteen or twenty kilometres from town.[94] And some eastern cities had far larger territories than these.

The accessibility of urban amenities depended not only on the physical distribution of the population but on psychological factors. The reluctance of country-people to make journeys into cities, visible through the perhaps somewhat distorting vision of Dio Chrysostom in his *Euboean Discourse,* may also have helped to cut their children off from schooling.[95]

Practical Inconveniences for the Writer and Reader

Papyrus or potsherd, wall-plaster or wax-covered wooden tablet, does it matter for the present enquiry what the Romans wrote on, or what they wrote with?[96] Only if a shortage of suitable materials made it additionally difficult to learn to read and write or to make use of writing. But that may indeed have been the case.[97]

Using and storing such writing materials as ostraca and wooden tablets was obviously tiresome and inconvenient by modern standards. But even an ostracon has advantages: durability and cheapness. And in the case of wooden tablets, we may doubt whether the Romans felt the disadvantages strongly, since even people who could certainly have afforded papyrus routinely used waxed tablets for many

94. I infer this mainly from the account of B. M. Levick, *Roman Colonies in Southern Asia Minor* (Oxford, 1967), 42–55.

95. For stress, perhaps somewhat exaggerated, on the psychological "non-relationship of town and village" in classical Syria, see P. Brown in D. M. Pippidi (ed.), *Assimilation et résistance à la culture gréco-romaine dans le monde ancien* (Paris & Bucharest, 1976), 214.

96. On the range of Roman writing materials there is a sizeable bibliography which has little to say about the practical or social implications of the physical facts. Most useful are J. Marquardt, *Das Privatleben der Römer* (2d ed., Leipzig, 1886), 800–823; W. Schubart, *Das Buch bei den Griechen und Römern* (2d ed., Berlin & Leipzig, 1921), 1–35; G. Pugliese Carratelli in *Pompeiana. Raccolta di studi per il secondo centenario degli scavi di Pompei* (Naples, 1950), 266–278; L. Wenger, *Die Quellen des römischen Rechts* (Vienna, 1953), 54–102; I. Bilkei, *Alba Regia* xviii (1980), 61–90; A. K. Bowman & J. D. Thomas, *Vindolanda: The Latin Writing-Tablets* (London, 1983), 32. Ink, incidentally, seems to have been easy to make: Bilkei 68.

97. The modern writer's and reader's greatest material advantages are of course those mentioned before, printing-presses and eye-glasses.

purposes.[98] Furthermore, waxed tablets could easily be reused.[99] Small tablets were constantly used for everyday purposes such as school exercises, letters and business documents.[100] They allowed one to write up to about fifty words a side,[101] and a multiple set of tablets, as many as ten in a codex form, was commonly used.[102] Except in a few unusually arid regions of the Empire, the material must normally have been available without much difficulty. Records for official storage were sometimes, so it appears, entered in special large-format codices.[103] But the convenient material for some purposes—long letters, and books of all kinds—was papyrus.

Papyrus was extensively used by the elite,[104] and all well-to-do Romans were familiar with it.[105] But in spite of some assertions to the

98. Roman wills were written on tablets (*Dig.* xxix.3, etc.); Caesar, for example, followed this practice (Suet. *DJ* 83).

99. According to H. Erman, *Mélanges [Jules] Nicole* (Geneva, 1905), 119–124, they were also more secure than papyrus texts.

100. See E. Sachers in *RE* (1932) s.v. "tabula," cols. 1881–86; L. Bove in *Atti del XVII Congresso internazionale di papirologia* (Naples, 1984), iii. 1189–93. For the numerous wooden tablets found in Britain, often illegible and consequently not well known, see Bowman & Thomas, *Vindolanda* 34–35.

101. See, e.g., *FIRA* iii no. 47. But a text twice this length could be accommodated.

102. Cf. G.E.M. de Ste. Croix in A. C. Littleton & B. S. Yamey, *Studies in the History of Accounting* (Homewood, Ill., 1956), 69 n.18. Martial xiv.4 mentions a quintuple tablet. A codex made up of nine tablets (ten originally) is illustrated by H. Widmann, *Archiv für Geschichte des Buchwesens* viii (1967), 587. For an eight-tablet codex from Herculaneum see Pugliese Carratelli in *Pompeiana*, 270–273 and fig. 26. A four-tablet codex appears in the famous "poetess" fresco from Pompeii: L. Curtius, *Die Wandmalerei Pompejis* (Cologne, 1929), pl. XI. For further examples see Bilkei, *Alba Regia* xviii (1980), 63–64. See Figures 4 and 5.

103. For census records (see the Altar of Domitius Ahenobarbus, above, p. 174 n.119) and for some official accounts (see Figure 6). For one or more large-format tablets from Herculaneum (27.5 × 23.5 cms) see A. Maiuri, *Par.Pass.* i (1946), 379.

104. Letters from magistrates to the Senate on *charta:* Suet. *DJ* 56. Papyrus was probably used for long and polished letters of the kind which were published in Cicero's correspondence (cf. Tyrrell & Purser's comments, vol. i [2d ed.], pp. 47–48; D. R. Shackleton Bailey, *Cicero's Letters to Atticus* i pp. 59–60). Pliny routinely wrote his letters on papyrus: *Ep.* iii.14.6, viii.15.2 (but there may also be a hint in the latter passage that some people would regard *charta* as a serious expense). Letters written between Tomi and Rome might be on papyrus (Ov. *Trist.* iv.7.7, v.13.30; cf. *Heroid.* xvii.20). For a serious papyrus shortage under Tiberius see Plin. *NH* xiii.89.

105. The elder Pliny errs in saying that rolls never exceeded twenty sheets (*NH* xiii.77; cf. E. G. Turner, *Greek Papyri. An Introduction* [Oxford, 1968], 4), but he is defended by T. C. Skeat, *ZPE* xlv (1982), 169–175, esp. 172. (The standard length was twenty sheets, totalling 320 to 360 cms.)

contrary it must have been quite expensive for most people's purses,[106] certainly outside Egypt, which remained the main source of supply. The price at Tebtunis in the period 45–49 seems normally to have been four drachmas a roll, and a single sheet might cost two obols— this at a time when skilled labourers earned about six obols a day, unskilled three. The price is analogous to one of, say, thirty to thirty-five dollars for a sheet of paper today.[107] The real price of papyrus would have been much higher in Greece or Italy, not to mention Spain or Britain, than in Egypt. It was not in most parts of the Empire a standard everyday material for ordinary citizens.[108] The use of parchment, spreading notably from the first century B.C. onwards,[109] does not seem to have improved matters radically. Hence the bland assumption of scholars that social class made virtually no difference to one's ability to find writing materials is ill-founded. And actual finished books written on papyrus were very expensive for most of the inhabitants of the Roman Empire.

Thus really convenient writing materials cannot have been as casu-

106. Papyrus was sometimes reused, but perhaps not often enough (given that the process of erasing a text was easy: Erman, *Mélanges Nicole* 119–121; M. Norsa, *Scrittura letteraria greca dal secolo IV a.C. all'VIII d.C.* [Florence, 1939], 23 n.2) to prove anything much about its value. However, it must be significant that, as most classical scholars know, the British Museum text of Aristotle's *Athenaion Politeia* was written on the back of some farm accounts; this was "late in the first or very early in the second century A.D.," according to P. J. Rhodes, comm. p. 4. Parallels for this are in fact reasonably plentiful: see Schubart, *Das Buch*, 163–164, 189. The attempt of N. Lewis (*Papyrus in Classical Antiquity* [Oxford, 1974], 129–134; cf. in similar vein T. C. Skeat in *Cambridge History of the Bible* ii [Cambridge, 1969], 59) to show that "in social milieux more elevated than that of a prosperous Egyptian villager the purchase of papyrus is not likely to have been regarded as an expenditure of any consequence" (133–134) is exaggerated and takes no account of the presumable differences between prices in Egypt and on the far side of the Mediterranean. Lewis 132 gives a valuable conspectus of the evidence.

107. Tebtunis: A. E. R. Boak, *Papyri from Tebtunis* i (= *P.Mich.* ii) (Ann Arbor, 1933), p. 98. At the same rate a single sheet might cost two obols: *P.Oxy.* xiv.1654. Wages: A. C. Johnson in *ESAR* ii (1936), 306–307.

108. It is probably a common notion that papyrus "came first in importance among ancient writing materials" until parchment took over (de Ste. Croix, *History of Accounting* 68), but this is a mistake which comes from an unduly Egyptian, or perhaps an unduly literary, view of antiquity. Lewis 90 also gives the wrong impression by describing papyrus as "the universal writing material." It would be hard to name any non-literary purpose for which papyrus was certainly the normal writing material in most of the Roman Empire.

109. Cf. de Ste. Croix 71, Skeat in *Cambridge History of the Bible* ii.66.

ally omnipresent as they are in our lives. Perhaps few of those Romans who had regular cause to write were inhibited by the cost or availability of materials. If literacy had shown any tendency to become more general, the difficulties might have been severe, though the production of wooden tablets and ostraca could have been increased. What remained very expensive for ordinary people were the materials, papyrus and parchment, which were practically necessary for the writing of any long text.

The Functions of Writing

Thus the Roman Empire was in some ways markedly unfavourable to the spread of Greek and Latin literacy and to the functioning of written procedures. Yet it would hardly be an exaggeration to say that the culture was characterized by the written word. In order to resolve this paradox we must now ask, as we have in previous chapters, what reading and writing were used for. We shall outline the common functions of writing which a person literate in Greek or Latin might encounter, with some attention also to people who were not literate in either of these languages. The geographical area to be taken into consideration is now enormous, and the most important change in the use of writing during the late Republic and under the principate is simply that writing spread dramatically across those wide areas of the western provinces which had been illiterate before the arrival of Rome.

Certain environments now presented large quantities of writing to the eyes of residents and passers-by, though the quantity would vary according to the occupation of the individual. Rome itself was such an environment; so too was Pompeii; so also were some provincial cities (such at least is the impression left by the extensive epigraphical remains of, for instance, Salonae and Ephesus).[110] This fact has contributed to misunderstandings about the level of literacy which was reached under the Roman Empire. Written texts were certainly commonplace in many people's lives. Yet they were not as commonplace as they are in an ordinary modern life, and in other places the written word was seldom or never seen, or if it was present it had very little direct effect: these were the environments inhabited by the majority of the population of the Roman Empire.

110. For Rome itself cf. M. Corbier, in *L'Urbs. Espace urbain et histoire. Actes du colloque (Rome, 8–12 mai 1985)* (Rome, 1987), 27–60, who extends the phenomenon to *la ville romaine* in general.

Work and Business Affairs

The range of specific functions was by now very wide, and they probably became more numerous in addition to spreading geographically.
We can conveniently begin with the practical realities of the world of
work and business affairs. It is plain that in managing his practical
affairs any well-to-do Roman or Greek was likely to make quite heavy
use of the written word. The running of an upper-class household,
with both town and farm property, had long involved the use of documents and the maintenance of more or less elaborate written records.
This would involve others besides the proprietor himself in acts of
writing. Varro recommended that the overseer of the slaves on an
estate, himself a slave, should be literate—practical advice which was
no doubt quite often followed.[111] And it was not only business matters in the most obvious sense that created paperwork: when Pliny
is on his estate at Tifernum he laments about the "country-people's
petitions" *(rusticorum libelli)* which he has to contend with;[112] it is
hard to imagine such petitions in Cato's time. It may be the case (the
hypothesis can hardly be tested) that a more bureaucratic style of
management tended to gain ground. In the third century Paulus can
assume that slaves will be listed in the records of the household's
slaves *(libelli familiae)* and on the ration lists *(cibaria)*.[113] The running
of the huge estates of Valerius Titanianus, in the third-century Fayum,
required extensive paperwork.[114] But the limits to the need for literacy
must also be observed. Cicero assumes that it is the overseer's job
to know the land, that of the *dispensator* (accountant) to "know
letters."[115] The case of P. Annius Seleucus, a wealthy but illiterate
businessman in first-century Pompeii, and also that of the fictional

111. *RR* i.17.4: "litteris atque aliqua sint humanitate imbuti." For the relationship between a landowner and such a trusted slave see, e.g., the often-discussed documents concerning L. Bellienus Gemellus and his slave Epagathus (turn of the first and
second centuries): I. Biezuńska-Malowist, *L'esclavage dans l'Egypte gréco-romaine* ii
(Wroclaw, 1977), 101–103.

112. Plin. *Ep.* ix.15.1. The farmers knew, no doubt from painful experience, that
their lord should be addressed in writing, as if he were a high official. All or most of
the writing must have been done for them by a hired scribe.

113. *Dig.* xxxii.99 pr. The word *cibaria* seems not be attested in this sense any
earlier.

114. As is vividly illustrated by the accounts in the papyrus roll *P.Mich.* xi.620
(239–240 A.D.).

115. Cic. *De rep.* v.3.5.

Hermeros, prosperous but at best semi-literate, should lead us to doubt whether written accounts were systematically kept in all sizeable enterprises.[116] However it is also important to notice that Seleucus' illiteracy did not absolve him from the necessity of dealing with documents.[117]

Much is known about the Roman law of obligations, but its social history has still to be written. One important development is that the shift towards the increased use of writing continued. Among upper-class Roman citizens written contracts were so much the norm by 44 B.C. that Cicero lists *stipulationes,* together with laws and wills, among "things which are done in writing."[118] Numerous texts refer to the recording of loans,[119] and most money that was lent by or to members of the upper class was probably recorded in writing, as indeed the term *novae tabulae* ("new account-tablets," meaning a general cancellation of debts), which was in circulation by the 50s B.C., confirms.

A vital question for us is the extent to which writing spread to the everyday transactions of skilled professionals, artisans and farmers. No answer can be more than impressionistic.

The figure of the *praeco* ("auctioneer" or "salesman") seems to be omnipresent in Latin writers, and those *praecones* who operated as private businessmen clearly played a major role in Roman commer-

116. For Seleucus see F. Sbordone, *RAAN* li (1976), 145–148. Hermeros: Petr. *Sat.* 58.7

117. This raises the question of signatures again. In the modern sense, they did not exist, as has often been remarked (e.g., by B. Kübler in *RE* [1931] s.v. "subscriptio," col. 491). The most important form of authentication was a seal, supported where necessary by the testimony of those who had witnessed the sealing: H. Steinacker, *Die antiken Grundlagen der frühmittelalterlichen Privaturkunde* (Leipzig & Berlin, 1927), esp. 76; M. Talamanca in *Enciclopedia del diritto* (1964) s.v. "documento e documentazione (diritto romano)," 551. A person's own handwriting could serve as evidence of authenticity (see esp. Suet. *Tit.* 3), and it was common for the originator of a document to append a brief statement to show that it really came from him or her. The statement included its author's name and thus came near to serving as a signature (see further H. C. Youtie, *ZPE* xvii [1975], 211–212). However, as in the case of Annius Seleucus, the principal's own handwriting was not at all necessary.

118. Cic. *Top.* 96: "non magis in legibus quam in testamentis, in stipulationibus, in reliquis rebus quae ex scripto aguntur." Admittedly the words "ex scripto" leave the role of writing in a *stipulatio* somewhat unclear. But for this period it is more false than true to say, as legal scholars often do (cf. A. Berger, *Encyclopedic Dictionary of Roman Law* [Philadelphia, 1953], 716), that *stipulatio* was an oral form of contract.

119. For example, Cic. *Att.* v.1.2 (the casual use of the term *nomen* implies a developed system of credit recorded in writing), v.21.11; Sall. *Cat.* 35.3; Gell. xiv.2.7; Scaevola in *Dig.* xx.1.34.1; Gaius in *Dig.* xxii.4.4 (cf. xx.1.4).

cial life which has no exact modern parallel. Though they might make use of writing,[120] the essence of their procedure was oral, and their importance plainly derived in part from the fact that it was natural for the Romans to buy and sell by means of spoken rather than written descriptions and by means of face-to-face dealings. The contempt of the well-born for *praecones*[121] should not obscure this fact.

The surviving documentation from outside Egypt, such as it is, suggests that transactions of modest size were seldom in ordinary circumstances put into written form.[122] Some striking exceptions are known. In the channel of an aqueduct near Tarentum, for instance, someone—probably the foreman of a work-crew—once scratched fifteen dates together with the names of the workmen present on the days in question.[123] Here we find a working man possessing both a certain degree of literacy and the inclination to use it for practical ends; and in fact these Tarentine scratchings fit easily into the framework we have already constructed: Italy had a corps of literate slaves who supervised the work of others. Of course some types of transaction had greater need of durable records than others: the incentive to make a written will may be strong for a person who buys and sells for cash without any written record. It is indeed probable that many ordinary people, especially in the more Hellenized and Romanized parts of the Empire, learned that they could use written documents for special purposes such as the making of wills—which they naturally did not have to write in their own hands—without acquiring the custom of frequent writing.[124] Perhaps we ought not to expect to find many accounts or other documents of financial transactions in the graffiti at Pompeii (the men of property had better things to write on for this purpose), but in any case we do not. Not many of the graffiti can be classified as utilitarian.

120. Cf. Lucian *Vit.auctio* 6.

121. This scarcely needs documenting: see Juv. iii.155–159, with E. Courtney's n.

122. In the waxed tablets from Dacia (*CIL* iii pp. 924–966) the smallest transactions amount to fifty and sixty *denarii* (nos. 12 and 5: reproduced in *FIRA* iii nos. 120, 122); these are loans. *FIRA* iii no. 137, another such tablet, records the sale of an ox (somewhere in or beyond Germania Inferior, probably in the period 47–58) for 115 sesterces, but those involved are mainly military (two centurions are witnesses), and that may make a difference.

123. See L. Gasperini in *Terza miscellanea greca e romana* (Rome, 1971), 180–182.

124. But it is important to notice that of the 119 wills catalogued by O. Montevecchi one at most was made by an artisan: *Aegyptus* xv (1935), 80 (the possible exception was *P.Oxy.* iii.646).

The Pompeian evidence deserves further discussion. The surviving archives of the financial agent L. Caecilius Iucundus, which consist of 153 wax tablets mostly belonging to the years 52–62, suggest that it was normal to write out receipts for considerable sums. The median sum realized in the recorded transactions was about 4,500 sesterces, the smallest sums 645 and 342 sesterces.[125] Some of those involved were illiterates, it seems, who had texts written for them.[126] The Pompeian wall-inscriptions appear to imply that while large transactions normally required the written word, smaller ones of the kind which the ordinary citizens and slaves carried out every day did not. For instance, two of the three offers of rental *(locatio)* painted on walls at Pompeii concern rather substantial properties.[127] Assertions made in the past that such things as advertisements for groceries and labels identifying the residents of buildings were common at Pompeii are unfounded.[128] Written advertising seems to have been of limited scope: it mainly consisted of electoral slogans, announcements of gladiatorial and other games, and a few notices aimed at the recovery of runaway slaves or horses.[129] While some inns at Pompeii identified themselves in writing, it appears that ordinary shops did not.[130] Certainly some small business matters which especially needed a permanent record were written down: a few graffiti record loans, for example.[131] It may be objected that the main medium the Pompeians used for recording financial matters was the wooden tablet, and that their wooden tablets have almost all perished. But the ninety or so writing-tablets discovered together at Murecine near Pompeii in

125. J. Andreau, *Les affaires de Monsieur Jucundus* (Rome, 1974), 91.

126. W. V. Harris, *ZPE* lii (1983), 107–108: eleven of Caecilius' seventeen male creditors wrote with their own hands; none of his five female creditors did so. But it is not completely certain that those who failed to write did so because they were illiterate.

127. For some details see Harris 105. By the late Republic those who put large properties on the market in this way were said to *proscribere:* Cic. *Att.* iv.2.7, etc.

128. Harris 105.

129. A stray horse advertised for in a painted text of twenty-eight words at Pompeii: *CIL* iv.3864 (cf. 9948). But if you wanted to catch a thief or a runaway, you would probably try a street-crier: cf. Dio Chrys. vii.123. A slave in Egypt: *P.Oxy.* li.3616 (with J. R. Rea's comments, which list the other evidence on this procedure; the only other surviving notice of this kind is *UPZ* i.121, which is some four centuries earlier). On written advertising in the Roman world see G. Raskin, *Handelsreclame en soortgelijke praktijken bij Grieken en Romeinen* (Louvain, 1936), 91–123.

130. It is hard to be sure. A shop in Martial has signs all over the doorposts (i.117.11), but it was a bookshop.

131. *CIL* iv.4528, 8203, 8204, 8310.

1959, all of them business documents, seem to confirm that only business matters of some importance were thus recorded.[132] The Pompeian evidence does not suggest that ordinary small shopkeepers or artisans or their ordinary customers wrote or read much or indeed at all in the course of business, or that they had to use writing through intermediaries to carry out their normal transactions.

Even in the highly bureaucratic environment of Egypt, ordinary farmers and artisans probably made little use of writing. In this context apprenticeship contracts are an especially intriguing category of papyrological text, since they take us well away from the social elite. It is quite remarkable to see apprenticeships being committed to writing in a fairly small and remote community such as Soknopaiou Nesos. However the majority of these contracts concern a single craft, namely weaving.[133] The special importance of such contracts, and the general inaccessibility of writing for this kind of artisan, are underlined by the fact that not one of the master weavers who made the surviving contracts was able to subscribe it in his own hand.[134]

The documentation of financial transactions in Egypt increases under Roman power, and it certainly enters into the lives of some of the poor. Leases of modest parcels of land, for instance, are recorded.[135] Such contracts sometimes brought together well-to-do persons who were accustomed to documentation and others for whom it was not an everyday affair.[136] And writing sometimes penetrated the operation of small enterprises to a remarkable degree. For instance, the proprietor of a bath establishment at Edfu in Upper Egypt in the first century A.D. used ostraca to write, or have written, some records about water jars.[137] In this case, however, the circumstances were exceptional, for the records were in Latin, and there must have been

---

132. For bibliography and legal discussion see L. Bove, *Documenti processuali dalle Tabulae Pompeianae di Murecine* (Naples, 1979) and *Documenti di operazioni finanziarie dall'archivio dei Sulpici* (Naples, 1984). Four of these documents show that when the security of defaulting debtors was sold off at Puteoli notice of the sales was given in *libelli* put up in a public portico (Bove, *Documenti di operazioni* 100–105).

133. See A. Zambon, *Aegyptus* xv (1935), 3–66; K. R. Bradley, *Historical Reflections* xii (1985), 316–317 (some twenty out of twenty-nine are for weaving).

134. Cf. Zambon 29 n.1; Youtie, *ZPE* xvii (1975), 204.

135. Thus *P.Oxy.* xli.2973 is a lease of 1¾ *arourai* (0.48 ha), xli.2974 of 2⅔ *arourai* (0.73 ha); but these are not typical sizes.

136. Thus *P.Yale* i.69 is a sublease of two rooms, but the property belongs to a Claudia Isidora who is "obviously wealthy," as the commentators note, p. 226.

137. H. C. Youtie, *AJA* liii (1949), 268–270, discussed this material. The purpose of the records was apparently to establish the bath attendants' responsibility for the jars.

some connection with the presence at Edfu of a military garrison. The military, like the rich, tended to bring with them the habit of using documents.

Both the Italians of Pompeii and the Greeks of Egypt undoubtedly used writing much more than the inhabitants of some backward parts of the Empire, and the information which they give us about the functions of writing cannot be applied to other populations. At the same time it is plain that in practically any province the well-to-do and some of the artisans made at least some limited use of writing.[138] In every province the representatives of the government gathered taxes, and the agents of the emperor administered his property, tending in each case to increase the need for documentation.[139] In every province there were merchants concerned with more or less long-distance trade, who commonly sent and received letters and dealt in amphorae and other containers whose contents were described in writing.[140] To a greater extent than before, other commodities were also inscribed: cheap terracotta lamps made in moulds frequently carried the manufacturer's name.[141]

The practical usefulness of literacy as a means of improving one's chances of making a livelihood must always have been recognized to some extent in the Greek and Roman worlds. Yet such recognition is not readily visible in the sources. "Habet haec res panem," says the crude freedman Echion in the *Satyricon*—"this thing has bread in it"; but although he has been speaking generally about the education of his son, what he has just mentioned is the mercenary potential of one particular subject—the law.[142] He goes on, it is true, to say that "let-

138. When M. I. Rostovtzeff (*The Social and Economic History of the Roman Empire* [2d ed., Oxford, 1957], ii.617 n.39) wrote that "accounts" had been preserved in graffiti from the large potteries of the Roman west (La Graufesenque and so on), he was in fact referring to lists of pots made in single time-periods (see most recently Marichal, *CRAI* 1981, 244–272; the earlier bibliography is extensive). These texts are written on ostraca.

139. Presumably it was an indirect effect of this influence that men who contracted to work for wages in the gold mines in Dacia did so in writing (*CIL* iii pp. 948–949). Each of the contracts contains an illiteracy declaration: ibid. nos. 9, 10, 11; 10 and 11 also appear in *FIRA* iii no. 150.

140. The practice of inscribing amphorae was not of course new. A fresh study is needed after that of M. H. Callender, *Roman Amphorae* (London, 1965). For some more up-to-date information see E. Rodríguez Almeida, *Il Monte Testaccio* (Rome, 1984), 173–271. For painted texts on amphorae as a form of advertising see R. I. Curtis, *Ancient Society* xv–xvii (1984–1986), 84– 86.

141. This practice was new in the Greek world in the late second century B.C. and spread widely under the principate: W. V. Harris, *JRS* lxx (1980), 128, 143.

142. Petr. *Sat.* 46.7.

ters are a treasure"; but what he is clearly supposed to be thinking
of is the possession not of general literacy, such as in the modern
world is a useful if minimal skill transferable from one occupation to
another, but of a particular skill which goes far beyond literacy. Parallel to this is the way in which, in Lucian's autobiographical essay
The Dream, a personified Paideia (Education), contending for young
Lucian's loyalty, dangles the worldly rewards;[143] for it is not his literacy which will be rewarded but his professional success as a rhetorician. These texts prove very little by themselves; they are simply the
nearest thing we possess to statements of the materialistic reasons for
obtaining education—and they refer, in effect, to the higher literary
education.

Slightly nearer to everyday life, perhaps, are the recommendations
of experts on architecture and midwifery that the practitioners of
these arts should be literate.[144] Relevant reading matter existed in
both fields, but such recommendations also imply that literacy was
not in practice assumed in the occupation in question, which in the
case of midwives is far from surprising.

Various types of legal document have already been discussed, but
something more needs to be said about legal procedures. To what
extent did the use of documentation in legal procedures spread?[145]
Most of the ways in which legal documents were used under the
Roman Empire were already known to earlier Romans, and the principal change is that the use of such documents spread to new segments
of the population. In certain regions, at least, the use of written
documents such as wills, marriage contracts and divorce settlements
became much more common during the first century A.D. and long
remained so. This development is well established for Greek Egypt.[146]
In the west, as Roman customs spread, the use of writing for such
purposes probably did so too. The commonplace character of a written
will in an Italian town under the principate is strongly suggested
by (among other evidence) dedications to men who did the actual

143. *Dream* 11–13. It is not in fact money that she offers.

144. Vitruv. *De arch.* i.1.4: the purpose is "uti commentariis memoriam firmiorem
efficere possit." On midwives see Soranus *Gyn.* i.3: ἐπιτήδειος δ᾽ἐστιν [πρὸς τὸ
γενέσθαι μαῖα] ἡ γραμμάτων ἐντός, ἀγχίνους, μνήμων, φιλόπονος . . . γραμμάτων μὲν ἐντός, ἵνα καὶ διὰ θεωρίας τὴν τέχνην ἰσχύσῃ παραλαβεῖν.

145. On the use of documentation in Roman private law see Steinacker, *Die
antiken Grundlagen,* esp. 66–122; Talamanca in *Enciclopedia del diritto* 548–561.
But their approaches are scarcely historical.

146. Wills: Montevecchi, *Aegyptus* xv (1935), 67–121. Marriage contracts and
divorces: Montevecchi, *Aegyptus* xvi (1936), 3–83.

writing.[147] However a testator could still announce his heirs or even make the whole will orally instead of committing their names to *tabulae*.[148]

Written contracts seem to have gained somewhat in status. Some Greek cities had long possessed archives for private contracts, and the use of such archives spread in the Roman period.[149] In some cities this filing of contracts became compulsory (which does not mean that all contractual agreements necessarily had to be in writing), with the presumable result that a document which was absent from the archive was likely to be held invalid. Indeed Dio Chrysostom, in a speech addressed to the Rhodians, seems to imply that even where registration is not compulsory contracts which are registered with a city have, in some way, greater validity than those which are not.[150] In this period, however, no such archivization of contracts seems to have spread to the west.[151]

One specialized kind of legal activity, petition to the emperor or provincial governor for legal redress, certainly came to be carried out largely by means of writing, through the submission of a *libellus*. This phenomenon will be discussed shortly in conjunction with civic uses of the written word. It leads, however, to another question: whether the limited centralization of the legal system which took place under the principate led to increased emphasis on written authority. A single instance will not allow us to settle this question, but a case mentioned by Pliny seems to express the logic of the hierarchical system. During

147. For a freedman copyist *(librarius)* of Venafrum "who wrote wills for twenty-five years without a lawyer," the chief reason for which he was honoured, see *CIL* x.4919 = *ILS* 7750. Philocalus, a schoolmaster at Capua, quite probably a freedman too, was honoured in part because he "wrote wills honestly *(cum fide)*": *CIL* x.3969 = *ILS* 7763.

148. Ulpian in *Dig.* xxviii.1.21. For the survival of oral wills throughout the principate see A. Watson, *The Law of Succession under the Later Roman Republic* (Oxford, 1971), 11–12. Concerning soldiers' wills cf. Florentinus in *Dig.* xxix.1.24.

149. The second-century inscription from Sibidunda in Pisidia published by G. E. Bean, *Anatolian Studies* x (1960), 71–72 no. 124 (= *SEG* xix [1963], no. 854), shows that such archivization was compulsory in some provinces, and that the (unidentified) emperor was now attempting to apply the requirement to Pisidia. The kinds of documents which would be archivized in this way varied from city to city.

150. *Orat.* xxxi.51. He mentions as examples sales contracts for land, for a ship or for a slave, loans, and manumission and gift documents. It may be that the reason the Severan jurist Callistratus answered the question whether the absence of a document told against the validity of a transaction was that Roman courts were now faced with the Greek practice; he said that it did not (*Dig.* xxii.4.5).

151. See Steinacker, *Die antiken Grundlagen* 77–78, 171.

his governorship of Bithynia-Pontus Pliny consulted Trajan about some criminals condemned at Nicomedia and Nicaea who had been released from punishments without any documentation.[152] The provincial governor seemed inclined to accept oral testimony and let them be, but Trajan insisted that they had been released "without any appropriate authority."[153]

It is an interesting speculation whether changes in the form of some legal documents reflect a certain limited extension in the use of writing. In Augustus' time or not long before, so it appears, the Romans began to use a new form of document for borrowing money. This was the *chirographum*, in other words a document written, nominally, though not always in reality, in the borrower's own hand.[154] Such documents became commonplace. This certainly suggests that, at least in Rome itself, the ability to write was growing commoner.

However literacy still did not matter greatly for the legal acts which the ordinary citizen was commonly called upon to perform. There were usually people available who could perform the act of writing for one, and it is symptomatic that, as we saw earlier, a man was not thought to be disqualified from the practical duties involved in being a guardian if he was illiterate, even if the woman he represented was literate or when other members of the family circle were literate.[155] The jurists said as much, recognizing at the same time that a man might know a fair amount about practical affairs without being literate.[156] In an upper-class family the guardian would always have been literate, but his responsibilities did not absolutely require this; and

152. The letters are Plin. *Ep.* x.31–32 ("nulla monumenta": 31.4).

153. *Ep.* x.32.1, 2.

154. The earliest more or less clear reference to the *chirographum* as a specific kind of document is Sen. *Contr. exc.* vi.1. Cf. L. de Sarlo, *Il documento oggetto di rapporti giuridici privati* (Florence, 1935), 35–36; Talamanca in *Enciclopedia del diritto* 551 (but neither lawyers nor lexica help much with the historical problems).

155. H. C. Youtie, *HSCPh* lxxv (1971), 168–169, whose best evidence was *P.Oxy.* xii.1463.17–22 (215 A.D.) (an illiterate *kurios;* see *P.Mich.* v.257.9–10 for another such case). See also *P.Oxy.* iv.716 (186 A.D.) (an illiterate *epitropos,* a freedman, in a family circle in which there was a fair amount of literacy).

156. Paulus, quoted by Modestinus in *Dig.* xxvii.1.6.19: "eius qui se neget litteras scire, excusatio [*from* tutela] accipi non debet, si modo non sit expers negotiorum." This text is admittedly problematic; see J. M. Fröschl, *ZSS* civ (1987), 94–102. Ignorance of the law resulting from lack of education naturally failed to arouse the sympathy of the jurists: cf. Ulpian in *Dig.* xiv.3.11.3, and in general xxii.6 (but cf. ibid. ii.1.7.4).

somewhat lower down the social scale it seems to have been a matter of indifference whether the guardian was literate or not.[157]

Civic and Political Uses

In earlier chapters we have explored some of the ambivalence of the civic and political use of writing in the ancient world. Written procedures assist control from above; yet they can give those who are underneath a means of asserting their rights. But it is only rather rarely at Rome that the latter possibility comes to the fore. When Caesar, as consul in 59, introduced the radically new practices of recording the hitherto confidential proceedings of the Senate and making the record public,[158] this was an attack on the power of the senatorial aristocracy—whose regime had only another ten years to run in any case. But the attack was a secondary one, and it did not lead to any wide dissemination of detailed political news.

The power of the Romans, who conquered many lands where writing was well-known, in other cases introduced or disseminated written culture. Without this wide diffusion of writing, political and administrative control would have been infinitely harder, probably impossible: the Roman Empire depended on writing. The affairs of magistrates and later of the imperial court, the taxation of citizens and provinces, the affairs of innumerable city governments, the maintenance of the armed forces—for all these writing was indispensable. Many people were thus more or less deeply involved in the writing and reading, and also in the delivery, storing, and retrieving of the resulting texts—an aspect of Roman life which historians have greatly neglected.[159] At the same time, the social limits of education and literacy remained quite narrow, almost everywhere and almost always. The smooth functioning of the political economy did not require otherwise.

Throughout the Greek and the Romanized parts of the Empire, statute law in its various forms was always written, and it was often

157. At least this was so in Greek Egypt—where writing was more important than in most places.

158. Suet. *DJ* 20.1: "inito honore primus omnium instituit ut tam senatus quam populi diurna acta confierent et publicarentur."

159. Cf. C. Nicolet, in *Culture et idéologie dans la genèse de l'état moderne* (Rome, 1985), 9–13, on the need for further study of the concrete processes of Roman governmental administration.

written up in public on bronze tablets. But Roman laws were still not kept in a formal archive in the late Republic, and they were not always inscribed.[160] The same applied to senatorial decrees: they had to be committed to writing and deposited in the state treasury, and they *might* be displayed to the public on bronze.[161] Under the late Republic a considerable effort was made to inscribe laws in other cities as well as in Rome, and a senatorial decree was always likely to be inscribed in any city which was directly concerned. The praetor's edict was posted.[162] The edicts, letters and rescripts of emperors, which came to be a major source of law, were by definition in writing, and the text was commonly put on public view—but they did not have to be,[163] and still less was there any requirement that such texts should be widely diffused. The haphazard care taken of official texts seems to be illustrated by the notorious fact that after 3,000 of the bronze inscriptions on the Capitol which contained senatorial decrees, treaties and *privilegia* were destroyed by fire in 69, Vespasian had to institute a search for other copies of the texts.[164] However the search itself is even more significant than the lack of a centralized archive; it suggests the symbolic as well as practical importance of the texts in question—as does Suetonius by calling them "the imperial power's finest and oldest equipment" or "record."[165]

Some clues to the real functions of civic documents might be obtained from a study of the precise locations where they were displayed in relation to the places which people actually frequented.[166] At Rome itself the functions of different parts of the city were widely

---

160. See C. Williamson, *Classical Antiquity* vi (1987), 173–174.

161. R. K. Sherk, *Roman Documents from the Greek East* (Baltimore, 1969), 9–13.

162. See F. von Schwind, *Zur Frage der Publikation im römischen Recht* (Munich, 1940), 50–52.

163. As the story in Suet. *Cal.* 41.1 confirms. At first Caligula did not publish the regulations about his new *vectigalia* (which a normal ruler would have wanted to make known; Caligula wanted the rules to be broken). This did not mean that they were invalid; it was just a great inconvenience, which the emperor remedied with one almost inaccessible posted copy.

164. Suet. *Vesp.* 8. On what was to be seen on the Capitol, both before and after the fire, see Williamson 165–166.

165. Suet. *Vesp.* 8: "instrumentum imperii pulcherrimum ac vetustissimum."

166. This topic requires a more detailed study than is possible here. For some comments and bibliography on the location of public notices see Corbier in *L'Urbs* 43–46. See also Williamson 179–180.

differentiated by the late Republic. The posting of senatorial decrees and other texts on the Capitol invites the question whether they were much in the public eye. During the last century of the Republic the Capitol had quite frequently been the scene of citizens' meetings, but the place had a more restricted role under the principate. The role as well as the topography of the forum area changed drastically between the time of Caesar and that of Trajan, and with those changes went changes in the significance of the texts on display. It seldom if ever occurred to anyone to display official or honorific texts in the Subura.[167] There was often a choice to be made about where to publish a text, and it is not surprising that under the principate the choice did not often express much governmental interest in communicating directly with ordinary citizens.[168]

The traditional way to communicate with a large public was through criers *(kerukes, praecones)*. The most significant fact about the *praecones* of Roman officials is perhaps simply that they were so numerous. They might be attached to the consuls, censors, praetors, curule aediles, quaestors or tribunes or to specially appointed *decemviri* or *curatores,* or to provincial governors. There were also of course official *scribae,* but it is significant that in fact none are attested in the service of the consuls or praetors: the form of communication which most magistrates needed to have provided by the state was not written but oral. They were full-time employees and had a fair amount to do: various *praecones* were responsible for announcing public meetings *(contiones)* and electoral assemblies, for bringing them to order, for announcing the results of voting, and for summoning the Senate, among numerous other duties. They were heavily involved in court procedures.[169] It is difficult to trace the historical development of these activities, but in any case they continued throughout the period under consideration. Naturally the public *praecones* of Rome had their counterparts in other cities.

Political control over what occurred in the provinces and beyond

167. G. Lahusen, *Untersuchungen zur Ehrenstatue in Rom* (Rome, 1983), 7–42, collects information about the distribution of such statues.

168. But occasionally emperors attempted to do this: cf. Corbier 52.

169. On all this see T. Mommsen, *Römisches Staatsrecht* i (3d ed., Leipzig, 1887), 363–366, etc.; W. Riepl, *Das Nachrichtenwesen des Altertums* (Leipzig & Berlin, 1913), 330–335; F. Hinard, *Latomus* xxxv (1976), 730–746 (who, however, can hardly be right to maintain that there was no distinction between public and private *praecones*).

depended heavily on correspondence. This involved in the first place correspondence with the officials of the Roman state itself. It is generally supposed that the republican magistrates and Senate did *not* exchange frequent letters with officials away from Rome—a notion which may be somewhat misleading.[170] At all events the principate brought some change: the emperor exercised power over his absent subordinates largely through correspondence, and indeed used texts on a large scale to deal with his subjects. The degree of his personal involvement in this paperwork is debated, but in any case his control over distant events, such as it was, depended upon it.[171] Most of the information he received about the army, about revenues, and about all other governmental affairs outside Rome itself was transmitted in writing, and so too were his instructions.

To an increasing extent the government possessed records about the citizenry. In the late Republic, proving that someone was or was not a Roman citizen was sometimes very difficult, but the principate brought the requisite archives into being: the Tabula Banasitana shows that under the Antonines the emperor's records of who had received Roman citizenship extended back to Augustus.[172] The latter had introduced the compulsory registration of Roman citizens at birth, thus for the first time making some use of the written word truly important for every one of them.[173] He was also responsible for provincial censuses.[174] None of this use of the written word required ordinary people to do any writing for themselves; all the surviving birth

170. Cicero's letters from Cilicia support the usual view, but there may have been quite a lot of mundane correspondence at lower levels, especially when armies were in the field. Note Caes. *BG* v.47.2 for important *litterae publicae* in his possession.

171. See in general F. Millar, *The Emperor in the Roman World* (London, 1977), 313–341. Efficient subversion also required letters: Tac. *Hist.* ii.86.

172. See the text in W. Seston & M. Euzennat, *CRAI* 1971, 472.

173. See F. Schulz, *JRS* xxxii (1942), 78–91; ibid. xxxiii (1943), 55–64, based on the registration document *FIRA* iii no. 2 (a waxed tablet of 62 A.D.) as interpreted by O. Guéraud: "eorum qui a lege Pap(ia) Popp(aea) et Aelia Sentia liberos apud se natos sibi professi sunt." Such is the evidence Roman historians have for major administrative changes.

174. Cf. W. Kubitschek in *RE* (1899) s.v. "census," cols. 1918–20. On the censuses taken in Gaul see F. Jacques, *Ktema* ii (1977), 285–328. Ulpian indicates the kind of information collected (*Dig.* l.15.4). The census taken every fourteen years in Egypt is first known with certainty in 19/20 A.D. (as shown by G. M. Browne, introd. to *P.Mich.* x.578), but it was probably preceded by a census in 11/12 (O. Montevecchi, *Aevum* i [1976], 72–75). It is attested down to 257/8 A.D.

certificates were probably written by professional scribes.[175] Death certificates also seem to have been compulsory in Egypt, at least for a certain period.[176] In reality, it seems extremely dubious whether these procedures were systematically enforced even in that bureaucratic land, let alone for non-Roman citizens elsewhere in the Empire.[177]

Provincial governors now naturally found themselves somewhat more involved with documents. Under the Republic there is no sign that they passed on any systematic records to their successors at all. Under the principate methods were still somewhat haphazard. One could find the census records of the province at the governor's head-quarters,[178] and probably records of criminal cases decided by previous governors.[179] On the other hand, when a criminal in Pontus claimed to have had his sentence reversed under a governor prior to Pliny, the lack of written evidence for the reversal does not seem to have caused Pliny any special surprise.[180] In Egypt the governor possessed quite complex records at a central archive in Alexandria (we do not know in detail what was kept there), and the *strategoi*, heads of

175. Cf. Schulz, *JRS* xxxiii (1943), 58; M. Hombert & C. Préaux, *Recherches sur le recensement dans l'Egypte romaine* (Leiden, 1952), 99. The latter collected some forty-seven documents in which the subscriptions are preserved. For surviving birth certificates see O. Montevecchi, *La papirologia* (Turin, 1973), 179–180. It is not likely that the obligation extended to the entire population of Egypt (cf. L. Casarico, *Il controllo della popolazione nell'Egitto romano* i [Azzate, 1985], 6).

176. See G. M. Browne, introd. to *P.Mich.* x.579, referring to a text afterwards published as *SB* xii.11112; and Casarico 21–22. According to Nicolet, in *Culture et idéologie* 22 (q.v. for further bibliography), death certificates were probably required of Roman citizens in general, from Augustus' time at least; but the argument is fragile.

177. Cf. Hombert & Préaux 40–41, who conclude that the system of census declarations was general, even though both the chronological and geographical distribution of the surviving declarations is very uneven (most are of the second century) and the total number of surviving texts seems small. They based their view on the scarcely compelling argument that the government ordered people to comply (cf. *Gnomon of the Idios Logos* secs. 44, 58–63).

178. Cf. Dio lix.22.3–4, concerning Caligula in Gaul.

179. Cf. Plin. *Ep.* x.31–32; the lack of documents releasing the condemned men was not fatal to their claim, in Pliny's eyes; but Trajan, as might be expected of the man at the centre, disagreed.

180. This was the case of the philosopher Flavius Archippus, discussed in Plin. *Ep.* x.58–60. The sentencing and the reversal (if it was genuine) had taken place many years earlier. But it is also important that to establish his claim Archippus relied on other documents, and that Trajan (60.1) clearly doubted that he had been formally absolved.

districts, also possessed such records.[181] Even subdivisions of the nomes (provinces) could have record-offices.[182]

The imperial government imposed itself through force and persuasion and by more or less general consent, but a good part of the effect was obtained by means of the written word. This last fact was not unnoticed. An extraordinary scene on the Anaglypha Traiani, a pair of reliefs set up in no less a location than the Forum Romanum (see Figure 6), shows soldiers systematically burning codices in the forum under official instructions, codices which evidently contained the records of sums owed to the imperial *fiscus* and to the state.[183] This was actually done by Hadrian and Marcus Aurelius, and probably by Trajan.[184] The emperors realized, in other words, that these records had become a hated symbol. Similarly, the resentment of the provincials sometimes focussed on the census, the written record which the Romans employed to impose taxation. Such was the case when some Gauls rebelled under Augustus.[185] Another way in which emperors used the written word to administer the Empire was the system whereby they responded to cities and individuals with letters and rescripts.

The government imposed itself psychologically as well as administratively. Written propaganda grew more elaborate and more important under the late Republic and the principate. There had already been some politically charged literature in the second century B.C., but it now grew in volume. Caesar's commentaries on his Gallic and civil wars performed the remarkable feat of simultaneously somewhat expanding the audience for propagandistic texts (this admittedly is inferential) and demonstrating great sophistication in the works

181. Cf. Turner, *Greek Papyri* 136 (the system became more complex under Hadrian), 138–139.

182. See R. H. Pierce, *Symb.Osl.* xliii (1968), 68–83. Village record offices: W. E. H. Cockle, *JEA* lxx (1984), 112.

183. For a recent discussion and bibliography see M. Torelli, *The Typology and Structure of Roman Historical Reliefs* (Ann Arbor, 1982), 89–118, who also discusses the comparable "Chatsworth Relief" (pl. iv.16).

184. Dio lxix.8.1, SHA *Hadr.* 7.6 (who mentions that the emperor forgave tax arrears in the provinces), *ILS* 309 (Hadrian); Dio lxxii.32.2, SHA *Marc.Aur.* 23.3 (Marcus). The Augustan precedent (Suet. *DA* 32) was rather different.

185. Liv. *Per.* 139. This event is alluded to in Claudius' speech, *ILS* 212 = *FIRA* i no. 43 ii.37–41. To analyse how this taxation system worked is not part of my intention; cf. W. Goffart, *Caput and Colonate: Towards a History of Late Roman Taxation* (Toronto, 1974), 9–21.

themselves. And it is precisely at the end of the Republic, in the years from 46 to 30, that we hear for the first (and last) time about propagandistic tracts, no doubt fairly simple ones, being disseminated among Roman soldiers. The principate, however, showed a mainly negative interest in the kind of written propaganda that appeared in literary form: emperors merely took action against what was hostile.[186] The *Res Gestae* started no tradition.

Most written propaganda was pitched at a simpler level, and much of the best propaganda was not written at all. Monumental inscriptions serving the interests of the powerful steadily proliferated: such texts explained who had erected or repaired a public building or temple; they identified the subjects of honorific statuary; and, on a more modest scale, they were written on milestones in order to identify the builder as well as to indicate mileage. To what extent any of these types of texts were actually read is, as always, debatable; but we should beware of assuming that the Romans had a modern degree of indifference to public inscriptions.[187] Inscriptions were genuinely important in the accretion of honours awarded to Caesar and later to Octavian.[188] There was some competition about who could put up a formal inscription in a public place, and though in 22 A.D. the leading men were still allowed to finance and put their names on public buildings, the emperors inevitably brought this to a halt.[189] The extreme indignation with which Pliny describes the inscription at the tomb of Pallas on the Via Tiburtina, which referred to the senatorial decree in the freedman's honour (passed more than forty years earlier), and his added indignation that the decree had originally been inscribed on bronze in a much-frequented place in the city, show that such monuments could possess a certain importance.[190]

186. Concerning censorship cf. M. I. Finley, *Times Literary Supplement*, 29 July 1977 (more fully in *Belfagor* xxxii [1977], 605–622); W. Speyer, *Büchervernichtung und Zensur des Geistes bei Heiden, Juden und Christen* (Stuttgart, 1981), 56–76; Corbier in *L'Urbs* 54–55. Concerning texts which defamed the *princeps* cf. G. Muciaccia in *Studi in onore di Arnaldo Biscardi* v (Milan, 1984), 61–78.

187. See Corbier 46–47.

188. In the former case much of the testimony is controversial, not least the decree in gold letters on silver tablets mentioned by Dio xliv.7, and the column inscribed "parenti patriae" which Suet. *DJ* 85.2 says the *plebs* set up in the forum (the latter must be substantially correct). Honorific inscriptions, including the *clupeus virtutis*, are mentioned in *Res Gestae* 34–35.

189. See Tac. *Ann.* iii.72. For another interesting case (gold letters again) see Suet. *Nero* 10 end.

190. Plin. *Ep.* vii.29, viii.6. It was put up "ad statuam loricatam divi Iulii," very

Some forms of written propaganda were aimed at taking simple messages to sizeable audiences of ordinary people.[191] Such were the placards which were carried both in triumphs and many other kinds of procession.[192] But it was above all coins which, potentially at least, could bring politically significant phrases before the eyes of the population at large. The effectiveness of this mechanism has been debated,[193] in isolation for the most part from the problem of literacy. The finer points of numismatic propaganda must have gone widely unnoticed, and for many people coin types were simply iconographic if they were noticed at all. It required recherché knowledge, as well as reading ability, to understand some of the coin legends of the late Republic; nor does this fact make the moneyers' choice of legends impossible to understand, for the obscurity of a message can make it impressive. But Jesus, a poorly educated provincial, is said to have referred the scribes and high priests to the *epigraphe* as well as to the portrait on "Caesar's" denarius,[194] and the creative use of coin legends from the late Republic onwards suggests that they were expected to carry an intelligible message to an audience of a certain size. This does not imply in any way that the masses were literate or that anyone imagined that they were. And there may have been a more specific audience, namely the army. The legions, as we shall see, included a very considerable number of literates and semi-literates. The upper order of Roman society and, later, the emperors possessed plenty of non-textual mechanisms by which to impress the masses: *panem, circenses,* and visual techniques such as coin types and public works, not to mention the imperial cult, could all be reasonably well understood by the wholly illiterate.

The further question arises whether ordinary citizens were expected,

---

probably in the Forum Iulium (cf. S. Weinstock, *Divus Julius* [Oxford, 1971], 87)—at all events in a "celeberrimus locus, in quo legenda praesentibus, legenda futuris proderentur" (viii.6.14). The inscription evidently did not last.

191. However Corbier, in *L'Urbs* 52, is quite mistaken to imply that the imperial power tried to communicate with the population at large by written means.

192. See P. Veyne, *Rev.arch.* 1983, 281–300.

193. Cf. G. G. Belloni in M. Sordi (ed.), *I canali della propaganda nel mondo antico* (*Contributi dell'Istituto di Storia Antica* iv) (Milan, 1976), 131–159; B. M. Levick, *Antichthon* xvi (1982), 104–116 (arguing, implausibly, that in the first century the *princeps* himself was the main audience); T. Hölscher, *Staatsdenkmal und Publikum* (Konstanz, 1984), 15–16; C. T. H. R. Erhardt, *Jahrbuch für Numismatik und Geldgeschichte* xxxiv (1984), 41–54 (literacy: 47).

194. Matthew xxii.20, Mark xii.16, Luke xx.24.

as citizens, to engage in written procedures. In the previous chapter we observed that while the late-republican Roman needed to be able to inscribe a few letters in order to exercise his voting rights, the great majority of male citizens never wrote anything in their civic capacity; and of course no woman ever did so. Grain distributions undertaken by the government in Rome from 123 B.C. onwards, and later by other cities in various parts of the Empire, generated some documents, especially since in Rome, as later in Oxyrhynchus, a citizen had to establish his right to be among the restricted number of beneficiaries.[195] How exactly this was done at Rome is disputed,[196] but it is clear that by Augustus' time the beneficiary possessed a tessera which was probably inscribed in some simple fashion. The extreme situation was reached in Egypt, where by the third century A.D. individuals— up to a total of 4,000 in the case of Oxyrhynchus—made rather elaborate written applications.[197] Many of the Oxyrhynchite applicants were illiterate and applied through intermediaries, thus making use of the written word without being able to understand it in detail.

Apart from members of his immediate circle, anyone who wished to make a request of the emperor or of a provincial governor normally presented it in writing. The approach might be by letter or, in the case of an ordinary petitioner, by *libellus*.[198] Going to his death, Caesar had his left hand full of such *libelli*.[199] For a city or for an educated man, composing an appropriate text would not as a rule be excessively difficult: whatever the result turned out to be, the channel of communication was a manageable one. It is hardly surprising that, as far as private citizens were concerned, those who most frequently gained imperial favours were literary men, orators, professors, and physicians[200]—men who were expert not only in matters which emperors thought important but also in expressing their desires in cogent written form. But a *libellus* might also come from unpretentious people: the fishermen of Formiae and Gaieta, for instance, who

195. E. G. Turner, *HSCPh* lxxix (1975), 18–20.

196. G. Rickman, *The Corn Supply of Ancient Rome* (Oxford, 1980), 244–249.

197. See esp. *P.Oxy.* xl.2892–2922, edited by J. R. Rea.

198. See Millar, *The Emperor in the Roman World* 242, on the difference of status implied in submitting a letter to the emperor and submitting a *libellus*. The practice seems to have become markedly commoner from the first decades of the second century (Millar 244), possibly as part of a general trend towards a greater use of writing in civic life.

199. Suet. *DJ* 81.8.

200. See Millar 491–507.

must have been unused to writing and were probably illiterate, once obtained a rescript from Antoninus Pius.[201] Provincial governors also received *libelli* from those they ruled. The most remarkable testimony concerning such documents is the papyrus containing an edict of the prefect of Egypt Subatianus Aquila, in which it is revealed that in three days of assizes at Arsinoe (capital of a nome), at some time in the period 208–210, he received no fewer than 1,804 petitions.[202] Special circumstances may have contributed to this extraordinary total. Petitioning the emperor was obviously a remote possibility for almost everyone. As to whether provincial governors often had experiences like the one Subatianus Aquila had at Arsinoe, it is hard to be sure. Nothing in any literary or legal source suggests that *libelli* were submitted in such large numbers. In the western provinces, at any rate, it is unlikely.[203]

Eventually the practice arose whereby the emperor arranged, when he issued a response to a petition, that it should be posted.[204] This was a matter of putting a single copy on display. In Egypt, and presumably elsewhere, the governor could issue instructions that a letter of his should be written up on a white board in the nome capitals and villages "in clear and easy-to-read letters."[205]

When Caesar was in power, someone wrote on the base of a statue of Brutus, the tyrannicide of 509 B.C., "utinam viveres!"—"if only you were alive!"[206] Political graffiti and posters (*libelli* again) are unlikely to have been a new phenomenon, but to judge from the amount of testimony from our period they probably became quite common in the more literate kind of city.[207] The fact that they were

201. Marcianus in *Dig.* i.8.4. Imperial procurators responded in writing and at length, but not only in this fashion, to the *coloni* on the emperor's African estates; the main inscriptions, often reproduced, are *CIL* viii.10570, 25902, 25943.

202. If the text of *P.Yale* i.61 is to be trusted. There is no parallel.

203. However in Italy a landed magnate might complain that he was being pestered by petitions while he was on a country estate: Plin. *Ep.* ix.15.1.

204. Cf. *P.Col.* vi.123, lines 1–2, 21: it was posted in the stoa of the *gumnasion* at Alexandria in 200, while the emperor was in Egypt.

205. *P.Yale* ii.175 (189/190 A.D.); cf. N. Lewis in *Studies in Roman Law in Memory of A. Arthur Schiller* (Leiden, 1986), 127–139.

206. Suet. *DJ* 80.6.

207. Graffiti: *CIL* iv.1074, 3726, etc. (Pompeii, where—as no doubt elsewhere—most graffiti had nothing to do with politics), and see J. Gascou, *Suétone historien* (Rome, 1984), 517–518; *libelli*, in the sense of short messages: Suet. *DJ* 80.3 (Rome) (cf. the βιβλία ἀνώνυμα of Dio xliii.47.6, which may, however, have been longer), Dio lv.27 (Rome), lvi.27 (Rome and elsewhere), lxi.16 (at Rome after the murder of

sometimes recorded or referred to by serious-minded historians suggests that a surprising degree of importance was attached to them: presumably another sign of the special potency of the written word. The electoral *programmata* of Pompeii (painted electoral endorsements of the last few years before 79 A.D.) are a related phenomenon, and although the surviving examples are confined to Pompeii, such texts were also used in Rome and other Italian cities.[208] Their functions are not always straightforward. In the case of the Pompeian *programmata* this is underlined by the fact that at the higher of the two levels concerned, the duumvirate, the elections were a formality—two candidates each year for two positions.[209] What was going on, therefore, was not persuasion of the electorate, but an assertion of something else—a claim of social standing.

However, those who were involved in local politics made use of writing; practically everywhere in the Empire local magistrates put local regulations into written form, were commemorated with honorific inscriptions, and maintained financial and other records. Rarely can any city official have been illiterate, and in this period our only evidence for official illiteracy concerns Egyptian villages. On the other hand it is very likely that in some provinces there existed decurions who were no better than semi-literate.

An important problem about the civic use of writing in the Roman Empire is to know how far the elaborate capillary bureaucracy which characterized the province of Egypt had counterparts elsewhere. It must have been a universal tendency of Roman officials under the principate to generate paperwork. Greek cities and probably many others retained copies of important official documents. But the state-dominated economy of Egypt and the traditions of the Ptolemaic

Agrippina), Suet. *Dom.* 13 (ἀρκεῖ on one of Domitian's arches). The only rebel who is said to have tried to use written propaganda to influence the unprivileged was T. Curtisius, a former praetorian guardsman who stirred up slaves in the area of Brundisium in 24 A.D.: "mox positis propalam libellis ad libertatem vocabat agrestia per longinquos saltus et ferocia servitia" (Tac. *Ann.* iv.27). (Perhaps it was in Rome that he got the idea of using *libelli*: Corbier in *L'Urbs* 56.) There are reasons to suspect that a few more slaves may have been literate in this region than in others (see below, p. 256); but in any case Curtisius, or Tacitus, seems to have been unrealistic.

208. *CIL* vi.14313 and 29942 and another inscription, also from Rome, described by S. Panciera, in φιλίας χάριν. *Miscellanea in onore di Eugenio Manni* (Rome, 1979), v.1641, all instruct *scriptores* of candidates to refrain from writing on the monuments in question. See further Riepl, *Das Nachrichtenwesen des Altertums* 341.

209. This was demonstrated by J. L. Franklin, *Pompeii: The Electoral Programmata, Campaigns and Politics, A.D. 71–79* (Rome, 1980), esp. 120.

kingdom were unique. Nowhere else did one have to obtain permission for so many actions or receipts for so many different kinds of payment, or record one's own official actions in such detail.

We should ask not only how much bureaucracy existed, but how far the people in the streets and in the fields became enmeshed in this world of bureaucratic writing. They indubitably did not have to write for themselves, but did they come into any close contact with official writing? It would depend on one's occupation. But for very many people, in spite of such official intrusions as the posting of edicts in villages and the occasional gathering of census information, such contact was slight except in abnormal circumstances.[210]

The army, however, came to be an especially bureaucratized milieu. Whereas there is a rather conspicuous lack of evidence about clerical functions in the army of the late Republic,[211] the army of the principate was almost modern in its love of documentation. Rosters of whole units of soldiers or of smaller detachments, pay records, records concerning military materiel, and letters about personnel are simply some of the largest categories of preserved documents. The phenomenon was widespread, probably universal among both legions and auxiliaries. How deeply it penetrated can be seen from the ostraca of Bu Njem, which give some of the correspondence and the daily rosters of an auxiliary unit stationed in the Tripolitanian desert in the mid-third century.[212] Military installations on the northern frontier have sometimes produced impressive quantities of pens and wooden tablets.[213] For a long period the honourable discharge and promotion to citizenship of an auxiliary or sailor was recorded not only at Rome but also on a bronze certificate, a so-called diploma, even though a considerable proportion of the recipients were illiterate or semi-literate. What any of this evidence may tell us about the literacy of soldiers is a question to which we shall return. And in spite of the wide range of military documentation, we should certainly beware of supposing that documentation was constantly present in every soldier's life.[214]

210. For some such cases see Millar, *The Emperor in the Roman World* 442.

211. See J. Harmand, *L'armée et le soldat à Rome de 107 à 50 av.n.è.* (Paris, 1967), 198–201.

212. See R. Rebuffat & R. Marichal, *REL* li (1973), 281–286.

213. E.g., Vindonissa (R. Laur-Belart, *Jahresbericht der Gesellschaft Pro Vindonissa* 1942/43, 32–39) and Sorviodurum (N. Walke, *Das römische Donaukastell Straubing-Sorviodurum* [Berlin, 1965], 58).

214. This is the implication of G. R. Watson in *ANRW* ii.1 (1974), 496, who says,

This desire for documentation led to the creation of specialized positions for military clerks. When in the second century Tarruntenus Paternus listed among the numerous specialists who were exempt from fatigues the more important kinds of *librarii* (clerks), he mentioned the ones who could teach—suggesting that some men recruited as *librarii* were no more than semi-literate—the clerks of the stores, of the savings-bank and of the heirless property;[215] there were clearly other categories as well. When the system was at its height, the legionary record office of the Third Legion *Augusta* at Lambaesis had twenty-two *librarii* and twenty-one *exacti* (a different species of clerk);[216] and this may well not have been the only office which this legion had at the time.[217] The epigraphical and papyrus evidence for military *librarii* is extensive. The position was a privilege from most people's point of view,[218] and evidently it was lucrative.[219] Once again we glimpse the document as a source of power.

Religious Uses

Long-established practices continued. Written prophecies circulated, though to judge by the papyri they were not copied in great numbers.[220] Religious dedications were inscribed, prayers were recited from book-rolls, complex magical spells circulated in written form. Other inscriptions told those who approached a shrine what to do and what not to do.[221] The establishment of the imperial cult made

---

e.g., that would-be recruits were "well-advised" to present letters of recommendation—a claim which is to say the least far from proved.

215. *Dig.* l.6.7

216. *ILS* 9100, discussed by M. Philonenko, *Revue africaine* lxix (1928), 429–435. The date is about 201.

217. However the system sometimes reconstructed by scholars is artificial and unhistorical: R. W. Davies, for instance, assumes (in *ANRW* ii.1 [1974], 312) that the *tabularium legionis* was *always* manned by about a score of *librarii* and *exacti*, and on the basis of very little evidence concludes that, beyond this, each legionary century had its own *librarius* (which is indeed possible).

218. Cf. *P.Mich.* viii.466, lines 21–32.

219. Hence there was a hefty fee to pay to enter their *collegium* at Lambaesis: *ILS* 9100.

220. Emperors and their subordinates greatly disliked them: cf. *P.Yale* ii.175. The well-known *Oracle of the Potter,* which evidently had a long history, appears in no more than three published papyri: see *P.Oxy.* xxii.2332, with the commentary of C. H. Roberts.

221. R. MacMullen, *Paganism in the Roman Empire* (New Haven, 1981), 11–13.

heavy use of epigraphical texts. Shrines and temples accumulated written material, so that, for instance, the temple of the river god Clitumnus in Umbria, which made use of written "fortunes" *(sortes),* also abounded by Pliny's time in inscriptions honouring the spring and the god.[222]

The written word itself continued to exercise some religious power: that is to say, it was sometimes felt to have some special solemnity about it which allowed people to bring about extraordinary results. The Sibylline Books were so authoritative that it was natural to use them, in 44, in a revolutionary attempt to make Caesar into a king.[223] And, to take another example as different from this one as possible, when a woman in a Greek romance was required to undergo an ordeal to prove her chastity, she might wear a written text of the oath she had sworn.[224] Books "marked down in unknowable letters" played a vital part in the initiation of the hero of *The Golden Ass.*[225] All this could be imagined because of some special quality which was thought to be inherent in a written text.

Intellectuals, meanwhile, produced a sizeable body of new writing about religious topics,[226] and they clearly to some extent both propagated and received their religious ideas by means of specialized books. From Lucretius to Porphyry, Greek and Latin authors on religious-philosophical subjects found a select but real audience. The main piece of evidence that such works might have some effect on a wider public is the work of an eccentric millionaire, namely the Epicurean treatise which Diogenes of Oenoanda had inscribed on the wall of a portico in his city in Lycia, an inscription now known to have been even more enormous than used to be supposed.[227] This inscription

222. Plin. *Ep.* viii.8: "legis multa multorum omnibus columnis omnibus parietibus inscripta." Cf. Ov. *Met.* viii.744–745.

223. On the importance of the Sibylline Books in the public life of the late Republic and early principate see K. Latte, *Römische Religionsgeschichte* (Munich, 1960), 160–161. In connection with Caesar: Cic. *De div.* ii.110; Suet. *DJ* 79 ("libris fatalibus"); App. *BC* ii.110; etc.

224. Achilles Tatius viii.12: she is then supposed to step into the shallow water of the Styx; if she is telling the truth, the water stays in place; if not, it rises to cover the tablet.

225. Apul. *Met.* xi.22.

226. Cf. MacMullen, *Paganism* 9–18.

227. According to M. F. Smith, *Anatolian Studies* xxviii (1978), 44, one of the two batches of doctrine by itself covered a distance of at least sixty-five metres and quite possibly 100 metres. The date is either Hadrianic or Severan.

was not entirely without parallels,[228] but it was all the same something of an oddity. Its originator was, we may surmise, under the influence of that Greek adoration of *paideia* which we have already met and shall meet again. Rather like Opramoas of Rhodiapolis, some forty miles away in the same province, he evidently believed in imparting knowledge to large numbers of his fellow-citizens and others, and in giving them some of the benefits of the written word.[229] One of the advantages of a stone inscription was evidently, in Diogenes' eyes, its durability.[230] However there do not seem to be many other authentic instances of intellectuals' using the written word to convey religious messages to large audiences;[231] Paul of Tarsus was a partial exception.

In spite of all this most ordinary people had no strong need to write or even to read in order to express their religious feelings or find out about the divine world. Visiting a shrine or uttering a prayer did not require one to read, nor did looking after a household *lararium* or attending a festival. A new cult would be propagated mainly by word of mouth.

It is Christian writings which suggest a coming change in the religious importance of the written word. Apparently it was the habit of religious and philosophical sects to maintain a measure of contact and coherence with the like-minded by exchanging letters. Diogenes of Oenoanda probably did something of this kind with his Epicurean friends.[232] It can reasonably be assumed that widely scattered Jewish communities sometimes corresponded with each other on religious matters. In any case some Christians began early on to attach special importance to letters and other pious writings.[233] Something of the kind was happening by the 50s and 60s, for otherwise the letters of

228. MacMullen 11 refers to an "outline" of doctrines about the Great Goddess still visible in a portico in Attic Phlya in the third century (Hippol. *Refutatio* v.20.5−7), implying that it was all textual; but much of it may have been pictorial.

229. On Opramoas see below, p. 244.

230. See fr. 2 col. iv, line 14−col. v, line 2 Chilton.

231. MacMullen 10 refers in this context to Paus. i.13.8 (a poem written by a local antiquarian at Argos) and to Philostr. *V. Apoll.* iv.30, where the hero encounters a young man in Elis who has written an oration praising Zeus—of which he is about to give a public reading, because that was the way you reached an audience if you were ambitious to do so.

232. M. F. Smith, *Anatolian Studies* xxviii (1978), 53; MacMullen 11 (who somewhat overstates the clarity of the evidence).

233. Cf. W. A. Meeks, *The First Urban Christians: The Social World of the Apostle Paul* (New Haven, 1983), 143, 146.

Paul would probably not have survived. The forcefulness of his writings may in fact have contributed to the new development.

Mercury invented letters, says Tertullian, which are necessary both for practical affairs ("commerciis rerum") and for our active concern with god ("nostris erga deum studiis").[234] If the latter phrase refers to *private* concern, we have here something new in the religious life of the Romans. It was not at all necessary for an ordinary Christian to read any text for himself, although the real enthusiast might of course wish to do so. For centuries the superstitious had been in the habit of turning to prophets, magicians and fortune-tellers[235] who were commonly armed with written texts. What was most strikingly new was the organized community and the gradual accumulation of a group of virtually unchangeable texts. Since these did not in the main possess magical or occult value, they could easily be transmitted within and between Christian communities and served as something of a fixed point. The written word thus came to exercise religious power in a somewhat novel way.

Commemoration

In more or less close contact with religious feelings and practices are some of the forms of personal commemoration which appear in epigraphical texts. Tombstones are the main topic here, though graffiti which simply record the writer's presence also deserve mention. There is nothing dramatically new in Roman commemorative texts—except once again for their vast diffusion over provinces where such things were unknown before.

Epitaphs could and no doubt normally did have both religious and social functions, as well as recording the existence of the deceased and the grief of the survivors. In the minds of some they seem to have conferred a certain kind of immortality or at least a prolongation of life,[236] thus in a sense acting as a substitute for what most Greeks and

234. *De corona* 8.2.
235. Cf. Theophr. *Char.* 16.6; Plu. *De superstit.* 3 = *Mor.* 166ab.
236. Cf. the ahistorical study of H. Häusle, *Das Denkmal als Garant des Nachruhms* (Munich, 1980). Propertius' well-known line "et breve in exiguo marmore nomen ero" (ii.1.72) cannot serve as a basis for any generalization. Diod.Sic. xii.13.2 was quoted above, p. 26. When Pliny (*NH* xiii.70) describes papyrus as the substance "qua constat immortalitas hominum" (this is his meaning, notwithstanding C. H. Roberts & T. C. Skeat, *The Birth of the Codex* [London, 1983], 8), he is expressing a literary point of view.

Romans believed in very little or not at all—a comfortable afterlife.[237] Such texts are notoriously formulaic. However the acuteness of feeling which lay behind some instances of epigraphical commemoration is suggested by the care which people sometimes took to arrange for their own tombs and epitaphs.[238] And the role of the written text in such commemorations was obviously vital, for nothing but the written name could identify the individual.

As inscribed tombstones proliferated in the environs of Greek and Roman cities in the first centuries B.C. and A.D., the notion is likely to have spread to many people who were at best on the edge of literacy—people who could not have written their own commemorations—that the written word could maintain the memory of the dead.[239] But social prestige was also involved. Memorializing the defunct with an inscription helped surviving family members to maintain or claim a certain social rank or respectability. The Roman and city elites favoured inscribed tombstones, and these therefore became to some extent a mark of status. Some families possessed social standing which was too secure to need this kind of support, but the enthusiasm of freedmen and, in some regions, of partially Romanized provincials for formal funerary inscriptions shows that these were valued for motives of status.[240] Most epitaphs were inscribed by skilled masons, who in many cases probably contributed to the formulation of the text, and this leads inevitably to the conclusion that an epitaph is far from guaranteeing that the deceased or even his or her survivors were themselves wholly literate.

Literature

In this period we begin to know far more about the circulation of literary works. Authors were numerous and prolific; it may seem that

237. On Roman views of the afterlife see esp. A. Brelich, *Aspetti della morte nelle iscrizioni sepolcrali dell'impero romano* (Budapest, 1937).

238. Augustus and Trimalchio (Petr. *Sat.* 71.12) wrote texts for their own tombs, but many others did too—one only has to consult the index of *CIL* vi under such phrases as *se vivo fecit, vivus fecit.* Cf. also Brelich 37–38. For the role of visual and epigraphical motifs attributing literary or intellectual distinction to the deceased in hinting at immortality cf. the speculative chapter entitled "l'héroisation par la culture" in H. I. Marrou, ΜΟΥΣΙΚΟΣ ΑΝΗΡ (Paris, 1938), 231–257.

239. As to whether, as has been claimed, peasants sometimes had epitaphs, see below, p. 275.

240. For the effects of this factor in one "barbarian" provincial milieu see Mócsy, *Gesellschaft und Romanisation in Moesia Superior,* esp. 228.

only the exceptionally inarticulate members of the Roman upper class refrained from literary composition.[241] A number of other writers are known who did not come from this social milieu,[242] and the tendency to poetize is widely visible in verse epitaphs and graffiti of undistinguished origin. Those Greek literary genres which had not already reached Rome by 100 B.C. did so soon afterwards, and some which had been thinly represented in Latin before, such as technical handbooks, multiplied freely. The extent of literary production is vividly illustrated by the enormous lists of Plutarch's and Suetonius' works; also, for instance, by the epitaph of a physician from Roman Smyrna, Hermogenes son of Charidemus, who wrote not only seventy-seven books on medicine but also a wide variety of historical and geographical books;[243] and if it were not for the accidental survival of the epitaph, he would be entirely unknown to us.

Even oratory became more bookish. In the first place, as the demand for polished speeches increased, speakers were more inclined to use texts written beforehand by themselves or others. In Cicero's time it appears that most of such speeches as were written out had already been delivered.[244] The purist Quintilian allows that a speaker may use notes, but holds that if a speech has been written out in full it should be memorized. By this time it was certainly common for orators to have at least something written down beforehand.[245] And during the late Republic the publication of speeches became far more frequent.

The geographical range of literature is certainly impressive. Many a Greek city fathered authors, and to a lesser extent so did the more

241. The broad array of minor writers can be tracked down in the standard works: W. Schmid & O. Stählin, *Geschichte der griechischen Literatur* ii.1, ii.2 (Munich, 1920–1924); M. Schanz & C. Hosius, *Geschichte der römischen Literatur* i (4th ed., Munich, 1927), ii (4th ed., 1935), iii (3d ed., 1922); H. Bardon, *La littérature latine inconnue* i–ii (Paris, 1952–1956). For one period see the more readable account of G. W. Bowersock, *Greek Sophists in the Roman Empire* (Oxford, 1969). The point here, however, is that *not* only those describable as sophists became authors.

242. Of well-known secular writers, Lucian perhaps has the clearest claim to artisan origins. The slaves Phaedrus and Epictetus are a special category. Vergil's social origin is disputed.

243. *CIG* 3311 = *IGRR* iv.1445 = *IGSK* xxiii.536.

244. Cic. *Brut.* 91. But Suet. *De gramm.* 3 may have slightly different implications: L. Aelius Praeconinus (a knight) got his name Stilo from the fact that "orationes nobilissimo cuique scribere solebat." The problem is complex and cannot be investigated here.

245. Quint. *Inst.* x.7.30–32. For practice in this period cf. Plin. *Ep.* v.13.6 ("recitavit libellum"), vi.5.6 ("Celsus Nepoti ex libello respondit et Celso Nepos ex pugillaribus": they are criticized, but because this was meant to be an *altercatio*).

advanced areas of the Latin empire. The papyri demonstrate the existence, in Greek provincial towns, of a recherché literary culture.[246] Furthermore, the audience for works of literature was plainly not confined to the upper elite. However the diffusion of literature remained much more oral than is often realized.

It is futile to conjure up the alleged "mass-production scriptoria of the big publishers of the ancient world,"[247] for neither "mass-production" nor indeed "publisher" is an appropriate notion. Books were of course frequently copied and distributed for profit,[248] and by one means or another works of literature spread to every city of the Empire—an event of fundamental importance. A poet's ambition to win world-wide fame could now be expressed with vast horizons:[249] the Colchians at the far end of the Black Sea and the Dacians will read him. But the limitations of Roman book-production and distribution must be recognized. The case is often cited of a work which was produced in an edition of 1,000 copies—the senator Aquilius Regulus' life of his son—although it was clearly an extreme case and the work itself was probably short.[250] Less often cited is the fact that

246. By way of example, one can cite from a recent volume of Oxyrhynchus papyri not only the expectable fragments of Euripides and Menander but also hexameters describing glass-blowing (*P.Oxy.* l.3536), a life of Isocrates (3543), and a piece of historical narrative regarded by its editor as belonging to a philosophical dialogue (3544), etc., etc. A study of R. A. Pack, *The Greek and Latin Literary Texts from Greco-Roman Egypt* (2d ed., Ann Arbor, 1965), reinforces the point over and over again.

247. T. C. Skeat's phrase, *PBA* xlii (1956), 189; this is not to dispute his conclusion that dictation was sometimes at least used in ancient book production, a question which has been studied further by P. Petitmengin & B. Flusin in *Mémorial André-Jean Festugière* (Geneva, 1984), 247–262. The desire of scholars to assimilate ancient book production to modern used to be deeply ingrained. According to L. Friedländer, *Roman Life and Manners under the Early Empire*, trans J. H. Freese, iii (London, 1909), 36, Atticus had numerous rivals, and hundreds of his scribes, writing from dictation at the same time(!), did the work of a printing press.

248. See in general H. Emonds, *Zweite Auflage im Altertum* (Leipzig, 1941), 17–23; V. Burr in *RLAC* (1959) s.v. "Editionstechnik," cols. 600–604; T. Kleberg, *Buchhandel und Verlagswesen*, trans. E. Zunker (Darmstadt, 1967); R. J. Starr, *CQ* xxxvii (1987), 213–223.

249. This occurs for the first time in Hor. *Od.* ii.20.13–20 ("me Colchus et qui dissimulat metum / Marsae cohortis Dacus . . .") (cf. E. Auerbach, *Literatursprache und Publikum in der lateinischen Spätantike und im Mittelalter* [Bern, 1958], 177–178), though the literary forerunners, Greek and Roman, were numerous (cf. R. G. M. Nisbet & M. Hubbard on ii.20.14).

250. Plin. *Ep.* iv.7.2 dwells on the lengths to which Regulus went in his mourning. According to Kleberg 62, editions of this size must have been not uncommon. R. Sommer, however, concluded from a careful discussion of the Ciceronian evidence (*Hermes*

when Varro's library was plundered during the proscriptions, quite a number ("aliquam multos") of the 490 "books" he had written disappeared.[251] This evidence shows that an author, even a wealthy one, might not bother to distribute copies of a book at all. The primary way of distributing books was not in any case by means of a trade of any kind, but through gifts and loans among friends.[252]

The books that were available were often poorly produced,[253] and for most people's pockets, though needless to say not for senators', they were likely to be quite expensive.[254] In such circumstances some book-owners got their own copies made.[255] The spread of book-dealers cannot have been fast: late-republican Verona had none, and a century and a half later the younger Pliny expected that such a flourishing and well-established provincial city as Lugdunum would be without; as it turned out, he was mistaken, but his expectation is also important evidence.[256]

An author at Rome who sought public attention normally put on a public reading, a *recitatio*.[257] It is hard for a poet to become famous, says M. Aper in Tacitus' *Dialogus*, for when does news of one of his readings fill Rome—let alone the provinces? The performance and the

---

lxi [1926], 412–414) that almost nothing can be known about the sizes of editions.

251. Gell. iii.10.17.

252. See the excellent demonstration by Starr, *CQ* xxxvii (1987).

253. Cic. *QF* iii.5.6; Seneca *De ira* ii.26.2. What less wealthy readers had to put up with can be imagined. Strabo xiii.609 writes of poor-quality copying in both Rome and Alexandria.

254. The small amount of important evidence is described by Kleberg 56–58, but his modern equivalents are potentially misleading and he draws the wrong conclusion (T. Birt, *Kritik und Hermeneutik, nebst Abriss des antiken Buchwesens* [Munich, 1913], 322, was much more pessimistic). The ordinary prices known are (1) five *denarii* for a work by Chrysippus which was probably quite short (Epictet. i.4.16); (2) five *denarii* for Martial book i (about 700 lines) in a "nice edition" (Mart. i.117.17); (3) one *denarius* for the *gracilis libellus* containing the 274 lines of Martial book xiii (xiii.3.2), which may be available at half-price (the poem's tone is playful, the value of the evidence uncertain). The magical books valued at 50,000 *denarii* in Ephesus (Acts xix.19) are also interesting. In Lucian *Pseudolog.* 30, 750 drachmas is an imaginable price for a rare book.

255. Phaedr. iv. prol.17–19. Cf. Birt 325–327.

256. Catull. 68.27–28 (and note the difficulties of buying books even in Rome in the same period: Cic. *QF* iii.4.5); Plin. *Ep.* ix.11.2 (where A. N. Sherwin-White misses the point in saying that Pliny's statement contrasts with the suggestion in ii.10.2 that a friend's verses will be read wherever Latin is spoken; such diffusion did not depend on bookshops). For books on sale in Brundisium: Gell. ix.4.1.

257. For details see G. Funaioli in *RE* (1914) s.v. "recitationes," cols. 435–446; Sherwin-White on Plin. *Ep.* i.13.

book work in tandem, as the *Dialogus* itself shows: its dramatic date is the day after Curiatius Maternus recited his tragedy *Cato,* and the interlocutors find him with the book in his hand, which he expects to publish.[258] But it is assumed to be the *recitatio,* not the book, which will make a man celebrated.[259] The custom of organizing such readings went back in some form well beyond Asinius Pollio, to whom the elder Seneca attributes its invention.[260] The effects of this custom on reading habits are hard to judge, but it can be guessed that for many in the audience the *recitatio,* taking up time and mental energy, acted as something of a substitute for personal reading. So too, perhaps, did the readings and performances which were a common feature of the symposia and dinner parties given by the Greek and Roman rich in the age of Plutarch and Pliny.[261]

But much more than this was involved in the oral transmission of literary works, as some remarks of Strabo's demonstrate. City people are affected by myths when they *hear* the poets telling of deeds of heroism; philosophy is for the few, poetry is more useful to the people and is able to fill theatres.[262] And Dio Chrysostom describes how, walking through the hippodrome, he encountered people playing the flute, dancing, performing tricks, *reading out a poem,* singing, and *recounting a history or tale.*[263] These vignettes are characteristic of the ancient world. Ample references show that street performers were well-known in the cities of imperial Italy.[264]

When Augustus found it impossible to sleep, "he summoned readers or story-tellers"[265] instead of reaching for a novel as a modern person might. The heavy reliance of the Roman upper class on readers is familiar,[266] and even for them it is clear that listening, instead of reading for oneself, always seemed natural.

258. Tac. *Dial.* 3.

259. *Dial.* 10.1–2: "mediocris poetas nemo novit, bonos pauci. quando enim rarissimarum recitationum fama in totam urbem penetrat?" That he is exaggerating his main point is irrelevant to mine.

260. Sen. *De contr.* iv praef.2. See Funaioli cols. 437–439; A. Dalzell, *Hermathena* lxxxvi (1955), 20–28.

261. See, e.g., Plu. *Quaest.Conv.* vii.8 = *Mor.* 711a–713f; Plin. *Ep.* i.15.2.

262. Strabo i.19–20.

263. Dio Chrys. xx.10.

264. See A. Scobie, *Aspects of the Ancient Romance and Its Heritage* (Meisenheim, 1969), 27–29, A. D. Booth, *Greece and Rome* xxvii (1980), 166–169.

265. Suet. *DA* 78.2.

266. Other evidence includes Plin. *Ep.* v.19.3, viii.1.2, ix.34, ix.36.4 (but compare v.3.2). Cf. F. di Capua, *RAAN* xxviii (1953), 66–70.

There was no such thing as "popular literature" in the Roman Empire, if that means literature which became known to tens or hundreds of thousands of people by means of personal reading. Even the best-known texts, those of Homer and Vergil (both of whom were very widely known), became familiar to school-children through dictation and recitation, not through school editions. As for works written expressly for the masses, there were none. When the elder Pliny dedicated his *Natural History* to Vespasian, he wrote that if he had simply published it, he could have defended it from the emperor's criticism by saying that it had been written for the lowly common-people, *humile vulgus,* for the crowd of farmers and artisans.[267] But the author is rhetorically pretending to abase his work in front of the dedicatee, and nothing much follows. No doubt some technical works were addressed to audiences which could be described from the point of view of an imperial flatterer as the *humile vulgus,* while from other points of view they would have been practitioners of respectable *artes.*

Equally useless as evidence for popular literature are the claims of Martial that Rome and even Britain are singing his verses;[268] these are the poetic pretensions to world-wide fame, not to be taken too seriously in Martial's case, which came from an already-long tradition.[269] Nor, rather obviously, can he be taken at his word when he writes that every old and young man and every chaste maiden at Vienna (Vienne) reads him ("it is said").[270] It has even been solemnly claimed that when the poet says that he is writing for those who watch the *ludi Florales,* a traditionally lubricious affair, he reveals that he expects a lower-class public;[271] this argument is not at all persuasive.

If no particular Roman book aimed successfully at a mass audience, may there not still have been genres of literature that did so? The Greek romance is the prime candidate. But the notion that it was truly popular[272] collides with two clear facts: the refined sophistication of

267. Plin. *NH* praef.6.

268. vi.60.1−2: "me manus omnis habet" (cf. v.16.2−3); xi.3.5.

269. E. E. Best, *CJ* lxiv (1968−69), 208−209, takes such texts far too literally, besides describing the centurion whom Martial imagines reading his works (xi.3.4) as "the lower ranks" of the army.

270. vii.88.3−4.

271. Best 208−209, referring to i praef.12−16 ("the identity of Martial's intended audience is plainly stated here"). Best's culminating argument (211) is that because Martial addresses poems to, e.g., an innkeeper and a charioteer, he counted such people among his readers. But this ignores literary convention (and in fact no innkeeper is addressed).

272. D. N. Levin, *Rivista di studi classici* xxv (1977), 18−29.

the authors' Greek,[273] and the relatively small number of papyrus fragments that survive.[274] We should rather see the romances as the light reading of a limited public possessing a real degree of education. As for Aesopic fables, they enjoyed some popularity, but Quintilian was surely being precise when he pictured the rustic and the uneducated *listening* to such stories.[275] It must also be by means of hearing that Strabo envisages the illiterate and uneducated absorbing the "myths" which they so much enjoy.[276] This is not to deny that there were some intellectually undemanding texts in circulation: Gellius describes how in the port of Brundisium he came across Greek books for sale, "full of wonders and tales."[277]

The libraries of the Hellenistic world had their Roman successors, in Italy and to a certain extent in the western provinces as well as in the east. Caesar was the first to plan a public library at Rome,[278] a scheme which was realized only after his death. Augustus' libraries and the modest number of others attested in various provinces[279] provide evidence of the reverence with which the Graeco-Roman upper class regarded the literary classics, and must to some degree have helped to make texts available to the learned and the respectable.[280] It would, however, be crudely anachronistic to suppose that the sum

273. This applies even to the non-"Attic" Chariton, in my view; see A. D. Papanikolaou, *Chariton-Studien. Untersuchungen zur Sprache und Chronologie der griechischen Romane* (Göttingen, 1973). Xenophon of Ephesus is a special case: see M. D. Reeve, *CQ* xxi (1971), 531–534. Cf. Reeve 538 on the romance-writers' stylistic polish.

274. Pack, *Greek and Latin Literary Texts*, musters a total of six papyrus fragments from among the five famous Greek novelists, with twenty-six other romance fragments in the anonymous section. The great addition since has been the *Phoenicica* of Lollianus (ed. A. Henrichs, Bonn, 1972). The *Iliad* and *Odyssey* have 605 entries in Pack, Euripides 75, anonymous historiographers 92.

275. Quint. *Inst.* v.11.19.

276. Strabo i.19, quoted above. On story-telling in antiquity see A. Scobie, *RhM* cxxii (1979), 229–259.

277. Gell. ix.4.3–4: "res inauditae, incredulae, scriptores veteres non parvae auctoritatis: Aristeas Proconnesius et Isogonus Nicaeensis et Ctesias et Onesicritus et Polystephanus et Hegesias; ipsa autem volumina ex diutino situ squalebant et habitu aspectuque taetro erant."

278. Suet. *DA* 44.

279. See C. Callmer in *Opuscula Archaeologica* iii (Skrifter utgivna av Svenska Institutet i Rom x) (1944), 167–185; C. Wendel in *RLAC* (1954) s.v. "Bibliothek," cols. 244–246 = *Kleine Schriften zum antiken Buch- und Bibliothekswesen* (Cologne, 1974), 176–178. But a new catalogue is needed.

280. In Gell. xix.5.4 the library of Tibur contains just the right work by Aristotle.

of these efforts had any large-scale effect on the diffusion of the written word.

Letters

The custom of private letter-writing probably grew stronger in late-republican Rome, and to some extent it spread through the western provinces together with other uses of written Latin. However, in spite of the considerable number of Greek and Latin letters that survive in one medium or another,[281] we can gain only a rather uncertain idea of how far down the social scale letters reached, and how far letters were relied upon by those who were capable of using them.

The typology of letters has been extensively studied: in antiquity they were classified into as many as forty-one different types, and it can be shown how Pliny's letters, if they are indeed real pieces of correspondence, fall into eight rather broadly defined categories.[282] In real life, while some letters had one single function (an invitation, a *consolatio*), others might have several different functions: conducting business affairs, conveying information, amusing the recipient, recommending a third party, seeking favours, and so on.

One little-noticed limitation is that most surviving letters were intended to cover a considerable distance: they seem not to have been used much for communicating with someone in the same city (as, before telephones dominated, they once were). This applied even to the circle of the letter-loving Pliny. Acknowledging a letter of recommendation, he says casually: "I would have recommended him to you, if you had been at Rome and I had been away."[283] In other words, the act of recommendation had been put into letter form only because the author was out of town: otherwise he would have done the recommending in person. This is all the more interesting because a letter of recommendation was a somewhat formal act which could gain impact from its written form. Letters of invitation preserved on papyri are also relevant here: not only are they rather few in number, they are often not self-contained—either sender or recipient or both are

281. Cf. P. Cugusi, *Evoluzione e forme dell'epistolografia latina nella tarda repubblica e nei primi due secoli dell'impero* (Rome, 1983), with bibliography of earlier work; unfortunately the author shows no interest in social history.

282. Cf. A. N. Sherwin-White, *The Letters of Pliny. A Historical and Social Commentary* (Oxford, 1966), 1–4, 42–52. But his categories (43–44) leave the actual functions of most of the letters in the dark.

283. Plin. *Ep.* vi.9.1; where Tacitus had written from we do not know.

left unnamed or are incompletely named. The natural conclusion from this evidence is that invitations, generally being local messages, were for the most part oral, but that an accompanying letter of invitation might also be used to add a dash of style.[284] This restriction in the way letters were used did not result from the lack of a public postal service, for the well-to-do overcame this difficulty for the purposes of long-distance correspondence and could have done so on a more local level. The reason is, rather, that the natural way of conveying a message was still to a considerable degree by word of mouth.

There were, however, frequent letter-writers on various social levels. At certain periods Cicero wrote to Atticus very frequently, sometimes even on successive days for weeks at a time.[285] He was a man of energy, and the pace of his letter-writing may also reflect some sense of isolation, but others are likely to have been equally prolific correspondents. On a lower social level too some people wrote quite frequently: there happens to survive a letter from a Greek-speaking soldier to his mother written on Phaophi twenty-fifth in which he mentions that he has already written to her three times that month.[286]

Some legionary soldiers wrote letters, but they were by no means the bottom rung of the social scale. At how low a social rank were letters written? The question may be misconceived, for social rank in itself did not make people into correspondents: occupation mattered more—so that we sometimes find slaves writing letters, and people of no social distinction writing to one another for business reasons, such as a pair of traders with Celtic names in London.[287] Women both sent and received letters, not only in high society but in the property-owning class in Greek Egypt.[288]

The idea of sending a message to an individual in writing was not confined to formal letters; that indeed was the purpose of many graf-

---

284. Cf. J. F. Oates, A. E. Samuel & C. B. Welles on *P.Yale* i.85. For the overall interpretation see U. Wilcken in L. Mitteis & U. Wilcken, *Grundzüge und Chrestomathie der Papyruskunde* (Leipzig & Berlin, 1912), i.1.419.

285. *Att.* ii.4–17 were written within scarcely more than a month in 59; vii.17–x.15 (sixty-seven letters) were written within about 100 days in 49; xii.12–xiii.20 (seventy-nine letters) in about 115 days in 45; etc.

286. *P.Mich.* iii.203; cf. H. Koskenniemi, *Studien zur Idee und Phraseologie des griechischen Briefes bis 400 n.Chr.* (Helsinki, 1956), 111–112.

287. Slaves: *P.Tebt.* ii.413. Traders in London: see K. Painter, *BMQ* xxxi (1966–67), 101–110 (Rufus Callisuni to Epillicus). This text is, however, unique.

288. Instances are listed by S. G. Cole in H. P. Foley (ed.), *Reflections of Women in Antiquity* (New York, 1981), 236.

fiti, and we could say pretentiously that these have a sub-epistolary function. Of course the graffito writer may have been writing without any real thought of an audience, or for his friends, or for all comers. In any case defining the social range of graffito writers has so far proved to be a practical impossibility.[289]

The author of a letter did not necessarily do the actual writing for himself or herself. This was true at all social levels. In the earliest part of their correspondence Cicero wrote to Atticus in his own hand, but later he often dictated, especially when he was very busy.[290] In Greek private letters the illiteracy formula, so often used in documents, was dispensed with and had no counterpart,[291] clearly because no one made the assumption that a private letter would be in the hand of its author. The majority of papyrus letters were not written by their own authors,[292] if author is really the right word for a person who sometimes relied on the scribe for phraseology as well as hand-writing; many of these people must have been semi-literates or illiterates who, however, knew how to make some use of the written word.[293]

Conclusion

It has been asserted that "the most natural form for the transmission or crystallization of a thought, at every social level and on every occasion, was the written form."[294] This claim is quite wrong, even for the most cultivated milieux. For the lower social levels, the mass of the population, it is remote indeed from the truth. Even for the highly educated, the spoken word retained a larger sway than is sometimes

289. Witness the great difficulties encountered by H. Solin in trying to analyse the background of the Herculaneum graffiti, *Cronache ercolanesi* iii (1973), 97–103.

290. Cf. D. R. Shackleton Bailey on Cic. *Att.* ii.20.5. By the time of xii.32.1 it was worthy of remark when Cicero wrote for himself.

291. J. L. White in White (ed.), *Studies in Ancient Letter Writing* (= *Semeia* xxii) (Chico, Calif., 1982), 95. The same volume also contains a checklist of all Greek letters in papyri (C.-H. Kim, 107–112).

292. Cf. Koskenniemi, *Studien zur Idee und Phraseologie* 114. Thus, at some social levels anyway, a wife would not be surprised to receive successive letters from her husband in entirely different hand-writing (even if she could tell the difference), as with *P.Mich.* iii.214 and 216.

293. *P.Mich.* inv.855, published by H. C. Youtie, *ZPE* xxvii (1977), 147–150, makes it tempting to say that by the standards of ordinary people, getting a letter copied was quite costly; in this text of the reign of Claudius a copy cost two drachmas.

294. A. Petrucci, *Studi medievali* x.2 (1970), 160; quoted with approval by G. Cavallo in M. Vegetti (ed.), *Oralità, scrittura, spettacolo* (Turin, 1983), 173–174.

recognized. Among the inhabitants of the Empire in general, though a few used writing heavily and though some knew how to use written texts without being literate, for most the written word remained inaccessible.

In manifold ways, however, the Roman world was now dependent on writing, particularly with respect to political and administrative power. The ability of the written word to overcome distance and its ability to engender respect become vitally important in a world empire. Rulers and states had made use of this double potential from early dates. Later the government of the Ptolemies had devised a system for exercising power which made much heavier use of documents than any previous one. In the Roman case both the practical and prestigious uses of writing were of vital importance to the exercise of power, under both the Republic and the principate. At Rome as in classical Greece, the increased use of the written word helped to spread rights to the citizens (and even to others). It not only enabled people to communicate but allowed them to claim rights and justice. However it also allowed those with power to exercise it more effectively, both by allowing Rome to control and administer its empire, and also by helping the well-to-do and the members of the various elites to maintain their superiority over the remainder.

Writing and the written word had other functions besides the readily intelligible ones listed in Chapter 2 and examined in this section. To what extent we should treat these other functions as "symbolic" is problematical. It seems obvious that inscriptions of many kinds had a symbolic meaning, and that those who composed official inscriptions or had them inscribed often meant, at some level, to say more than the words actually written. The same applies to epitaphs and to some kinds of religious inscriptions. Private letters can mean a little, or sometimes a great deal, more than they say (practically impossible for a historian to know). Yet it remains hard to define what is symbolic and what is not. Curse-tablets may be thought of as highly symbolic, for they were commonly addressed to divine beings and followed set forms; but they also said quite graphically what was meant.

We might hypothesize that some circumstances which called for the written word called for it to be used with especial tact or moderation (the authors of the duumviral *programmata* at Pompeii did not want to *say* that they were flattering future office-holders). In other cases it was the known existence of the texts (the inscriptions on the Capitol, for instance), more than their actual contents, which possessed importance. In contexts of this kind the written word was likely to assume a meaning quite different from its apparent one.

Schooling

The history of schooling among the Romans is in need of a comprehensive revision. Some received ideas—such as the notion that Roman schooling invariably fell into three clear-cut phases, superintended in turn by the *ludi magister* (or *grammatistes* or *litterator*), the *grammaticus* and the *rhetor*—have recently come under attack. Here, however, only those problems which concern instruction in reading and writing can be considered. In particular we must investigate the accessibility of elementary education.

A pervasive system of schools is a prerequisite for mass literacy. But is it not possible, all the same, that a large number of people in the Roman world learned to read and write without attending a school? We must be careful not to exaggerate the parallelism of ancient and modern practice. The children of wealthy Romans very often received their education, or at least the early stages of it, from tutors.[295] Among the elite it was also a commonplace that parents had a specific obligation to teach reading and writing to their own sons (no known text applies this obligation to daughters); this was a presumed duty, not an impossibly remote ideal.[296] How far this idea penetrated the society at large is unknown: it appears in Plautus, but not in any other non-aristocratic text until late antiquity.[297] Working fathers and poorly educated mothers may have thought that teaching letters was a task for the schoolmaster. Quite certainly the teaching of elementary reading and writing was part of what went on in schools;[298] these skills had not normally been acquired beforehand. It is likely in fact that most people outside the upper class relied on schools for the elementary education of their children. The education of slaves, too—when it took place at all—might be carried out in a regular school.[299] In

295. See, e.g., Suet. *De gramm.* 17 (Verrius Flaccus, tutor of Augustus' grandsons); Plin. *Ep.* iii.3.3; and in general Quintil. *Inst.* i.2.

296. Plu. *Cat.Mai.* 20; Nepos *Att.* 1; Val.Max. ii.7.6; Suet. *DA* 48, 64.3; cf. Cic. *Att.* viii.4.1.

297. Plaut. *Most.* 126; Heliod. *Aeth.* i.13.1.

298. See L. Grasberger, *Erziehung und Unterricht im klassischen Altertum* ii (Würzburg, 1875), 254–321; Marrou, *Histoire* 391–397; S. F. Bonner, *Education in Ancient Rome* (Berkeley, 1977), 165–188.

299. A. D. Booth, *TAPhA* cix (1979), 11–19.

short, we have no reason to suppose that the Romans somehow transmitted literacy in great quantities without the help of great quantities of formal schooling.

The difficulties of tracing the distribution of Roman schools are compounded by obscure terminology. A three-stage division of the kind mentioned above, which is canonical in the modern literature,[300] is far too rigid. What, for instance, is the function of a *magister?* Martial imagines the sad fate of a poet's works:[301] the schoolmaster will use him for dictation, so that he will come to be hated by the "tall maiden and the virtuous boy." These children must be eleven- or twelve-year-olds, at least, and no longer learning to read and write; yet the teacher is a *magister.*[302] On the other hand Quintilian sees everything beyond basic reading and writing as the domain of the *grammaticus.*[303] And the suspicion must be strong that men who called themselves *grammatici* sometimes taught plain reading and writing.[304] The term *litterator* seems to have been applied both to elementary teachers and tutors and to *grammatici,*[305] quite probably because the functions were often indistinct. It is only in fact from the second century A.D. that the sequence *litterator–grammaticus–rhetor* becomes visible.[306] Hence the difficulties of locating elementary teachers in the Latin literary and epigraphical evidence are even greater than might initially be supposed. The Greek terminology has

300. See Marrou, *Histoire,* esp. 389–390 (however in 597 n.1 he expressed some hesitation on this point).

301. viii.3.15–16: "oderit et grandis virgo bonusque puer."

302. In Gell. xvi.6.5 a man who is evidently a *grammaticus* (expounding Vergil) is addressed as *magister.*

303. *Inst.* i.4.1

304. Such is the view of A. D. Booth, *Florilegium* i (1979), 1–14, who is to be credited with questioning the existence of a fixed tripartite system. But his arguments are not decisive, for it is not clear that what Orbilius taught Horace, to the accompaniment of beatings, was the *elementa* (the passage in question is *Epist.* ii.1.69–71). Plin. *Ep.* ii.14.2 does not particularly concern "elementary" teaching. It is true, however, that Galen (*Scripta Minora* ii.25 Marquardt–Müller–Helmreich) and Ausonius (*Prof.* viii.10–13—"primis in annis," x.11–13) record *grammatici* as their first teachers.

305. E. W. Bower, *Hermes* lxxxix (1961), 462–477, esp. 469–474. A. D. Booth, *Hermes* cix (1981), 371–378, strains the evidence in attempting to show that a *litterator* was very seldom an elementary teacher.

306. Cf. Apul. *Flor.* 20.3. SHA *Marc.* 2.2–4 gives the sequence *litterator* (plus *comoedus, musicus, geometra*), *grammaticus, orator; Verus* 2.5 gives *grammatici, rhetores, philosophi.* In Diocletian's Price Edict the ascending grades of teacher are *magister institutor litterarum* (etc.), *grammaticus, orator* (etc.): S. Lauffer (ed.), *Diokletians Preisedikt* (Berlin, 1971), 124–125.

similar complications: a *didaskalos* may be an elementary teacher, but he may be on a much more advanced level;[307] or he may be the teacher of an apprentice, or even a Christian catechist.

A recent book claims that there existed "a dense network of schools" throughout the Empire.[308] The authors even assert that the imperial government created this network—a grotesque misconception. An incautious phrase of H. I. Marrou's may be to blame, namely his assertion that, from Vespasian's reign on, the Roman Empire pursued "an active policy of intervention and patronage" with regard to schools.

It is true that from time to time emperors or their agents did things in favour of elementary schoolmasters,[309] the clearest case being the regulations governing the mining community of Vipasca (in Lusitania), in which it is laid down that, as far as the imperial agent in charge of that community is concerned, schoolmasters are to be untaxed.[310] It also appears that by Vespasian's reign some *magistri* and all or most *grammatici* were free from civic obligations *(munera)* in the cities.[311] Vespasian laid down, and Hadrian repeated, that these privileged persons should be exempt from billeting. Between 198 and 211, however, it was decreed that a man had freedom from civic obligations only if he taught in his own city; if he went elsewhere, he lost his exemption at home.[312] Caracalla took the exemption away from elementary schoolmasters entirely.[313] Ulpian confirms this, adding the

---

307. See the examples in Harris, *ZPE* lii (1983), 97 n.43. Add *IG* xiv.798 (Naples), pointed out and commented on by J. Christes, *Sklaven und Freigelassene als Grammatiker und Philologen im antiken Rom* (Wiesbaden, 1979), 154.

308. "Una fitta rete scolastica": G. F. Gianotti & A. Pennacini, *Società e comunicazione letteraria in Roma antica* (Turin, 1981), iii.128.

309. It is not likely that the παιδευταί who received tax privileges in a document from Ephesus (of triumviral date) published by D. Knibbe, *ZPE* xliv (1981), 1–10 (= *IGSK* xvii.4101), included elementary teachers, though K. Bringmann maintains (*Epigraphica Anatolica* ii [1983], 52) that the Latin original referred to *grammatici*. The latter shows that the document was a *senatus consultum* and argues that it applied to the whole Empire.

310. *ILS* 6891 = *FIRA* i.105, line 57 *(ludi magistri)*. It is probably of Flavian or early second-century date.

311. *Dig.* l.4.18.30 (Arcadius Charisius).

312. *Dig.* xxvii.1.6.9 (Modestinus). This is incorrectly described as a confirmation by Marrou, *Histoire* 434; his account of the actions of subsequent emperors from the Gordians onwards is not accurate. Later on, however, he recognizes the import of the *Digest* passages cited in the next two notes.

313. *Dig.* l.4.11.4: "eos, qui primis litteris pueros inducunt, non habere vacationem divus magnus Antoninus rescripsit."

proviso that provincial governors should avoid burdening such men excessively.[314] In any case this is all very limited as a policy for primary education, and the more active concern of the emperors and their officials was entirely for advanced teaching.[315] As to how far the cities of the Empire went in supporting schoolmasters, and how much private philanthropy contributed, we shall consider region by region.

First, however, it is important to observe how wretched the physical conditions of schooling were in the Roman Empire, and how elementary schoolmasters continued to be despised by articulate opinion.

Roman schools were, as far as we can tell, physically makeshift. Those normally hideous but at the same time strangely inspiring educational edifices which appear in every modern centre of population have no counterparts in Roman archaeology or indeed in any written source concerning the Roman Empire. We need to be on guard against missing something, and someone might suggest that the *gumnasia* which characterized Greek cities were important for elementary schooling (the notion is not at all plausible). But Pompeii is extremely suggestive. Though an attempt has been made to show that the town possessed a number of schools,[316] there is no strong evidence that any particular building was devoted to this purpose,[317] and the very notion may be anachronistic. No school has been identified at Ostia either. The famous painting from the house of Iulia Felix at Pompeii which illustrates a school scene seems to show that it took place at the edge of the forum, partly in a portico.[318] The edge of a forum was a natural place for such an activity.[319] Something that was in or practically in the street was normal,[320] and the most that was likely to be provided as an aid to privacy was a *pergula*[321]—whatever

314. *Dig.* l.5.2.8 (quoted below, p. 241 n.350).

315. Marrou 435–437 gives a succinct account of imperial activity in this field.

316. M. della Corte, *Studi romani* vii (1959), 622–634.

317. Harris, *ZPE* lii (1983), 109–110.

318. *Le pitture antiche d'Ercolano e contorni* iii (Naples, 1762), 213, very often reproduced, e.g., in Daremberg-Saglio s.v. "ludus, ludimagister," fig. 4647; Bonner, *Education* 118. It is described by W. Helbig, *Wandgemälde der von Vesuv verschütteten Städte Campaniens* (Leipzig, 1868), no. 1492.

319. Cf. Liv. iii.44.6; Dion.Hal. *AR* xi.28.3. Cf. Bonner 119.

320. Martial ix.68; Dio Chrys. xx.9 (the teachers of letters sit in the street with the boys, and "nothing in this great crowd," he optimistically says, "hinders them from teaching and learning"). On the troublesome phrase "extremis in vicis" (Hor. *Epist.* i.20.18)—a place where teaching takes place—see S. F. Bonner, *AJPh* xciii (1972), 509–528, who concludes that its meaning is "at the ends of the streets."

321. Cf. Suet. *De gramm.* 18.2, etc.

that was exactly (probably the sort of delimited and sometimes covered space which is often to be found outside a café in France or Italy).[322] This relative lack of privacy may not have been invariable, and nothing compels us to think that in cold climates Roman schoolmasters taught outdoors all year round. But this sort of physical arrangement was very probably the norm, partly no doubt for financial reasons, partly perhaps for reasons of publicity,[323] certainly in part because public opinion feared the sexual corruption of the boys which was somewhat expected in a school setting.[324] In any case the physical ambience would usually have been unconducive to learning; and it accurately symbolized the lack of interest in elementary education on the part of both society in general and the authorities in particular. Very few Roman texts suggest the existence of schools large enough to require the presence of several masters at once.[325]

The contempt which Greeks and Romans so often expressed for those who taught reading and writing is more difficult to analyse than may appear at first glance. The first difficulty is always to know whether this contempt was felt outside the upper class;[326] that the well-to-do belittled those who, while more or less sharing the culture of the elite, sold their knowledge for pathetic sums of money, is scarcely surprising. Among those who wrote books, the attitude was certainly pervasive,[327] and the number of epitaphs which commemorate *ludi magistri*, *grammatodidaskaloi* and the like is remarkably small. We may conclude that the occupation was avoided by almost all educated people who could afford to do so, and the implication of Quintilian

322. See Bonner, *Education* 120, for a discussion of this problem.

323. Cf. Liban. *Orat.* i.102.

324. This is a persistent theme. See Quint. *Inst.* i.2.4–5, 3.17; Plin. *Ep.* iii.3.3–4; Juv. x.224 (see E. Courtney's commentary for further references). The Capuan *magister ludi litterari* Philocalus was pointedly described in his epitaph (*CIL* x.3969 = *ILS* 7763) as having behaved "summa cum castitate in discipulos suos."

325. Sen. *Contr.* i praef. 2 implies the existence of a largish school, in this case with more than 200 pupils. It was probably at Corduba (in spite of L. A. Sussman, *The Elder Seneca* [Leiden, 1978], 20; see M. Griffin, *JRS* lxii [1972], 6) and the school of a *grammaticus*. But Seneca was under temptation to exaggerate the school's size. The inscription of Lycian Xanthus discussed below raises the strong possibility that quite a number of Greek cities continued to have fairly populous schools.

326. For their views in this period see Cic. *Tusc.Disp.* iii.12.27, *Fam.* ix.18.1; Plu. *De vitando aer.al.* 6 = *Mor.* 830a; Tac. *Ann.* iii.66.3, etc. Cf. Plin. *Ep.* iv.11.1 (a senator now teaching rhetoric!).

327. Cf. Justin xxi.5; Dio Chrys. vii.114; Juv. vii.198 (the contrast consul-*rhetor*); Lucian *Men.* 17; etc.

that some men became teachers who had themselves not progressed much beyond the *primae litterae* is likely to be accurate.[328]

Whether the cost of schooling seemed easily tolerable to the family of an artisan or a shopkeeper or a small farmer is hard to judge. Our sources about such matters are wretched. According to the one usable figure concerning school fees, which refers to a rather modest school in Venusia, the boys brought along eight *asses,* half a denarius, each month.[329] It is hard to imagine that anyone except the very poorest can have been deterred by this expenditure; yet many people lived on a few *asses* a day or quite outside the nexus of cash.

In these circumstances, which social strata made use of elementary schooling? On one occasion Martial implies that in Rome itself some slaves went to school,[330] and from this a scholar has drawn the quite unjustified conclusion that elementary schools simply "peddled craft literacy" to poor and slave children. Children who were destined for liberal education moved, according to this theory, straight from home tuition to a more or less advanced *grammaticus.* But this cannot be right. There is no reason to believe that all schools were socially equivalent in the ancient world any more than they are in class-ridden modern societies. Furthermore, Martial was writing about a place and time, *urbs Roma* in the first century, which had a far larger percentage of slaves, and a vastly greater need for educated slaves, than any other city in the Empire.[331] Meanwhile some at least of those who were comfortably off sent their sons to elementary schools. When Quintilian and Dio urge the benefits of schooling instead of private tutoring for the sons of the elite,[332] they may not, it is true, have meant to include the very earliest stage. But it must be significant that the school exercises, apparently of the third century and later, which are

328. *Inst.* i.1.8. However some schoolmasters certainly had pretensions: thus in a third-century text published by F. G. Kenyon, *JHS* xxix (1909), 29–31 (cf. Painter, *BMQ* xxxi [1966–67], 110), a schoolmaster refers to Pythagoras teaching letters (great men had done it).

329. Hor. *Sat.* i.6.75, with the reading "octonos . . . aeris." Cf. E. Fraenkel, *Horace* (Oxford, 1957), 3. The reading "octonis . . . aera" produces a leaden line and is not to be countenanced (Marrou, *Histoire* 598–599, and Bonner, *Education* 149–150, make unduly heavy weather of this). Juv. x.116 is humorous exaggeration.

330. Booth, *TAPhA* cix (1979), 11–19, discussing Martial x.62.1–5. iii.58.30–31 also refers to slaves who attended a *paedagogium,* a kind of institution which will be described below.

331. Cf. A. C. Dionisotti, *JRS* lxxii (1982), 121 n.72.

332. Quint. *Inst.* i.2; Dio lii.26.1.

printed in *Corpus Glossariorum Latinorum*[333] assume that the boy who attends school comes from a family which has a good supply of slaves at home.[334] In view of the high price of papyrus, it is intriguing that of the 225 surviving texts written by beginning pupils in Greek Egypt, fully 96 were on papyrus:[335] most of these must have been written by offspring of the well-to-do.

As to how much girls went to school, it is hard to discover. Some have claimed that they attended as much as boys,[336] but a system so free of gender bias could be believed in only if there were strong evidence. Martial twice alludes in a matter-of-fact way to the presence of girls in schools,[337] which is probably enough evidence for the city of Rome in his own time, though it is of course far indeed from showing that girl pupils were as numerous as boys. A certain number of girls probably attended in some of the towns of imperial Italy, though there is no explicit evidence to that effect.[338] Some testimony from Xanthus in Lycia, to be considered shortly, suggests that there were some girl pupils in the more cultivated kind of Greek city, as there definitely were at Xanthus in the second century.[339] Thus Dionysius of Halicarnassus saw nothing incongruous in describing the famous Verginia attending a school in Rome.[340] In a small Greek town in Egypt in the second century, girls' schooling was not unknown.[341] But none of this should obscure the practical certainty that almost everywhere male pupils vastly outnumbered female ones. The proportion of girls in the

333. Vol. iii, ed. G. Goetz.

334. Cf. Dionisotti 93. One text, Plin. *NH* ix.25, mentions the son of a *pauper* attending a *ludus litterarius* (at Puteoli under Augustus).

335. For the catalogue see J. Debut, *ZPE* lxiii (1986), 253–263 ("acquisition des rudiments"); eighty-one were on ostraca, forty-four on *tabellae*.

336. Marrou, *Histoire* 391. Cf. Pomeroy, in Foley, *Reflections* 310, who declares that "the Romans . . . sent their daughters to school."

337. viii.3.15–16: a schoolmaster *(magister)* dictates poetry to a reluctant audience—"grandis virgo bonusque puer." In ix.68.1–2 a *ludi magister* is addressed as "invisum pueris virginibusque caput." Val.Max. vi.1.3, and also *CIL* vi.2210 (= *ILS* 4999) and 6327, refer to *paedagogi* who taught girls; but it may have been home-teaching in each case (cf. Bonner, *Education* 39, for Roman *paedagogi* as teachers).

338. The funerary monument of Philocalus, the *ludi magister* of Capua, represents him with two other figures, one female (see the photograph in Bonner 43). But as Marrou pointed out (ΜΟΥΣΙΚΟΣ ΑΝΗΡ 47; cf. pl. II), she is supporting Philocalus' elbow and should therefore be seen as his wife or daughter.

339. Cf. also Philostr. *Imag.* i.12.3.

340. Dion.Hal. *AR* xi.28.3.

341. *P.Giss.* iii.80 and 85.

Roman Empire as a whole who ever attended a school can never have been more than very small.

By modern standards, moreover, many Romans seem to have been unambitious about the age at which children should learn to read and write. Quintilian criticizes those who think that boys should not be "taught letters" before the age of seven,[342] but even he refers to what can be learned before that age with the disparaging phrase "quantulumcumque est," "however little it is."[343] Seven seems to have been the normal age for sending a boy to school for the first time.[344] Since rather inefficient methods of teaching reading and writing were common (not to mention the lack of elementary primers for children), progress must often have been slow. Dionysius describes how the boys were taught the names of the letters *before* their forms,[345] and Quintilian confirms that this was usual (he himself disapproved).[346] It is no great surprise to encounter boys of ten and thirteen still learning to read and write.[347]

During the reign of Antoninus Pius, a flatterer told the Romans that "everything [in the Empire] is full of gymnasia, fountains, propylaea, temples, workshops and schools."[348] This adulatory text is written from the particular point of view of the prosperous inhabitants of Greek cities. It is important evidence for an ideal believed in by many men of this class, but it tells us nothing whatsoever about the experience of the Romans as a whole. Nor should Juvenal's rhetorical statement that the whole world now has "Graias nostrasque . . . Athenas," schools of higher education in Greek and Latin, be cited to show any more than that there was a modicum of Greek and Latin education in the western provinces.[349]

---

342. *Inst.* i.1.15–24.

343. i.1.18.

344. Cf. Juv. xiv.10.

345. Dion.Hal. *De comp.verb.* 25.211.

346. *Inst.* i.1.24. For a general account of teaching at this level see Bonner, *Education* 165–178.

347. At Heracleopolis (hardly *caput mundi,* but still Greek): C. Wessely, *Studien zur Palaeographie und Papyruskunde* ii (Leipzig, 1902), 27 (lines 5 and 7).

348. Ael.Arist. *To Rome* 97.

349. Juv. xv.110. E. Courtney takes the phrase in an abstract sense, "the culture of Greece and Rome," but his own parallels show this to be unjustified. Marrou, *Histoire* 426, proclaimed that Juvenal's words are "so profound and so exact"; in reality the line is vague but at the same time somewhat misleading. Bonner in turn gives a misleading impression (*Education* 156–159) by bundling together all levels of education. No one would doubt that the elite was interested in promoting higher education, but that shows nothing about its policy towards primary education.

The evidence at our disposal concerning the distribution of schools consists of incidental references, mainly in inscriptions. Moreover, a single reference to a schoolmaster is no guarantee that a town possessed a continuously functioning school over a long period; nor does silence mean that any particular locality lacked a school; for many Italian towns, and even for such an important provincial centre as Lugdunum, no schoolmaster is attested. All we can hope to discover is what *kinds* of towns possessed schools. Most villages, it should be noted at once, were very probably without them. From this period only one text seems to give good evidence that some small settlements had schoolmasters: Ulpian mentions among those who teach "the first letters" both those who teach in cities *(civitates)* and those who teach in *vici.*[350] However, the difference between a *civitas* and a *vicus* was primarily juridical, and even this text does not go far towards demonstrating the widespread existence of village schools.

In Rome itself, the amount of schooling that went on is quite unknown. When Suetonius says that at one time, apparently in the late Republic, there had been more than twenty *scholae* in the capital,[351] he was plainly not thinking about ordinary "street" schools, but about higher-level and often no doubt small establishments. In many of the towns of Italy, by the first century A.D., schools are attested. Evidence about Pompeii and Capua has already been mentioned, and from literary texts and inscriptions we can add a number of other places to the list.[352]

---

350. *Dig.* l.5.2.8: "Qui pueros primas litteras docent, immunitatem a civilibus muneribus non habent: sed ne cui eorum id supra vires indicatur, ad praesidis religionem pertinet, sive in civitatibus sive in vicis primas litteras magistri doceant." It is possible that the last words are interpolated: G. Rotondi, *Scritti giuridici* (Milan, 1922), i.476, rejected "sive in civitatibus" to the end; G. Beseler, *ZSS* 1 (1930), 33, rejected "sed ne" to the end. In Hor. *Epist.* i.20.18 "extremis in vicis" probably refers to city streets, as we saw earlier.

351. *De gramm.* 3.4.

352. On Beneventum cf. Suet. *De gramm.* 9.1. Vicetia: *De gramm.* 23.1. For a *grammaticus* at Brundisium in the second century see Gell. xvi.6.1–12. Other *grammatici* (cf. Christes, *Sklaven und Freigelassene* 152–153) are known from Verona (*CIL* v.3433; but in v.3408 = *ILS* 5551, from the same city, the *ludus publicus* is more likely to concern gladiators than schoolboys), Comum (v.5278), Urbs Salvia (ix.5545) and Beneventum (ix.1564); at one time Capua had a *grammaticus Graecus* (x.3961). A *praeceptor* at Brixia: *CIL* v.4337; a *didaskalos* at Naples: *IG* xiv.798. A "[magiste]r" or "[praecepto]r litterarum" at Aquileia: *Archeografo triestino* 1891, 392 (and in *Mitteilungen der Central-Commission* xvii [1891], 38 n.3); another *praeceptor* there: A. Calderini, *Aquileia Romana* (Milan, 1930), 331. Whatever the exact functions of *paedagogi* attested at Vicetia (*CIL* v.3157) and Bergomum (v.5144),

However a famous letter from Pliny to Tacitus suggests how scattered schools may still have been in their time. Comum, which we might think of as a town fairly typical of Trajanic Italy in terms of both wealth and culture, lacked a school for boys until Pliny himself proposed to the local men—the leading citizens, we presume—that they should hire teachers *(praeceptores);* he offered to contribute a sum equal to one-third of what they could collect.[353] Pliny's narration leaves many things unclear, including whether elementary instruction was truly lacking beforehand; the incident arose from concern over a boy who was still *praetextatus* but studying at Milan—no infant therefore.[354] We do not know the result of Pliny's proposal. Two things are definite, however: teachers were hired "publicly" in other cities;[355] and this public hiring involved some degree of endowment, as Pliny intended should be the case at Comum. There must have been other such philanthropic acts, and the third-century jurist Marcianus casually mentions bequests "in eruditionem puerorum."[356] But only one other gift for primary or secondary education is specifically known from anywhere in the Empire.[357] In any case it is remarkable that education was in such a bad state in Trajanic Comum,[358] and nothing in Pliny's letter suggests that he intended to have anything like free or universal education provided, even for boys.[359]

In the more civilized of the western provinces—that is to say, Narbonensis, Baetica and Africa Proconsularis—the situation was probably similar. If, as seems likely, the school which the elder Seneca attended was at Corduba and not at Rome, it was impressively large

their presence implies organized schooling. Concerning Puteoli see below. There is evidence concerning teachers in other Italian cities under the late Empire.

353. Plin. *Ep.* iv.13.

354. Sherwin-White (on iv.13.3) was in error to say that "rhetorical," i.e., advanced, education was in question. The words *praetextatus* and *puer* (sec.3) show this, and "multis in locis" (sec.6) and "statimque ab infantia" (sec.9) confirm it.

355. Pliny sees that endowments are misused "multis in locis . . . in quibus praeceptores publice conducuntur": iv.13.6.

356. *Dig.* xxx.117.

357. The very fragmentary inscription *CIL* x.1838 (Puteoli) might refer to another case, but again the *ludus* was more probably gladiatorial.

358. Bonner, *Education* 109, takes Pliny's action to be "an excellent example of that enlightened attitude to education which became so manifest under Nerva and Trajan." This is fantasy.

359. In fact it is assumed that fees will be paid: iv.13.5 ("adicere mercedibus"). The point of the endowment was probably to allow the hiring of a well-qualified *grammaticus*.

by Roman standards. It can be assumed that none of the cities in
these provinces was ever very long without a schoolmaster. In Gallia
Comata, in Spain outside Baetica, and in Numidia, inscriptions suggest that the main towns (such as the tribal capitals in Gaul and
Spain) possessed schools of various kinds, and that only they possessed them. In Gaul, for instance, Augustoritum (Limoges), chief
town of the Lemovices in Aquitania, was once the home of a man who
was described in his epitaph as "artis grammaticae doctor, morumque
magister."[360] Among the meagre inscriptions of Augustoritum his
presence is striking. The only other teacher who is attested in the same
province at any time in this period lived at Elimberris (Auch), capital
of the Ausci and only a few miles outside Narbonensis.[361] In the whole
of the rest of Gallia Comata the only other evidence for schools is
from Durocortorum (Rheims)—a mention in Fronto[362]—and perhaps from Augusta Treverorum (Trier).[363] In the German provinces,
there is no direct evidence at all for *grammatici* or *ludi magistri*. Yet
such people must have existed. Colonies and military centres such as
Colonia Agrippinensis (Cologne), Mogontiacum (Mainz) and Augusta
Rauricorum (Augst), with plentiful Roman citizens of substantial
income, cannot have been altogether without schools. It so happens
that Suetonius, describing the activities of Caligula on the Rhine,
mentions a *litterarius ludus;*[364] he does not name the location, which
might well be Mainz. This reference underlines the fragility of the epigraphical evidence. Even in Gallia Narbonensis, where schools must
have been relatively quite numerous, the relevant inscriptions are
few.[365] But two useful facts emerge from this discussion. One is that

360. If that is the correct text: see *CIL* xiii.1393.

361. *CIL* xiii.444 is the tombstone of a freedman C. Afranius Clarus Graphicus
(significant name) who is described as *doctor, librarius* and *lusor latrunculorum*. He
was probably a *grammaticus*.

362. Fronto *Ep.* fr. vi (p. 240) Van den Hout (cf. ii.175 Haines): "illae vestrae
Athenae." Context is completely lacking.

363. *CIL* xiii.3694, 3702 (a *grammaticus Graecus*) (but these could be fourth-
century inscriptions); H. Nesselhauf & H. Lieb, *Bericht der Römisch-germanisch
Kommission* xl (1959), 124–125 no.6 (a *schola;* but it may not have been a school).

364. Suet. *Cal.* 45.3.

365. *IG* xiv.2434 (Massilia) refers to a γραμματικὸς Ῥωμαϊκός. *CIL* xii.714.12
shows that the *scholastici*, probably schoolboys, had twenty seats reserved in the
amphitheatre at Arelate. A girl aged seven is referred to as *scholastica* in xii.1918
(Vienne). Once again the *ludus* mentioned in E. Espérandieu, *Inscriptions latines de
Gaule (Narbonnaise)* (Paris, 1929), no. 186, from Arausio, is more likely to have been
gladiatorial than educational.

the scatter of "school" inscriptions in all these provinces is thinner than in the Greek world. The same applies to the remainder of the western provinces.[366] The other is that such inscriptions of this type as there are all belong to important towns and never to small settlements.

We turn to the eastern provinces. Marrou believed that the Hellenistic school system, the scope of which he greatly exaggerated, continued to function under the principate.[367] In reality the number of Greek children who went to school probably declined from the first century B.C. on, in the period—not coincidentally—of Roman power. This seems a reasonable inference from the fact that the endowments for primary education which we meet in the Hellenistic period, some of which may have continued to function under the Romans, had few successors. The last evidence for a subsidized *grammatikos* in the Hellenistic period seems to date from the 70s B.C. in Priene.[368] No philanthropic act concerning elementary education was known of until 1981. An inscription from Xanthus in Lycia, published in that year, revealed that in the mid-second century A.D. Opramoas, a Lycian grandee of extreme wealth who was already known from other inscriptions, provided long-term funding for the education of the local citizens' children.[369] This is all the more remarkable because he apparently provided for both girls and boys. The event was separated by only a few years from Aelius Aristides' assertion that the Empire was full of schools, and it is to be assumed that in reality others besides Opramoas made some such benefactions. However the Opramoas text is unique among all the numerous philanthropic inscriptions of the eastern Empire.

Nor did the cities themselves carry the burden. They sometimes gave immunity to *grammatici* and to sophists, as we know from a letter which Antoninus Pius wrote to the common council *(koinon)* of

366. For the Pannonian evidence, such as it is, see I. Bilkei, *Alba Regia* xx (1983), 67–74. For Spain: L. Sagredo & S. Crespo, *Hispania Antiqua* v (1975), 121–134.

367. Cf. Marrou, *Histoire* 422–430.

368. *I.v.Priene* 112.

369. A. Balland, *Fouilles de Xanthos* vii (Paris, 1981), no. 67 (= *SEG* xxx [1980], no. 1535). According to lines 24–29, the benefactor educates and feeds (παιδεύει τε καὶ τρέφει) all the children of the citizens for sixteen years; the cost appears not to be mentioned. The date is after 152 (Balland 189–190). For Opramoas as the benefactor see Balland 186–187; against: J. J. Coulton, *JHS* cvii (1987), 171–178. How many of the inhabitants of Xanthus and its territory remained outside the citizen body is unknown.

the province Asia limiting the numbers of exemptions according to the size of the city in question.[370] The permitted range was from three *grammatici* and three *rhetores* in the smallest cities to five of each in the largest. But there is little to suggest that any ordinary Greek city of this period took the large extra step of publicly financing elementary education. Only one example of such financing is known, a *grammaticus* named Lollianus of the mid-third century who was paid—at least he was supposed to be paid—by the city of Oxyrhynchus.[371] In a petition to the emperors Valerian and Gallienus, Lollianus asserted that earlier emperors had instructed the cities to pay salaries to *grammatici*.[372] This was probably a limited and fairly recent development, for Ulpian had thought it necessary to specify that it was indeed legitimate for decurions to pay salaries "ob liberalem artem."[373] As we shall see later, there are hints that in Egypt the level of Greek literacy may have been somewhat on the rise in the Severan period; but the connection of Lollianus and his predecessor with any such development is likely to have been at most indirect, for they were hardly employed to provide elementary education—Lollianus' pretensions and standing were substantially above the level of a *grammatodidaskalos*.

No city whose inhabitants were Greek or thoroughly Hellenized, even if it was quite small, can have lacked at least one school,[374] and normally no doubt there were several. Consistent with this is the papyrus evidence showing elementary teachers in this period at Caranis, Oxyrhynchus, Heracleopolis and probably Hermoupolis (the last three were capitals of nomes),[375] but not by any means in the majority of Greek settlements in Egypt or indeed in really small places at all.[376] What was lacking, however, in most communities throughout the Greek world was the will to allocate public or philanthropic funds to schooling for the children of the poor. It is simply assumed in the

370. *Dig.* xxvii.1.6.2 (Modestinus).

371. *P.Coll.Youtie* ii.66; the text is also in *P.Oxy.* xlvii.3366.

372. Lines 12–16. The editor, P. J. Parsons, holds that Lollianus was probably inventing this.

373. *Dig.* l.9.4.2.

374. Harris, *ZPE* lii (1983), 98–99.

375. Caranis: *P.Mich.* viii.464.10 (Caranis in 99 A.D. must have been a place with thousands of inhabitants; cf. *P.Ryl.* iv.594, etc.); Oxyrhynchus: *P.Oxy.* xxxi.2595.10; Heracleopolis: *SB* iii.268; Hermoupolis: *P.Giss.* ii.80 and 85. Cf. Harris 98 n.50.

376. Naturally no definite conclusion can be drawn from what may be a fortuitous lack of evidence about other places. On the other hand, we must not infer the existence of organized schooling in a particular community from finds of literary papyri.

pseudo-Plutarchan treatise on the upbringing of children that parents have to pay for their children's education themselves, if anybody is going to, and that this is the natural order of things.[377]

The office of *paidonomos,* "supervisor of boys," might in theory help us to judge the social extent of Greek education. It was once claimed that wherever it exists this office shows that the city had provided for elementary education.[378] Though the area in question is limited to the province Asia and areas very close to it, many cities are involved and the claim would be important if it were valid.[379] But we have no reason to see the *paidonomoi* as officials who were responsible for ensuring that *all* the free boys in their cities received education just as if they had been modern school inspectors.[380] However they are not irrelevant to literacy. The existence of the office indicates the real enthusiasm of many Greeks for *paideia* and also a certain tendency to think that the state should be involved in promoting it. Yet the *paidonomoi* had other concerns besides literary education, including games, parades, and religious cults.[381] Nor have we any reason to believe that they attempted to bring into the schools boys who would not otherwise have attended.

The ideal of *paideia* lived on in the Greek cities. Diodorus Siculus, in a passage discussed earlier,[382] praised subsidized education for all the sons of citizens. It is no surprise to find another Greek, in a very different geographical context (Oxyrhynchus, under Domitian), promising in his marriage contract to provide his sons with "the education suitable for free boys";[383] propertied Greeks gave high priority to such things. But no one really undertook the effort which would have been necessary to extend literacy to the mass of the free population.

The governmental attention almost all went to higher education. This may seem strange, but it was a rational enough choice from the point of view of well-to-do Greeks and Romans. They could easily

377. Ps.-Plu. *De lib.educ.* 11 = *Mor.* 8e.

378. E. Ziebarth, *Aus dem griechischen Schulwesen* (2d ed., Leipzig & Berlin, 1914), 39.

379. In *ZPE* lii (1983), 101 n.62, I listed the evidence for the existence of the *paidonomia* at twelve cities from Nicomedia to Termessus in the late Republic or principate. It probably existed at many other cities in this region.

380. Ziebarth cited Ps.-Plu. l.c. and Athen. vi.262b to show that "one tried" to make schools available to the poor. Neither text helps.

381. Harris 101.

382. xii.12–13.

383. *P.Oxy.* ii. 265.24: [τὴν πρέ]πουσαν ἐλευθέροις παισὶ παιδείαν.

arrange for the elementary instruction of their own children, but education at higher levels was a more difficult matter. To ensure the availability of competent *grammatici* and *rhetores* was important to them for broad cultural and social reasons. But the *paideia* which the elite so much respected led hardly anyone to the conclusion that effective primary education for the mass of the poor was worth promoting or subsidizing, even for boys.

As for the education of slaves, the most detailed scholarly discussion of the subject is written in an optimistic tone, in conformity with the dominant tradition of modern work on ancient slavery.[384] An important element in the argument is the *paedagogium*, "antiquity's most systematic and durable plan for educating slave children."[385] The *paedagogium* is held to have been a regular institution which trained young slaves in, among other things, reading and writing, in every wealthy Roman household.[386] The model would perhaps have been the educational system which Crassus set up, in a spirit not at all altruistic, for the very numerous slaves in his possession.[387]

It is true that several imperial writers mention *paedagogia* in the houses of the rich. However, while Seneca leaves the function of the *paedagogium* unclear, for Pliny it is a place where slaves happen to sleep; and for Ulpian *paedagogia* are not places but people—waiters or trainee waiters.[388] It is likely enough that the *paedagogium* was a common feature of an opulent household for all or most of the period for which the imperial *paedagogia* are attested, which is from Tiberius to the Severans. What is unclear is what sort of training usually went on in these non-imperial *paedagogia*. Sometimes no doubt there was instruction in reading and writing, but what is mentioned most often by the sources is training in the preparing and serving of food;[389] and this was probably the main preoccupation. No text supports the notion that they provided "systematic" elementary education parallel to what was available outside.[390] More probably—

384. C. A. Forbes, *TAPhA* lxxxvi (1955), 321–360.

385. Forbes 334.

386. Cf. Marrou, *Histoire* 391, Bonner, *Education* 45.

387. Plu. *Crass.* 2.

388. Sen. *De tranq.an.* i.8; Plin. *Ep.* vii.27.13; Ulp. in *Dig.* xxxiii.7.12.32. Two inscriptions mention *paedagogi puerorum* in non-imperial households: *CIL* vi.7290, 9740 (and see further S. L. Mohler, *TAPhA* lxxi [1940], 275–276).

389. Colum. i praef.5; Sen. *Ep.* 47.6; Juv. v.121–123.

390. In addition Suet. *Nero* 28.1 and Tertull. *Apol.* 13 make it clear that *paedagogia* were associated with pederasty.

though this too is conjecture—slave children learned to read and write either when, in a large household, particularly careful or humane masters took thought for the matter, in which case the young slave might be sent to school outside the household,[391] or when other literate slaves made an effort to transmit literacy in order to help slave children along the path to manumission. In this connection the de facto independence of a certain proportion of freedman and slave families is obviously important.

In the imperial household slave education was probably more systematic, since the need for administratively competent and other educated slaves was so great. The existence of special buildings for the training of slaves on the Palatine and on the Caelian, though their precise functions are not known, points in the same direction.[392] Both were of substantial size. The *paedagogium* on the Palatine, if that is its correct identification, has yielded a large quantity of slave graffiti—unfortunately of not very informative content. In any case an organized effort was very probably made to impart literacy and a modicum of literary education to some members of the imperial *familia*.[393] But from the *paedagogium* on the Palatine to the life of the ordinary farmworker, labourer or domestic servant of slave status was a very great distance.

Levels of Literacy

An International Elite

Within the elites of the established Graeco-Roman world a degree of written culture was a social necessity, and an illiterate male would have been regarded as bizarre.

391. As had happened to Hermeros, Petr. *Sat.* 58.13.

392. On the establishment on the Palatine see esp. H. Solin & M. Itkonen-Kaila, *Paedagogium* (Helsinki, 1966) = V. Väänänen (ed.), *Graffiti del Palatino* i (Acta Instituti Romani Finlandiae iii); in favour of the traditional identification, proposed by F. Lenormant, see pp. 68–78 (Solin). But it seems unlikely that it duplicated the function of the establishment on the Caelian (cf. F. Coarelli, *Roma* [Rome & Bari, 1980], 144).

393. H. Solin, *L'interpretazione delle iscrizioni parietali. Note e discussioni* (Faenza, 1970), 23 n.17, supposes that one of the tasks of the *paedagogium* was to teach its denizens to write perfect Latin and Greek—which is far from certain—and observes, more cogently, that the linguistic forms and "relatively stable orthography" of the graffiti show that the writers had received some education. For the inscriptions

Not that a man who belonged to this social class would necessarily have to do much writing or even reading for himself, for there were suitably trained slaves available. This was presumably the reason why, according to Quintilian, the respectable *(honesti)* often did not take care about writing well and quickly. (It is evident from the context that he is referring to handwriting, not to literary style).[394] Though very little autograph writing of upper-class Romans survives, certain specimens fit in with Quintilian's comment. It appears that the prefect of Egypt Subatianus Aquila added in his own hand the words *errosthai se boulomai,* "I wish you good health," to an official document he issued in 209.[395] His handwriting is a barely legible scrawl, by comparison with the other hands in the same text. Even more striking, because it involves longer sentences and men whose first language was Greek, is the agreement of 111 A.D. between the heirs of the very wealthy Alexandrian Ti. Iulius Theon concerning the distribution of his slaves. The main text is neatly written, but the two sons and the grandson, who wrote the last four lines, did so very negligently.[396] That is natural enough, since the occupations of the listed slaves include shorthand writer, amanuensis, and scribe. In other words, the Iulii Theones had no pressing need to write neatly.

Something like aristocratic negligence may lie behind an anecdote told about Herodes Atticus, Athenian Croesus in the reigns of Antoninus Pius and Marcus Aurelius—though the story ended in the opposite of negligence. Herodes was told that his son was "bad at letters" and had a poor memory. He therefore named twenty-four slave boys after the twenty-four letters of the alphabet, so that his son would learn the letters through growing up with the slaves. However, perhaps nothing more can be detected in this than a plutocrat's reaction to a mild case of dyslexia in his son.[397]

---

of imperial *paedagogi puerorum* (one of whom was named T. Flavius Ganymedes: *CIL* vi.8970) see Mohler, *TAPhA* lxxi (1940), 267; on the institution *a Capite Africae* on the Caelian, Mohler 271–273 (though the author's view that it was just like a modern boarding school is indefensible). In 198 no fewer than twenty-four "paedagogi puerorum a Capite Africae," all imperial freedmen, made a dedication to the emperor (*CIL* vi.1052).

394. *Inst.* i.1.28: "res quae fere ab honestis . . . neglegi solet, cura bene ac velociter scribendi." In i.1.29 he implies that such people would write for themselves mainly "in epistulis secretis et familiaribus."

395. *P.Graec.Berol.* 35, with W. Schubart's comments.

396. *P.Oxy.* xliv.3197.

397. Philostr. *V.Soph.* ii.1.10 (δυσγράμματος). At all events the son, by name

Further hints that the literacy of male members of the upper class might in a few cases be uncertain are to be found a little later than this in two passages in Cassius Dio. In the discourse about imperial policy which he puts into the mouth of Maecenas, he recommends that the sons of the senatorial and equestrian orders should attend schools together,[398] before going on to study horsemanship and weapons. The point is that they should learn what will make them useful to the ruler. But what are the failings of the upper class which Dio wishes to counteract? One is apparently the haphazard education which the sons of senators and knights received as a consequence of being educated mainly at home.[399] The other passage concerns M. Oclatinius Adventus, a consul appointed by Macrinus in 217, of whom Dio says that "through lack of education he could not read."[400] This is part of an elaborate joke at Oclatinius' expense: he had been a scout but he could not see; he had been a "letter-carrier" (that is, a *frumentarius,* another military function) but was unable to read. What facts lie behind this it is impossible to tell: more probably a lack of the full literary education than actual semi-literacy or illiteracy.

Cassius Dio, in any case, and not Oclatinius was typical of the Graeco-Roman elite in his high, even fervent, regard for education and literary culture. Not only literary texts, but epitaphs and funerary monuments too, make it clear that this was the general attitude.[401] The virtues ascribed to people in epitaphs are, it may be presumed, at least to some degree those which were really admired—and devotion to letters, to *studia,* to eloquence, to the Muses, is attested in abundance.

It was in fact a repugnant thought to upper-class Greeks and Romans that a man of their own class might be illiterate. When, therefore, open-minded and energetic officials, such as Q. Sertorius or Cn. Iulius Agricola, set about raising the sons of worthy provincials to participation in political responsibility, they took thought for schooling. Sertorius did this in Spain in the 70s B.C.,[402] as did Agricola in

---

Bradua, grew up to be *consul ordinarius* in 185 (for the family background see W. Ameling, *Herodes Atticus* [Hildesheim, 1983], i.95–96).

398. Dio lii.26.1: ἵνα ἕως τε ἔτι παῖδές εἰσιν ἐς τὰ διδασκαλεῖα συμφοιτῶσι.

399. Cf. Quint. *Inst.* i.2.

400. lxxviii.14.1: ὑπ' ἀπαιδευσίας.

401. On the funerary monuments of the Roman period with scenes of intellectual life and on the accompanying inscriptions see Marrou, ΜΟΥΣΙΚΟΣ ΑΝΗΡ, esp. 222–230.

402. Plu. *Sert.* 14.3: he brought the sons of the best families from all the tribes to

Britain in the 80s A.D.[403] Others almost certainly followed a similar policy in the western provinces during the period of Agricola and Tacitus, for Tacitus regards what Agricola did as beneficial but not strange. By Tiberius' time the most aristocratic youths of the Gallic provinces had been gathered at Augustodunum for the pursuit of *studia liberalia.*[404] Wealthy locals no doubt helped the process along,[405] and the possession of a modicum of literary culture presumably became, as the Neumagen "school" relief of the late second century suggests, a source of prestige.[406] In the east, meanwhile, the Romans can seldom have been in the position of encouraging education, for the propertied class almost everywhere had long believed that at least a minimum of written culture was essential for a Hellene of any pretensions.

Wealth itself was never an absolute guarantee of literacy; the newly wealthy might be very uneducated. The most striking case known is that of P. Annius Seleucus, plainly a freedman, who appears in a waxed tablet from Pompeii, a document of 40 A.D. which was written on behalf of Seleucus by his slave Nardus because the former "said that he did not know letters."[407] Since a sum of 100,000 sesterces interest *a month* is mentioned, Seleucus clearly possessed or at least had access to very large amounts of money. In Petronius the wealthy freedman Hermeros is portrayed as being semi-literate: he says cheer-

Osca and put them under Greek and Roman teachers, in order to give them a share of power when they grew up.

403. Tac. *Agr.* 21.2: "principum filios liberalibus artibus erudire." Demetrius of Tarsus, a *grammaticus*, is likely to have been involved (cf. R. M. Ogilvie & I. A. Richmond ad loc.).

404. Tac. *Ann.* iii.43.

405. Something of this can be glimpsed in Suet. *De gramm.* 3: a wealthy *eques Romanus* paid a *grammaticus* an enormous salary to teach somewhere in the provinces—Osca (Huesca), according to a good emendation by R. P. Robinson (the "Oscan" name of the *eques* (Aeficius) suits the place well). The *grammaticus* in question is not of course likely to have been teaching reading and writing, and neither are the famous *doctores* who, Suetonius goes on to say, taught in Gallia Togata.

406. The Neumagen relief: W. von Massow, *Die Grabmäler von Neumagen* (Berlin & Leipzig, 1932), no.180 and pl. 27, often illustrated elsewhere: E. M. Wightman, *Roman Trier and the Treveri* (London, 1970), pl. 14a; Bonner, *Education* fig. 9. The monument (dated by von Massow 285 to the 180s) was highly elaborate; the "school" relief which forms part of it shows a seated teacher between two seated pupils of adolescent age and a third standing one. It seems to proclaim the care of the deceased for his own education or that of his sons. The contention of Marrou, ΜΟΥΣΙΚΟΣ ΑΝΗΡ 214, that the monument is that of the teacher seems much less likely.

407. See the text in Sbordone, *RAAN* li (1976), 145–147.

fully that he knows only the monumental style of lettering ("lapidarias litteras scio")—block letters which were the first lessons at school, but which were not the script of ordinary business documents.[408] However, it is to be assumed that such wealthy illiterates and semi-literates were nouveaux riches and that their sons received at least a minimum of conventional education.

In this Greek and Roman elite, women may have been virtually as literate as men, but the evidence is not decisive. There were some practical reasons to educate daughters at least to this level, since most of them would have to run large households. For what the silence is worth, no illiteracy is explicitly known among such women. A few of them became intellectuals, and some engaged in financial and business affairs in which reading and writing were useful though not indispensable. Literary allusions make it plain that at Rome an intelligent woman of the upper class was often able to acquire a good conventional education, and was expected to do so, so that she would become "litteris Graecis Latinis docta," as Sallust says of the Sempronia who was famous for her role in the Catilinarian affair.[409] As for Greece, a story about Eurydice, mother of Philip II of Macedon, which is told in a pseudo-Plutarchan work,[410] probably reveals the attitude of a well-to-do Greek man of letters under the Roman Empire: Eurydice was "thrice-barbarous" and an Illyrian—and illiterate, but she became so concerned for the education of her children that she learned letters. The implications are that it is "thrice-barbarous" for a Greek woman of good social position to be illiterate, and that such a woman can remedy the defect. Funerary reliefs demonstrate, and some Pompeian portraits of women confirm, that some literary education was thought to be desirable for a woman of good family.[411]

But it is hard to be sure that the conformity which characterized the

408. Petr. *Sat.* 58.7. There is no parallel for *lapidariae litterae*. R. W. Daniel, ZPE xl (1980), 158–159, can hardly be right to see an allusion to the script of business documents.

409. Sall. *Cat.* 25.2.

410. Ps.-Plu. *De lib.educ.* 20 = *Mor.* 14b–c. Apparently the author did not realize who Eurydice was. On the textual problems see most recently L. Robert, *REG* xcvii (1984), 450–451.

411. On girls and women reading or writing or carrying book-rolls in Roman funerary reliefs cf. Marrou, ΜΟΥΣΙΚΟΣ ΑΝΗΡ nos. 1, 8, 11, 13, 68, 71, 84, 106, 111, 156, 157, 163, 165, 167, 192 (these are or seem to be from Rome), 154 (Capua), 15, 104, 166, 168 (Narbonensis), 52 (Carthage), 72 (Tarraco), 193 (unknown provenance). For the Pompeian portraits, see below, p. 263 n.459.

education of upper-class boys extended to girls; the standard ambitions which prompted the education of sons scarcely applied to daughters. All or most daughters at this level will have depended on the
uncertainties of private teaching of one kind or another, and very
many of them were married at twelve, thirteen and fourteen. It is
likely that such a system left some women no better than semi-literate.

Soldiers

The recruiting practices introduced by Marius presumably guaran-
teed that in the late Republic a sizeable proportion of the legionaries
were illiterate. However even in the late Republic, soldiers were sometimes the owners of a certain amount of property,[412] and as cultural
levels gradually rose in the first century B.C., the number of illiterates
in the army may possibly have declined. Yet when we encounter, as we
do on several occasions during the civil wars at the end of the Republic, attempts to propagandize legionaries by means of written texts,
we do not have to suppose that many of them could read easily for
themselves.[413] The normal means of propagandizing both ordinary
civilians and ordinary soldiers remained oral, but when it was a question of tampering with the loyalty of someone else's army, a discreet
method had to be found, even if it could reach only a limited proportion of the audience.

Under the principate the military environment must have given a
certain impetus to writing, not only because it created documentation
but because it gave young men opportunities for advancement and,
incidentally, having removed them from their families, gave them an
incentive to become letter-writers.

While many illiterate auxiliary soldiers are known from papyri, I
have found only one illiterate legionary (a veteran in fact) in the sur-

412. Harmand, *L'armée et le soldat* 256; P. A. Brunt, *Italian Manpower, 225
B.C.–A.D. 14* (Oxford, 1971), 410.
413. In 46 Caesar tried to subvert both the local and Roman troops of Scipio
Nasica in Africa by means of brief *biblia,* with some success; Nasica replied in kind
(Dio xliii.5; cf. *Bell. Afr.* 32). Octavian tried the same technique on Antony's army in
44 (App. *BC* iii.44: many *biblia*), as the Caesarians did against Brutus before the
second Battle of Philippi (Dio xlvii.48.1). When Antony had such leaflets shot into
Octavian's camp outside Alexandria in 30 (which, incidentally, shows what a light-
weight object a *biblion* could be), Octavian read them out to the soldiers himself (Dio
li.10.2–3).

viving evidence.[414] The number of existing documents which were
written by legionaries other than those who held clerical posts is
not vast, and private letters do not in any case employ the illiteracy
formula (so that we often do not know who did the actual writing).
However legionary soldiers must very commonly have been fully literate or semi-literate; legionaries on the Rhine, for example, were
able to scratch their names on the underside of their drinking vessels.[415] The difference between the two kinds of soldier is striking. It
tends to support those who hold that legionaries were quite often
recruited from solid property-owning families. It has become clearer
in recent work that, in some provinces at least, such families made a
definite contribution.[416] Of course some legionaries must in fact have
been illiterate even at the height of the Empire, but a high proportion
of those recruited may well have had some elementary schooling.[417]

The auxiliaries, recruited in provincial territories which were often
far from the centres of education, must sometimes have been ignorant
of Greek and Latin at the outset of their service. There is ample testimony that many of them could not write properly. A particularly interesting document in this context is a book of receipts for hay-money,
written by and on behalf of cavalrymen of the squadron Veterana
Gallica in Egypt in 179.[418] On the generous assumption that those
who are not said to be illiterate or "slow writers" wrote for themselves, forty-two of the sixty-four sufficiently preserved texts (66%)
were made out for illiterates or (in one case) for a "slow writer." Thus
perhaps as many as 34% of these cavalrymen were subscription-
literate, which would be an interestingly high figure.[419]

414. In *P.Mich.* ix.551 (Caranis, 103 A.D.), the sale of a donkey.

415. B. Galsterer, *Die Graffiti aus der römischen Gefässkeramik aus Haltern*
(Münster, 1983), 55–57.

416. See G. Forni in *ANRW* ii.1 (1974), 391 (summarily); and M. Speidel in
ANRW ii.7.2 (1980), 743–744 = *Roman Army Studies* i (Amsterdam, 1984), 60–61.

417. A casualty list of the legion III Cyrenaica, probably of 115–117 A.D., is of
interest here: *CPL* no. 110 = R. O. Fink, *Roman Military Records on Papyrus* (Cleveland, 1971), no. 34 (see the latter for bibliography). It was drawn up by "someone not
at all accustomed to writing" (Fink 160), perhaps just because of heavy casualties.

418. *P.Hamb.* i.39, published in full for the first time by Fink 283–306.

419. Some illiterates may not have been declared as such. On the other hand,
"Casis Apitus" (= Cassius Habitus?) in Fink no. 32 was not altogether illiterate, since
after he had allowed most of the illiteracy formula to be written on his behalf, he
added in his own hand Κασις Απιτος ελαβον. In no. 33 Heliodorus son of Serenus, a
"slow writer," wrote at the end of the receipt Ηλιοδωρος ελαβα ως προγιται, con-
firming in effect that he was semi-literate.

The receipt ostraca from Pselcis give a similar impression;[420] but on a closer examination it emerges, not surprisingly, that literacy correlates with military rank. Almost all of the eleven men of known rank who were illiterate were ordinary soldiers; the only significant exception was a standard-bearer.[421] Of those of known rank who were called in to write for others, six were ordinary soldiers, eight officers. It appears that about two-thirds of this small sample of ordinary auxiliary cavalrymen in Egypt were illiterate or semi-literate, but that no senior rank was open to such a man. However even the ordinary soldiers were, culturally speaking, Greek, and economically they were by no means impoverished (although they may have come from impoverished families).[422] But many auxiliaries in other parts of the Empire continued to be recruited among more barbarous ethnic groups, and those recruited in the west in particular are likely to have been much less literate than the ones serving in Egypt who provide most of the evidence.

Slaves

The highly educated slave is a familiar phenomenon, as is the successful freedman who can be assumed to have received at least a moderate amount of education before he was manumitted. Many

420. U. Wilcken, *Griechische Ostraka aus Aegypten und Nubien* (Leipzig & Berlin, 1899), contains a number of receipts with some or all of the illiteracy formula preserved, and many others written by someone other than the recipient himself, presumably in all or most cases because of illiteracy (these are late second- or early third-century texts): nos. 1129* (asterisks mark the cases in which the illiteracy formula is used), 1130, 1131, 1132*, 1136*, 1139*, 1141*. These texts are reprinted in Fink no. 78, as are the similar texts *SB* iii.6957, 6958, 6960, 6961*, 6962, 6964, 6966, 6974*; *O.Bodl.* (= *O.Tait*) ii.2004, 2009, 2011(?)*, 2014, 2016, 2020, 2021, 2030*, 2035, 2038. For the likelihood that these documents come from a cavalry cohort, very possibly II Ituraeorum, see Fink 311. In the approximately forty instances in which it is possible to tell whether the recipient was literate, fourteen (35%) show that he was. Other evidence: *P.Vindob.* L135, published by H. Harrauer & R. Seider, *ZPE* xxxvi (1979), 109–120, is a Latin debt certificate of 27 A.D. issued by an auxiliary cavalryman to an auxiliary soldier, both of whom are said to be illiterate. *SB* vi.9248 (= Fink no. 79) (second century) is another receipt written for an apparently illiterate cavalryman. An illiterate marine: P. M. Meyer, *Juristische Papyri* (Berlin, 1920), no.37 = *FIRA* iii no. 132 (166 A.D.).

421. *SB* iii.6962 = Fink no. 78.37 (178 or 210 A.D.).

422. There seems to be no investigation of the origins of the auxiliary soldiers in Egypt beyond R. Marichal, *L'occupation romaine de la Basse Egypte* (Paris, 1945), 27–33.

members of the higher ranks of the teaching profession were, especially in Rome itself, freedmen or slaves.[423] There was need everywhere for a number of slaves who were literate in varying degrees, and every man of wealth would require some such—and not only for materialistic reasons, to judge by the fondness for conversation with educated slaves which is discernible in Horace and Pliny.[424] Thus it was quite natural that in Flavian Rome, as we have seen, slaves were sometimes sent to school. But while the *paedagogium* may have provided some education for slaves in the imperial household in Rome itself, there was no generalized system for instructing slaves in elementary literacy.

As for the countryside, Varro thought it was useful to have a bailiff *(vilicus)* who could read and write[425]—something which his readers evidently did not take for granted and which was not always the ideal even on large estates.[426] His head shepherd *(magister pecoris)* is supposed to be literate enough to use the book about ovine medicine which he carries around with him.[427] Interesting local circumstances in the extreme southeast of Italy, at Tarentum and in the Salento— namely the prevalence of types of stone which can be inscribed even by a semi-skilled mason—show that the desire for commemoration, and for a sort of literacy too, affected a considerable number of slaves in this area where slave labour was abundantly used.[428]

None of this, however, should lead us to imagine that slave-owners

---

423. See Christes, *Sklaven und Freigelassene*. A Hadrianic writer, Hermippus of Berytus, wrote at least two books περὶ τῶν ἐν τῇ παιδείᾳ διαπρεψάντων δούλων (Suidas ii pp. 673–674 Adler).

424. Hor. *Sat.* ii.6.65–76; Plin. *Ep.* ix.36.4.

425. *RR* i.17.4.

426. Cf. Cic. *De rep.* v.3.5; Colum. i.8.4 (quoted below).

427. *RR* ii.2.20 (there could hardly be more forceful testimony of the care some Roman magnates devoted to their estates). On the other hand, Columella's book vii makes no such supposition. In *Terza miscellanea greca e romana* 178–179, Gasperini published two epitaphs of slave shepherds, *gregarii*, from outside Tarentum (N3 = *AE* 1972 no. 102, and N4, with photos). He remarks on the rarity of such texts, comparing *CIL* xi.7586. The two Tarentine texts are strikingly crude in execution, partly no doubt for the reason about to be mentioned in the text.

428. On the materials used in this region and their effects on the inscriptions see G. Susini, *Arch.Stor.Pugl.* xxii (1969), 45–48; and Gasperini 174 n.1. The latter estimates that in this area 30–40% of the persons commemorated were slaves, which might suggest that the level of slave literacy was similar to the level in the free population. We have already encountered some unusual evidence for literate rural slaves in this region, above, p. 216 n.207. They will always have been a small minority.

had more than a very small proportion of their slaves taught to read and write, or that many slaves managed to learn independently. There were always some people who were enslaved when they were already literate adults or adolescents. Down to the Mithridatic Wars, especially, this was very common; but after the Augustan era it was usually as a slave that the slave learned letters or did not.

The case of the rich freedman P. Annius Seleucus and his slave Nardus is symptomatic: Nardus is literate and probably something of a specialist; Seleucus, like most slaves and ex-slaves, does not know letters.[429] In an imaginary household in Campania, it is the exceptionally promising adolescent slave who can divide by ten and read at sight.[430] Even the prosperous freedman Hermeros prides himself on simply knowing *lapidariae litterae*,[431] block letters.

All or most of the literate slaves who have been mentioned here were exceptional in some way. Even the ones who held the most responsible jobs on the estates of Varro and his friends were an elite among farm slaves. And Columella remarks, somewhat ambiguously, that even an illiterate bailiff can manage affairs "quite nicely" *(satis commode)* provided that he has a retentive memory. He cites an earlier expert as saying that an illiterate bailiff "brings coins more often than he brings the [account] book" because his illiteracy makes it harder for him to falsify the accounts.[432] Since the wealthy and cerebral Columella was fairly content with an illiterate in such a job, it may be assumed—indeed it is obvious—that even the higher-ranking slaves on Roman farms were commonly unable to read or write.

"Any slave acquired a higher value if he [or she?] became literate," says a recent writer,[433] implying that in consequence very many of them were taught to read and write. And literacy did undoubtedly add to a slave's market value, at least at one time, as is confirmed by the fact that during the Republic literate slaves who were for sale were apparently labelled "litterator."[434] Crassus is said to have made large

429. See above, p. 251.

430. Petr. *Sat.* 75.4. Trimalchio says that he kissed the slave "non propter formam, sed quia frugi est: decem partes dicit, librum ab oculo legit." In *Sat.* 28.6–7 we are told of a *libellus* at Trimalchio's front door which threatens a slave with 100 lashes if he goes out without permission, which nicely illustrates the use of writing to control those who in many cases would not have been able to read the message.

431. *Sat.* 58.7.

432. Colum. i.8.4, speaking of the encyclopaedic Celsus, who wrote under Tiberius.

433. Bonner, *Education* 37.

434. Suet. *De gramm.* 4.

profits by having slaves trained as readers and clerks, among other occupations.[435] But we should avoid the assumption that Roman slave-owners in general were constantly preparing their slaves for market, and if any large slave-owner had ever decided to arrange instruction for all his male slaves the investment might have been rash.[436]

The essential facts remain these: for the daily tasks which most slaves performed, slave-owners are unlikely to have seen any advantage in a slave who knew how to read and write; at the same time there were special functions which a literate slave could fulfil, and there was frequently more incentive for a slave to learn to read and write than there was for a person born into a family of free peasants.

The educated male slave was never a cause for much remark. At the same time, a male or female slave in a menial occupation—such as the groom in a story told by Dio Chrysostom, or the servant-girl Palaistra in pseudo-Lucian's *Ass*—is expected to be illiterate.[437]

In this as in many other respects, the further we move from Rome and other centres, the less we know. Epigraphical evidence is seldom informative, and for the purpose of this argument there is no point in accumulating the relatively small number of slave epitaphs. It is true that the number of freedman epitaphs is impressively large, and indeed freedmen may have been particularly fond of written commemorations which could serve as a sign of their new status.[438] Even graffiti—and some of those at Pompeii were undoubtedly written by slaves, which should surprise no one[439]—so far at least hardly modify or add to the outline which has already been drawn. The papyri show what we would expect: some literate slaves, but no reason to think that they were commonplace.

Limited though the amount of slave literacy was, it strongly influenced the shape of the entire educational system. The essential point is obvious enough: since it was easy for well-to-do Romans and for officials to acquire or train slaves with clerical skills, they had no practical need to take thought for the elementary education of the free-

435. Plu. *Crass.* 2.

436. Seneca counts it as an indulgence and a *beneficium* when a master gives some liberal education to a slave (*De ben.* iii.21.2), but this does not help us, since he is speaking of something more than basic literacy.

437. Dio Chrys. ii.15 (because the slave was literate, he was able to pass himself off as free); Ps.-Luc. *Ass* 11 (Palaistra does not know letters).

438. Possibly this is why Hermeros is shown boasting about his knowledge of *lapidariae litterae*—this was the script of tombstones.

439. Some examples are listed in Harris, *ZPE* lii (1983), 108 n.99.

born.[440] A large proportion of Roman clerical work was carried out by slaves and freedmen, and this very fact came near to precluding the literacy of the majority of the free-born population.

Italy

The preceding discussion has already brought out some of the most significant testimony about the extent of literacy during the late Republic and the principate. An attempt will now be made to estimate the level of literacy achieved in each of three large regions of the Roman Empire. Although we shall generalize about each region, we must also keep in mind that in each of them literacy without doubt varied considerably between town and country.

Concerning Rome and Italy, we have already considered language variety (no serious impediment to literacy in this case), urbanization (comparable to that of other advanced pre-modern populations) and schooling (apparently sketchy, by the same standard); and we have noticed the crucial shortage of public and philanthropic concern over elementary education. All this evidence might lead us to conclude that the level of male literacy was well below the 20–30% range which prevailed in, say, England of the period 1580–1700. And the evidence we have so far encountered about Roman women suggests that their literacy was below, perhaps far below, 10%.

The only substantial arguments in favour of the more optimistic views of Roman literacy which scholars have sometimes embraced are that the functions of writing were so extensive as to create a "written culture"—which is true—and that this culture required very extensive literacy—which does not follow. In Rome itself, there must always have been tens of thousands of literate people; we only have to think of the senatorial and equestrian orders and their numerous more or less direct dependants, of prosperous tradesmen, of the prae-torian guard, of the proliferating imperial "household," and of the trusted slaves of the well-to-do. However nothing in the civic or economic lives of the ordinary citizens should lead us to think that the proportion of literates was high in the population as a whole. In Italy outside Rome men of property were evidently quite educated or at least barely literate throughout this period,[441] and in most towns there

---

440. Cf. W. V. Harris, *Quaderni di storia* xxvii (1988), 16–17.

441. Consider the use of book-rolls and diptychs as marks of prestige in the funerary sculpture of first-century B.C. Volaterrae: Nielsen in Bruun, *The Romanization of Etruria* 263–404 (they are exclusively male attributes).

would have been some literate people lower down the social scale. As in Rome, however, nothing we know about the use of literacy indicates that it reached the mass of the population.

Surviving Roman graffiti certainly help to show that in many places there was more than scribal literacy. It has in fact been maintained that the great majority of them, whether at Pompeii, Rome, Ostia or Condatomagus or on the Magdalensberg, were written by people of "low social condition."[442] Tens of thousands of texts were visible on the walls of Pompeii at the moment of its destruction. There is, however, no need to assume that they were mainly of "low" social origin. They *may* for the most part have been written, over several years, indeed decades, by a few hundred literate slaves and by schoolboys from highly respectable families.[443] Curses and obscenities were not necessarily the exclusive preserve of the poor, nor do the poor have to have been the primary audience for written announcements of gladiatorial games.[444]

Nor are the electoral endorsements *(programmata)* which were painted on the walls of many Pompeian houses to be cited as evidence of truly widespread literacy.[445] The written word had without question penetrated deeply into the civic processes of Pompeii, and most influential voters must have been at least semi-literate, which would have enabled them to receive the message which the *programmata* were sending. The endorsers *(rogatores)* themselves, who included such modest social groups as fishermen, dyers and mule-drivers,[446] were not necessarily literate, for the actual writers, as in the case of the gladiatorial announcements, were skilled professional sign-painters whose work was characterized by formality, competence, and correct orthography. Most of the endorsers were trade groups or individuals who are not likely to have been impoverished. The desire of those who paid for such signs was not only to influence the elections but also to assert their own status, as is neatly confirmed by the discovery that the highest elections, for the duumvirate, were a formality—each year there were as many places as there were candi-

---

442. Cavallo in Vegetti, *Oralità, scrittura, spettacolo* 175.

443. In some cases it can be seen that the same hand produced a number of graffiti: H. Solin, *S & C* v (1981), 310.

444. Both notions were implied by A.-M. Guillemin, *Le public et la vie littéraire à Rome* (Paris, 1937), 78.

445. As they often are: cf. above, p. 169 n.99.

446. *CIL* iv.826; 864; 97, 113.

dates.[447] The fishermen, dyers and mule-drivers sought association with the leading men of the town and knew (as one could hardly help knowing) that written endorsements could contribute to this cause; whether any of them were fully literate cannot be discovered.

Almost all graffiti leave the status, sex and occupation of the writer and of the expected reader or readers indeterminate. Less is to be learned from them about the volume of literacy than has sometimes been realized.[448] The argument that plentiful graffiti signify a modern level of literacy is fallacious, as many parallels indicate. In 1857, for instance, during the Indian Mutiny, great quantities of graffiti were to be seen in some Indian cities,[449] though the country's population was overwhelmingly illiterate.

A remarkable group of Pompeian graffiti (there are analogues from other sites) consists of literary and quasi-literary texts: quotations from the poets or verse compositions of the writer's own.[450] "Arma virumque cano" is ubiquitous, and the first word of *Aeneid* ii ("conticuere") quite common; Vergilian phrases are quoted on more than twenty other occasions. But we seldom find either Vergil or doggerel in locations which are at all revealing about literacy; almost all this verse comes from large houses or from public places where anyone may have written, including the poor but also the children of the well-to-do.[451] Thus while some Pompeians reveal a passion for verse, and while the *Aeneid* shows every sign of having been genuinely famous, nothing emerges about mass literacy.

A comprehensive study of the physical location of Pompeian graffiti would be a large undertaking in itself and one which could yield only impressionistic results. The presence or absence of graffiti in small dwellings may be attributable to diverse causes. It is possible that there was a relative shortage of graffiti in really small units. In the

447. See above, p. 216.

448. We need not consider here labels identifying the owners or residents of buildings (they are rare), price lists in shops and taverns (I know no authentic case of such a graffito), offers of small property to rent (practically non-existent); on all this see Harris, *ZPE* lii (1983), 105.

449. C. Hibbert, *The Great Mutiny* (London, 1978), 81, 221.

450. Cf. M. Gigante, *Civiltà delle forme letterarie nell'antica Pompei* (Naples, 1979). It is impossible to tell how many of the verse compositions which are not known to us from other sources were original.

451. Mild exceptions: *CIL* iv.733 (a sort of apotropaic couplet, known from other sources, in Greek, painted in a *taberna*), 2213 ("contiquere" in a brothel), 4665 (the same in a smallish house).

great houses they are common, and also in those which have eight to ten small rooms on the ground floor and some more space upstairs. A unit with four or five rooms on the ground floor (and some upstairs) may or may not have some short graffiti;[452] and it can be conjectured that such a house would have been inhabited by a not especially prosperous artisan or shopkeeper and that someone in such a family was likely to have been semi- or fully literate. The masses of the Pompeian poor would sometimes have lived in rooms within such units, sometimes in smaller units, sometimes in the countryside or in the streets.

Another relevant body of material consists of the 153 waxed tablets of the Pompeian financial agent L. Caecilius Iucundus.[453] Some of Iucundus' clients wrote receipts for him in their own hands, but others were represented by intermediaries, who used such formulae as "I wrote at the request of . . ."—that is, they do not use an explicit illiteracy formula. Illiteracy, however, was apparently the reason for this use of third parties,[454] for the clients in question do not seem to have been simply absent.[455] Of the seventeen male creditors who were called upon to provide receipts, eleven (65%) did so with their own hands.[456] Of the five female creditors, not one wrote for herself— a disparity which supports the view that those who failed to write these documents for themselves were illiterate. However the clients of Iucundus were far from being a cross-section of the Pompeian population: they were people with considerable if not exactly splendid assets to sell at auction; the median sum realized was about 4,500 sesterces.[457] These documents are thus consistent with, and in fact require, the view that the literacy rate of the male inhabitants of Pompeii was far, far

452. See Harris 106 for examples.

453. They are to be found in *CIL* iv Suppl. i (3340). Many are reproduced in *FIRA* iii and in Andreau, *Les affaires de Monsieur Jucundus*.

454. As Mommsen suggested, *Hermes* xii (1877), 104–105. He is followed by G. Cavallo in *Alfabetismo e cultura scritta nella storia della società italiana* (Perugia, 1978), 121–122. For an illiterate involved in financial transactions at Puteoli in 38 see G. Purpura in *Atti del XVII Congresso internazionale di papirologia* (Naples, 1984), iii.1248–54.

455. This emerges from Tab. XXIV, where the creditor Umbricia Antiochis, who failed to write for herself, was among the *signatores;* and in the other cases also, the words "habere se dixsit" are applied to the creditor, who thus seems to have been present.

456. Males who wrote for themselves: VI, XX, XXI, XXVI, XXVIII, XXXII (Latin in Greek letters), XXXIII, XXXVIII (ineptly written and poorly spelled), XLV, L, LVIII (inept too); those who did not: VII, XVII, XXVII, XXX, XXXV, XLVI.

457. Andreau, *Les affaires de Monsieur Jucundus* 91.

lower than 65%. While only one of the male creditors who sold goods for a sum above 3,511 sesterces failed to write his own receipts—and this very roughly indicates an economic level above which it was unusual for a male Pompeian to be unable to write—the female creditors' total failure to write, even though they were not from impoverished backgrounds,[458] strikes a sinister note. Is it possible that the level of women's literacy at Pompeii was very low indeed?

The question brings to mind a series of more or less well-known Pompeian paintings of women holding pens and writing-tablets. At least six of these are known to have existed, most of them in fairly large houses, one or two in quite modest surroundings.[459] This image originated in classical Athens, but its presence on the walls of an ordinary Pompeian house invites speculation about the owners' thoughts concerning the education of women. The obvious inferences are two. One is that in a certain number of reasonably prosperous Pompeian families (at or just below the level of the decurionate, we might guess), a woman's ability to write was thought to be an attraction or an asset. The second is that a woman of this social class was not presumed to be literate—it was a definite attribute if she was.

Returning to the graffiti, we must note that they give very little indi-

458. All four of the sums they are known to have realized were well above the median level just mentioned: HS 11,039 (Tab. XXV), 8,562 (XL), 6,456½ (XXII) and 6,252 (XXIV). It seems very unlikely that it was some kind of social inhibition that prevented the women from writing.

459. Six of these are listed in various ways by K. Schefold, *Die Wände Pompejis* (Berlin, 1957), 130, 158, 168 (as wife of Terentius Neo; this is a double portrait, with the man holding a papyrus roll; see Figure 5), 171–172, 202; cf. 249 (this last is given as "Muse oder Dichterin mit Scrinium"). The exact original location in Pompeii of the seventh (Naples inv. 9084), an attractive portrait often reproduced—e.g., in T. Kraus, *Lebendiges Pompeji* (Cologne, 1973), pl. 213—is in my view still problematical (cf. A. Allrogen-Bedel in *Neue Forschungen in Pompeji* [Recklinghausen, 1975], 118–119). The relatively modest houses are the Casa dell'Ara Massima (VI.16.15— "di non grandi proporzioni": M. della Corte, *Case ed abitanti di Pompei* [3d ed., Naples, 1965], 88), which was elaborately decorated with wall-paintings; and the House of L. Cornelius Diadumenus (VII.12.26–27—"non molto vasta": della Corte 202, but also extensively decorated). Caution is required in interpreting the portraits of "Terentius Neo" and his wife; he is sometimes thought to have been a baker, but the portraits are probably Tiberian (D. L. Thompson in *Pompeii and the Vesuvian Landscape* [Washington, D.C., 1979], 78), and the subjects' social standing cannot be judged accurately (Thompson 79 comments that "those Pompeians who could read and write were proud of their accomplishments"). Also worth mentioning here are other scenes of women reading papyrus rolls (Helbig, *Wandgemälde* nos. 1866–68) and the numerous representations of Muses.

cation of the occupations of the writers. Artisan occupations that appear include those of fuller, weaver, pastry-cook, perfumer and a repairer of shoemakers' tools.[460] These texts gain some interest from the fact that none of the men in question had any special need to use writing in their working lives; but how typical these individuals were remains unknown.

A final intriguing feature of the Pompeian graffiti is their orthography. In contrast with the inscriptions carved or painted by professionals, which in Italy under the principate show a high degree of accuracy in spelling, most graffiti have spelling mistakes after the first two or three words.[461] By this period Latin orthography was not simply a matter of personal taste,[462] and the rules were of course known to a certain number of Pompeians, as many inscriptions confirm. Presumably schoolmasters did their best to impose uniform spelling. Their widespread failure in this respect may imply that while the fully literate section of the population may have been small—no larger, in any case, than the range below 20% for male literacy suggested earlier—there was a substantial group of semi-literates, people who could write only with some difficulty.[463]

Several thousand of the Pompeians alive in 79 must have had some writing ability,[464] but perhaps not more than two or three thousand. They would have included all male members of the curial class, and some but not all of the artisans and tradesmen in more skilled occupations. The level of literacy among women in the latter social group was probably low. A substantial though very uncertain number of slaves living in the town must have been literate. Among the country-people, levels of literacy were presumably lower.

460. The fuller Cresce(n)s wrote *CIL* iv.4100, 4102–04, 4106–07, 4109, 4112–13, 4115, 4117–18, and 4120 and probably other graffiti. Weavers: 8258–59. The others: 1768–69, 2184, and 1711, respectively.

461. Taking at random a section of *CIL* iv (8873–9172) which offers fifty texts with three or more complete and intelligible Latin words, I find that 74% of these mostly very brief texts make at least one definite orthographical error.

462. See V. Väänänen, *Le latin vulgaire des inscriptions pompéiennes* (rev. ed., Berlin, 1958), 12–13.

463. As far as I know, no palaeographer has systematically investigated the degree of graphic skill or ineptitude which Pompeian or other Roman graffito-writers show.

464. The commonplace nature of reading at Pompeii seems to be emphasized by the forum scene in the paintings from the House of Iulia Felix in which four figures (but two may be attendants or onlookers) are reading a text or texts posted in the forum (see Figure 7). However the texts concerned would have been ones of considerable civic or business importance.

How did other Italian towns compare with Pompeii? The graffiti are uniquely exuberant by contrast with Herculaneum or Ostia or any excavated site. This might be explained in various ways. However Pompeii differed from most other towns in two important respects: it had somewhat stronger contact with the Greek world, and it was richer. The district flourished agriculturally and commercially and was on the edge of what the Roman elite regarded as desirable villa territory.[465] Literacy at Pompeii was in fact probably above the Italian norm.[466]

Other prosperous cities are also likely to have contained a higher proportion of literates than Italy as a whole. Among the cities of the Tenth Augustan Region, for example, Aquileia's entry in the long-outdated *Corpus Inscriptionum Latinarum (CIL)* contains over 1,000 Latin inscriptions, and Verona and Brixia have more than 600 each. In fact regional variation is to be expected, with Campania and the Tenth Region likely to have been more literate than the regions in the far south.

The density of the surviving inscriptions in a given region may serve as a rough indication of the level of literacy which prevailed there in the period of maximum epigraphical activity, which in Italy ran from about 50 A.D. to 250. The possible objections to this claim are easy to formulate: one region may have had a stronger epigraphical tradition than another; one may simply have been richer than another (neither of these factors is unrelated to the level of literacy itself); one may have had suitable stone more readily available than another; one may have experienced more demand for building materials in post-ancient times than another; one may have a longer history of antiquarian research than another. Finally, population density varied from region to region, and to an extent that cannot be measured.

Notwithstanding the inevitable defects of the *CIL*, Table 3 summarizes the regional densities of monumental inscriptions. The figures in this table may correspond approximately to the relative literacy of the various regions. The ranking is at least plausible: Liguria and Lucania are likely on other grounds to have been the least literate parts of Italy,

---

465. Cf. R. C. Carrington, *JRS* xxi (1931), 110–130, which still gives the best overall impression of the territory.

466. However even at Pompeii scribes plied for hire, to judge by the scene in the Iulia Felix paintings which shows one working in the forum: *Le pitture antiche d'Ercolano* iii.213, pl. xli. Cf. Harris, *ZPE* lii (1983), 111 n.113. This must have been a common scene in every town.

Table 3. Monumental Latin inscriptions per 1000 sq kms in Augustan regions

Region		Inscriptions per 1000 sq kms	
I	Campania	410.9	(100.0)
VI	Umbria	275.7	(67.1)
V	Picenum	205.1	(49.9)
IV	Samnium	156.6	(38.1)
X	Venetia	119.6	(29.1)
VII	Etruria	118.0	(28.7)
II	Apulia	73.6	(17.9)
XI	Transpadana	70.8	(17.2)
VIII	Aemilia	69.5	(16.9)
IX	Liguria	42.9	(10.4)
III	Lucania	18.5	(4.5)

Sources: Numbers of inscriptions: *CIL* v, ix, x, xi (but I have omitted the imperial government's milestones). Areas of regions: J. Beloch, *Die Bevölkerung der griechisch-römischen Welt* (Leipzig, 1886), 431.

Note: The unweighted regional average is 141.9; the standard deviation is 111.0. The figures in parentheses represent an index in which the density in Campania is 100.

Note: The names of the regions do not of course correspond perfectly to the ethnic divisions. Even though the relevant sections of *CIL* are severely out-of-date, it is unlikely that its relative incompleteness varies much from region to region; one might guess, on the basis of recent publications, that it contains between one-half and two-thirds of the published texts in most regions.

Campania to have been the most literate. If the ranking is generally valid, its most interesting result would be the relatively high level of literacy which was to be found in the formerly Oscan and Osco-Umbrian areas of central and east-central Italy.

After all this we can give only very rough estimates of the extent of literacy in Rome and Italy. The most important considerations which should cause us to suggest figures which diverge from the 20–30% male literacy and the less than 10% female literacy projected above, lead to a lower estimate. In order of importance, these factors are the evident feebleness of the school system and the general shortage of interest in financing it, the lack of any imperatives which might have led the well-to-do to take an interest in the education of the free-born poor, and the evidence for the illiteracy or semi-literacy of some well-to-do freedmen. The chief considerations on the other side are, again in order of importance, the mass of the Pompeian graffiti; the clearly artisan origin of some of these texts; the great wealth of late Republican and imperial Italy, which gave some people a relatively large amount of leisure for learning to read and write; and the spread of numerous functions of literacy to many different regions (in particular it is worth recalling the written petitions handed to Pliny by the country-people of Tifernum). I conclude that the overall level of literacy is likely to have been below 15%.

The Western Provinces

Parts of the western provinces gradually took on the cultural character of Italy, and we must suppose that by the first century A.D. the levels of literacy were as high in Narbonensis and Baetica; the cities of north Africa need not have been significantly behind.

So much might be hazarded without reference to any statistics. But in fact a rough measure may again be sought in the relative density of inscriptions, shown in Table 4. The same reservations apply as with the Italian figures discussed above, with some added difficulties: some of the provinces in question came under Roman control sooner than others;[467] the differences of terrain are even more severe (Raetia and Noricum obviously had lower population densities than some other provinces); and the adequacy of *CIL* itself also varies.[468]

While these statistics may give a quite accurate ranking of provinces by literacy (and to produce such a ranking is of course their *only* function), there are some surprises. The high position of Numidia stems mainly from the presence of the army, but Dalmatia's rank may seem remarkable, since the province never seems to have had even a single legion posted in it after 86 A.D.;[469] its showing is largely a result of the prodigious epigraphy of the city of Salona. Baetica, on the other hand, occupies a strangely low rank. It is tempting to think that the relative dearth of local epigraphists in the period when *CIL* was being produced, together with the distance from Berlin and Vienna, has depressed the ranking of all the Spanish provinces.[470] With this reservation the figures in this table suggest that only Africa Proconsularis, Numidia, Dalmatia and Narbonensis are likely, as provinces, to have reached Italian levels of literacy (individual cities elsewhere may also have done so).

467. Dacia is too anomalous and is omitted.

468. Furthermore, some provinces, especially in North Africa, made considerable epigraphical use of other languages.

469. J. Wilkes, *Dalmatia* (London, 1969), 114.

470. I have not attempted to calculate the total number of published texts. For bibliography see Bérard et al., *Guide de l'épigraphiste* 78–82.

Table 4. Monumental Latin inscriptions per 1000 sq kms in selected western provinces

Province	Inscriptions per 1000 sq kms
Africa Proconsularis	127.3
Numidia	94.3
Dalmatia	62.7
Narbonensis	55.6
Pannonia	28.7
Noricum	24.8
Baetica	21.7
Sardinia	20.2
Mauretania Caesariensis	18.9
Belgica and Germany west of the Rhine	18.3
Aquitania	11.2
Lugdunensis	10.3
Lusitania	9.6
Tarraconensis	7.8
Britannia	5.7
Raetia	5.2
Mauretania Tingitana	3.3

Sources: Numbers of inscriptions: *CIL* ii, iii, vii, viii, x, xii, xiii (milestones omitted). Areas of provinces: J. Beloch, *Die Bevölkerung der griechisch-römischen Welt* (Leipzig, 1886), 444, 448, 460, 461 (Sardinia, the Spanish, Gallic and Danube provinces).
Note: The unweighted average is 30.9; the standard deviation is 33.7.
Note: The relevant volumes of *CIL* are severely out-of-date; I have acted as if they were equally so. For consistency's sake I have accepted the provincial boundaries given in *CIL*. I estimate Africa Proconsularis at 110,000 sq kms, Numidia at 100,000, Mauretania Caesariensis at 120,000, Mauretania Tingitana at 40,000, Britain at 200,000.

In the less advanced provinces, literacy must in the main have been confined to small and specific social groups. The representatives of the imperial power and those soldiers who were literate accounted for a high proportion of the inscriptions and of the literacy in such provinces as Britain and Pannonia.[471] Another literate group consisted of

471. In Britain very few inscriptions come from the south, the midlands or East Anglia, and less than 20% of the total from south of Chester. The total in R. G. Collingwood & R. P. Wright, *The Roman Inscriptions of Britain* (Oxford, 1965), is 2,314, including many small fragments which would not have been admitted to an ordinary corpus. "Of the 2,216 stones included in *RIB* I (excluding milestones), 1,914 came from areas under military occupation," according to J. C. Mann, *JRS* lxxv (1985), 205. Mann briefly attempts to explain much of this phenomenon by reference to the shortage of "good building stone" in the southeast (204), and no doubt this made some difference; but the purchasers of tombstones are unlikely to have been

the local men of power, whom Roman officials, as we have seen, made some effort to Romanize. In the more prosperous cities everywhere this group was gradually joined by a flourishing local bourgeoisie, and the economic prosperity of these cities during most of our period was accompanied, as in Italy, by the presence of successful freedmen. In every city some of the more ambitious merchants and artisans also came to be literate or semi-literate. In the countryside, meanwhile, literacy is unlikely to have extended much beyond landowners and their specialized slaves.

The conjectural nature of these judgements is obvious. They happen in fact to coincide with, or even be more optimistic than, the judgement of an expert on the epigraphy of the Danubian provinces and its social background. In Pannonia, he concludes, illiteracy was widespread and perhaps even extended far enough up the social scale to reach some of the decurions.[472]

Nor does anything in the evidence from Britannia contradict this interpretation. Graffiti are known from practically every province,[473] but the informal inscriptions from Britain—writing-tablets and other texts as well as the graffiti themselves—are especially informative. The reason is the remarkable care with which the most inconsequential-seeming pieces of writing from Britannia have been recorded.[474] Almost all such texts are naturally brief, and most commonly they are either religious dedications or simply owners' (less frequently, makers') marks. Many can be tied to military personnel or to others whose presence was a result of the military occupation. Most interesting of all are those texts—not known in great numbers—which can be firmly tied to artisans in non-military contexts or to incompletely Romanized Celts. A glass-maker's name found in London and in

---

highly sensitive to prices, and much of the explanation must be cultural. The cultural backwardness of Britain emerges very clearly from A. A. Barrett, *Britannia* ix (1978), 307–313 (no literary allusions apart from a very few to the *Aeneid*). On Pannonia see Bilkei, *Alba Regia* xviii (1980), 73.

472. Mócsy, *Pannonia and Upper Moesia* 262–263.

473. Important bodies of material from the western provinces include that from la Graufesenque mentioned above (which led A. Petrucci, *Bullettino dell'Archivio paleografico italiano* ser. 3 i [1962], 118, to the conclusion that literacy was widely diffused in the more prosperous western provinces); R. Etienne et al. (eds.), *Fouilles de Conimbriga* ii (Paris, 1975), 143–205; Galsterer, *Graffiti aus der römischen Gefässkeramik;* R. Egger, *Die Stadt auf dem Magdalensberg* (Vienna, 1961).

474. See the annual accounts of epigraphical discoveries in *JRS* xi (1921) to lix (1969) and subsequently in *Britannia*.

Chichester and a joiner's square with the owner's name on it from Canterbury show, on any common-sense understanding, that some such men were at least semi-literate.[475] A dedication to Apollo by "Corotica, the daughter of Iut(i)us" found in Wiltshire and a Rutland dedication to a local deity by "Mocuxsoma" show that some indigenous people who were partially Romanized had adopted Roman habits of writing, though not necessarily that they were fully literate themselves.[476] Very occasionally a longer text emerges: for example, a writing-tablet, mentioned earlier, which bears a Latin letter from a man with a Celtic name to one of his slaves.[477]

Evidence of this kind has, however, led to some misunderstanding of the level of literacy which prevailed in Roman Britain. Unawareness of ancient educational conditions, tinged perhaps by patriotic optimism, has allowed some exaggerations. One scholar maintains that "even artisans could write Latin,"[478] and it is true that *some* artisans could write a kind of Latin. But most probably could not, not to mention the real mass of the indigenous population.[479]

Definite evidence about the literacy of women in the western provinces is slight. Nothing really suggests that women's literacy was anomalously strong, and nothing points to their having had easy access to schools. A few texts imply that quite large numbers of women were expected to be able to read. One such group of texts is to be found on spindle whorls from Gaul which are inscribed in Gallic or Latin or a mixture of the two (thus the intended readers are of local descent). The Latin ones bear such messages as "Salve tu puella" and "Salve soror," and the messages which can be understood are all addressed to women.[480] Such texts resemble those which are sometimes written on drinking vessels or sling bullets in being anonymous

---

475. The glass-maker: R. P. Wright, *JRS* lv (1965), 224 no. 16, and lix (1969), 239 no. 24; the joiner's square: H. Chapman, *Antiquaries' Journal* lix (1979), 402–407 (also mentioned and illustrated by M. W. C. Hassall, *Britannia* x [1979], 351 no. 32).

476. These texts: R. P. Wright, *JRS* lii (1962), 191 no. 4 and 192 no. 6.

477. Found in London; see above, p. 230 n.287.

478. S. Frere, *Britannia* (3d ed., London, 1987), 303. Cf. R. M. Ogilvie & I. A. Richmond on Tac. *Agr.* 21.2; J. Morris, *Londinium* (London, 1982), 221–222.

479. According to D. Ellis Evans, in *ANRW* ii.29.2 (1983), 977, "a very small percentage" of the population of Roman Britain was literate.

480. This material was described and discussed most recently by W. Meid, *Gallisch oder Lateinisch?* 13–26, and in *ANRW* ii.29.2 (1983), 1029–43. For the Latin texts see A. Héron de Villefosse, *BACT* 1914, 213–230. Some fifteen texts are known, mostly from the territory of the Senones and Aedui. They are conventionally dated to the third or fourth century (Meid 13 = 1030), but might be earlier.

and brief and often piquant. All of them give some simple pleasure to the person who has them written or decides to write them. The reader whom chance selects may or may not be at least semi-literate, but the inscribed spindle whorls presuppose that the female users of such objects may be able to read. This is only a hint at the extent of female literacy and no basis for any conclusion, especially as the texts of this general type are not numerous. It is only by reference to general considerations such as have been discussed before that we can make even a hypothetical estimate of women's literacy in the western provinces: even at the height of the Empire, no more than a very small minority of them are likely to have been able to read and write.

In semi-literate cultures it is very common for people's recorded ages to end in five or zero, so that the proportion of the population which appears to be of such ages far exceeds the natural 20%; too many people seem to be twenty, twenty-five, and so on. This also occurred on a large scale in the Roman Empire,[481] and a skilful attempt has been made to correlate this fact with Roman illiteracy.[482] The strong tendency of the Romans to round their ages[483] does indeed provide a degree of confirmation that many of them were illiterate.[484] An attempt can then be made to trace the variations of age-rounding by class, gender, and region; the result which possesses most interest for the social history of literacy is that soldiers who are commemorated in inscriptions of the city of Rome were much more prone to age-rounding than Italian decurions (though less so than ordinary civilians).[485] This tendency gives a very strong hint that in spite of

481. See A. Mócsy, *AAASH* xiv (1966), 387–421.

482. R. P. Duncan-Jones, *Chiron* vii (1977), 333–353, and *ZPE* xxxiii (1979), 169–177.

483. See especially *Chiron* vii (1977), 343. Even where the practice was least prevalent, in Italy (not counting Rome), about 54% of the ages given in male epitaphs are rounded to a figure ending in five or zero.

484. Duncan-Jones 351 sets out the statistics of both age-rounding and illiteracy in ten modern countries and calculates the correlation. He remarks on the fact that "in modern cases where rounding exceeds an index level of 30 (the Roman average by area is much higher, about 55), illiteracy of 70% or more is also found" (347). (These index levels mean that 44% and 64%, respectively, of the ages are rounded.) But the practical difficulties of reckoning the lapse of years accurately were considerable under the Roman Empire (cf. Duncan-Jones 336, who does not succeed in disposing of this counterargument). And whereas in modern times, even in the third world, a literate person is likely to be reminded of his or her precise age from time to time, in antiquity there was little need for precision in this matter.

485. Duncan-Jones 338–339. Soldiers have an index of 37.9, Italian decurions one of 15.1, and civilians not specified as freedmen or slaves one of 48.4.

the shortage of specific evidence for illiteracy among the praetorians and legionaries, it was not uncommon.[486] In geographical terms age-rounding was least common in Italy, in Gaul, in Rome itself and in Africa Proconsularis and Numidia.[487] This pattern corresponds reasonably well to the relative density of monumental Latin inscriptions. But it hardly needs much emphasis that this method of measuring relative literacy is at best very approximate.

It is doubtful whether we can reach a final numerical judgement of much value about literacy in all or parts of the western provinces. But the epigraphical statistics presented above, especially when they are compared with the parallel figures from Italy, together with all the other negative considerations which have been presented, make it unlikely that the overall literacy of the western provinces even rose into the range of 5–10%.

This conclusion does not make nonsense of all that has been written about the *oeuvre éducatrice* of Rome, but it gives that accomplishment a new definition. By the end of the first century A.D. all the western provinces contained not only the descendants of Roman colonists but a segment of the truly indigenous population which was acquainted with the Latin language and with every other important aspect of Roman culture. Writing was a routine part of their experience. Such provinces had never before, with the possible exception of Africa Proconsularis, experienced the degree of literacy which they now attained. Nor was this literacy limited to a small aristocratic, priestly, or clerical elite. In cities everywhere there were literate artisans as well as landowners. The social structure in these cities came to resemble that of the Italian cities, complete with prosperous freedmen. However this new literacy was numerically very restricted. By contrast with what happened in early modern states, the western provincials were in all likelihood poorly provided with schools. And in fact nothing in the society or economy of the western provinces required more than a low level of literacy. There was no special effort to educate more than a very few of the local population, and the

486. However the tendency of women's ages to be rounded more than men's in most parts of the Roman Empire should not be tied closely to the difference between women's and men's literacy, but rather to the general subordination of women, which also limited their level of literacy.

487. Duncan-Jones 343 lists regions in ascending order of the tendency to round male ages: Italy, Gaul, Rome itself, Africa Proconsularis and Numidia, Mauretania (an explicable anomaly), Dalmatia, Spain, Moesia, Germany, Dacia, Pannonia, Noricum.

notion fostered by some Greeks that every male should know letters never took hold.

In the Roman world the connection between elementary literacy and public libraries was slight. However, it was not because of poverty that the provincial cities in the west, with known exceptions only at Carthage and Timgad, lacked the public libraries which are attested in Italy and the Greek east. The reason was that in the west it made no sense to make books available, even in a symbolic way, to the citizens at large. The Latin culture which Rome exported was far-reaching but it was by no means democratic.

The Greeks

The Greeks carried their ideal of *paideia* with them everywhere, and we can discuss the literacy of all Greeks in one section provided that we keep in mind that many people lived on the fringes of Greek culture.

It appears that the ideal of universal education for the free, or for free males, which had never been tried in practice in more than a few cities, lost ground after the advent of Roman power. In the eyes of Diodorus Siculus, writing in the third quarter of the first century, it was, as we saw earlier, a splendid conception. His praise for Charondas' scheme of subsidized education for all the sons of citizens (Charondas was not thought to have gone so far as to include daughters) is emphatic. Two centuries later at Xanthus, it was still perhaps not entirely eccentric of the wealthy Opramoas to attempt to put such a scheme into effect. The deep respect of the Greek elite for traditional *paideia* is easily visible under the Roman principate, and no member of this elite would have found it difficult to appreciate Aelian's story about the Mytilenaeans of old, who punished some rebellious allies by forbidding them to teach their sons letters or *mousike*.[488] The distaste of an educated Greek for illiteracy is visible, as we noticed earlier, in Longus' insistence on making his young goatherd and shepherdess literate, counter to all plausibility. Aelius Aristides provides some explicit evidence that Greeks saw schools as essential elements in flourishing cities. But since financial assistance for basic schooling was almost unknown among the Greeks under Roman power, the literate element in the population probably decreased.

Whether the Greek cities continued to be the most literate places in

488. *VH* vii.15: "thinking this the worst of punishments."

the Mediterranean world is doubtful. Rome, some other Italian cities and some provincial cities in the west which came to participate in the Latin cultural tradition may have been on the same level or higher. The surviving epigraphy is our only basis for comparisons. While a few cities, such as Ephesus, produced a very large number of inscriptions,[489] an ordinary Greek city, like many a western city, gives us a hundred or a few hundred epigraphical texts. As for entire provinces or even parts of provinces, the lack of modern corpora of Greek inscriptions makes it difficult to compare the east with the west. It is evident, nonetheless, that there was much variation in the rate at which inscriptions were produced during the Roman period. If we take Boeotia as an average region of old Greece, we find 2,969 texts in the old volume of *Inscriptiones Graecae,* which is the equivalent of 1,151 per 1,000 square kilometres of territory, a much greater density than that of Latin inscriptions in Campania. Even if we were to halve the figure to eliminate classical and Hellenistic inscriptions (which in reality are a smaller proportion than this), the density is still very high.[490] If on the other hand we take the section of Lydia covered in a recent volume of *Tituli Asiae Minoris,* we find 600–700 texts for the period of the Roman Empire, or about 75–90 per 1,000 square kilometres, a density similar to that of Latin inscriptions in one of the more Romanized provinces of the west.[491]

As usual, direct literary evidence about the diffusion of literacy is slight. Four texts may be mentioned which throw some rather fitful light on the subject. One of them, from Artemidorus' handbook on dreams, does no more than suggest that the author was aware of the existence of many adult illiterates, for, according to him, to dream that one is learning letters has different meanings for those who know them and for those who do not.[492] Two passages of Lucian are slightly more illuminating, though each is problematical. When Lucian imagines a fraudulent professor of rhetoric, he describes him as saying to the neophyte orator "forge ahead . . . even if, as is very common

489. There are somewhat more than 5,000 items in *Die Inschriften von Ephesos* i–vii = *IGSK* xi–xvii, but this total of course includes the Hellenistic texts.

490. *IG* vii.504–3472; there are many others in the addendum. The volume was published in 1892. The area was 2,580 sq kms, according to Beloch, *Bevölkerung der griechisch-römischen Welt* 161.

491. v.1, published in 1981, covers about 8,000 sq kms in northeastern Lydia (see the map at the end of that volume). R. MacMullen's valuable note on this material (*ZPE* lxv [1986], 237–238) somewhat overstates the area.

492. Artemid.Dald. *Oneir.* i.53.

[koinotaton], you don't know how to write your letters."[493] Now Lucian is plainly not reporting on general social conditions but waxing sarcastic about orators and their teachers. What in any case would it mean to say that being unable to write was "very common"? But at least Lucian in all likelihood knew that there was a mass of Greeks who were illiterate. In another passage, an imaginary dialogue between Athenian *hetairai,* Drosis cannot read and must ask Chelidonium to read out her lover's farewell letter;[494] but that hardly tells us anything about the literacy of *hetairai,* let alone any other social group.

More informative, perhaps, is the recommendation of Soranus, quoted earlier, to the effect that to be a suitable midwife a woman should be acquainted with *grammata* so that she can read and thus add theory to practice.[495] It would hardly be surprising if Soranus attached more importance to theory than any actual Greek midwife did, but his remarks imply not only that some midwives were, as we would have expected, unable to write, but also that there was nothing fantastical in supposing that a woman of very ordinary social rank might at least be able to read. This does not mean that many Greek women could do so, and it is once again the most competent practitioners of a skilled occupation who are in question. We have seen signs before that in antiquity medical knowledge was especially likely to be transmitted through reading.[496]

A further point needs to be made about social rank, with respect to the inscriptions and particularly epitaphs. In theory a peasant, a shepherd or a goatherd might be commemorated by an epitaph, but only epitaphs in great numbers can indicate, even indirectly, the literacy of a social class. Epitaphs for Greek peasants are in any case rare—no more than a drop in the ocean of Greek epigraphy.[497]

Occasional Greek inscriptions commissioned by guilds of men who followed a menial occupation—porters, for example, did this in a number of cities—imply that these labourers knew something about

---

493. Lucian *Rhet.praec.* 14.

494. *Dial.meretr.* 10.2–3. Chelidonium undertakes to write a graffito (using charcoal) about the philosopher who is corrupting the ex-lover Cleinias.

495. Soranus *Gyn.* i.3, quoted above, p. 203 n.144.

496. Above, p. 82.

497. For shepherds and goatherds see L. Robert, *Hellenica* vii (Paris, 1949), 153–154; but when an epitaph says simply "Manes, a shepherd serviceable (χρήσιμος) to his masters," it is not difficult to guess who commissioned it. A "peasant": L. Robert, *RPh* ser.3 xxxi (1957), 20 (on *SEG* i.459, a four-line verse (!) inscription from Philomelion in Phrygia: more likely a country gentleman).

the functioning of written texts and about their prestige.[498] However, just as in the case of the Pompeian *programmata,* these texts give practically no useful information about the literacy of the porters themselves.

Concerning one province with many Greek and more or less Hellenized inhabitants, Egypt, our source material is relatively abundant. The number of surviving Greek papyri from Egypt increases sharply after the advent of Roman power, and the number of documents referring to illiteracy increases accordingly. The old discussion of Calderini counted 440 such documents belonging to the period between 100 B.C. and 200 A.D.,[499] the great majority being later than 30 B.C.; and many more have been published since her study. Other documents throw rays of light on the subject without actually using the illiteracy formula.

The Greek papyri show with reasonable clarity which social groups were literate in that language in Egypt, which groups hovered on the edge of illiteracy, and which were predominantly illiterate.[500] The analysis of such documents is complicated by the fact that in some cases those who are declared to be illiterate were illiterate in Greek but able to write in Egyptian.[501] A further complication, already mentioned, is that persons who may on some particular occasion rely on the writing of an intermediary *may* in fact be able to write, and even those who are declared to be illiterate may be able to read and even to write after a fashion. And as we have observed, what seems to be an autograph letter may well have been written by an undeclared third party.

At all events most of the males of the "gymnasium" class—essentially the Greek townsmen who possessed some substantial property and were the sons of other such persons—were literate. A few, however, belonged to the intermediate group of the "slow writers," such as a fisherman—fortunate to be in the gymnasium class—who is

498. A guild of porters at Tarsus: T. R. S. Broughton, *AJA* xlii (1938), 55–57 (one inscription); L. Robert, *BCH* ci (1977), 88–92 (another), qq.v. for other evidence concerning Calymnos, Smyrna, Alexandria Troas, Cyzicus and Perinthus.

499. R. Calderini, *Aegyptus* xxx (1950), 15.

500. This material was catalogued, insofar as it was known in 1913, by E. Majer-Leonhard, and afterwards studied by R. Calderini and by H. C. Youtie (see above, p. 10 nn.31–32).

501. According to N. Lewis, *Life in Egypt under Roman Rule* (Oxford, 1983), 81, "many" who were illiterate in Greek, "especially members of the priestly class," could write in demotic; but such an assertion is entirely relative.

attested in a document of the year 99.[502] These men formed an elite which made a real effort to maintain its own Greekness. In the towns and large villages a certain number of artisans (some of whom belonged to the gymnasium class) were literate, but many others were not, so that, for instance, every one of the master weavers who appears in apprenticeship contracts is said to be illiterate. As this example shows, such artisans did make occasional use of the written word, but there was no necessity for them to write with their own hands, and it is evident that many of them took a negligent or wholly uninterested attitude towards the education of their sons in *grammata*. At best, such a family might have some literate and some illiterate members.[503] Thus all sorts of more or less skilled manual workers appear among the illiterate segment of the population,[504] and instances of such artisans' writing for themselves are rare indeed.[505] Their use of written texts even through intermediaries was naturally fairly limited: very seldom, if ever, did they make written wills.[506] As is to be expected, some freedmen and slaves were literate[507]—but this fact provides no evidence whatsoever about the literacy of the mass of the free-born, except to show that it was not at all necessary to the functioning of the economic system that such people should know how to read

502. No member of the gymnasium class is known to have been an illiterate until 285 A.D. (*P.Oxy.* xlvi.3295). *P.Flor.* i.4 (245 A.D.) refers to an illiterate who is classified as a "twelve-drachma man," a privileged group wider than the gymnasium class (cf. E. Bickermann, *Archiv für Papyrusforschung* ix [1928], 39–40; S. L. Wallace, *Taxation in Egypt from Augustus to Diocletian* [Princeton, 1938], 119, 403–405); cf. *PSI* iii.164 (287 A.D.). The fisherman: *P.Tebt.* ii.316 = *Chrest.* 148. Youtie's otherwise excellent account of literacy in Graeco-Roman Egypt pays too little attention to the class element in its distrubution. His comment that "scribes were indispensable, literacy was not" (*HSCPh* lxxv [1971], 169) obscures the obvious but important fact that well-to-do Greek males were normally able to read and write.

503. However, E. Wipszycka, *Rev.Et.Aug.* xxx (1984), 280, was not right to say that this was true at all social levels with the effect that literacy was just a matter of individual choice; neither the men who were members of the gymnasium class nor the poor had much choice in the matter.

504. Calderini, *Aegyptus* xxx (1950), 25–26.

505. Thus a text such as *P.Lond.* iii.164 i and k (212 A.D.), which were subscribed in part by Philantinous, a weaver, is quite unusual. *BGU* iv.1065 (97 A.D.) was subscribed by a goldsmith in a somewhat clumsy hand.

506. Cf. Montevecchi, *Aegyptus* xv (1935), 77, 79–80.

507. See Biezuńska-Malowist, *L'esclavage dans l'Egypte* ii. 98–105, for some instances of slaves in administrative employment. Instances of freedmen subscribing documents: *P.Oxy.* xxxviii.2857.34–37 (134 A.D.) (an unskilled effort: see pl. v in that volume); *PSI* v.473 (168 A.D.).

and write. Almost all the free-born poor in Egypt must have been illiterate, for our very extensive documentation scarcely produces a counter-instance.

Outside the larger and more prosperous settlements the level of literacy must have been still lower. It is evident that in the villages, where schools were probably uncommon, literacy was an accomplishment of a select few (some of whom not only were literate but also had a taste for literature). There was no requirement that village elders *(presbuteroi komes)* should be literate, and the village chiefs *(komarkhai)* who appeared in the third century were commonly illiterate.[508]

We might expect that a village clerk *(komogrammateus)* should have been literate in Greek, if any village official was. In practice he did not have to be, as emerges from H. C. Youtie's investigation of the case of Petaus, the village clerk of Ptolemais Hormou and other villages during the years 184–187.[509] Petaus could sign a document with the standard formula *Petaus komogrammateus epidedoka,* "I Petaus, village clerk, have submitted (this)," but at some period of his tenure he was still trying to learn to do this independently of a model to copy from, for the papyrus *P.Petaus* 121 appears to be a work-sheet on which he ineptly practised writing the formula.[510] It is clear that even if he could read Greek, which is very possible, he was virtually unable to write it—except that in a sense he could write enough.

This point is illustrated by what happened in an official investigation he undertook.[511] A complaint was made against another village clerk in the region, Ischyrion of Tamauis, to the effect that he was unfit for his job because he was a bankrupt debtor and illiterate. The local prefect *(strategos)* deputed Petaus, who was evidently thought to be a capable man, to examine the matter. He reported that all was well because Ischyrion was not in fact illiterate, "but signs all the village papers which he submits to the *strategos* and others."[512] It would be interesting to know how far this part of Petaus' answer satisfied his superiors; presumably he knew what he was doing, in which case we

508. The first comarch to appear in the documents is illiterate: *P.Oxy.* xliv.3178 (248); and in a slightly later text all of the eight mentioned are illiterate: *P.Flor.* i.2 (265).

509. H. C. Youtie, *Cd'E* lxxxi (1966), 127–143. The texts are gathered in *P.Petaus.*

510. See pl. XIX(a) in *P.Petaus.*

511. See *P.Petaus* 11.

512. I follow here the revised reading of *P.Petaus* 11, lines 35–37, given by Youtie, *GRBS* xii (1971), 240 n.8: μὴ εἶναι δὲ καὶ ἀγράμματον αὐτόν, ἀλλὰ ὑπογράφειν οἷς ἐπιδίδωσι στρα(τηγῷ) καὶ ἄλλοις βιβλίοις τῆς κωμογρα(μματείας).

can see that these superiors defined the literacy which they required the village clerks to possess as signing ability. In other words, Ischyrion, like Petaus, was at most semi-literate, but he could still do his job because literacy was routinely supplied for him by an underling. On the other hand, it would have been a reproach against Ischyrion if he had been totally illiterate. This evidence makes it probable that many village officials in Antonine Egypt were illiterate or semi-literate.

After all this it comes as no surprise when Origen, whose main experience was in the city of Alexandria, asserts that the majority of people—he is thinking of the Greeks in general—are "unlettered and somewhat rustic,"[513] and while it would be misguided to treat such a remark as the conclusion of a social investigation on Origen's part, and we can scarcely tell what he meant by illiteracy, his observation has some value as an antidote to the narrow social vision of some modern commentators.[514] It is probable that the population of Alexandria was more literate than the Greeks and the Greek-speaking inhabitants of the rest of Egypt, except perhaps those of the larger towns.[515]

It is certain that the women of Roman Egypt were less literate than the men. We commonly encounter in the papyri illiterate women who are members of families in which men are literate;[516] the converse is rare.[517] Women seem to receive letters more often than they send them, and this fact has been interpreted as a sign of their lower level of literacy,[518] a reasonable conclusion notwithstanding the fact that many letters were written by intermediaries. Some women in families

---

513. *Contra Cels.* i.27: πολλαπλασίους οἱ ἰδιῶται καὶ ἀγροικώτεροι τῶν ἐν λόγοις γεγυμνασμένων.

514. Wipszycka, *Rev.Et.Aug.* xxx (1984), 280, gives the wrong impression when she writes of "une connaissance très généralisée de l'écriture" in Egypt under the principate.

515. Cf. Pomeroy in Foley, *Reflections* 312. However, as we have seen (above, p. 13), a small-town environment may be at least as favourable to literacy as that of a metropolis.

516. See *BGU* iv.1107 = *Sel.Pap.* i.16 (13 B.C.) (the woman has a literate brother); *P.Mich.* ix.554 (Domitianic) (an illiterate woman with a slow-writing sister and a literate brother); *P.Fayum* 100 (99 A.D.) (two with literate husbands, lines 21–22 and 27–29); *P.Oxy.* xvii.2134 (about 170 A.D.) (literate son); *P.Amh.* ii.102 (180 A.D.) (the husband is a "slow writer"); *P.Tebt.* ii.399 (second century A.D.) (literate husband).

517. A literate wife with an illiterate husband: *P.Oxy.* xii.1463; cf. Youtie, *ZPE* xvii (1975), 216. It is intriguing that the wife was an Oxyrhynchite, the husband an Alexandrian.

518. Cole in Foley, *Reflections* 235.

of gymnasium rank were illiterate,[519] and lower down the social scale literates must have been very few indeed. Schoolboys continued to copy out sexist witticisms about female education.[520] The exceptional nature of women's literacy is illustrated by the petition which the evidently well-to-do Aurelia Thaisous wrote to the Prefect of Egypt in 263 in which she based her claim to privileges in part on the fact that she was able to write easily.[521] This was a source of pride to her, and she expected it to make a favourable impression on the Prefect.[522] From the sum of the evidence known to him Youtie concluded that "illiteracy in women was traditional at all levels of society."[523] This is hardly true about the daughters of the very best families, but otherwise it cannot be faulted.

The evidence we have been considering about the limited social range of literacy in Roman Egypt is confirmed by the tendency of lenders to be more literate than borrowers, lessors more literate than lessees, and in general for well-to-do males to be more literate than everyone else.[524] All this implies that the decision whether or not to have a boy taught to read and write was strongly influenced by the expense—which would hardly need saying but for persistent lack of realism on this subject among scholars. However, we must not lose sight of the fact that the illiterates who were involved in the transactions just referred to were, in spite of their illiteracy, making use of the written word.

A cardinal question is whether these conclusions drawn from the papyri have any value for the rest of the Greek world. The segment of the population of Egypt that spoke Greek was not a social cross-section: there was a huge population, made up largely of peasants, which knew little or nothing of the immigrants' language. Some of

519. *P.Oxy.* xxxviii.2858 (171 A.D.). In *P.Oxy.* vii.1028 (86) a woman of this class added her signature in what the editor called "rude uncials."

520. *P.Bouriant* 1, lines 146–153: ἰδὼν γυναῖκα διδασκομένην γράμματα εἶπεν· οἷον ξίφος ἀκονᾶται. The subject is Diogenes, the date of the papyrus the fourth century A.D. (but the phrase must have been recopied over many generations).

521. *P.Oxy.* xii.1467.

522. Cf. Youtie, *ZPE* xvii (1975), 221. And she did in fact receive the *ius trium liberorum* for which she had applied; Youtie, *HSCPh* lxxv (1971), 168.

523. *HSCPh* lxxv (1971), 170.

524. Calderini, *Aegyptus* xxx (1950), 25. In *P.Mich.* xii.633 (of about 30 A.D.), to take one instance from among many, the lessor of thirteen *arourai* of land (3.58 hectares) is at least signature-literate (however, he writes in what the editor calls an "awkward, angular style") while the three lessees are illiterate.

those who knew Greek hovered between the two cultures, but others, perhaps particularly in Alexandria and in the *metropoleis,* remained enthusiastically Greek. Their Hellenism, to judge from the books they read and had copied, was real. In consequence of all this we should not suppose that the Greeks of the old Greek cities were in general more successful at diffusing literacy through the population than the Greeks of Egypt. Some cities with powerful educational traditions, such as those in the area of the eastern Aegean and the adjacent coast, the area where the office of *paidonomos* was widespread, may have done better. But nothing that is known about Greek schools outside Egypt would lead us to suppose that under the Roman Empire they had a significantly greater impact than the schooling we know of from the papyri.

Another eastern province for which the evidence about literacy is relatively good (by the undemanding standards we are compelled to apply) is Judaea, although this evidence does not primarily concern Greek or Latin literacy. But it was in particular connection with Judaea in the first century A.D. that a scholar made the startling claim that, in the Near East, "writing was an essential accompaniment of life at almost all levels."[525] He based this assertion on three passages in the gospel of Matthew. In these texts Jesus is shown as attempting to clinch an argument by saying "Have you not read that . . . ?" (The original remark would have been in Aramaic; the original act of reading would have been in Hebrew.) The implication of this is supposed to be that the individual, or at least the male individual, in the Judaean street or field could be expected to have read the sacred writings. However such evidence is valueless as evidence for extensive literacy, because on each of the occasions in question Jesus was reportedly addressing an audience specifically made up either of Pharisees or of the "chief priests and elders."[526] *They* presumably had read.[527] The

---

525. C. H. Roberts in *Cambridge History of the Bible* i (Cambridge, 1970), 48 (cf. 49). He continues, however, with the obscure words "to an extent without parallel in living memory."

526. Matt. xii.3, xix.4 (Pharisees in each case), xxi.42 (chief priests and elders). There are parallel texts in the other synoptic gospels.

527. A passage in the gospel of John may be more useful: Jesus taught in the Temple, and "the Jews" said: "How does this man know letters, not having studied?" (vii.14–15—but perhaps this means "How does he know the scriptures?"), the implication being that a person of Jesus' social standing would not be expected to know how to read. Jesus is shown reading in Luke iv.16–17, writing in the (probably fictional) passage John viii.6–8.

mirage of mass literacy in first-century Judaea, which would be very much at odds with what we know of Greek literacy, begins to fade.[528]

The most eccentric large bodies of ancient written material, from the point of view of the social historian, consist of the Safaitic and Thamudic graffiti briefly discussed in the section "Spoken and Written Languages." They are so numerous that they might seem to suggest a relatively high level of literacy in those populations. But once the chronology, functions, and character of these texts are taken into consideration, no more than the appearance of anomaly remains.

Change

Since the period which we have been considering here is very long, it is natural to look for changes within it. But even when it seems reasonably obvious that levels of literacy changed—surely, for instance, there was a rise in literacy among Roman citizens between 250 and 100 B.C.—the fact can be hard to establish. The same applies to the decline in literacy which probably took place among the inhabitants of the Roman Empire between 200 A.D. and 400.

The functions of writing certainly expanded, and not only in the sense that it came to be widely used in regions where it had been practically unknown before. An example of this from political life is the creation of the *acta senatus* in 59 to record what had never been formally recorded before. Another is the registration of the births of Roman citizens. But most of the things which Romans now did with writing, they had already done before 100 B.C., at least on a small scale. Roman culture was already at that date in a phase of transition from orality to reliance on the written word. The transition continued but never reached modern proportions: from the point of view of the upper class there was no point in carrying the change any further than it had gone by, say, 14 A.D., and in any case it could not have happened without radical changes in the educational and social systems and some major unimagined change in the technology used for reproducing the written word.

The number of literate inhabitants of the Roman world must have tended to rise in the first centuries B.C. and A.D. as Romanization took hold of backward provincial regions. The speed and thoroughness

528. But this topic will not be dealt with here. S. Safrai, in H. H. Ben-Sasson & S. Ettinger (eds.), *Jewish Society through the Ages* (New York, 1969), 148–169, gives an account of elementary education in the Talmudic period.

with which the Italians and provincials became Latinized has sometimes been overestimated, but a large-scale Latinization did occur,
and it created the possibility, duly realized on a modest scale, of Latin
literacy.

But did the Greeks and Romans themselves become any more or
less literate in the same period? We have noticed reasons to think that
in the Greek world, or at least in some Greek cities, the high point had
already passed by the second half of the first century B.C.: an apparent
fall-off in educational foundations points in this direction. To set
in the other scale is the great increase in the production of Greek
papyrus texts in the first and second centuries A.D.[529] At any rate there
can hardly have been any significant decrease in literacy in Egypt at
this time. The growth in the production of papyri and ostraca stemmed
from several different roots: bureaucratization, a greater use of writing
in business transactions, a greater fondness for literary texts. Remote
as the Fayum was from Athens, Pergamum and Antioch, it is tempting
to suppose that this increased use of written texts was a widespread
phenomenon in the Greek part of the Empire. The educational philanthropy of the Hellenistic period would then appear as one geographically limited cause of an increase in literacy, and at the same
time as a symptom of attitudes which themselves assisted elementary
education. The lack of such philanthropy under the Roman Empire
was an impediment, but meanwhile other causes—those identified a
moment ago in connection with the papyri—somewhat increased the
volume of literacy. And in some parts of the Greek world—the case
of the Saittae region of Lydia has recently been studied—the production of inscriptions increased in the first century A.D. and until the
170s[530]—a fact which could be explained in various different ways. It
may well be loosely related to the level of literacy.

No easily identifiable factor worked on the Romans and Italians
themselves in the first century B.C. to produce the same effect. There
are some hints of an improvement, such as the use of written propa-

529. For a curve representing the production of datable papyri and ostraca, see
R. MacMullen, *AJPh* ciii (1982), 234–235. It reaches its high point in the period
140–160 A.D. The registers of various types of legal documents compiled by Montevecchi (see above, p. 118 n.10) show how in general they proliferated from Augustus
onwards. Cf. also the list of Oxyrhynchite leases compiled by J. Rowlandson in the
commentary on *P.Oxy.* l.3589: the number rises quite steeply from 103 onwards and
declines after 323.

530. See MacMullen, *ZPE* lxv (1986), 237–238. The sample is quite small (405
datable inscriptions in *TAM* v.1).

ganda on soldiers during the 40s and 30s; but they are nothing more than hints. However the great increase in epigraphical production in Rome and Italy from the time of Augustus onwards, perhaps even more from the mid-first century A.D., makes it likely that at least a slightly higher proportion of the population was able to read and write.[531] This is as far as hypotheses may legitimately go.

531. Nothing seems to support the contention of S. Hornshöj-Möller, *Aegyptus* lx (1980), 197, that Roman literacy was already in retreat in the second century A.D.

8   Literacy in Late Antiquity

After the foundation of Constantinople in 324, the emperor wrote to Eusebius to order fifty parchment volumes *(somatia)* of scripture for the churches of the new capital.[1] His action had no kind of classical precedent, and it stemmed from an important cultural change, the rise of a state-sponsored religion which relied heavily on the written word. But at the same time the emperor's letter hints at the continuity of ancient conditions, for he ordered books which the faithful would for the most part hear read aloud, and he expected that fifty volumes would cater for the spiritual needs of the capital city.

There had probably been some decline in literacy in the Empire as a whole before 324. Thus we must start a little earlier, from the mid-third century, and ask how far, when, why, and with what consequences literacy declined in the late Roman Empire.[2] It is evident that the level of literacy did in fact fall in the area of the classical Roman Empire between the third and the seventh centuries. The decline of city elites and of the production of inscriptions on stone, mostly accomplished by the early fifth century, make this plain enough. Formal proof is not possible, however; and, as we shall see, there were new literate groups and new uses of writing. There were also provinces where the decline was slow or even imperceptible.[3]

1. Euseb. *Vita Const.* iv.36.

2. The only discussions of late-antique literacy which offer any detail at all are the sketches by G. Cavallo (esp. in *La cultura in Italia fra tardo antico e alto medioevo* [Rome, 1981], ii.523–538; and in M. Vegetti [ed.], *Oralità, scrittura, spettacolo* [Turin, 1983], 166–186). For Egypt, however, see E. Wip[s]zycka, *Rev. Et.Aug.* xxx (1984), 279–296.

3. Cavallo, in Vegetti 183, suggests that the supposed shift in the meaning of the term *illitteratus* away from "uncultivated" to "unable to read and write" (for which see H. Grundmann, *Archiv für Kulturgeschichte* xl [1958], 21–24), a shift which is thought to have taken place in the fifth or early sixth century, is an indication of the decline, the point being that a smaller achievement was now required to substantiate one's claim to be *litteratus*. But the reality of the shift is quite dubious, and it is likely that the terms in question had always, in certain contexts, referred to basic literacy.

The changes which we are about to examine are closely bound up with a huge array of political, economic, and religious developments— many of them the subject of current historical controversy. Our purpose here is simply to follow, as far as possible, the fate of literacy and illiteracy, and to make some suggestions about the place of the written word in late antique society. We move from about 250 to the early fifth century, but the latter date is far from being a natural barrier everywhere, and we must also consider some later trends; papyrus texts in particular will take us briefly as far as the sixth century and even beyond.

The decline of the cities and that of the prosperous city elites are to some extent separate phenomena, each with its complicated history. Regional variations are enormous. Nonetheless it is plain that from the mid-third century until Diocletian's time there was a period of severe difficulty for cities in many parts of the Empire: the relative scarcity of privately and municipally financed buildings of this period is sufficient proof. The extreme thinning out of private inscriptions in all or most parts of the Empire shows that city elites and the more prosperous sorts of artisans and tradesmen were in serious difficulties. Signs of economic strength returned under the tetrarchs at the end of the third century. Developments after that time vary greatly from region to region, and even to some degree within regions. Recent work has in fact tended to bring out a noteworthy economic revival in some places during the fourth century,[4] and long-distance trade seems to have revived somewhat.[5] In other words, the pervasive and permanent deterioration in the imperial economy came only in the late-fourth or the fifth century.

The decline of cities was perhaps especially uneven in the western Empire, but in the end it occurred in all the provinces there. Whether or not cities and individuals were already building less under the Severan emperors, the trend is widely visible throughout Italy and the west in the second half of the third century. Part of the explanation is no doubt that resources were gradually transferred to the imperial power and to great magnates, but at all events the prosperous bour-

4. The most convincing case has been made by C. Lepelley, *Les cités de l'Afrique romaine au Bas-Empire* i–ii (Paris, 1979 – 1981); but the African provinces were of course free of barbarian invasions longer than practically any European province.

5. Cf. J. Rougé, *Recherches sur l'organisation du commerce maritime en Méditerranée sous l'empire romain* (Paris, 1966), 312–319. For other forms of exchange and distribution in this period see C. R. Whittaker in P. Garnsey, K. Hopkins & C. R. Whittaker (eds.), *Trade in the Ancient Economy* (London, 1983), 174–178.

geoisie which had maintained a certain literate and literary culture during previous centuries was by the end of the third century severely attenuated. Some cities, such as Augusta Treverorum (Trier), flourished more in the fourth century than ever before. Indeed the fourth century saw some recovery, especially in north Africa, and older generalizations about fourth-century decay have turned out to be inapplicable to some areas. This should not, however, obscure either the fact that most Italian cities, for instance, never returned to the prosperity of the high Empire or recovered from the destruction of city life brought about by the invasions of the early fifth century.[6]

The results of all this are reflected in the inscriptions. Whereas the annual production of Latin inscriptions throughout the Empire increased steadily from Augustus' time until Septimius Severus, thereafter it fell abruptly—though under Valerian and Gallienus it was still above the Julio-Claudian level, and even in the years 268–284 it was not much below the level of Tiberius' reign.[7] This suggests, plausibly enough, that the economic decline of the inscription-commissioning classes had a somewhat delayed effect—in other words, they went on for a time putting up inscriptions they could scarcely afford. There was perhaps some recovery in the production of inscriptions under the tetrarchs and Constantine, but if so it was in good part because of governmental activity. A new decline occurred later in the fourth century.

In the Greek half of the Empire, it would be extremely difficult to put together any overall statistics of epigraphic production, but there was undoubtedly some decline between, say, 250 and 450.[8] However

6. For reasons to be cautious about the decline of cities in the Latin Empire in the fourth century, see C. R. Whittaker, *Opus* i (1982), 171. While it is plainly dangerous to rely on the individual perceptions of contemporaries on this subject, for northern Italy the well-known passage of Ambrose in which he refers to "tot . . . semirutarum urbium cadavera" in Aemilia (*Ep.* 39.3) still requires attention, notwithstanding its Ciceronian model. Concerning the cities of Italy see esp. B. Ward-Perkins, *From Classical Antiquity to the Middle Ages* (Oxford, 1984).

7. See S. Mrozek, *Epigraphica* xxxv (1973), 113–118; his statistics are reproduced and commented on by R. MacMullen, *AJPh* ciii (1982), 243–245.

8. In *ZPE* lxv (1986), 237–238, R. MacMullen shows that the Greek inscriptions of the upper Hermus valley in Lydia, a high proportion of which are dated, decline abruptly soon after 250; taking into account the economic factor, he all the same observes a decline in "the impulse to commit some message to writing in a public and more or less permanent form." In north-central Syria, however, after a similar decline, Greek inscriptions reappear from 324 A.D., and continue until 609 (L. Jalabert, cited by MacMullen, *l.c.*). It is probable that many such variations are to be found in the eastern provinces.

the decline of the eastern cities came more slowly than in the west; after serious and readily detectable troubles in many places in the third century, there was, to judge crudely by the amount of known construction, a considerable recovery in the fourth century which in some places lasted until the sixth.[9]

A clear feature of third-century epigraphy is the very severe decline in the number of freedmen who are attested; they were far fewer and probably poorer too. The demand for slaves probably decreased, and so did the ability of freedmen and slaves to accumulate resources. Although freedmen had possessed a reputation for philistinism, they had contributed to the economic and intellectual vigour of the elite which they emulated and which their sons sometimes entered. From the time of Alexander Severus, imperial freedmen begin to appear drastically less in the inscriptions,[10] and so too does the sevirate, the para-magistracy for which well-to-do private freedmen had for so long competed.

The effects of these and related changes on the overall level of literacy were not simple. In the fourth century there were far fewer literate freedmen than there had been 200 years earlier; but just for that reason perhaps a free-born male had more chance of rising to a high political and social position with the assistance of notarial skills. Hence Libanius is able to list men who rose by this means from very modest beginnings—probably exaggerated for effect—to the highest political offices.[11] John Chrysostom too, himself a successful rhetorician, envisages the son of poor parents as being able to rise by means of rhetoric.[12] For this kind of social mobility to be possible, as it was in the fourth-century east, there must still have been some elementary schools accessible to fairly poor people. It should not, however, be

9. See provisionally E. Patlagean, *Pauvreté économique et pauvreté sociale à Byzance, 4ᵉ–7ᵉ siècles* (Paris & The Hague, 1977), 232–233.

10. See P. R. C. Weaver, *Familia Caesaris* (Cambridge, 1972), 25–26, 301.

11. Liban. *Or.* xlii.23– 25; cf. lxii.10. Flavius Philippus, praetorian prefect in the east c. 344–351, was the son of a sausage-maker, he says. Datianus, who reached the consulship in 358, was the son of a bath-attendant; while Domitianus, praetorian prefect in the east in 353–354, was the son of a manual labourer. On all this cf. D. Nellen, *Viri litterati; gebildetes Beamtentum und spätrömisches Reich im Westen* (Bochum, 1977), 98–102. Of course Libanius disapproved of such extreme social mobility. Flavius Optatus rose from being a schoolmaster (but an unusual one: he taught the son of the emperor Licinius) to holding the patriciate and the consulship under Constantine; but this is a different kind of case (cf. Liban. *Or.* xlii.26–27).

12. John Chrys. *Adv.oppugn.* iii.5 (= *PG* xlvii.357). His own parents were far from destitute.

thought that the system sent large numbers of the sons of the poor to school.

Old and New Functions of the Written Word

The first question, and a difficult one, is whether in these times writing came to play a different part in economic life. The papyri show that in Egypt certain kinds of business documents, leases and sales contracts, were much less used in the fourth century, and especially after the 330s, than they had been in the third.[13] The main cause of this change may have been a sheer contraction of economic activity, but documentation may also have come to be regarded as less necessary. The decline of banking in the Roman Empire in the decades around 300, a complex problem in itself,[14] is likely to have meant in the end that city-dwellers had rather less to do with documents. It might admittedly be argued that nothing in the extensive remains of late-antique law suggests that written business procedures gave way to oral ones, but this kind of evidence might easily fail to reflect ordinary life. For the time being we should leave somewhat open the question whether, say, a loan or sale of a given size was by Theodosian times less likely to be recorded in writing; but the hypothesis is a reasonable one. The effective management of one of the large and dispersed estates characteristic of late antiquity required, as before, some use of documentation, but there is no means of telling whether the same kinds of records went on being kept and to the same degree: another somewhat open question.

It seems to be an unquestioned historical axiom that the late Roman Empire was also more bureaucratic than the principate and

13. Thus leases from Oxyrhynchus number forty-nine in the third century, fifteen in the fourth (only three of them later than 335) (*P.Oxy.* l.3589 comm.). In the catalogue of sale contracts compiled by O. Montevecchi, now out of date but still highly informative, the following are the ratios of third- to fourth-century documents: slave sales, 15:2 (*Aegyptus* xix [1939], 14–16); animal sales, 9:6 (ibid. 33–50); building sales, 37:7 (*Aegyptus* xxi [1941], 97–98); land sales 36:6 (*Aegyptus* xxiii [1943], 17–18); "oggetti vari," 12:2 (ibid. 244–261). An example of a category of document which peters out in this period (last document 308 A.D.) are those concerning wet-nursing: M. Manca Masciadri & O. Montevecchi, *I contratti di baliatico* (Milan, 1984). Labour and service contracts, never very numerous, peter out after 200, but multiply again under and after Justinian: O. Montevecchi, *I contratti di lavoro e di servizio nell'Egitto greco romano e bizantino* (Milan, 1950).

14. Cf. J. Andreau in A. Giardina (ed.), *Società romana e impero tardoantico* (Rome & Bari, 1986), i.601–615.

supported a greater number of bureaucrats.[15] The further inference has been drawn that in some places at least, and in Egypt above all, late-antique society "required" very widespread literacy.[16] But the apparent growth in bureaucracy turns out on careful inspection to have been something rather different. The imperial freedmen and slaves of the period down to Severus Alexander came to be replaced by free officials, but the amount of "paperwork" which was generated by governments probably decreased to a notable degree between 250 and 400—with a reversal under the tetrarchs and Constantine—and continued to decrease later. The constant struggle of the emperors to maintain and extend their control over the machinery of government did not create a new bureaucracy in a world which had not previously possessed one; for it was a struggle which had been going on in one form or another since Augustus. What it produced from the second half of the third century was a transfer of bureaucratic functions to the army, and in the fourth century a certain number of new jobs for senior officials such as the *agentes in rebus,* the corps of inspectors to whom Constantius II gave considerable power.[17] After Constantine it is also clear that a man could rise to the extreme heights of political office through a bureaucratic career even if his origins were lower-class, and the existence of these new upward paths in the government may have had some important effects on attitudes towards education.

However, the questions which are important from the point of view of the functions of the written word are whether the bureaucracy as a whole generated more or less paperwork, and whether this paper-work impinged on people's lives in new ways.

The last provincial census which the Roman government carried out in Egypt was in 257–58, and no census is likely to have been completed in any province after the reigns of Valerian and Gallienus until the time of the tetrarchs. The new census of Diocletian was extremely detailed (to this extent we may accept the hostile testimony of Lactantius),[18] and in general the amount of documentation engendered by the taxation system which Diocletian devised must have

15. Cf., e.g., M. I. Finley, *Ancient Slavery and Modern Ideology* (London, 1980), 146; Marrou, *Histoire* 446.

16. Wipszycka, *Rev.Et.Aug.* xxx (1984), 280; hence she finds the obviously limited diffusion of literacy "paradoxical."

17. Concerning them see A. Giardina, *Aspetti della burocrazia nel basso impero* (Rome, 1977).

18. Lactant. *De mort.pers.* 23.1–4.

been large by any ancient standard.[19] The amount of detail which officials gathered probably varied from region to region. But in any case
this taxation system soon died of its own complexity, at least in Egypt,
where our knowledge is best, and this perhaps happened even before
Diocletian's abdication.[20] What replaced it in that province were suc-
cessively cruder systems, which relied on much lower levels of information and presumably of documentation; it is probable that by
341–42 the government had ceased to differentiate between the levels
of tax to be paid on different qualities of land.[21] The so-called "library
of properties," the register of properties on which an accurate new
census might in theory have been based, is attested no more after 319.[22]

For most provinces there is no secure way of discovering the degree
of complexity involved in Diocletian's system of taxation,[23] but the
system was perhaps simpler in many provinces than it was in Egypt.
We have plentiful details from only one other area: nine cities in the
eastern and southeastern Aegean which have produced epigraphical
records of property declarations of the late-third or early-fourth centuries.[24] These records were certainly complex, but they concern a
small comfortably-off segment of the population—and a region of
limited size which had a centuries-long tradition of relatively high literacy. It has been plausibly suggested that since these records committed to stone such fluctuating details as the numbers of sheep and
pigs owned, they may have served as marks of social distinction
for the owners who appeared in them.[25] In short, these are further
instances in which the ostensible message of an inscription is not its
only message. The tetrarchic government unquestionably made heavy
use of writing in order to set up a new fiscal system; but this did not
mean that henceforth there was a regular cycle of paperwork all over
the Empire.

19. The prefect of Egypt ordered that the taxation edict be sent to "every village or
place whatsoever" (*P.Cair. Isidor.* 1, line 16).

20. For the date see J. Lallemand, *L'administration civile de l'Egypte de l'avènement de Dioclétien à la création du diocèse (284–382)* (Brussels, 1964), 36–37,
185–186. For the Diocletianic system see Lallemand 168–182.

21. Lallemand 37, 184–185.

22. Lallemand 188.

23. A summary account: A. H. M. Jones, *The Later Roman Empire, 284–602*
(Oxford, 1964), i.61–66.

24. See W. Goffart, *Caput and Colonate: Towards a History of Late Roman Taxation* (Toronto, 1974), 113–121.

25. Goffart 121.

The administration of Egyptian towns in the late-third century and for much of the fourth century involved impressive quantities of documentation. Some of the documents in question are of a thoroughly mundane and day-to-day kind, such as a list of watchmen at Oxyrhynchus or the receipts given to comarchs (village officials) for workmen sent in for state service;[26] however such documents do in fact normally concern matters of considerable local importance. In any case documents generated by the administration of the towns eventually grow much rarer. The trend is clear from the 340s and very marked indeed in the last third of the century.[27]

To what extent parallel developments were taking place elsewhere in the Empire we cannot tell. A recently published edict of Valentinian I from Apulia shows the government making a fervent attempt to use improved local recordkeeping, including monthly reports *(mestrui breves)*, for purposes of tax-gathering.[28] In the long term, however, say between the Severan period and the early fifth century, there was plainly a general decline in the administrative use of writing on the city level. It is hinted at by such changes as the ruling of 293 that illiterates could serve in the decurionate. The decline was gradual. In a region where the evidence has received a recent and thorough survey, the north African provinces, there are still some signs of municipal offices at work in the second half of the fourth century.[29] That probably ceased to be the case in all the regions which were affected by barbarian invasions in the fifth century.

Rome received its first systematic law code for many centuries in 291 with the *Codex Gregorianus,* which was followed in or soon after 294 by the *Codex Hermogenianus* (neither of course survives).[30] This innovation might be thought to represent the investing of still

26. Watchmen: *P.Oxy.* i.43 (295). For the comarchs' receipts see the references given by Lallemand, *L'administration civile* 135 n.2, which are especially interesting because, as she remarks, most comarchs were illiterate.

27. See the documents cited by Lallemand 96–138.

28. A. Giardina & F. Grelle, *MEFRA* xcv (1983), 249–303.

29. Thus at a small town in Africa Proconsularis whose full ancient name is not known, the record offices, which were very old, were in some way repaired or restored in the period 368–370 (*CIL* viii.27817 = *ILS* 5557: "tabularia antiquissima"; cf. Lepelley, *Cités* ii.106). At Thubursicu Numidarum in the same province in 397 or 398 there were *notarii* who were probably employed by the city (August. *Ep.* 44; Lepelley ii.216).

30. The fragments are in *FIRA* ii.653–665. See in general L. Wenger, *Die Quellen des römischen Rechts* (Vienna, 1953), 534–536.

greater authority in the written word. Caution is required, however, for the codes were presumably nothing more than compilations of existing texts, and they were a matter of convenience in a period of extensive new legislation rather than products of a novel attitude towards written law. Furthermore, it appears that it was private, not governmental, initiative which led to their being compiled. Yet regardless of the exact status of the authors, it seems a safe assumption that these codes were meant to be legal guides for the use of officials.[31]

The convenience of this new form of legal reference book was made possible by the spread of the codex book at the expense of the bookroll, a change which was going on apace at the end of the third century.

The degree to which judicial proceedings depended on the written word is a question rendered especially complex by the changes which took place in the judicial structures themselves, including the emergence of military and ecclesiastical jurisdiction. Judicial documents in Egyptian papyri appear to decrease in number in the latter part of the fourth century in parallel with the administrative documents just mentioned. But the trend is incomplete; for example, in 390 an illiterate wage-earner could still think it worthwhile to have a petition written when he had been assaulted.[32] The knowledge was widespread even at this date that to obtain legal redress it was necessary to submit a complaint in writing.

Until the 250s the Roman army regularly compiled elaborate written records, such as the documents on ostraca written during that decade by the auxiliary unit at Bu Njem. In the standard collection of military records on papyrus, texts which come from Dura Europus as well as from Egypt, they are still numerous in the 240s and 250s but cease completely after 256 until a dubious fragment appears in 293.[33] The bureaucratic system of the army broke down under Valerian and Gallienus. It revived again under the tetrarchy, and proper military rosters briefly reappear.[34] But although later papyri tell us a great deal about the army, the detailed bureaucratic records of the earlier period are never equalled. By this time the army had long been involved in the civilian administration and paperwork of the provinces, a trend

31. Cf. T. Honoré, *ZSS* ciii (1986), 168–169.

32. *P.Oxy.* xlix.3480.

33. See R. O. Fink, *Roman Military Records on Papyrus* (Cleveland, 1971); but his definition of what constitutes a military record is a restrictive one. The 293 document: Fink no. 86 = *P.Grenf.* ii.110.

34. *P.Mich.* x.592, 593.

which had begun in the Severan period and accelerated in the mid-third century.[35] But military affairs in the strict sense probably passed their peak of bureaucratization in the third century.

Vegetius, writing after 383, but perhaps not long afterwards, expressed the following opinion: "Since there are many offices in the legions which require educated soldiers *[litteratos milites]*, it is appropriate that those who test the recruits should examine the stature, physical strength and mental alertness of all of them; but in some cases skill in note-taking [if this is what *notarum peritia* means] and practice in arithmetic is selected."[36] Yet nothing in this text supports the view that the army's paperwork was now much more extensive; the army had had a bureaucratic side to it, and had needed some literate recruits, for several centuries. It had now absorbed some functions which had once been fulfilled by civilians; that is all. Indeed, it would not have been surprising if Vegetius had put heavier emphasis on the need for clerical skills. As for his belief that a written roster was still drawn up daily in the legions, the papyrus evidence strongly suggests that this was wishful thinking or a piece of outdated information from an old source.

In the realm of literary and quasi-literary texts, a change had now occurred which may have important implications for the ways in which such texts were used. Gradually the book in codex form superseded the papyrus roll.[37] The literary codex was already known in the first century A.D., but in the second century more than 98% of the Greek literary texts which we possess were still written on rolls (the percentage might have been notably lower outside Egypt, but there is no specific reason to think so). In the third, fourth and fifth centuries the figures sink to 81%, 26% and 11%, respectively. One group in Egypt, however, had already long given its allegiance to the codex: the Christian biblical papyri of the second century, which are few (eleven are now known), are exclusively from codices.[38] From roughly 300 A.D.

---

35. See R. MacMullen, *Soldier and Civilian in the Later Roman Empire* (Cambridge, Mass., 1967), 54–70.

36. ii.19: "quoniam in legionibus plures scholae sunt quae litteratos milites quaerunt, ab his qui tirones probant in omnibus quidem . . . sed in quibusdam notarum peritia, calculandi computandique usus eligitur."

37. The best account of the facts is now that of C. H. Roberts & T. C. Skeat, *The Birth of the Codex* (London, 1983).

38. These figures are all from Roberts & Skeat 36–37, 40–41 (but according to G. Cavallo, *SIFC* ser.3 iii [1985], 120–121, the total of extant codices earlier than 300 A.D. is even smaller than they suppose). For the dominance of the codex outside

the total production of literary texts in Egypt declined markedly, and those that were produced were mainly in codex form.

In order to understand this change we have to consider these two phenomena together: the overwhelming preference of the Christians for putting their holy books into codex form, and the much slower decision of those who wrote and commissioned non-Christian writings to change to the codex, a decision made during the last decades of the third century and the first decades of the fourth. It is plain, first of all, that there was an economic advantage, for though a codex uses more space for margins, it allows both sides of the papyrus or parchment to be used.[39] This explanation might be sufficient by itself, were it not for the curious behaviour of the Christians: it is hardly credible that they alone were cost-conscious (the cost advantage of the codex was there all along), or that it was by coincidence that the codex came to be dominant even for pagan texts in a period in which the numbers and influence of the Christians were rapidly increasing.

One theory has it that the Christians preferred codices to book-rolls because, being of the lower orders, they were accustomed to codices and regarded upper-class book-rolls with suspicion.[40] This cannot be right: the Christians who made most use of books must in the main have been quite familiar with book-rolls (and what passes for "popular" literature was in fact almost all written on rolls, at least in Egypt, where virtually all our evidence comes from), whereas the more plebeian of the Christians came from backgrounds in which no books of any kind were in regular use.[41] This last fact may have been

Egypt see, e.g., J. Scheele, *Bibliothek und Wissenschaft* xii (1978), 25–33, on the evidence of Augustine.

39. T. C. Skeat, *ZPE* xlv (1982), 173–175, has calculated somewhat artificially that a 44% saving of paper is involved, and a 26% saving of cost if the labour of writing is taken into account. The suggestion of Cavallo, in Vegetti, *Oralità, scrittura, spettacolo* 182–183, that late-antique books were actually more expensive since they were not copied by slaves but by paid scribes is not convincing.

40. G. Cavallo, in Cavallo (ed.), *Libri, editori e pubblico nel mondo antico* (Rome & Bari, 1975), 83–85, and in *SIFC* ser.3 iii (1985), 118–121.

41. Cavallo's view seems to be partly based on the misconception that a text such as Lollianus' *Phoenicica*, which is known to us from a codex, was written for the "basso popolo." It is far-fetched to suppose that such a book as Bodmer Codex XXVII (of the late third or early fourth century; the papyrus is described by A. Carlini, *Mus.Helv.* xxxii [1975], 33–40) was intended for readers of a low social level (Cavallo, *Libri* 108): it is a text of Thucydides! The comparison of the codex with modern paperbacks (85) is completely inappropriate, there being no mass education and therefore no mass public to appeal to. For a conclusive demonstration that "popular"

important: many Christians felt no conscious attachment at all to the old written culture and may for this reason have been especially willing to jettison the old kind of book. But for the positive attraction of the codex form we have to look elsewhere. It certainly made it possible to encompass a longer text within a single physical "book"—an entire *Iliad* or *Aeneid,* for instance, which previously required a number of rolls each.[42] But the suspicion must remain strong that the Christians saw some other specific advantage in the codex form, and, as others have suggested, this is likely to have been the greater ease with which a particular passage can be found in a codex.[43] To find the passage which you want to read to the faithful or use against your opponent in a theological squabble, you would commonly have had to unroll up to ten feet of papyrus. How much easier to mark a page and turn to it immediately![44] It is interesting that in the lists of second-century codices that are unconnected with Christianity or Judaism, of which seventeen are currently known, six or more are texts which may have been needed for consultation and quotation more than for ordinary reading.[45] Some are also texts which are likely to have been wanted in "one-volume" editions, such as Plato's *Republic.* Thus the codex had a number of advantages over the book-roll, and it should in general have made it easier for people to read literary texts. It certainly made it easier to look things up in a technical handbook, or in a legal textbook or in a collection of enactments such as was to be

literature (romances, the *Acta Alexandrinorum,* the Oracle of the Potter, the *Sortes* of Astrampsychos) was almost always written on rolls see Roberts & Skeat 69–70.

42. Cf. E. G. Turner, *The Typology of the Early Codex* (Philadelphia, 1977), 82–84; Roberts & Skeat 71–73.

43. C. R. Gregory, *Canon and Text of the New Testament* (New York, 1912), 322–323; F. G. Kenyon, *Books and Readers in Ancient Greece and Rome* (2d ed., Oxford, 1951), 114–115.

44. The technique is vividly illustrated in August. *Ep.* 29.4–10, an account of a sermon: "codicem etiam accepi et recitavi totum illum locum," etc. Against the theory that ease of consultation and quotation was the vital consideration, T. C. Skeat argues (*Cambridge History of the Bible* ii [Cambridge, 1969], 70) that without chapter divisions in the text it would have been as hard to find a passage in a codex as in a roll; but the vital difference, plainly, is that one can put markers between the pages of a codex. Skeat's notion (72) that the codex became the prevalent form of book among the Christians because "some leading figure in the early church . . . succeeded . . . in imposing its use" is entirely without substance, and also fails to explain why pagans too eventually turned from the one form to the other.

45. Roberts & Skeat 71; cf. Turner 89–90.

found in the new legal codes of the 290s.[46] The victory of the codex over the book-roll was natural in an age in which religious books were gaining in relative importance, and in which consultation and quotation instead of independent and disinterested reading were becoming commoner.[47]

The copying and the practical availability of secular literary texts underwent a decline which probably started in many places in the third century. The steep decline in the production of literary papyri in Egypt comes in the fourth century (the peak was in the second century),[48] and while there is no way of measuring this trend in other places it was presumably one which affected the whole Empire. This was at the same time a symptom of and a cause of a profound cultural change, an extensive loss of awareness of past achievements in history-writing, in philosophy, in all genres of imaginative literature, and eventually in mathematics. Of course the break was far from complete: some authors continued to be quite widely available, and there were learned men in both east and west long after the period we are now considering. When Macrobius wrote the *Saturnalia,* he was evidently not short of books. Nonetheless, the discontinuity was real. While it is obviously risky to connect the literary knowledge of any individual Roman with this trend, it is at least worth considering whether the limitations of the reading of such an active mind as, say, that of Lactantius (born about 240) were caused in part by the sheer unavailability of texts.[49] Particularly striking are the limits of Lactantius' knowledge of Latin prose authors, even Cicero, who had much to offer him. The life span of Lactantius is admittedly a rather early

46. Concerning the transfer of the texts of the classical jurists from roll to codex see F. Wieacker, *Textstufen klassischer Juristen* (*Abh.Gött.* ser.3 no. 45) (Göttingen, 1960), 93–119.

47. The increasing use of parchment instead of papyrus is another important change, but its implications for this inquiry are unclear. The most recent scholarship on the topic includes R. Reed, *Ancient Skins, Parchments and Leathers* (London & New York, 1972), 86–117; Roberts & Skeat 5–10. Its increased diffusion may be partly attributable to growing difficulties in obtaining papyrus supplies.

48. Kenyon, *Books and Readers* 37; W. H. Willis, *GRBS* ix (1968), 210: 636 manuscripts are dated to the third century, 204 to the fourth; P. Lemerle, *Le premier humanisme byzantin* (Paris, 1971), 57–60 (but at Constantinople imperial copyists kept many works alive).

49. R. M. Ogilvie, *The Library of Lactantius* (Oxford, 1978), with the conclusions summarized at 109–110. He contrasts Lactantius' reading with that of Tertullian (born about 160). Jerome, however, seems to have been better read than Lactantius.

period for the decline in the circulation of pagan literature. Later on, however, the trend becomes very clear. Many if not all the works of Cicero were impossible to find even in a considerable town such as Hippo in Augustine's time.[50] When later writers such as Libanius and Gregory of Nyssa complain of the shortage of copyists, they are probably referring to a serious and widespread problem.[51]

The diffusion of new literary works became even more narrowly restricted than it had been in the high Empire. In the literary world of the late fourth century and of Sidonius Apollinaris, well-to-do intellectuals obtained their books by borrowing them from their acquaintances and having them copied, and friends might send copies of their own works; booksellers are seldom mentioned.[52]

Certain other important functions of writing went into uneven retreat. Practically all kinds of honorific and commemorative inscriptions, from texts honouring emperors to brief epitaphs, decreased in the mid-third century, revived to some extent under the tetrarchs, and declined again during the middle or late fourth century. The main cause was probably economic, but the result was in any case that the habit of using the written word for a variety of such purposes declined.

In matters of religion, however, written words continued to gain importance, in a trend already observable in the second century. Because a large proportion of our evidence for this trend concerns Christianity, we are bound to consider in what may seem disproportionate detail the functions of the written word among the Christians, who were a small minority until Constantine adhered to their cult. But from 312 Christianity began to affect everyone, directly or indirectly, and we ought therefore to trace the early stages of Christian attitudes towards the written word, all the more so since they have not always been clearly understood. At the same time, pagan religion also

50. August. *Ep.* 118.9. Augustine's very poor knowledge of Greek (*Ep.* 118.2.10), which in previous centuries would have been thought inexcusable in a man of intellectual pretensions, is evidence of, among other things, a decline in the circulation of Greek books in the Latin world.

51. Liban. *Ep.* 347.1, 605.2 (cf. 569.2); Greg.Nyss. *Ep.* 12, referring to Antioch and Cappadocia, respectively.

52. Cf. P. Petit, *Historia* v (1956), 484–486; and A. F. Norman, *JHS* lxxx (1960), 122–126, on the circulation of books in Libanius' circle (which was also influenced by political factors); bookdealers are referred to in *Or.* i.148, *Ep.* 428.3, etc. On conditions in the west cf. M. Kraemer, *Res libraria cadentis antiquitatis Ausonii et Apollinaris Sidonii exemplis illustratur* (Marburg, 1909), 67–73. Sidonius refers to a bookseller *(bybliopola)* (*Ep.* ii.8.2, v.15), but in the latter passage at least his function is that of a private copyist whose work is checked in detail by Sidonius himself.

seems to have been making greater use of writing; it is probable, for instance, that most of the surviving Greek magical papyri from Egypt date from the third and fourth centuries[53] because of a real growth in the use of such texts (there is really no way of knowing whether this was also true elsewhere).

Religious beliefs began to be expounded and fought about in writing to a much greater extent than ever before, chiefly by the Christians and the more articulate among their opponents. The degree of importance which written propaganda assumed in the minds of the antagonists is illustrated by the fact that under Maximinus (presumably therefore in the eastern Empire only) the government circulated the memoirs of Pontius Pilate to every province with instructions that they should be exhibited "everywhere, both in the country and in the cities."[54] The effects, especially in country districts, are likely to have been slight.

But we should not see writing and the book as the main means of Christian propaganda in the first three centuries.[55] A clear indication of this is the fact that its missionaries wrote few if any translations of the scriptures into languages other than Greek and Latin in this period,[56] even though Christianity was soon in touch with many provincial populations speaking mainly their own indigenous languages.[57] Also to be set against the admitted importance of the written word in Christian devotions is the strikingly small number of papyrus fragments of books of the New Testament dating from earlier than 200.[58] We know from Eusebius that even in Palestine obtaining books of scripture was not always a straightforward matter: his friend Pamphilus, who was an enthusiast for distributing them, had to copy many codices himself.[59] The illusion that Christianity was spread mainly by means of the written word is possible only for those who exaggerate the literacy of the high Empire.

53. A.-J. Festugière, *Les moines d'Orient* i (Paris, 1961), 25 n.5.

54. Euseb. *HE* ix.5.1.

55. With Cavallo in Vegetti, *Oralità, scrittura, spettacolo* 181.

56. The western aspect of this naturally mystified one who wanted to see Christianity as an essentially text-reading religion: H. I. Marrou in *La scuola nell'occidente latino dell'alto medioevo* (Settimane di Studio del Centro italiano di studi sull'alto medioevo, xix) (Spoleto, 1972), 137–138.

57. Cf. Iren. *Contra haeres.* iii.4.

58. E. A. Judge & S. R. Pickering, *Prudentia* x (1978), 1–13 (four definite instances); Roberts & Skeat, *Birth of the Codex* 40–41 (five instances).

59. Jerome *Adv.Rufin.* 1.9.

For professional holy men and women in the new cult the sacred texts had wide-ranging importance, and they were felt to be a powerful means of contact with the divine. It is natural to suppose that this aspect of Christianity was largely an inheritance from Judaism.[60] In any case the Christians soon developed their own habit of attachment to the written word, encouraged no doubt by their physical remoteness from one another and perhaps also by a certain Graeco-Roman tradition of awe for what was written down. Even an outsider might know that they were devoted to sacred books.[61] The holy writings gathered more and more authority, and by the time Hippolytus was writing in the early third century, if not earlier, they were so important that they began to be the subject of learned commentaries.[62] And scriptural authority was felt to be a valid weapon in favour of religious beliefs which in most people's eyes departed from all reasonableness.[63]

There was a continuous production of pious books. From the time of the death of Polycarp in the 160s and of the Lugdunum persecution (177), the executions of Christians were the subject of both genuine and spurious pamphlets recounting the sufferings of the victims.[64] While most of the famous authors of Christian tracts were of more or less bourgeois origin,[65] less educated authors also put together works of theological polemic and accounts of miracles. By Diocletian's time a Christian community of some size in, for instance, Thessalonica or Cirta would have a body of written material in its possession, and this was regarded by the government as a suitable target when persecution began.[66] The authority attributed to the canonical writings grew to be immense: Christ appears on some fourth-century sarcophagi displaying or simply holding a book-roll (see Figure 8).[67] Augustine

60. Cf. J. Leipoldt & S. Morenz, *Heilige Schriften* (Leipzig, 1953), 116–117.

61. Lucian *Peregr.* 11–12 (with reading aloud).

62. Cf. Euseb. *HE* vi.22–23.

63. See, e.g., Hippolytus *Contra haer.* (= *Contra Noetum*) 9 (p. 251 Nautin).

64. See Euseb. *HE* iv.15; Cypr. *Ep.* 27.1; etc.

65. A. Kneppe, *Untersuchungen zur städtischen Plebs des 4. Jahrhunderts n. Chr.* (Bonn, 1979), 169.

66. Cf. *Martyr Acts of Agape, Eirene and Chione* 5.1 = H. Musurillo (ed.), *Acts of the Christian Martyrs* (Oxford, 1972), 286–290: the Christians have so many parchments and book-rolls and writing-tablets and volumes and σελίδες (pages?) of writing; the scene is Thessalonica under Diocletian. Also *Acta Munati Felicis* in *Gesta apud Zenophilum* (CSEL xxvi), 188, concerning events at Cirta in 303.

67. See F. Gerke, *Christus in der spätantiken Plastik* (3d ed., Mainz, 1948), figs. 48, 49, 52, 53, 61, 70, 71.

explains that Christian miracles are to be believed in because they have scriptural authority: "those miracles are all recorded, as we know, in utterly truthful [*veracissimis*] books. There we are told what happened, and the beliefs which the miracles were intended to support."[68]

This emphasis on the importance of the scriptures encouraged fables about feats of memorization. The origin and significance of such stories are not wholly clear, but it seems most likely that they were invented or exaggerated, as the case may be, in a culture in which some people who had had little opportunity to learn to read believed fervently that they should be closely familiar with holy writings. It was also a world in which many people, some of them of undoubted intelligence, could believe such fables.[69] At all events the proto-monk Antony, according to Augustine, remembered scripture in spite of being illiterate.[70] A blind Egyptian mentioned by Eusebius is a degree less fabulous: he is said to have known whole books of scripture by heart, but he had committed them to memory before he was blinded.[71] And there were genuine efforts at memorization: at Oxyrhynchus in the late fourth century, and presumably in other places as well, it was laid down that a deacon must learn by heart certain specific portions of scripture, and a presbyter still more.[72] It was almost implicit that such men could read, but at the same time their memories were being prepared to take some of the place of books.

We must always beware of underestimating the capacity of the best ancient memories. The classical "art of memory" was still alive in the early fourth century, as we know from Augustine and Martianus Capella.[73] This, however, although it was indeed a product of and a mark of a semi-oral culture, was a rational system which formed part of the careful training of the orator. No doubt it worked. But it had nothing to do with the world of Christian miracles and in any case would hardly have enabled anyone to perform the stupendous feats of memory about which the Christian authors just cited had fantasies.

68. August. *CD* xxii.8.

69. This is not to deny that stories of this kind may be true (cf. above, pp. 31–33, on feats of memory)—but in fact none of the ones cited here is credible as it stands. Their lack of truth makes them *more* useful as historical evidence, as E. Wipszycka remarks, *Rev.Et.Aug.* xxx (1984), 290.

70. August. *De doctr.Christ.* prol.4 (*PL* xxxiv.17): "sine ulla scientia litterarum." For similar stories of somewhat later date see Wipszycka 290, 293.

71. Euseb. *De mart.Pal.* 13.7.

72. See the Coptic papyrus published by F. Rossi, *Memorie della R. Accademia delle Scienze di Torino* ser. 2 xxxvii (1885), 84.

73. F. A. Yates, *The Art of Memory* (London, 1966), 46–53.

The attitudes of the Christians towards the written word and its functions were necessarily somewhat complex. A persistent tradition of theirs emphasized that Peter and the other apostles were uneducated,[74] as indeed they very probably were. This example was always available, so that Origen (implicitly) and Clement of Alexandria (more openly) could assert that lack of education was no impediment to eternal salvation.[75] Indirectly this must in the end have had some effect on education. Celsus charged that the Christians turned children away from their teachers, and although elementary education was not the main religious battleground, anything which kept children away from the available teachers was bound to have some effect on literacy.[76] The dilemma of the Christian with some education is expressed by Tertullian: learning *litteratura* (to read and write competently) is important, but the conventional education is permeated with paganism.[77] In some later Christian quarters a positive spiritual value was attached to ignorance, and the monk Antony was respected for, rather than in spite of, his illiteracy.[78] The abbot Arsenius, at one time the tutor of Arcadius and Honorius, praised the merits of uneducated and probably illiterate Egyptian peasants.[79] While conventional ecclesiastics needed at least to be able to read (though in fact it was possible for them to be illiterate),[80] and some of them, like some Christian laymen, felt the powerful attractions of the old literary culture, they could be complacent about, or at any rate content with, the

74. Acts iv.13 (John and Peter are ἀγράμματοι καὶ ἰδιῶται); Orig. *Contra Cels.* viii.47 (the same description); Jerome *In Matth.* iv.19–20 (they were fishermen and *illitterati*); cf. Rufin. *Apol. contra Hieron.* ii.37–38 (*CCSL* xx.112); August. *CD* xviii.49.

75. Orig. *Contra Cels.* i.27, vi.14 (cf. iii.50); Clem.Alex. *Paed.* iii.11.78 (the latter, however, is enough of an intellectual to say that faith is learned *even* without letters).

76. Orig. *Contra Cels.* iii.55–58. He replies by merely denying that the Christians have turned children away from teachers who teach things which are σεμνότερα (the ἄσεμνα were such things as comedy).

77. *De idololatria* 10.

78. See Athanas. *Vita Antonii* 1, 72, 73; August. *De doctr.Christ.* prol.4; Sozomen *HE* i.13. *Adv.Iudaeos* 10 (*CCSL* iv.278) is characteristic: "sine litteris disserit scripturas eis." There seems to be no adequate discussion of the early history of holy ignorance; however there is some material in Festugière, *Les moines d'Orient* i. 75–91; and J. Saward, *Perfect Fools* (Oxford, 1980), 1–47.

79. *Apophth. Patrum* in *PG* lxv.88–89. For a conflict between an abbot's fondness for three pious books and his desire to be without possessions see *Apophth. Patrum* in *PG* lxv.188 (he got rid of them).

80. For illiterate clergy see below, p. 320.

educational backwardness of the ordinary faithful[81]—just because this was the age of faith, not of reasoning. "Creditur piscatoribus."[82]

By the end of the fourth century the religious prestige which had once attached to oracles had shifted to other texts—principally the Bible, but also the *Aeneid*. Hence there arose gospel cleromancy, dipping into the text at random for guidance about the future, and *sortes Vergilianae* (which were very probably a novelty in the 390s).[83] The most famous occasion on which the Bible was used in this way was in a garden in Milan in 386: Augustine heard a child's voice saying "Tolle, lege" ("Take it up and read"), opened his codex at random, and found his instructions in Romans xiii.13–14.[84] This sort of procedure may not have been at all common among Christians or pagans, but it was known to a sizeable public, and in the Christian elite at least it was taken very seriously.

An effort was certainly made in the fourth-century church, in Egypt and perhaps elsewhere, to see to the elementary education of some of those who made an occupation out of religion. While solitary ascetics could be illiterate and indeed many monks in organized communities must have been so too,[85] Pachomius emphasized that all novice monks were to be instructed in reading (he naturally assumed that some of the new recruits would be illiterate)[86]—a fact which is all the more

81. Clem.Alex. *Paed.* iii.11.78; Orig. *Contra Cels.* i.27, vi.14. Similar attitudes persisted: John Chrys. *Adv.oppugn.* iii.12 (*PG* xlvii.368); Pelagius on *I Cor.* i.19 (*PL* Suppl. i.1184).

82. Ambros. *De fide* xiii.84.

83. See P. Courcelle, *Recherches sur les Confessions de Saint Augustin* (2d ed., Paris, 1968), 188–202; Y. de Kisch, *MEFR* lxxxii (1970), 321–362. H. Dessau, *Hermes* xxvii (1892), 582–585, saw that the *sortes Vergilianae* belong to the period of the *Historia Augusta*'s composition. Note esp. August. *Ep.* lv.37 (*CSEL* xxxiv.2.212).

84. August. *Conf.* viii.29 ("nihil aliud interpretans divinitus mihi iuberi, nisi ut aperirem codicem et legerem quod primum caput intervenissem"). The advice he received was entirely familiar to him, but now had supernatural authority.

85. Wipszycka, *Rev.Et.Aug.* xxx (1984), 293, is quite wrong to say that monks "must" have been able to read the Bible. The collected *Apophthegmata Patrum* certainly do not suggest that they were constantly engaged in Bible-reading.

86. *Praecepta* 139–140 (*PL* xxiii.82 and A. Boon, *Pachomiana Latina* [Louvain, 1932], 49–50): "si litteras ignorabit, hora prima et tertia et sexta vadet ad eum qui docere potest . . . et etiam nolens legere compelletur"; cf. Basil of Caesarea *Regulae Fusius Tractatae* 15 (not crystal clear). The ideal spread: in sixth-century Arles, Caesarius maintained that all female religious should learn to read and write (*Regula Sanctarum Virginum* 18.6), and Aurelian said that all monks should learn *litterae* (*Regula ad monachos* 32).

interesting because Pachomius himself, far from being a direct heir of classical Greek culture, wrote and no doubt usually spoke in Coptic.[87] The rule assumes in any case that personal reading is of considerable day-to-day importance to Pachomius' monks. Athanasius tells holy virgins to have books in their hands at dawn.[88] In the west, on the other hand, Augustine says that many (holy men, he means) live by themselves through faith, hope, and charity, "sine codicibus";[89] and the Rule of Benedict takes cognizance of illiteracy without making any attempt to eliminate it.[90]

But for the ordinary Christian, though the authority of the written word was in the background, there was no need for personal reading. This statement may seem to run counter to the instructions of Christian teachers from Clement of Alexandria and Hippolytus onwards, who in fact tell the faithful laity to make a habit of reading the scriptures for themselves.[91] But these are the instructions of men of letters (the new type of letters), and men moreover of metropolitan background (Alexandria, Rome, Carthage), implicitly addressing Christians who are comfortably off and quite educated, those who can read such works of spiritual instruction.[92] There could be no question of aiming such a requirement at all the faithful. It was obvious to everyone that not all the faithful could read what, say, Clement of Alexandria wrote, or even understand it if it was read to them.

87. On the continuing or even increased importance of reading and writing in the monastic life of Egypt in the sixth and seventh centuries see Wipszycka 293–295.

88. Athanas. *De virginitate* 12.

89. *De doctr. Christ.* i.39: "homo itaque fide et spe et caritate subnixus eaque inconcusse retinens non indiget scripturis nisi ad alios instruendos."

90. Benedict *Regula* (*CSEL* lx) 58.20. The applicant to the order must make his *petitio* in writing, but it can be written for him if he does not know letters—"et ille nobicius signum faciat et manu sua eam super altare ponat." Marrou, *Histoire* 477, was highly misleading in saying that this rule dealt with the education of the novices.

91. Clem.Alex. *Paed.* ii.10.96 (dawn is the hour for prayer, reading and good works, not for sex); Hippolytus: see H. Achelis, *Die ältesten Quellen des orientalischen Kirchenrechtes* (Leipzig, 1891), 126–127; H. Duensing, *Der aethiopische Text der Kirchenordnung des Hippolyt* (Göttingen, 1946), 136–139; Leipoldt & Morenz, *Heilige Schriften* 118. See also Cyprian *De zelo et livore* 16, Novatian *De bono pudicitiae* 14.

92. On the social origins of early patristic texts cf. Kneppe, *Untersuchungen zur städtischen Plebs* 169, and (specifically concerning Clement) R. MacMullen, *Historia* xxxv (1986), 323. For John Chrysostom's concern to get his quite atypical congregation actually to read the scriptures which they possessed see *Hom. in Ioann.* 32.3 (*PG* lix.187–188); cf. *De Lazaro* 3.1–4 (*PG* xlviii.991–996).

The church's leaders recognized that if Christian writings were to have much effect on the masses they would have to be transmitted orally. In the second century the scriptures were normally *heard*.[93] Arius wrote a popular presentation of his doctrine in the poem *Thaleia,* but much of its effectiveness apparently derived from the fact that it could be sung.[94] The attitude of a prelate actually faced with the inability of the faithful to read for themselves is revealed by Cyril of Jerusalem in the fourth century: he recognizes as a matter of course that some Christians cannot read the holy scriptures, and tells them to learn by heart a short summary of the dogma.[95] In Augustine's time, pamphlets describing miraculous events (aretalogies) were read out to the faithful.[96] These were all ways in which the church brought the written word to bear on its partly illiterate public.

A resolute attempt was once made to show not only that Clement and others recommended personal reading of the scriptures, but that it was actually normal among early Christians.[97] However, it is useless to invoke in favour of this position such texts as Eusebius' description of the boyhood training of Origen, whose father exercised him at length in the scriptures.[98] The other evidence cited is if anything even less relevant. We have already seen some of the evidence that Christians en masse, like the rest of the population, included a high proportion of illiterates.

Other cults also possessed holy texts, but even when we make allowances for the vastly better preservation of Christian writings it is hard to resist the impression that Christianity made particularly heavy use of the written word, and the question thus arises whether this contributed to its success. And in fact the enthusiasm of the church's leaders for holy writings had a certain pragmatic basis. The authoritativeness of the written word had great value: it gave the leaders a measure

---

93. Iren. *Contra haeres.* ii.27.2; Orig. *Contra Cels.* iii.50.

94. Athanas. *Or.contra Arian.* i.7 (*PG* xxvi.24), *Epist. de Syn.* 15 (*PG* xxvi.705); see further A. H. M. Jones, *The Later Roman Empire* ii.964; M. L. West, *JThS* xxxiii (1982), 98–105 .

95. Cyril Hieros. *Cat.* v.12 (*PG* xxxiii. 520–521).

96. August. *CD* xxii.8.

97. A. von Harnack, *Ueber den privaten Gebrauch der Heiligen Schriften in der alten Kirche* (Beiträge zur Einleitung in das Neue Testament v) (Leipzig, 1912). See also Leipoldt & Morenz, *Heilige Schriften* 118–120. The sectarian nature of the argument is obvious.

98. Euseb. *HE* vi.2.7–10. The father was a man of property as well as being a zealot and future martyr.

of control and a means of maintaining cohesion—hence unending reams of instruction about both doctrine and behaviour.[99] The theological tract and the sermon are the characteristic forms of writing of the new age.

The acute logorrhoea which afflicted a number of Christian writers, most conspicuously John Chrysostom and Augustine, is also suggestive in itself. It may be connected with a certain improvement in the availability of secretaries who could take down shorthand *(notarii)*. But well-to-do Romans had never been short of secretarial assistance, and some other explanation is needed. The essential fact is perhaps that ecclesiastical writers usually did not write for a critical audience, indeed hardly *wrote* for an audience at all. The book trade seems to have shrunk since earlier Roman times, and the main methods by which most patristic writings were diffused were, besides donation, the depositing of texts in a library such as the one belonging to the church of Hippo, which of course had a collection of Augustine's works, and the lending of copies so that interested individuals with sufficient resources could have their own copies made.[100] The papyri show, not surprisingly, that in Egypt at least such works had a relatively modest circulation.

Elementary Education

Many of the well-to-do continued to set a high value on education. The tradition can still be heard in the classic speech on the subject delivered at Augustodunum in 298 by the rhetorician Eumenius,[101] and it continued long afterwards to produce men of letters quite as polished as those of earlier times; one has only to read, for instance, the letters of Sidonius Apollinaris to see that this was still true even in the troubled Gaul of the 460s and 470s. However the strength of this tradition did very little for elementary education. As in earlier times,

99. An example of the latter kind of writing is Cyprian's *De habitu virginum* (*PL* iv.451–478), evidently the work by which, according to his biographer, he controlled them "velut frenis quibusdam lectionis dominicae" (Pontius *Vita Cypr.* 7.4 = *PL* iii.1547).

100. Cf. August. *Serm.* 23.8, etc.; Possidius *Vita August.* 18 (*PL* xxxii.49); Scheele, *Bibliothek und Wissenschaft* xii (1978), esp. 76–78.

101. *Pan.Lat.* ix (= iv). See *C.Th.* xiii.3.1 and 4 for the privileges of *grammatici* and *professores litterarum* under Constantine, and xiv.1.1 for the importance officially attached to liberal education in 360. On the number and power of rhetoricians in the fourth century see R. MacMullen, *RSI* lxxxiv (1972), 5–6.

much of the elite made sure that its own sons were reasonably well educated, but the upper orders made very little or no attempt to assist the education of the masses.[102] The insignificant amount of philanthropic assistance that went to elementary education under the high Empire has no late-antique counterpart. Nor should the very occasional appearance in the sources of a *schola publica* or *municipalis* make us think of a modern kind of school with publicly financed operations, least of all an elementary school.[103]

In this as in earlier periods some people learned to read and write without going to school at all. Direct evidence for this is, however, quite thin, and the extent of such teaching is largely a matter of guesswork. Presumably the very rich employed private tutors for the earlier phase of education;[104] and when a literate family could not afford to send a child to school or when the father (or other relative) was a particularly didactic personality[105] a child might, especially in Greek milieux, learn to read and write at home. Nevertheless third- and fourth-century sources often describe the most elementary teaching as being performed by a schoolmaster of some kind.[106] Macarius-Symeon, for instance, takes it for granted that one goes to a specific place for the first stage of learning letters.[107] This was probably the normal experience, in the cities of both the eastern and the western

102. Neglect of this reality led Marrou, *Histoire*, esp. 439, to give a very unbalanced account of late-antique education.

103. It was in the *schola publica* at Carthage that Augustine taught rhetoric (*Conf.* vi.7.11). For the *municipales scholae* at Vesontio and Lugdunum see Auson. *Grat.* 7.31.

104. Paulinus of Pella, grandson of Ausonius, seems to have learned the *prima elementa* at home (*Eucharist.* 65 = SC ccix.64)—this must have been in Burdigala—before going to school at the age of six, where he studied Greek first (ibid. 74–76) (cf. Auson. *Ep.* xxii.45–50 = 75.45–50 Prete; R. A. Kaster, *TAPhA* cxiii [1983], 332–333). This is a lofty social milieu.

105. This may have been the case with Hypatius in fourth-century Phrygia, since his father, who taught him letters, was a *scholastichos*, i.e., a highly educated man (Callinicus *Vita Hypat.* 1 = SC clxxvii.72).

106. See the sources discussed by Kaster 325–328; as he points out, they are of uneven value. Kaster's notion (338) that when members of the upper class learned the *prima elementa* at school they did so from a *grammaticus*, while the *ludi magister* catered to "the lower levels of the population," is unsupported by evidence and runs straight into the fact that, unless the expression is understood in a very relative way, the "lower levels" did not send their sons to school in significant numbers, as far as we can tell (Kaster 340 hedges his view). This is not to deny that schools differed in social character.

107. *Hom.* 15.42 (= *PG* xxxiv.604).

provinces, for the sons of moderately prosperous families and of poorer families which showed unusual educational ambition.[108] We also know that elementary teaching was sometimes carried on by men whose primary occupation was not teaching at all[109]—individuals who would therefore be practically impossible to identify in the inscriptions as teachers. Thus while a certain proportion of late-antique literacy may have been imparted outside schools, its extent must in fact have been closely linked to the vicissitudes of the school system.

Diocletian's Price Edict suggests that elementary schoolmasters continued to be poorly paid, for it stipulates that they were to receive fifty *denarii* a month for each pupil, one quarter of the rate for Greek and Latin *grammatici* and for *geometrae*.[110] This probably meant an income much lower than a craftsman's.[111] But the real significance of this social neglect remains, as in earlier periods, somewhat obscure: its main effect might have been to make elementary education accessible, not indeed to the masses, but at least to a surprisingly large number of people. On the other hand not many of the literate can have been tempted to become schoolmasters.

The economic difficulties of the third century without much doubt reduced the amount of schooling that took place in the Roman Empire, and the troubles of the late fourth-century Empire, especially in the west, must have had a drastically negative effect. Cultural and religious changes also undermined the system, such as it was. It is a commonplace that late-antique education at the secondary and higher levels involved forms of Greek and Latin that were conservative, artificial, and increasingly distant from the languages of everyday life.[112] The Greek of Nonnus and the Latin of Sidonius Apollinaris were not the most practical forms of the respective languages for men who

108. At least the case of Augustine is fairly clear. The son of a *curialis* who was quite well-to-do, in spite of "admodum tenuis" (*Conf.* ii.3.5) (see B. D. Shaw, *P & P* cxv [1987], 8–10), he learned to read and write at school in Thagaste: *Conf.* i.13.20 (cf. i.9.14).

109. Cypr. *Ep.* 61.1; Greg.Nyss. *Contra Eunom.* i.49 (i.39 Jaeger).

110. *Diokletians Preisedikt*, ed. S. Lauffer, pp.124–125.

111. Cf. A. H. M. Jones, *The Later Roman Empire* ii.997. Contemptuous texts about schoolmasters: Liban. *Or.* xlii.26; SHA *Quadr.Tyr.* 14.1. The new expression χαμαιδιδάσκαλος ("outdoor teacher," in effect) in Diocletian's Edict expresses this contempt.

112. Concerning forms of Latin see Grundmann, *Archiv für Kulturgeschichte* xl (1958), 22.

lived in sixth-century Egypt or fifth-century Gaul (although they were highly functional from the point of view of the social elite, as any historian of education who has read Veblen will recognize). In any case the question which concerns us most is not whether practical-minded parents lost interest in the higher literary education, but whether the teaching of the *elementa* lost some appeal even among pagans. And in fact there is no reason to believe that it did. Christianity, on the other hand, did serve to weaken the traditional system of elementary education, as we shall shortly see.

In the more civilized regions of the western Empire, many or all towns of moderate size probably continued to have schools under the tetrarchs and at least through most of the fourth century. Forum Cornelii, a town of modest size in northern Italy, had a *magister litterarum* in the time of Diocletian's persecution (he was murdered by his pupils);[113] Parentium, a similar place, had a *magister puerorum* in the late fourth or early fifth century.[114] We know from Augustine (born in 354) that Thagaste had an elementary school when he was young, and Madaurus must have had one too.[115] Iomnium, a fairly insignificant place on the coast of Mauretania Caesariensis, had a *magister liberalium litterarum* at some date in the early period of the Christian Empire.[116] Tetradius, one of Ausonius' students, became a teacher, presumably a *grammaticus,* in the not very important Aquitanian town of Iculisma.[117] Notwithstanding all this, some sense of a decline in basic education may eventually have made itself felt; at least a Christian writer of the late fourth century or slightly later remarks that the tradition of educating children in letters and readings "per neglegentiam obsolevit."[118]

There is even a slender thread of testimony that girls sometimes went to school in the western provinces. A recently published Latin textbook of the late third or the fourth century shows that some

113. Prudentius *Peristeph.* 9.21–24.

114. *Inscr.It.* x.2.58 (= *ILCV* 719) and 74, both commemorating the donations of a Clamosus (perhaps the same man in both cases, or perhaps father and son as suggested by Kaster, *TAPhA* cxiii [1983], 342). Incidentally, the man's *nom parlant,* "Shouter," is scarcely likely to allude to Martial v.84.1–2 (in spite of Kaster), and hence does not show that his teaching "had some contact with the classical tradition."

115. *Conf.* i.13.20, ii.3.5.

116. *ILS* 7762.

117. Auson. *Ep.* 11 is addressed to him; in lines 22–23 Iculisma is treated as something of a backwater.

118. Ps.-Ambrose *Comm. in Epist. ad Eph.* iv.11–12 (*PL* xvii.409d).

girls attended.[119] Ausonius refers in an entirely casual way to the fact that his daughter went to school;[120] in his exceptionally cultivated milieu such a practice was clearly normal. It is overwhelmingly probable, however, that without any improvement in the social position of women girl pupils continued to be heavily outnumbered by boys.

In the more backward provinces of the western Empire and in those which were worst affected by military action from the third century on, it is to be assumed that schools were even more sparse than they were in Italy and other privileged regions.

Similarly, in the eastern Empire many cities continued to possess schools for a long period. Both Maximinus' government and Eusebius assumed that they were widespread.[121] Throughout the fourth century towns which were at most of the second rank quite commonly seem to have had the services of schoolmasters (once again the evidence is very spasmodic). This was probably the occupation of the "teacher of wisdom" Aurelius Trophimus whose verse epitaph, dating from the first half of the fourth century, survives from some small place in central Phrygia.[122] Tavium in Galatia, the third most important town there but no metropolis, had the services of a schoolmaster in the time of Libanius,[123] and Seleuceia on the Euphrates (Zeugma) had a school at some point during the fourth century which was attended by the ten-year-old son of a Latin-speaking army officer.[124] Under Valens a Christian priest from Edessa, one Protogenes, was exiled to Antinoopolis in Upper Egypt and, being literate, had opened a school there;[125] but the significance of this fact is unclear, because it may imply that Antinoopolis, now a relatively important place, had previously not had a school at all. There are extremely few if any explicit references to schools in the papyri after 300.[126] Even in a large and vigorous city such as Antioch, the social range of those who went to school seems to have been decidedly limited, to judge from a passage in one of

119. A. C. Dionisotti, *JRS* lxxii (1982), 97 (line 1).

120. *Ep.* 22.33.

121. Euseb. *HE* ix.5.1, 7.1.

122. *SEG* vi.137, lines 4 and 28; cf. Kaster, *TAPhA* cxiii (1983), 342.

123. Liban. *Ep.* 1080.

124. *AE* 1977 no. 818. Such seems the only reasonable interpretation of the words "amb. in sco." The boy had been going to school for only two months when he died at the age of ten.

125. Theodoret *HE* iv.18.8. His avowed aim was proselytization.

126. A *grammatodidaskalos: Stud. Pol.* xx. 1117 (Heracleopolis). For *didaskaloi*, not characterized further, see *SB* xii.10981, *BGU* iv. 1024.

Libanius' orations in which he contrasts the person who has been to school with the goldsmith—who must typically have been one of the most prosperous of all craftsmen.[127] The late-antique epitaphs of Corycus, in Cilicia, mention no fewer than 120 occupations, including all the more prosperous kinds of artisan and tradesman, but no schoolmaster,[128] which suggests that none existed or at best that such men were impoverished and poorly regarded. The claim that in the late Empire villages possessed elementary schools is most misleading.[129] No evidence for the existence of such schools in the fourth or fifth century is cited, and if they did exist they were certainly not the norm.

In practice the fathers of the church accepted with complete equanimity the ignorance of the lay poor. Spreading education beyond what must have seemed its naturally established boundaries was not a matter of concern to them. Neither the church nor the new political order which it superintended gave any help to elementary education (except, as we have seen, in the case of professional holy men). The claim of a modern apologist that the Christians felt an "interest in educating the poor" is entirely spurious.[130] Another apologist's claim that the pre-Constantinian church was "the great elementary teacher among the Greeks and Romans" has no foundation whatsoever.[131] It can be inferred from a comment of Julian's that the Christians had not even devised a school programme that substituted Christian writings for the detested pagan classics.[132] A tentative step in that direction taken by an isolated individual under Valens, the Protogenes of Edessa just mentioned, has, rather surprisingly, no known parallels in either

127. Liban. *Or.* lxiv.112. Nonetheless, the goldsmith knows about the houses of Priam and Laius—from dance performances.

128. Cf. W. V. Harris, *ZPE* lii (1983), 95.

129. A. H. M. Jones, *The Decline of the Ancient World* (London, 1966), 348. He probably did not mean to say that many villages had them.

130. W. H. C. Frend, *Martyrdom and Persecution in the Early Church* (Oxford, 1965), 212. The passage of Tatian to which he alludes (*Or.* 30) shows nothing of the kind.

131. This was claimed by von Harnack, *Ueber den privaten Gebrauch* 60. In the *Constitutiones Apostolorum* iv.11 (= F. X. Funk [ed.], *Didascalia et Constitutiones Apostolorum* [Paderborn, 1905], 233), a fourth-century text, the instruction to educate children in "sacred letters" is perfunctory and clumsily modelled on a phrase of Paul's. It has no practical significance.

132. Julian *Adv.Galil.* 229e. He challenges the Christians to select some of their children and educate them in their scriptures, and predicts that they will grow up to be as ignoble as slaves.

the Greek or the Latin part of the Empire.[133] Hence the fourth-century Christians were left with no system which could be fully satisfactory to them.

Some suggested that Christian parents should commit even those of their sons who were not going to be monks to monastic communities for training. Both Basil of Caesarea (somewhat cautiously) and John Chrysostom endorse this notion.[134] But there is no sign or likelihood that the idea was taken up, and later Chrysostom seems to assume that education will be the parents' own responsibility.[135] None of the admonitions of Christian writers that the pious should read the scriptures led to the kind of practical measures in favour of reading which some Protestant churches took in later times. And although the church cared for the orphans of its community in a way which was practically without precedent in the ancient world, it did not organize schools for them.[136]

The skeletal and anaemic system of schools which existed in the early Roman Empire did not die in the third century or even in the fourth. It did not succumb to the initial seizure of power by the Christians. But it inevitably grew still weaker under the influence of economic and political developments, and eventually under the influence of the antieducational priorities of the Christians.

A Real Decline

The limitations of the evidence about the extent of literacy in late antiquity not only preclude useful statistics but also make it difficult, in some regions, to see even the general long-term trend. The relatively large quantity of documentary papyri which survive from sixth-century Egypt stand as a warning that literacy may not have declined steadily in every part of the Roman world. But there are some probabilities, and that is usually the best that historians can hope for.

Illiteracy in the strict sense of the term did not yet affect the men of

133. Marrou, *Histoire* 467, 475. However for children destined for a monastic existence, Basil of Caesarea and Jerome devised a program of elementary education which excluded pagan texts: Marrou 473 (see esp. Bas. *Reg.fus.tract.* 15.3 = *PG* xxxi.954).

134. Bas. *Reg.brev.tract.* 292 (*PG* xxxi.1288); John Chrys. *Adv.oppugn.* iii.18 (*PG* xlvii.380) (but clearly the very young are not in question).

135. In *De inani gloria:* see esp. 19, 22 (*SC* clxxxviii.104, 106). The audience is well-to-do.

136. Marrou, *Histoire* 466.

great power and wealth, the level above the mere decurions, except perhaps in the case of some particularly uncouth army officer. There was, however, a much greater division between the well-educated members of the upper elite and the other members of the same social order, many of whom were military men. Soldiers of more or less peasant origin who rose to high office, such as the emperor Galerius, may have been only just literate.[137] However the notion lived on for a time that a member of the upper elite ought properly to be capable of discussing and writing in a somewhat polished style. Therefore, Constantine and Valentinian I, who lacked the full classical education,[138] made sure that their sons received it.

Writing in Constantinople for an upper-class audience, John Chrysostom assumes that everyone takes care to have his sons taught letters.[139] No member of the upper elite is known to have been illiterate in the fourth century, although the possibility cannot be completely excluded. When Libanius praises Julian for having ended the employment of "barbarians" as provincial governors, he admits that though the barbarians had no *nous* they "knew how to write quickly."[140] According to Libanius, Julian reinstated "men filled with poetry and prose." Even in the high Empire, as we saw earlier, writing quickly and well was not in fact a universal accomplishment in the upper class. However there is a certain change of tone in the fourth century; and when Ammianus, praising Valentinian, describes him as "scribens decore,"[141] he seems to hint at new conditions; in earlier centuries this would have been an undignified or at best a trivial reason for praising a distinguished Roman.

The earliest indication that this literacy was somewhat in retreat on the outer fringes of the ruling class is the decision made by the tetrarchs in 293 that men who were "expertes litterarum"—which must mean

137. Galerius was born in Dacia Ripensis of "parentibus agrariis," according to *Epit. de Caes.* 40.15, and had been a "pastor armentarius, unde ei cognomen Armentarius fuit." His nephew, the later emperor Maximinus Daia, is made the subject of the same topos in Lactant. *De mort.pers.* 19.6: "sublatus nuper a pecoribus et silvis, statim scutarius," etc. (cf. 18.3). But the author's religious hatred deprives this of value. The HA describes Bonosus, a usurper in the period 267–272, as a military man; as a boy "litterarum nihil didicit" (*Quadr.Tyr.* 14.1).

138. Constantine was "litteris minus instructus" in youth; *Exc.Val.* 2.

139. John Chrys. *De inani gloria* 18 (*SC* clxxxviii.102).

140. *Or.* xviii.158. MacMullen, *RSI* lxxiv (1972), 7, should not have cited this text to show that under Julian provincial governors knew "at most" how to read and write.

141. "venusteque pingens et fingens"; xxx.9.4.

illiterates, not simply men of limited literary culture—could nonetheless serve as decurions.[142] This does not by any means show that illiteracy "reigned" among decurions,[143] but neither is it likely to have been a response to an isolated case. The decision might be interpreted as a consequence of the evasion of the decurionate by the well-to-do; in other words, a less prosperous kind of person may now have been holding the office. It is unfortunate that nothing precise is known about the background of the first illiterate town councillor attested in Egypt, who appears little more than a decade after the tetrarchs' edict.[144] In any case the decurionate still, under the tetrarchs, seems to have implied substantial ownership of property, and truly widespread evasion of the office came only later.[145] Therefore the provision of 293 does suggest that a social group which had been largely immune from illiteracy in previous times now contained more illiterate members.

There is not even a known instance of female illiteracy in high-ranking Roman society in the fourth century—though in reality some women such as Constantine's mother Helena who had risen from a very low social stratum by virtue of a man's career must have been illiterate or semi-literate. When Augustine describes the ideal wife as "litterata, vel quae abs te facile possit erudiri,"[146] the suspicion must be strong that he is thinking of basic literacy and implying that at his social level a woman of marriageable age (she would be very young by modern standards) might easily lack that qualification.

As to the diffusion of literacy at lower social levels, there are optimists to be found among the historians of this period as of others. An authority on the barbarian west has maintained, for instance, that there the ability to read and write "was always a necessity, especially

142. *Cod.Iust.* x.32.6.

143. As asserted by MacMullen 7.

144. *P.Thead.* 32 (= G. M. Parássoglou, *The Archive of Aurelius Sakaon* [Bonn, 1978], no. 15), lines 1–12 (308 A.D.). See further H. C. Youtie, *HSCPh* lxxv (1971), 175 n.49. *P.Sakaon* 15 is held by M. Drew-Bear, *Cd'E* lix (1984), 319–320, to be the only certain evidence for an illiterate *bouleutes* in Egypt. An artisan named Caecilianus, a weaver, who was *duovir* at Abthugni in the province of Byzacena in 303, was thought by A. H. M. Jones, *The Later Roman Empire* ii.860, to have been "apparently illiterate" because he had a *scriba* write official letters for him. But this by no means shows that he was illiterate, and it is clear at least that he was able to read (see Lepelley, *Cités* ii. 273).

145. Jones ii.738, 741; cf. W. Langhammer, *Die rechtliche und soziale Stellung der Magistratus municipales und der Decuriones* (Wiesbaden, 1973), 262–278.

146. August. *Soliloq.* 1.10.17.

in the towns," his principal argument being that otherwise people would not have troubled to put up inscriptions.[147] But these inscriptions are very few by the standards of the classical city, and even the epigraphical culture of earlier times did not depend on mass literacy (the arguments do not need to be repeated). The assertion of A. H. M. Jones that craftsmen and shopkeepers, as well as those still further down the economic scale, were "for the most part illiterate"[148] is a more plausible conjecture.

The illiteracy of the lay poor follows inevitably from the lack of subsidies for elementary education. In the huge expanse of homiletic and other literature, no late-antique author encourages people to pay for a schoolmaster or put up a school-building. Some of the resources which went to support the church had the effect of teaching reading and writing to clerics and monks who would otherwise have remained illiterate, and so to some extent we are dealing with a shift of literacy from one social location to another, rather than with a decline.

It is craftsmen and shopkeepers—apart from women, who throughout this study remain more elusive than men—who are the most difficult to be sure about. They had been a partly literate, partly semi-literate, partly illiterate social stratum in the high Empire, and so they probably continued to be in the fourth-century west, and still later in the east. There were small-town schools in the fourth century where a mason or a baker might send his sons if he had some ambition for them. And Vegetius assumed that it was possible to recruit literate soldiers, who are most likely to have come from this social level.

Whether the literacy of slaves declined can only be conjectured. But while the majority of them had always been illiterate, it seems to indicate something new that Augustine can solemnly recount as a miracle the case of a slave who learned to read.[149] For a slave it was now an extraordinary accomplishment.

The fate of literacy in the western provinces must have varied greatly

---

147. P. Riché, *Education et culture dans l'Occident barbare, VI–VIIIᵉ siécles* (Paris, 1962), 60–61. He in fact recognizes some of the limitations of the school system.

148. Jones ii.997.

149. *De doctr.Christ.* prol.4. For a story of a free person learning to read by means of a miracle see *Historia Monachorum* 30, set in Egypt; see also H. Hyvernat (ed.), *Les actes des martyrs d'Egypte* (Paris, 1886–87), 180, a story set in an Egyptian village (cited by Wipszycka, *Rev.Et.Aug.* xxx [1984], 290).

according to the survival or decline of cities in particular regions. The decline in the number of preserved inscriptions after the mid-third century varies from severe, for example in Italy, to very drastic, for example in Upper Moesia; variations within provinces are common, and a substantial number of cities still regularly saw new inscriptions erected until around 400.[150] These facts can give only a faint indication of what was happening to literacy. It is probable, however, that there was some overall decline from the middle of the third century onwards, which became more severe after the barbarian invasions of the early fifth century. A hundred years later, full literacy was quite rare outside clerical and monastic circles. A sermon of Caesarius of Arles (d. 542) dramatizes the problem as it existed in his time in a relatively civilized region: reading the scriptures is, ostensibly at least, set before the faithful as an obligation, but it is recognized that not only *rustici* but even well-to-do merchants *(negotiatores)* may be unable to read for themselves. When illiterate merchants need writing in their work, they hire *mercennarios litteratos,* and they are told to do the same to hear the holy writings. There is no thought that the church should tell, or help, anyone to learn to read.[151]

In the eastern part of the Empire the decline was also gradual, and there was of course no overwhelming series of barbarian invasions to intensify it in the fifth century. In Egypt, as we saw in the previous chapter, there is some evidence that illiteracy was already spreading up the social scale by the time of Diocletian. In 285 we encounter for the first time a member of the gymnasium class who was illiterate.[152] In 320 the will of the legionary centurion Valerius Aion was witnessed by seven other centurions, three of whom are declared to be illiterate, which had once been a rare condition at this rank.[153] At the very beginning of the fourth century, one Aurelius Demetrius, who had held important offices at Arsinoe, makes the surprising declaration

150. For Upper Moesia see the graph in A. Mócsy, *Gesellschaft und Romanisation in der römischen Provinz Moesia Superior* (Amsterdam, 1970), 200.

151. Caes.Arel. *Serm.* 6.1–2 (*CCSL* ciii.31–32); cf. 8.1 (*CCSL* ciii.41).

152. *P.Oxy.* xlvi.3295. R. Calderini, *Aegyptus* xxx (1950), 26, mentions an illiterate gymnasiarch of the third century, but presumably she was alluding to *P.Flor.* i.63, which in fact gives evidence of no such thing, as was shown by U. Wilcken, *Archiv für Papyrusforschung* iv (1908), 448. The official who had *P. Panop.Beatty* 1 line 182 written in the year 298 thought it worth specifying that the man needed for a certain task should not only possess great understanding and wealth but also be skilled in letters: the first two qualities did not by themselves quite guarantee the third.

153. *SB* xii.11042 = *P.Col.* vii.188.

that he is illiterate—a case which is all the more interesting because he does so in a petition to the prefect of the province; in other words, he knew well how to make use of the written word to seek redress, and shame did not prevent him from declaring his illiteracy.[154] Again it is of interest—though since the context is a village the fact does not cause great surprise—that a man as locally powerful as Aurelius Sakaon of Theadelphia was illiterate; he flourished in the 310s and 320s, and he too was experienced, indeed skilled, in the use of written texts.[155]

On the other hand, the small decrease in the number of private letters on papyri from the third century to the fourth (a recent check-list has 224 items from the third century, 205 from the fourth)[156] suggests that in the prosperous class from which most of these letters emanated there was little if any decline in literacy, at least until the era of Theodosius. In the period 325–350 a well-to-do woman in Hermoupolis could possess at least simple literacy.[157] The serious overall decline in the number of papyri comes somewhat spasmodically in the mid-fourth century; from the 370s to the 470s it is almost continuous.[158] Thereafter, somewhat surprisingly, there is a reversal—a steady increase lasting far into the fifth century. The immediate cause of the fourth-century decline is plainly a dramatic decrease in the amount of official and other administrative activity.[159] The depopulation of certain sites at the edge of the desert (Theadelphia, Soknopaiou Nesos) may also have contributed.[160] Admittedly the decline in the number of papyrus documents does not prove with certainty that literacy

154. *P.Oxy.* i.71, with the comments of H. C. Youtie *ZPE* xvii (1975), 206. Demetrius had been high priest and superintendent of the *annona*.

155. *P.Strasb.* i.42; *P.Thead.* 21; etc. Cf. Parássoglou, *Archive of Aurelius Sakaon* passim. In an Oxyrhynchus document of 316 one carpenter could subscribe while another was illiterate: *P.Oxy.* i.53. I know of no one who was so clearly an artisan who subscribed a document later than this.

156. G. Tibiletti, *Le lettere private nei papiri greci del III e IV secolo d.C.* (Milan, 1979), 6–22.

157. See K. A. Worp, *Das Aurelia Charite Archiv* (Zutphen, 1980). She belonged to an emphatically Hellenic family, and she prided herself on writing (Worp 9). Worp 2 suggests that she learned from her mother.

158. The most recent figures are provided by R. S. Bagnall & K. A. Worp in *Miscellanea Papyrologica* (Papyrologica Florentina vii) (Florence, 1980), 13–21.

159. R. Rémondon in *Atti dell'XI Congresso internazionale di papirologia* (Milan, 1966), 140–142; Bagnall & Worp 13; notwithstanding the objections of Wipszycka, *Rev.Et.Aug.* xxx (1984), 282–283.

160. Cf. Wipszycka 282.

declined in the same period—and it has recently been claimed that literacy in some sense or other was undiminished in Egypt between the fourth century and the seventh.[161] It is vastly more natural, however, to suppose that a society which felt far less need for administrative documents, and also for new copies of literary texts, found the arts of reading and writing themselves less important and less worth imparting to the young.

It is intriguing to see that in a period when we should strongly suspect that literacy was in decline, the "slow writers" begin to reappear. In the entire period from 212 to 390 only one person is declared to be a slow writer in a papyrus text,[162] but from the latter date such people begin to be mentioned frequently once again. That might be a meaningless change of convention; more probably, the intervening period corresponds roughly to the high point of literacy in the history of Roman Egypt.

But the high point was more probably earlier in most other provinces of the eastern Empire. The typicality of Egypt in this respect is by no means to be assumed. However the testimony about schoolmasters which has already been mentioned, and the state of the Greek cities, suggest that there was no radical decline during the fourth century in the number of those who learned to read and write. If the Greek epigraphical evidence for the fourth to sixth century were in a more orderly condition, it might give us some indication here. But we must be careful not to take possibly isolated groups of inscriptions as definite evidence. The epitaphs of Corycus, in Cilicia, for example,[163] which show that the more prosperous artisans and tradesmen there were familiar with the use of writing for personal commemoration—though not in fact that they were literate—have few parallels in the provinces of Asia Minor. The shortage of copyists in the late fourth century, the relative silence in the evidence about fifth- and sixth-century schoolmasters—it is on such very indirect indications that we have to depend.

A loose indication of this kind is provided by the fact that in 439 Theodosius II in Constantinople found it advisable to rule that a man who could not even subscribe his will could nonetheless make a valid

---

161. Wipszycka 295.

162. *PSI* ix.1037 (301 A.D.), with the comments of H. C. Youtie, *GRBS* xii (1971), 249.

163. I discussed this material in *ZPE* lii (1983), 93–95.

one.[164] Earlier governments had assumed that by and large the men of property, those whose wills were a subject of concern, were able to subscribe them—which did not of course mean that they were fully literate. Now even this limited accomplishment could not be assumed; this is likely to have been a fairly recent change.

Apologists for Christianity have sometimes implied that the bookish nature of the cult meant that ancient Christians were notably more literate than pagans.[165] As far as lay people are concerned, this supposition is quite unlikely. The ordinary Christians were sometimes instructed to read the scriptures for themselves, but, as we have seen, no one seems to have thought that this applied to the social classes which were normally illiterate. In the age in which the Christians were still a tiny sect of enthusiasts, Origen and Clement of Alexandria had admitted that in general the Christians were uneducated, as was perfectly natural. This was how matters were perceived in Alexandria, and there is likely to have been still less literacy among Christians in many other places. From the time of Constantine onwards, as adherence to the cult became less a matter of personal enthusiasm, the degree of a Christian's literacy was determined still more than before by the usual considerations of class, gender and personal ability. The continuing lack of a specifically Christian educational program in the fourth century may in fact have put the Christians at a disadvantage in this respect.

Christian Latin, it has been said, "was a Latin that invited literacy—it had the simplicity and uniformity of an ideological language."[166] In practice, however, the invitation was extended only to those who devoted their lives to religion, and even in this age such people were relatively few.[167] The same scholar's further claim that "behind Augustine's vast output in Hippo, we can sense the pressure

164. *N.Th.* xvi.3: "quod si litteras testator ignoret vel subscribere nequeat, octavo subscriptore pro eo adhibito eadem servari decernimus"; cf. xvi.6.

165. Leipoldt & Morenz, *Heilige Schriften* 115–120; Marrou in *La scuola nell'occidente latino* 136. Cf. F. Steinmann, *Klio* liii (1971), 353–360, who seeks to explain the high level of literacy supposedly revealed by the eighth-century Coptic papyri from Djeme (Upper Egypt) by arguing that Christianity required the laity to read the scriptures for themselves; in fact the legal documents in question have no claim to represent a cross-section of the population (cf. the comments of Wipszycka, *Rev.Et.Aug.* xxx [1984], 287).

166. P. Brown, *JRS* lviii (1968), 90.

167. Brown's observation that "to participate fully" in late-antique Christianity required literacy is applicable neither to laymen—still less laywomen—nor even to

of the need to extend this religious literacy as widely as possible" is an acute observation insofar as it distinguishes religious literacy—that is, the religious function of the written word—from other kinds; but it runs up against the awkward fact that neither Augustine nor any other influential ecclesiastic ever even considered the problem of mass illiteracy—which is hardly surprising, since they had jettisoned the Greek cultural traditions which alone might have led them in that direction. For holy men and women the texts were of such importance that, as we have seen, monastic rules required the recruits to learn letters. Hence Christianity did lead to the instruction in reading (at least) of some people who would not otherwise have learned. But this effort, together with the struggle to maintain a literate clergy, exhausted the interest of the Christians in supporting literacy.

From the point of view of the leaders of the church, it was desirable that the clergy in general should at least be able to read. Levels of clerical literacy probably varied from region to region. In Greek-speaking Egypt, where writing had long been relatively commonplace, clerical illiteracy, though not unknown, seems to have been unusual in the fourth and fifth centuries. The great majority of those clerics whose knowledge or ignorance of writing comes into view in this period could write.[168] The significance of an illiterate Christian "reader" in Egypt has been much discussed, but if he was really illiterate in Greek he would not have been at all a surprising phenomenon in a junior rank of the clergy which did not necessarily have to do any reading.[169] In the north African provinces further west, of all the catholic bishops called upon to subscribe in 411, only one is said "to have been igno-

---

monks. For illiterate clergy in early fifth-century Africa, who were admittedly disapproved of, see below.

168. At some date which, according to Wipszycka 288, can hardly be later than the third century, the so-called Canons of the Apostles (T. Schermann, *Die allgemeine Kirchenordnung* [Leipzig, 1914], 25) envisaged that in Egypt a bishop might be unable to write. However, in her search for illiterate clergy Wipszycka found only two in fourth-century documents (both deacons) (*SB* vi.9622 = Parássoglou, *Archive of Aurelius Sakaon* no. 48, *P.Würzb.* 16), and none at all in the fifth century. Pointing out the large number of clerical subscriptions from this period, she reasonably concluded that the Greek-speaking Egyptian clergy of this time were highly literate. For further arguments, of varying value, in favour of this view see Wipszycka 289–290.

169. The text is *P.Oxy.* xxxiii.2673 (304 A.D.). He may have been literate in Coptic: C. H. Roberts, *Manuscript, Society and Belief in Early Christian Egypt* (London, 1979), 65. But see most recently and most convincingly G. W. Clarke, *ZPE* lvii (1984), 103–104.

rant of letters," a certain Paulinus, bishop of Zura.[170] Other evidence
from the same region implies that while it was thought better to have
literate deacons than illiterate ones, some did not make the grade.[171]
Outside relatively cultivated provinces such as these, the level of clerical education is likely to have been notably lower.

One effect which Christianity seems to have had in some regions
was to further the diffusion of literate languages. In the west, at least,
it is clear enough that it had the effect of spreading the use of Latin.[172]
That must have made literacy at least faintly accessible to new populations. It is also worth observing that in the same general period
literacy in other languages became more readily available in certain regions, through the development of Coptic (demotic Egyptian
written in an adaptation of the Greek alphabet which was easier to
learn than the traditional script),[173] and through the development of
Syriac as a written language.

However Christianity served to weaken the ancient reverence for
humane *paideia* which had undoubtedly had some positive effects,
over many centuries, on the general educational level of the more
Greek and Hellenized inhabitants of the Empire. It is impossible to
tell what effects mass Christianity by itself would have had on literacy
in a time of economic and political stability. In the event its overall
effect on reading ability is unclear (while the functions of reading
underwent some change), but its effect on literacy as it is understood
in this book was very probably negative.

There is no prospect of quantifying the changes which took place in
the diffusion of literacy in late antiquity. An accumulation of evidence
shows that literacy did indeed decline, but the decline may not have
been as severe as might be imagined; for nothing like mass literacy
had ever been attained in the high Empire, and literacy by no means
disappeared in late antiquity. Some decline can be observed even in
the third century, and even decurions were affected. Though evidence
is very limited, it is likely that literacy was in definite retreat in many
regions in the last decades of the fourth century and the first decades
of the fifth. What occurred was not a simple retreat of literacy into the
upper elite; not only did there continue to be specialists of various

170. *Gesta Collationis Carthaginiensis anno 411* i.133 = CCSL cxlixA.112.
171. *Codex Canonum Ecclesiae Africanae* in H. T. Bruns (ed.), *Canones Apostolorum* (Berlin, 1839), i.169. The date is 401.
172. C. C. Smith in *ANRW* ii.29.2 (1983), 945–946.
173. Cf. Wipszycka, *Rev.Et.Aug.* xxx (1984), 286.

social ranks who used writing in their work, but there was an almost entirely new social location for the written word among the more professionally and the enthusiastically pious of the Christians. However the degree to which Christianity actually encouraged people to learn to read and write has sometimes been greatly exaggerated, and not even the rise of a partially literate monasticism gave any powerful stimulus to the overall level of literacy. The functions of literacy tended to shrink. Meanwhile the system of schools, never extensive or robust even at the height of the Roman Empire, weakened still further, especially in the west, and they failed to receive the official or the philanthropic assistance which alone could have enabled them to have a widespread impact. In these circumstances the level of literacy inevitably declined from the craftsman's literacy of the high Empire, though this may have continued for a long time in certain parts of the Greek world, down to the marginal kind of literacy which was to prevail until the Middle Ages were far advanced.

Conclusion

> there thou mayst brain him,
> having first seized his books . . .
> > Remember
> first to possess his books; for without them
> he's but a sot, as I am, nor hath not
> one spirit to command. They all do hate him
> as rootedly as I. Burn but his books . . .
> > —Caliban, in *The Tempest* III.ii.85–92

Recapitulation

Writing spread from one function to another in archaic Greece and Italy, in ways which are almost entirely veiled from us. We can, however, see that writing was not only useful but, in its various Greek and Italian forms, easy, and also that in appropriate surroundings it was impressive and even solemn and even quasi-magical. Hence while the earliest uses of writing may have been severely practical commercial ones, very early texts also served to identify the owners of the objects on which they were inscribed, to perpetuate the memory of the dead, or to dedicate some artifact to a god. All these may have been practical purposes too, but they required the written word to do something other than transcribe an oral message. Partly this is a matter of overcoming time: the graffito *goes on* saying whom the vase belongs to, the epitaph *goes on* saying that a man or woman lived; the dedication *goes on* proclaiming that so-and-so offered this to such-and-such a god. Writing therefore gives power to an utterance by providing a number of repetitions, potentially a very large number of repetitions. Even a few such repetitions may be important, if, for example, they transmit a poem which in previous times would have been lost with the death or old age of the person who composed it.

During the late seventh and sixth centuries, the functions of writing proliferated. Letters in the epistolary sense may have been known much earlier, but at all events they were probably a known phenomenon by the time the *Iliad* was written down, and certainly they were by the late sixth century—though they are likely to have remained a very specialized form of communication. But as the functions—and also the number of literate and semi-literate people—grew, the written word became deeply embedded in the civic life of many Greek cities. This is the age of the first written laws, of the first coin legends, and of the first officials charged with creating written records. Hipparchus of Athens is the first Greek known to have used writing for outright political propaganda, and within a few years the Athenians were exorcising presumptuous politicians by writing their names on ostraca.

As a result of such innovations, together with the growing use of written texts in the precincts of the gods, very large numbers of Greek men—practically the entire male population of the cities and many country-dwellers in addition—must have been aware, by the end of the sixth century, that writing existed. Many must also have been aware by now, as some must have realized from the earliest phase of the history of Greek writing, that you could use writing through intermediaries: others could write for you (Polycrates' *grammatistes* may be the earliest attested case, which is not to say that Polycrates was illiterate), others could read for you or pass on to you the information they received from reading. However in the same general period, in the sixth century in all likelihood, came the birth of the school in which boys could "learn letters," if their parents paid for them to do so—a form of social organization which plainly must have given a powerful impetus to the volume of literacy.

During the high classical period of Athens and of the Greek *polis* in general, the functions of writing continued to multiply, in connection above all with legal and business procedures and with the public life of the city. Between the 420s and the 360s in particular this process can be observed taking place at Athens. Meanwhile historiography and technical handbooks emerge into the daylight, and books of many kinds circulate more extensively. The trading of books begins to be attested. In general we can say that by 323 a certain number of men in Greek cities spent a lot of time with written texts, and many lives were affected by operations carried out in writing. As a result of the increased importance of writing, Plato and others argued that all the sons and even daughters of the citizens should receive schooling in letters, though as far as is known no city yet acted on this recommendation.

However the reputation of the written word in classical Greece was by no means entirely positive. Even among the educated it often seems to have generated suspicion: Greeks quite frequently perceived letters and other documents as instruments of deceit. Together with the sort of reasoned criticism of the use of writing which is put forward in the *Phaedrus* (for which admittedly we have no close parallel), such views may have operated on a conscious or unconscious plane to inhibit the conversion away from oral culture.

The Hellenistic Greeks, in particular those who ruled and administered the Ptolemaic empire, developed the bureaucratic uses of writing far beyond what had been known in the classical era. For the first time Greeks held large states together, and they depended on the written word to do so. But the great Hellenistic innovation concerned elementary education: in a few cities, at least, individual philanthropists sought to bring it about that all the free boys, and in some instances girls as well, attended school.

From a very early period, written texts seem to have fulfilled functions beyond what was practical. The associations of writing will have depended partly on the reader or viewer, but the natural impressiveness of the written word in a society with limited literacy was enhanced by connections with what was sacred, what was hallowed by respect (the Homeric poems), and what was official. Nor is it likely that this impressiveness diminished much, for though a man who dwelt in a classical or Hellenistic city would have found no particular strangeness in the written word, the association of writing with political power may well have tended to grow closer.

The functions of writing in early Italy are even harder to pin down than in archaic Greece. Owners' names on vases and other objects, religious dedications and other surviving texts fail to tell a clear tale. The writing-tablets which rulers and merchants may have exchanged are not directly attested, and the impression we gain that religious uses were particularly important at Rome could in fact be mistaken. In the fourth century B.C. matters become somewhat clearer as the functions of writing known to us from inscriptions broaden out; in addition, it is plain that from this time onwards texts of various kinds were vital to the effectiveness of Rome's military and political power. The broadening of the functions of writing continued throughout the Republic, with a greatly increased quantity of evidence from the time of Polybius and of the *leges tabellariae* onwards.

Under the late Republic and the principate the use of writing spread still further, both in terms of functions and in terms of geography, as those European provinces which were substantially without literacy before the Roman conquest started to undergo Romanization. During this period the range of functions becomes so wide that some scholars have slipped into the supposition that a Roman city was practically modern in its use of writing and might contain, for example, masses of advertisements and newspapers. The full range of writing, best though not completely illustrated by the epigraphy of Pompeii, is indeed by the Julio-Claudian period very great. The Romans used written receipts and kept written accounts, wrote up political slogans, organized their armed forces by means of a mass of documentation, kept records of who became a citizen, circulated the texts of magical spells and books advocating religious beliefs, abused each other and protested love to each other in graffiti, wrote letters, and, in great numbers, commemorated the dead.

Gradually during late antiquity, and at greatly varying rates in different regions, many of the classical functions of writing lost importance or disappeared altogether. This trend very clearly applies to governmental uses of the written word. Proving a negative—such as that writing was *not* now used for this purpose or that—is of course usually difficult, but it is apparent that in almost every sphere of life and in very many regions writing was used less in the fifth century A.D. than it had been in the period before 250. Religious practice forms the great exception; though Christianity did not require ordinary believers to read with their own eyes for the sake of religion, and though Christianity probably had a negative effect overall on the literacy of the inhabitants of the Empire, it did place the reading of the sacred texts near to the centre of the lives of both men and women who were dedicated to the cult.

Even when the Greeks and Romans had advanced beyond their archaic phases, they still held on to oral procedures to a greater extent than is commonly realized. This is true both in the sense that the literate retained some non-literate ways of doing things and in the sense that the majority stayed illiterate. Both political persuasion and the diffusion of literature remained oral to an important degree throughout antiquity. Although much of our evidence for this persistence of orality is indirect—for the unwritten word is usually short-lived—it is clear that great numbers of men exercised their rights and fulfilled their duties as citizens, made their livings, and satisfied their religious needs with little or no personal reading or writing.

Oral procedures lived on, automatically so to speak, because no economic, social or religious force ever required otherwise or brought into being a system of popular education, except for relatively brief periods in relatively few places. Written communication suffered from considerable inconveniences by modern standards, and could be expensive. Some forms of writing could also arouse suspicion.

Thus there occurred a transition away from oral culture. This was, however, a transition not to written culture (in the sense in which modern cultures are written cultures) but to an intermediate condition, neither primitive nor modern. In this world, after the archaic period, the entire elite relied heavily on writing, and the entirety of the rest of the population was affected by it. But some of the marks of an oral culture always remain visible, most notably a widespread reliance on and cultivation of the faculty of memory.

In these circumstances it seems perfectly natural that nothing like mass literacy ever came into being in antiquity. A critic might suggest that this conclusion is no more than the result of an accumulation of somewhat fragile arguments, but in reality the basis is solid. It consists in the first place of the comparative argument: literacy on a large scale is the product of forces such as did not exist in antiquity; and a society which is about to bring forth mass literacy shows symptoms, in particular an ample and expanding school system, which we cannot find in the ancient evidence. Behind this lie the "negative" facts about the ancient world: not only the lack of techniques which would have permitted mass diffusion of written texts, and the weakness in antiquity of the ideological notion that all citizens (or all believers) should be able to read and write, but also the slackness of demand for a literate workforce, a demand which, insofar as it existed, was met in good part by slaves.

As for the specific testimony about semi-literacy and illiteracy in antiquity, interested scholars have sometimes drawn correct conclusions, but more often they have treated as socially marginal what was in fact commonplace and indeed typical (the lives of country-people, artisans, slaves, women). It has also been supposed by many scholars that schooling was universal or nearly so, another point of view which cannot be sustained.

The most that we can hope to do is to give estimates of the likely levels of literacy prevalent in given populations at given periods, paying due attention to the existence of semi-literates, and frankly recognizing the degree of uncertainty that attaches to all such estimates.

There is not the least reason to suppose that literacy spread quickly in Greece in the eighth or seventh century. If it was the possession of some of the well-to-do and of a few technicians and artisans, as seems most likely, the proportion of the population that was involved was minute. In the sixth century, however—by the end of it at any rate—signs emerge at Athens of craftsman's literacy, that state of affairs in which many, or even a majority of, skilled craftsmen, as well as members of the social elite, are literate while the mass of the population, including almost all women, are not. The clearest sign that literacy of this kind existed is provided by the rules which governed Athenian ostracism, at least from the 480s onwards: they seem to indicate that at least 15% of the adult male population reached the level of semi-literacy or some higher level, and that a very substantial proportion of this 15% was able to write easily. Therefore, we can probably take it that 5% *or more* of the total adult population (including women and slaves) was literate according to our definition. The next most important pieces of evidence for the spread of literacy before the end of the archaic period are the schools of Chios and Astypalaea. It is exceedingly difficult to define an upper limit, but on comparative grounds it would be surprising if more than 10% of the population of Attica (male and female) was really literate by the time of the Persian Wars. An increase presumably took place during the succeeding century and a half, but since there was no radical social, economic, political, technological, religious, or—finally—educational change (with regard to primary education), the increase is not likely to have been dramatic, and it certainly stayed within the range of craftsman's literacy. Given that women's literacy probably remained on an extremely low level, the overall rate is not likely to have risen much above 10–15%. What did change was that by the mid-fourth century the literate had far more cause to use their ability, in particular their reading ability. How far any of this reflected conditions in the rest of Greece is another obscure question: the more advanced areas, which probably included the southeastern Aegean, would have had at least as much literacy as Athens; but at the other extreme, which Sparta may well represent, there were cities in which very few indeed were fully literate and very little use was made of the written word.

These conclusions will be highly unpalatable to some classical scholars. Let it be stressed therefore that they cannot be invalidated by reference to more or less ordinary Greeks whom we may observe in the act of reading or writing. A contrary view would have to explain why and how a mass of members of the thetic class learned to read and write, for that is what such a view would imply.

It is likely that a notable change occurred in the Hellenistic era, a change which may have had its most powerful effects in those cities which were already the most literate. In particular the educational philosophy which lay behind the known acts of quasi-egalitarian educational philanthropy put into effect at Teos and elsewhere is likely to have had some results. The real impetus for such measures is hard to define, but it is clear that at this time many Greeks (certainly not just in the four cities that are known to have been involved) believed that schools should be subsidized. The Teos foundation is the only one which is known to have aimed at the education of *all* the children of the city, and neither there nor elsewhere is this aspiration likely to have been fulfilled. But these cities may have seen literacy on an "early-modern" scale, perhaps even at a level of 30–40% among the free-born men—though hardly on that level among women, even at Teos. The foundations probably did not outlast the Aegean crisis of the 80s B.C., and under Roman power the cause of universal education among the citizens of Greek cities seems seldom to have been revived.

When the literacy of the Romans and Latins first extended beyond a few people who had a specialized need for writing is impossible to judge. This had without serious doubt happened by the end of the fourth century B.C. Further growth throughout the middle Republic can be inferred from the ways in which writing was used. However— and this is true all the way through the republican epoch—we know even less about schooling than we do in classical Greece, and there is not the least reason to think that schools included the mass of the population in their clienteles. The earliest indication that Roman citizens may have reached a relatively high level of literacy are the *leges tabellariae* of the 130s, which required voters to make use of extremely simple written texts. This was not populist legislation, but there was now at least a solid minority of literate citizens. Women were presumably less literate than men, and once again the combined literacy level in the period before 100 B.C. is unlikely to have much exceeded 10%. The problem is further complicated by the influx of slaves in unprecedented numbers, slaves who were sometimes literate and who did a large proportion of such clerical work as needed to be done.

In the Roman Empire as a whole, the degree of literacy is likely to have varied widely from one region to another. A major limitation was that a large proportion of the provincial population did not even have a grasp of spoken Latin or Greek. Latin literacy spread into every province in the west, as Greek literacy had earlier spread in the east (and not only there), but in many areas indigenous languages dominated in spoken usage. Meanwhile schools remained for the most part unsupported by communities or even by philanthropists, and what they taught was to very many people of little or no practical value. The direct evidence bearing on literacy continues in most areas to be slight. While the evidence from Pompeii, in particular, suggests that something of the order of craftsman's literacy had been achieved there by 79 A.D., Pompeii was probably more literate than some other Italian towns and much more so than most places in the western provinces. Even at Pompeii one could be simultaneously well-to-do and semi-literate or illiterate. In the western provinces, with the possible exception of the areas where neo-Punic was the chief spoken language, literacy was probably almost entirely confined to the cities' social elites and to those who had some special practical need for reading or writing. As for women's literacy in Italy and the west, nothing would lead us to doubt, and some hints in the evidence confirm, that it was even more limited than that of men. In the provinces the level of women's literacy is likely to have been well under 5%.

Among the Greeks the old respect for *paideia* lived on under Roman power. It remained unthinkable that a man of property (unless perhaps he was a freedman) or a man with any claim to distinction in city life could be illiterate. That of course leaves the mass of the population unaccounted for. The overall level of literacy may have declined somewhat from the Hellenistic age, with less philanthropic assistance now being directed towards primary education. There are hints in the evidence that literacy was limited, at best, among artisans. Small farmers and the poor will generally have been illiterate.

Late antiquity presents us with the hardest problems, partly because of regional variations in the fate of cities and their economies, partly because of the difficulty of relating literacy to known changes in the economic and social structures. The problematic extent of late-antique bureaucracy and the growth in the religious use of the written word complicate matters further. However it is probable that the system of primary education, never at all strong, eventually grew weaker. And while literacy may not have declined significantly until the late fourth century A.D. or even later, there are suggestions of a decline in some places as early as the third century. Working against the decline was the rise of religiously inspired reading, which led people of modest social standing to use and transmit their literacy or semi-literacy. But while Christianity encouraged the religious to read, it tended to strengthen the forces which operated against secular literacy.

Levels of literacy were low in classical antiquity by comparison with those prevailing in the most educated countries of the last 200 years. That is entirely to be expected, for each society achieves the level of literacy which its structure and ethos require and its technology permits. What might be considered remarkable is that with no technological advantages, as far as writing was concerned, over the Egyptians or Phoenicians—except the alphabet itself—the Greeks and Romans used the written word, and diffused knowledge of how to read and write, as much as they did.

Why was it, then, that the classical world achieved so much higher a level of literacy than the Near East? The simplicity of the alphabet is an explanation which is not to be scorned, for whatever may be said about the simplicity of Phoenician script or about the ability of the masses to learn scripts which are less straightforward than Greek (Hebrew, Arabic, Japanese), the fact remains that it was the users of the simple but comprehensive Greek script who first went a definite step beyond scribal literacy. Yet this explanation (whether it is strictly "technological determinism" or not) fails to account fully for what happened. After all, the Greek and, later, the Roman alphabets reached many regions where they did not proceed to gain anything like the diffusion or usage that Greek writing obtained in Greece. The Greeks themselves were vastly illiterate from Byzantine times until the nineteenth century.

Therefore we are compelled to consider other causes. It would be possible and perhaps even correct to take refuge in loose generalities about the Greek and the Roman mentalities. However the Greeks enjoyed a particular advantage in addition to the excellence of their alphabet, namely that as a people they prospered greatly between the eighth century B.C. and the fourth, and in a special way: new wealth was diffused widely, relatively speaking and at least in some states, through the citizen body. There was a material basis for the self-confidence of the citizens of Greek city-states, there were resources to pay for teachers, and there was a degree of leisure for learning and maintaining the skills of reading and writing. Thus a reciprocal process came into being, for literacy obviously helped men to create wealth. And as a final speculation we may add that the physical diffusion of the Greeks themselves, from Afghanistan to the Atlantic, was an additional incentive to written communication.

Some Consequences

What were the consequences of these Greek and Roman levels of literacy? This question is different from asking what follows from a population's or an individual's first learning to read and write. Even the latter problem turns out to be very difficult to answer when it is approached by means of a large amount of evidence instead of by pure conjecture.[1] Thus we are in no position to be dogmatic about the effects of selective *alphabétisation*. Concerning the results of the literacy and the illiteracy of the Greeks and Romans, we can give no more than hypothetical and interim answers.

On the economic plane, literacy of the kind that prevailed in the more literate parts of the ancient world undoubtedly assisted trade, even though there was no necessity for a man of trade to do his own writing. The accumulation of technical information committed to writing also presumably had some positive economic effects.

"The primary function of written communication is to facilitate slavery," a great anthropologist has claimed;[2] and it is easy to see that writing can serve systems of political and social hegemony in many different ways. Writing certainly assisted hegemony in the Greek and Roman world, to a certain extent. Newly armed with writing, the Greeks set up colonies in the lands of others along vast stretches of the Mediterranean and Black Sea coasts, securing their power in organized *poleis*. (The role of writing in the early organization of cities seems, however, to have been quite subsidiary.) Later on, especially from the sixth century onwards, those Greeks who were able to afford education used the written word to promote their own political interests, and ignorance of writing came to be seen as a disqualification for office. Athens used meticulous written records in ruling its short-lived fifth-century empire. Closely linked with political power within the city was cultural hegemony, which came to depend in part on a direct knowledge of texts. A particular form of the dominance of the text—

1. Cf. S. Scribner & M. Cole, *The Psychology of Literacy* (Cambridge, Mass., 1981), 6–8 passim.

2. See above, p. 38. The reference is to domination in general, not to chattel slavery as such.

or rather of men who made use of texts—was the bureaucratic government of the Ptolemies.

Rome in turn would have found it entirely impossible to extend its power much beyond Latium if it had not been for the written word, and in this case too the upper order maintained its power over the rest of the community partly by its superior command of written texts. Here once again the cultural hegemony of a social class, more pronounced in this instance because it included a knowledge of classics in a foreign tongue, maintained stability. The more or less centralized power of the emperors became possible when it became possible in organizational terms to control the whole Empire and particularly the senatorial officials and the armies; this control was achieved largely by means of letters and other documents. Conversely, the weakening of the educational system and of the system of written communication hastened the decline of the late Roman Empire.

There is much to be said in support of such a point of view. The theory that literacy facilitates exploitation perhaps applies with especial force to societies which combine a high degree of literacy among the elite and the servants of the elite with a high degree of illiteracy in the rest of the population. In a Greek or Roman city, rousing the rabble had to be done mainly in speech and mainly in public. Meanwhile the educational system, insofar as such a thing existed, tended to have socially conservative effects, reinforcing class distinctions and serving as an additional brake on social mobility. If we wanted to place the various political cultures of the Greeks and Romans somewhere on the spectrum between "open" and "closed," we could not properly say that any of them, with minor and occasional exceptions, was near to being open, and the Romans always lived in a society that was quite closed. For in practical terms access to elementary education was limited, and access to the rhetorical education which was the mark of the elite was very restricted indeed.[3] It should be obvious that in Greece and to an even greater extent in the Roman Empire the illiteracy of the masses contributed to the stability of the political order, much as it has done, *mutatis mutandis,* in many other historical contexts. The Japanese official who in the 1720s commented explicitly on the helpfulness of mass illiteracy from the point of view of the government was making a point of obvious validity.[4] The distur-

3. On the importance of the latter question cf. L. Stone, *P & P* xlii (1969), 73–74.

4. R. P. Dore, *Education in Tokugawa Japan* (London, 1965), 215, referring to an utterance of Ogyū Sorai (1666–1728).

bances caused by the spread of literacy, on the other hand, have been numerous and varied.[5]

But there is much more to say about the political and social effects of limited literacy. These effects should not in any case be exaggerated: class distinctions and social ossification do not *depend* on the exploitation of literacy by the privileged; they are just intensified if the privileged can use writing, the others not. But most important in the Graeco-Roman context is that while limited literacy could have socially conservative effects, it could also help to create and defend the rights of the citizens. In other words, the "primitivists" described in Chapter II seem to have gone too far in decrying the political and social effects of literacy. Limited literacy did not create a highly democratic culture in antiquity (which would have been a most paradoxical consequence), but it did have the effect of helping citizens to establish and maintain their rights. Being able to read documents for oneself and being able to write one's own *libellus* did not guarantee anything, but it was better than being unable to do so. Euripides was not by any means entirely mistaken when he made Theseus pronounce that written laws gave every citizen equality before the law. It at least gave some citizens a degree of security which they would not otherwise have had. It may even have given them a degree of protection against tyrants, in the sense that literate citizens were harder to keep under control than illiterate ones. Opposition to Roman emperors often took written form, and such texts were sometimes taken seriously enough to be suppressed.

Writing, in short, can serve as an instrument of class hegemony or of individual domination. But when the ability to use it spreads to any sizeable social group, that group is likely to develop a stronger sense of its own rights; this does not of course by itself guarantee the creation or survival of freedom or even of *libertas*. We cannot say "the more literacy, the more freedom,"[6] for too much else is involved in securing freedom; but the conviction of Paulo Freire and others that a

---

5. Cf. N. Z. Davis, *Society and Culture in Early Modern France* (Stanford, 1975), 189–226 ("Printing and the People" down to 1600); Stone 84–86 (England in the eighteenth century).

6. What we may call the classic liberal position was succinctly stated by J. Chall, *Harvard Educational Review* xl (1970), 274: "that's the greatness of reading—that it can make the individual free. Once you have the tool of literacy, even if you were given it only in order to get you to think in a certain way, you can use it to think your own thoughts."

literate population is more likely than an illiterate one to resist oppression is hard to contest.

This discussion could advance from historical facts and hypotheses to a philosophical consideration of freedom and civil order. Writing facilitates domination over both external and internal populations, especially if they are illiterate. With regard to internal populations, it also facilitates the development of many other things: written laws which may have positive effects, a more complex economic life which may give rise to economic growth, civil peace, a certain degree of social mobility for men of talent. Caliban felt himself controlled by the medium of the written word, and the domineering Prospero did indeed control him, by magic. This was hardly an undesirable result.

There cannot be the least doubt that writing was an indispensable instrument of imperial domination. Whether in fact the specific kind of literacy which came into being in the Greek and Roman world is a prerequisite for empire is, however, dubious, in view of the earlier empires of the Near East. At all events the empires of Greek and Roman antiquity all depended heavily on writing and documents.

From this brief sketch we can turn briefly to some of the intellectual consequences of Greek and Roman literacy. No results are likely to have followed in an automatic fashion, and a proper answer to this question would require a full consideration of all the other factors which influenced the development of ancient intellectual life.

We should remind ourselves here of the practical difficulties which continued to inhibit the accumulation of information and the exchange of ideas even when literacy had made considerable progress. We have noted the inconvenience and the expensiveness, for most people in antiquity, of obtaining books. It would be quite unrealistic to suppose that literacy by itself led ordinary literate Greeks and Romans to a knowledge of the outside world or of novel ideas, still more to think that it led them to critical modes of thinking.[7] Presumably most literate Greeks and Romans used their knowledge of reading and writing for nothing more than practical or mundane purposes.

A lover of paradoxes could describe the intellectual and cultural consequences of the limited spread of literacy, as well as the political and social ones, in negative terms. It could be argued that the effect of literacy was to give certain texts a privileged position which stifled cre-

---

7. As to how little a world-view may be changed by literacy cf. K. A. Lockridge, *Literacy in Colonial New England* (New York, 1974), 4.

ativity and diversity. The text of Homer permeated the minds of educated Greeks for a millennium, and in general the authoritative voices from the past were the poets whose works were written down. It was notoriously the aspiration of most Greek and Roman authors to stay quite close to their precursors while practising in one way or another the art of *variatio*. And the effects of establishing certain texts as classics went beyond literature. It might, for instance, be thought to have assisted conservatism in religion (it was Homer and Hesiod, according to Herodotus, who taught the Greeks about the gods), at least as far as the educated were concerned.[8]

In technical fields, too, the authority of what the books said may have been unduly heavy and may have distracted attention from the possibilities of independent investigation. Certainly the majority of ancient writers on technical matters seem to have a very bookish attitude towards their subjects: this is true of most of the surviving writers on farming and on military matters, and Galen for instance treats the writings of Hippocrates with profound respect.

This argument about the intellectual effects of Greek and Roman literacy only has to be stated for its weakness to become visible. The accumulation of texts was a necessary though not sufficient condition for many of the literary and intellectual achievements of the classical world. The writing down of ideas, whether they were philosophical or scientific or historical, served as a resource and a challenge to those who came afterwards. They could ignore the challenge only with some difficulty (they might of course fail to live up to it, as happened in historiography after Thucydides and Polybius). Perhaps we should rather say that, *being Greeks,* they could not ignore such a challenge: in other words, the mentality of the Greeks was particularly inclined towards certain kinds of intellectual development, and this inclination was not a consequence—not in any case a direct consequence—of literacy. The agonistic and the inquisitive aspects of this mentality are highly visible in the earliest period of Greek literature. But the material which Greek and Roman minds worked on partly consisted of written texts, and this permitted the development of refined systems of philosophy and the accumulation of information. It did not stifle thought. Galen, to take one example out of very many, though he revered Hippocrates, also typically wrote: "I shall interpret those

8. For some remarks about the immutability of sacred texts, and its limits, see B. V. Street, *Literacy in Theory and Practice* (Cambridge, 1984), 136–137.

observations [of his] which are too obscure, and add others of my own, arrived at by the methods he wrote down."[9] And literacy enabled the Greeks to create a literary tradition which remained vigorous over a span of many generations.

To trace the possible influences of ancient patterns of literacy on the intellectual history of Greece and Rome would require a separate investigation, especially as that history has in some fundamental respects been strangely neglected. We would have to ask innumerable specific questions about the works of ancient authors, and general ones too about the development of language and logic, about verbal precision, about the invention of fiction, about scepticism and rationalism, about attitudes towards the past and towards the outside world, in other words questions about the entire intellectual style of the Greeks and Romans.

The written culture of antiquity was in the main restricted to a privileged minority—though in some places it was quite a large minority—and it coexisted with elements of an oral culture. This written culture certainly helped to widen class differences, as well as having the overwhelmingly important effect of enabling empires to be built. Access to the privileged world of writing was automatic for some and variously difficult for others. The Greeks and Romans would have become very different people if, *per impossibile,* they had achieved mass literacy. As it was, they achieved something much more limited, with consequences for the community which were complex and not all beneficial. If fortune set the individual among the literate, that was a golden gift.

9. *De usu partium* i.8 (iii.21 Kühn). G. E. R. Lloyd, *Science, Folklore and Ideology* (Cambridge, 1983), examines the question whether written authorities inhibited critical inquiry, and concludes from studying Pliny, anatomical writers and Soranus that the effects were varied (see esp. 116).

Bibliography

I. Works Primarily Concerned with Greek and Roman Literacy or Education

Beck, F. A. G. *Greek Education. 450–350 B.C.* London, 1964.

———. *Album of Greek Education.* Sydney, 1975.

———. "The Schooling of Girls in Ancient Greece." *Classicum* [Sydney] ix (1978), 1–9.

Best, E. E. "The Literate Roman Soldier." *Classical Journal* lxii (1966–67), 122–127.

———. "Martial's Readers in the Roman World." *Classical Journal* lxiv (1968–69), 208–212.

———. "Literacy and Roman Voting." *Historia* xxiii (1974), 428–438.

Bilkei, I. "Schulunterricht und Bildungswesen in der römischen Provinz Pannonien." *Alba Regia* xx (1983), 67–74.

Bonner, S. F. "The Street Teacher: An Educational Scene in Horace." *AJPh* xciii (1972), 509–528.

———. *Education in Ancient Rome.* Berkeley, 1977.

Booth, A. D. "Elementary and Secondary Education in the Roman Empire." *Florilegium* i (1979), 1–14.

———. "The Schooling of Slaves in First-Century Rome." *TAPhA* cix (1979), 11–19.

———. "Some Suspect Schoolmasters." *Florilegium* iii (1981), 1–20.

———. "Douris' Cup and the Stages of Schooling in Classical Athens." *Echos du monde classique* xxix (1985), 275–280.

Boring, T. A. *Literacy in Ancient Sparta.* Leiden, 1979.

Bower, E. W. "Some Technical Terms in Roman Education." *Hermes* lxxxix (1961), 462–477.

Boyaval, B. "Le cahier de Papnouthion et les autres cahiers scolaires grecs." *Rev.arch.* 1977, 215–230.

Burns, A. "Athenian Literacy in the Fifth Century B.C." *JHI* xlii (1981), 371–387.

Calderini, R. "Gli ἀγράμματοι nell'Egitto greco-romano." *Aegyptus* xxx (1950), 17–41.

Cartledge, P. A. "Literacy in the Spartan Oligarchy." *JHS* xcviii (1978), 25–37.

Cavallo, G. "Dal segno incompiuto al segno negato. Linee per una ricerca su alfabetismo, produzione e circolazione di cultura scritta in Italia nei primi secoli dell'impero." In *Alfabetismo e cultura scritta nella storia della società italiana. Atti del seminario tenutosi a Perugia il 29–30 marzo 1977.* Perugia, 1978, 119–145.

———. "Scrittura, alfabetismo e produzione libraria nel tardo antico." In *La cultura in Italia fra tardo antico e alto medioevo.* Rome, 1981, ii.523–538.

———. "Alfabetismo e circolazione del libro." In M. Vegetti (ed.), *Oralità, scrittura, spettacolo.* Turin, 1983, 166–186.

Cole, S. G. "Could Greek Women Read and Write?" In H. P. Foley (ed.), *Reflections of Women in Antiquity.* New York, 1981, 219–245.

Cristofani, M. "Rapporto sulla diffusione della scrittura nell'Italia antica." *S & C* ii (1978), 5–33.

Forbes, C. A. "The Education and Training of Slaves in Antiquity." *TAPhA* lxxxvi (1955), 321–360.

Freeman, K. J. *Schools of Hellas.* London, 1907.

Grasberger, L. *Erziehung und Unterricht im klassischen Altertum.* Vols. i–iii. Würzburg, 1864–1880.

Harris, W. V. "Literacy and Epigraphy, I." *ZPE* lii (1983), 87–111.

———. "L'analfabetismo e le funzioni della parola scritta nel mondo romano," *Quaderni di storia* xxvii (1988), 5–26.

Harvey, F. D. "Literacy in the Athenian Democracy." *REG* lxxix (1966), 585–635.

Johnston, A. "The Extent and Use of Literacy: The Archaeological Evidence." In R. Hägg (ed.), *The Greek Renaissance of the Eighth Century B.C.: Tradition and Innovation.* Stockholm, 1983, 63–68.

Maehler, H. "Die griechische Schule im ptolemäischen Aegypten." In E. Van't Dack et al. (eds.), *Egypt and the Hellenistic World. Proceedings of the International Colloquium, Leuven, 24–26 May 1982.* Louvain, 1983, 191–203.

Majer-Leonhard, E. ΑΓΡΑΜΜΑΤΟΙ. *In Aegypto qui litteras sciverint qui nesciverint ex papyris graecis quantum fieri potest exploratur.* Frankfurt-a.-M., 1913.

Marrou, H. I. "L'école dans l'antiquité tardive." In *La scuola nell'occidente latino dell'alto medioevo* (Settimane di Studio del centro italiano di studi sull'alto medioevo, xix). Spoleto, 1972, 127–143.

———. *Histoire de l'éducation dans l'antiquité.* 7th ed. Paris, n.d.

Mohler, S. L. "Slave Education in the Roman Empire." *TAPhA* lxxi (1940), 262–280.

Nieddu, G. F. "Alfabetismo e diffusione sociale della scrittura nella Grecia arcaica e classica: Pregiudizi recenti e realtà documentaria." *S & C* vi (1982), 233–261.

———. "Testo, scrittura, libro nella Grecia arcaica e classica: Note e osservazioni sulla prosa scientifico-filosofica." *S & C* viii (1984), 213–262.

Sagredo, L., & S. Crespo. "La enseñanza en la Hispania romana." *Hispania Antiqua* v (1975), 121–134.

Schmitter, P. *Die hellenistische Erziehung im Spiegel der Νέα Κωμῳδία und der Fabula Palliata.* Bonn, 1972.

———. "Compulsory Schooling at Athens and Rome?" *AJPh* xcvi (1975), 276–289.

Vogt, J. "Alphabet für Freie und Sklaven." *RhM* cxvi (1973), 129–142. Reprinted in *Sklaverei und Humanität. Ergänzungsheft zur 2. erweiterten Auflage.* Wiesbaden, 1983, 17–27.

Wipszycka, E. "Le degré d'alphabétisation en Egypte byzantine." *Rev.Et. Aug.* xxx (1984), 279–296.

Youtie, H. C. "Pétaus, fils de Pétaus, ou le scribe qui ne savait pas écrire." *Cd'E* lxxxi (1966), 127–143. Reprinted in *Scriptiunculae.* Amsterdam, 1973, ii. 677–698.

———. "Ἀγράμματος: An Aspect of Greek Society in Egypt." *HSCPh* lxxv (1971), 161–176. Reprinted in *Scriptiunculae* ii. 611–628.

———. "Βραδέως γράφων: Between Literacy and Illiteracy." *GRBS* xii (1971), 239–261. Reprinted in *Scriptiunculae* ii. 629–651.

———. "'Because They Do Not Know Letters.'" *ZPE* xix (1975), 101–108. Reprinted in *Scriptiunculae Posteriores.* Bonn, 1981, i.255–262.

———. "Ὑπογράφευς: The Social Impact of Illiteracy in Graeco-Roman Egypt." *ZPE* xvii (1975), 201–221. Reprinted in *Scriptiunculae Posteriores* ii.179–199.

Ziebarth, E. *Aus dem griechischen Schulwesen.* 2d ed., Leipzig & Berlin, 1914.

II. General Works on Greek and Roman History (books of tangential relevance omitted)

Achelis, H. *Die Ältesten Quellen des orientalischen Kirchenrechtes.* Leipzig, 1891.

Allrogen-Bedel, A. "Herkunft und ursprünglicher Dekorationszusammenhang einiger in Essen ausgestellter Fragmente von Wandmalereien." In *Neue Forschungen in Pompeji.* Recklinghausen, 1975, 115–122.

Andreau, J. *Les affaires de Monsieur Jucundus.* Rome, 1974.

———. "Declino e morte dei mestieri bancari nel Mediterraneo occidentale (II–IV d.C.)." In A. Giardina (ed.), *Società romana e impero tardoantico.* Rome & Bari, 1986, i.601–615.

Annibaldis, G., & O. Vox. "La più antica iscrizione greca." *Glotta* liv (1976), 223–228.

Astin, A. E. *Cato the Censor.* Oxford, 1978.

Auerbach, E. *Literatursprache und Publikum in der lateinischen Spätantike und im Mittelalter.* Bern, 1958.

Bacchielli, L. "Le pitture dalla Tomba dell'altalena di Cirene nel Museo del Louvre." *Quaderni di archeologia della Libia* viii (1976), 355–383.

Bagnall, R. S., & K. A. Worp. "Papyrus Documentation in Egypt from Constantine to Justinian." In *Miscellanea Papyrologica* (Papyrologica Florentina vii). Florence, 1980, 13–23.

Balland, A. *Fouilles de Xanthos* vii. *Inscriptions d'époque impériale du Létoôn.* Paris, 1981.

Balogh, E. "Voces paginarum. Beiträge zur Geschichte des lauten Lesens und Schreibens." *Philologus* lxxxii (1927), 84–109, 202–240.

Bardon, H. *La littérature latine inconnue.* Vols. i–ii. Paris, 1952–1956.

Barrett, A. A. "Knowledge of the Literary Classics in Roman Britain." *Britannia* ix (1978), 307–313.

Barruol, G. "La résistance des substrats préromains en Gaule méridionale." In D. M. Pippidi (ed.), *Assimilation et résistance à la culture gréco-romaine dans le monde ancien.* Paris & Bucharest, 1976, 389–405.

Bartoccini, R. "Frammento di legge romana rinvenuto a Taranto." *Epigraphica* ix (1947), 3–31.

Bean, G. E. "Notes and Inscriptions from Pisidia, II." *Anatolian Studies* x (1960), 43–82.

Beard, M. "Writing and Ritual. A Study of Diversity and Expansion in the Arval Acta." *PBSR* liii (1985), 114–162.

Beazley, J. D. *Athenian Black-Figure Vase-Painters.* Oxford, 1956.

———. *Attic Red-Figure Vase-Painters.* 2d ed. Oxford, 1963.

———. *Paralipomena.* Oxford, 1971.

Bekker-Nielsen, T. *Bydannelse i det romerske Gallien.* Arhus, 1984.

Belloni, G. G. "Monete romane e propaganda. Impostazione di una problematica complessa." In M. Sordi (ed.), *I canali della propaganda nel mondo antico* (Contributi dell'Istituto di storia antica iv). Milan, 1976, 131–159.

Beloch, J. *Die Bevölkerung der griechisch-römischen Welt.* Leipzig, 1886.

Bénabou, M. *La résistance africaine à la romanisation.* Paris, 1975.

Bentley, R. *A Dissertation upon the Epistles of Phalaris.* London, 1699.

Bérard, F., et al. *Guide de l'épigraphiste.* Paris, 1986.

Berger, A. *Encyclopedic Dictionary of Roman Law.* Philadelphia, 1953.

Bernand, A., & O. Masson. "Les inscriptions grecques d'Abou-Simbel." *REG* lxx (1957), 1–46.

Berneker, E. "χειρόγραφον." In *RE* Suppl. x (1965), cols. 126–127.

Beseler, G. "Romanistiche Studien." *ZSS* l (1930), 18–77.

Besevliev, A. *Untersuchungen über die Personennamen bei den Thrakern.* Amsterdam, 1970.

Bianchini, M. "La συγγραφὴ ed il problema delle forme contrattuali." In A. Biscardi et al. (eds.), ΣΥΜΠΟΣΙΟΝ 1974. Athens, 1978, 245–258.

Bickermann, E. "Beiträge zur antiken Urkundengeschichte." *Archiv für Papyrusforschung* ix (1928), 24–46.

Biezuńska-Malowist, I. *L'esclavage dans l'Egypte gréco-romaine.* Vol. ii. Wroclaw, 1977.

Bikerman, E. *Institutions des Séleucides.* Paris, 1938.

Bilkei, I. "Römische Schreibgeräte aus Pannonien." *Alba Regia* xviii (1980), 61–90.

Birt, T. *Die Buchrolle in der Kunst.* Leipzig, 1907.

———. *Kritik und Hermeneutik, nebst Abriss des antiken Buchwesens.* Munich, 1913.

Blegen, C. W. "Inscriptions on Geometric Pottery from Hymettos." *AJA* xxxviii (1934), 10–28.

Boardman, J. *Athenian Black Figure Vases.* London, 1974.

———. *Athenian Red Figure Vases. The Archaic Period.* London, 1975.

Boegehold, A. L. "The Establishment of a Central Archive at Athens." *AJA* lxxvi (1972), 23–30.

Bogaert, R. *Banques et banquiers dans les cités grecques.* Leiden, 1968.

Bonner, R. J. "The Use and Effect of Attic Seals." *CPh* iii (1908), 399–407.

Bonner, R. J., & G. Smith. *The Administration of Justice from Homer to Aristotle.* Vols. i–ii. Chicago, 1930–1938.

Booth, A. D. "Allusion to the Circulator by Persius and Horace." *Greece and Rome* xxvii (1980), 166–169.

———. "Litterator." *Hermes* cix (1981), 371–378.

Bove, L. *Documenti processuali dalle Tabulae Pompeianae di Murecine.* Naples, 1979.

———. "Documentazione privata e prova: Le tabulae ceratae." In *Atti del XVII Congresso internazionale di papirologia.* Naples, 1984, iii.1189–1200.

———. *Documenti di operazioni finanziarie dall'archivio dei Sulpici.* Naples, 1984.

Bowersock, G. W. *Greek Sophists in the Roman Empire.* Oxford, 1969.

———. *Roman Arabia.* Cambridge, Mass., 1983.

Bowman, A. K., & J. D. Thomas. *Vindolanda: The Latin Writing-Tablets.* London, 1983.

Bradeen, D. W. *The Funerary Inscriptions (The Athenian Agora* xvii). Princeton, 1974.

Bradley, K. R. "Child Labour in the Roman World." *Historical Reflections* xii (1985), 311–330.

Brann, E. "Late Geometric Well Groups from the Athenian Agora." *Hesperia* xxx (1961), 93–146.

Bravo, B. "Une lettre sur plomb de Berezan': Colonisation et modes de contact dans le Pont." *Dialogues d'histoire ancienne* i (1974), 111–187.

Brelich, A. *Aspetti della morte nelle iscrizioni sepolcrali dell'impero romano.* Budapest, 1937.

Bretone, M. "Il giureconsulto e la memoria." *Quaderni di storia* xx (1984), 223–255.

Bringmann, K. "Edikt der Triumvirn oder Senatsbeschluss? Zu einem Neufund aus Ephesos." *Epigraphica Anatolica* ii (1983), 47–76.

Brixhe, C., & G. Neumann. "Découverte du plus long texte néo-phrygien: L'inscription de Gezler Köyü." *Kadmos* xxiv (1985), 161–184.

Broneer, O. "Excavations on the North Slope of the Acropolis, 1937." *Hesperia* vii (1938), 161–263.

Broughton, T. R. S. "A Greek Inscription from Tarsus." *AJA* xlii (1938), 55–57.

Brown, P. "Christianity and Roman Culture in Late Roman Africa." *JRS* lviii (1968), 85–95.

———. "Town, Village and Holy Man. The Case of Syria." In D. M. Pippidi (ed.), *Assimilation et résistance à la culture gréco-romaine dans le monde ancien.* Paris–Bucharest, 1976, 213–220.

Brugnone, A. "Defixiones inedite da Selinunte." In *Studi di storia antica offerti dagli allievi a Eugenio Manni.* Rome, 1976, 67–90.

Bruneau, P. "Tombes d'Argos." *BCH* xciv (1970), 437–531.

Bundgård, J. A. "Why Did the Art of Writing Spread to the West? Reflexions on the Alphabet of Marsiliana." *Analecta Romana Instituti Danici* iii (1965), 11–72.

Burnett, A. "The Coinages of Rome and Magna Graecia in the Late Fourth and Third Centuries B.C." *Schweizerische Numismatische Rundschau* lvi (1977), 92–121.

Burr, V. "Editionstechnik." In *RLAC* (1959), cols. 597–610.

Calabi Limentani, I. "Modalità della comunicazione ufficiale in Atene. I decreti onorari." *QUCC* xvi (1984), 85–115.

Calhoun, G. M. "Documentary Frauds in Litigation at Athens." *CPh* ix (1914), 134–144.

———. "Oral and Written Pleading in Athenian Courts." *TAPhA* l (1919), 177–193.

Callender, M. H. *Roman Amphorae.* London, 1965.

Callmer, C. "Antike Bibliotheken." In *Opuscula Archaeologica* iii (Skrifter utgivna av Svenska Institutet i Rom x) (1944), 145–193.

Camp, J. M. Review of *Studies in Attic Epigraphy . . . Presented to Eugene Vanderpool. AJA* lxxxvii (1983), 113–115.

Cantineau, J. *Le nabatéen.* Vols. i–ii. Paris, 1930–1932.

———. *Grammaire du palmyrénien épigraphique.* Cairo, 1935.

Cantineau, J., et al. (eds.), *Inventaire des inscriptions de Palmyre*. Beirut & Damascus, 1930–1975.

Carlini, A. "Il papiro di Tucidide della Bibliotheca Bodmeriana P. Bodmer XXVII." *Mus.Helv.* xxxii (1975), 33–40.

Carrington, R. C. "Studies in the Campanian Villae Rusticae." *JRS* xxi (1931), 110–130.

Carter, L. B. *The Quiet Athenian*. Oxford, 1986.

Cartledge, P. A. "Spartan Wives: Liberation or License?" *CQ* xxxi (1981), 84–105.

Casarico, L. *Il controllo della popolazione nell'Egitto romano*. Vol. i. Azzate, 1985.

Cavallo, G. "Note sulla scrittura greca corsiva." *Scriptorium* xxii (1968), 291–294.

———. "La nascita del codice." *SIFC* ser.3 iii (1985), 118–121.

——— (ed.). *Libri, editori e pubblico nel mondo antico*. Rome, 1975.

Chadwick, J. "The Berezan Lead Letter." *PCPhS* xix (1973), 35–37.

Chapman, H. "A Roman Mitre and Try Square from Canterbury." *Antiquaries' Journal* lix (1979), 402–407.

Christes, J. *Sklaven und Freigelassene als Grammatiker und Philologen im antiken Rom*. Wiesbaden, 1979.

Civiltà del Lazio primitivo. Rome, 1976.

Clarke, G. W. "An Illiterate Lector." *ZPE* lvii (1984), 103–104.

Cockle, W. E. H. "State Archives in Graeco-Roman Egypt from 30 B.C. to the Reign of Septimius Severus." *JEA* lxx (1984), 106–122.

Coldstream, J. N. *Geometric Greece*. London, 1977.

Cole, S. G. "New Evidence for the Mysteries of Dionysos." *GRBS* xxi (1980), 223–238.

Colonna, G. "Una nuova iscrizione etrusca del VII secolo e appunti sull'epigrafia ceretana dell'epoca." *MEFRA* lxxxii (1970), 637–672.

———. Contribution to "Il sistema alfabetico." In *Atti del colloquio sul tema l'Etrusco arcaico*. Florence, 1976, 7–55.

———. "'Scriba cum rege sedens.'" In *L'Italie préromaine et la Rome républicaine. Mélanges offerts à Jacques Heurgon*. Rome, 1976, i.187–195.

———. In C. M. Stibbe et al., *Lapis Satricanus* (= Archeologische Studiën van het Nederlands Instituut te Rome, Scripta Minora v). The Hague, 1980.

Corbier, M. "L'écriture dans l'espace public romain." In *L'Urbs. Espace urbain et histoire. Actes du colloque (Rome, 8–12 mai 1985)*. Rome, 1987, 27–60.

Coulton, J. J. "Opramoas and the Anonymous Benefactor." *JHS* cvii (1987), 171–178.

Courcelle, P. *Recherches sur les Confessions de Saint Augustin*. 2d ed., Paris, 1968.

Courtney, E. *A Commentary on the Satires of Juvenal.* London, 1980.

Cousin, G., & C. Diehl. "Cibyra et Eriza." *BCH* xiii (1889), 333–342.

Crawford, D. J. *Kerkeosiris. An Egyptian Village in the Ptolemaic Period.* Cambridge, 1971.

Crawford, M. H. *Roman Republican Coinage.* Cambridge, 1974.

Crifò, G. "La legge delle XII Tavole. Osservazioni e problemi." In *ANRW* i.2 (1972), 115–133. Reprinted in *Libertà e uguaglianza in Roma antica.* Rome, 1984, 91–123.

Criscuolo, L. "Ricerche sul komogrammateus nell'Egitto tolemaico." *Aegyptus* lviii (1978), 3–101.

Cristofani, M. "Appunti di epigrafia etrusca arcaica. Postilla: la più antica iscrizione di Tarquinia." *ASNSP* ser.3 i (1971), 295–299.

———. "Appunti di epigrafia etrusca arcaica, II." *Arch.Class.* xxv–xxvi (1973–74), 151–165.

———. "L'alfabeto etrusco." In *Popoli e civiltà dell'Italia antica.* Vol. vi. Rome, 1978, 403–428.

———. "Appendice. Le iscrizioni." In *Materiali per servire alla storia del Vaso François* (= *Bollettino d'arte,* Serie speciale i) (1981), 175–178.

——— (ed.). *Civiltà degli etruschi* (Florence exhibition catalogue). Milan, 1985.

Cugusi, P. *Evoluzione e forme dell'epistolografia latina nella tarda repubblica e nei primi due secoli dell'impero.* Rome, 1983.

Cunningham, I. C. *Herodas. Mimiambi.* Oxford, 1971.

Curtis, R. I. "Product Identification and Advertising on Roman Commercial Amphorae." *Ancient Society* xv–xvii (1984–86), 209–228.

Curtius, L. *Die Wandmalerei Pompejis.* Cologne, 1929.

Cuvigny, H. "La surveillance des récoltes (γενηματοφυλακία)." *Cd'E* lix (1984), 123–135.

Dalzell, A. "C. Asinius Pollio and the Early History of the Public Recitation at Rome." *Hermathena* lxxxvi (1955), 20–28.

Daniel, R. W. "Liberal Education and Semiliteracy in Petronius." *ZPE* xl (1980), 153–159.

Davies, J. K. *Athenian Propertied Families, 600–300 B.C.* Oxford, 1971.

Davies, R. W. "The Daily Life of the Roman Soldier under the Principate." In *ANRW* ii.1 (1974), 299–338.

Debut, J. "Les documents scolaires." *ZPE* lxiii (1986), 251–278.

de Kisch, Y. "Les sortes Vergilianae dans l'Histoire Auguste." *MEFR* lxxxii (1970), 321–362.

della Corte, M. "Pompei—Continuazione degli scavi in via dell'Abbondanza." *Not.Sc.* 1916, 155–58.

———. "Scuole e maestri in Pompei antica." *Studi romani* vii (1959), 622–634.

———. *Case ed abitanti di Pompei.* 3d. ed. Naples, 1965.

Delorme, J. *Gymnasion. Etude sur les monuments consacrés à l'éducation en Grèce*. Paris, 1960.

de Romilly, J. *La loi dans la pensée grecque*. Paris, 1971.

de Sarlo, L. *Il documento oggetto di rapporti giuridici privati*. Florence, 1935.

de Ste. Croix, G. E. M. "Greek and Roman Accounting." In A. C. Littleton & B. S. Yamey (eds.), *Studies in the History of Accounting*. Homewood, Ill., 1956, 14–74.

Dessau, H. "Ueber die Scriptores Historiae Augustae." *Hermes* xxvii (1892), 561–605.

Devréesse, R. *Introduction à l'étude des manuscripts grecs*. Paris, 1954.

di Capua, F. "Osservazioni sulla lettura e sulla preghiera ad alta voce presso gli antichi." *RAAN* xxviii (1953), 59–99.

Dionisotti, A. C. "From Ausonius' Schooldays?" *JRS* lxxii (1982), 83–125.

d'Ipolito, F. "Das ius Flavium und die lex Ogulnia." *ZSS* cii (1985), 91–128.

Dornseiff, F. *Das Alphabet in Mystik und Magie*. 2d ed. Leipzig & Berlin, 1925.

———. "Hesiods Werke und Tage und das alte Morgenland." *Philologus* lxxxix (1934), 397–415. Reprinted in E. Heitsch (ed.), *Hesiod*. Darmstadt, 1966, 131–150.

Dover, K. J. *Lysias and the Corpus Lysiacum*. Berkeley, 1968.

Dow, S. "The Athenian Calendar of Sacrifices. The Chronology of Nikomakhos' Second Term." *Historia* ix (1960), 270–293.

Drew-Bear, M. "Les conseillers municipaux des métropoles au IIIᵉ s. ap.J.C." *Cd'E* lix (1984), 315–332.

Drijvers, H. J. W. *Old-Syriac (Edessean) Inscriptions*. Leiden, 1972.

Duensing, H. *Der aethiopische Text der Kirchenordnung des Hippolyt*. Göttingen, 1946.

Duncan-Jones, R. P. "Age-Rounding, Illiteracy, and Social Differentiation in the Roman Empire." *Chiron* vii (1977), 333–353.

———. "Age-Rounding in Greco-Roman Egypt." *ZPE* xxxiii (1979), 169–177.

Easterling, P. E. "Books and Readers in the Greek World. 2. The Hellenistic and Imperial Periods." In *Cambridge History of Classical Literature* Vol. i. Cambridge, 1985, 16–41.

Edelstein, E. J., & L. Edelstein. *Asclepius: A Collection of the Testimonies*. Baltimore, 1945.

Eder, W. "The Political Significance of the Codification of Law in Archaic Societies: An Unconventional Hypothesis." In K. Raaflaub (ed.), *Social Struggles in Archaic Rome*. Berkeley, 1986, 262–300.

Egger, R. *Die Stadt auf dem Magdalensberg*. Vienna, 1961.

Ellis Evans, D. "Language Contact in Pre-Roman and Roman Britain." In *ANRW* ii.29.2 (1983), 949–987.

Emonds, H. *Zweite Auflage im Altertum*. Leipzig, 1941.

Erhardt, C. T. H. R. "Roman Coin Types and the Roman Public." *Jahrbuch für Numismatik und Geldgeschichte* xxxiv (1984), 41–54.

Erman, H. "La falsification des actes dans l'antiquité." *Mélanges [Jules] Nicole.* Geneva, 1905, 111–134.

Etienne, R., et al. (eds.). *Fouilles de Conimbriga.* Vol. ii. Paris, 1975.

Falbe, C. T., J. C. Lindberg, & L. Müller. *Numismatique de l'ancienne Afrique.* Vol. ii. Copenhagen, 1860.

Faraone, C. A. "Aeschylus (*Eum.* 306) and Attic Judicial Curse Tablets." *JHS* cv (1985), 150–154.

Ferrandini Troisi, F. "'Pesi da telaio.' Segni e interpretazioni." In *Decima miscellanea greca e romana.* Rome, 1986, 91–114.

Festugière, A.-J. *Les moines d'Orient.* Vols. i–iv. Paris, 1961–1965.

Fink, R. O. *Roman Military Records on Papyrus.* Cleveland, 1971.

Finley, M. I. *Studies in Land and Credit in Ancient Athens, 500–200* B.C. New Brunswick, N.J., 1952.

———. *The Use and Abuse of History.* London, 1975.

———. "Censura nell'antichità classica." *Belfagor* xxxii (1977), 605–622.

———. *Ancient Slavery and Modern Ideology.* London, 1980.

———. "Le document et l'histoire économique de l'antiquité." *Annales E.S.C.* xxxvii (1982), 697–713.

Fiumi, E. "Contributo alla datazione del materiale volterrano. Gli scavi della necropoli del Portone degli anni 1873–1874." *SE* xxv (1957), 367–415.

Flory, S. "Who Read Herodotus' *Histories?*" *AJPh* ci (1980), 12–28.

Forni, G. "Estrazione etnica e sociale dei soldati delle legioni nei primi tre secoli dell'impero." In *ANRW* ii.1 (1974), 339–391.

Fraenkel, E. *Rome and Greek Culture.* Oxford, 1935. Reprinted in *Kleine Beiträge zur klassischen Philologie.* Rome, 1964, ii.583–598.

———. *Horace.* Oxford, 1957.

Franklin, J. L. *Pompeii: The Electoral Programmata, Campaigns and Politics,* A.D. *71–79.* Rome, 1980.

Fraser, P. M. *Ptolemaic Alexandria.* Vols. i–iii. Oxford, 1972.

Frederiksen, M. W. "Changes in the Pattern of Settlement." In P. Zanker (ed.), *Hellenismus in Mittelitalien.* Göttingen, 1976, 341–355.

Frere, S. *Britannia.* 3d ed. London, 1987.

Friedrich, J. *Kleinasiatische Sprachdenkmäler.* Berlin, 1932.

Frier, B. W. *Libri Annales Pontificum Maximorum: The Origins of the Annalistic Tradition.* Rome, 1979.

———. "Roman Life Expectancy: Ulpian's Evidence." *HSCPh* lxxxvi (1982), 212–251.

Fuhrmann, M. *Das systematische Lehrbuch.* Göttingen, 1960.

Funaioli, G. "Recitationes." In *RE* (1914), cols. 435–446.

Furley, D. J. "The Purpose of Theophrastus's *Characters.*" *Symb.Osl.* xxx (1953), 56–60.

Galsterer, B. *Die Graffiti aus der römischen Gefässkeramik aus Haltern.* Münster, 1983.

Gandz, S. "The Dawn of Literature. Prolegomena to a History of Unwritten Literature." *Osiris* vii (1939), 261–522.

García y Bellido, A. "Die Latinisierung Hispaniens." In *ANRW* i.1 (1972), 462–500.

Garlan, Y. "Greek Amphorae and Trade." In P. Garnsey et al. (eds.), *Trade in the Ancient Economy.* London, 1983, 27–35.

Garnsey, P. D. A. "Where Did Italian Peasants Live?" *PCPhS* n.s. xxv (1979), 1–25.

Gascou, J. *Suétone historien.* Rome, 1984.

Gasperini, L. "Il municipio tarentino. Ricerche epigrafiche." In *Terza miscellanea greca e romana.* Rome, 1971, 143–209.

Gastaldi, S. "La retorica del IV secolo tra oralità e scrittura." *Quaderni di storia* xiv (1981), 189–225.

Gentili, B. "Poesia e comunicazione nell'età ellenistica." In *Studi in onore di Aristide Colonna.* Perugia, 1982, 123–130. Virtually repeated in *Poesia e pubblico nella Grecia antica.* Rome & Bari, 1984.

Georgiev, V. I. "Thrakisch und dakisch." In *ANRW* ii.29.2 (1983), 1148–94.

Gerke, F. *Christus in der spätantiken Plastik.* 3d ed. Mainz, 1948.

Gernet, L. "La création du testament." *REG* xxxiii (1920), 123–168, 249–290. Reprinted as "La loi de Solon sur le 'testament,'" in *Droit et société dans la Grèce ancienne.* Paris, 1955, 121–149.

———. "Sur les actions commerciales en droit athénien." *REG* li (1938), 1–44. Reprinted in *Droit et société dans la Grèce ancienne,* 173–200.

Gerov, B. "Die lateinisch-griechische Sprachgrenze auf der Balkanhalbinsel." In Neumann & Untermann (see below), 147–165.

Gianotti, G. F., & A. Pennacini. *Società e comunicazione letteraria in Roma antica.* Vols. i–iii. Turin, 1981.

Giardina, A. *Aspetti della burocrazia nel basso impero.* Rome, 1977.

Giardina, A., & F. Grelle. "La Tavola di Trinitapoli. Una nuova costituzione di Valentiniano I." *MEFRA* xcv (1983), 249–303.

Gigante, M. *Civiltà delle forme letterarie nell'antica Pompei.* Naples, 1979.

Glotz, G. *Ancient Greece at Work.* Trans. M. R. Dobie. London, 1926. Originally published as *Le travail dans la Grèce ancienne.* Paris, 1920.

Goffart, W. *Caput and Colonate: Towards a History of Late Roman Taxation.* Toronto, 1974.

Gómez-Moreno, M. *Misceláneas.* Madrid, 1949.

Gomme, A. W. et al. *A Historical Commentary on Thucydides.* Vols. i–v. Oxford, 1945–1981.

Gorges, J. G. "Centuriation et organisation du territoire. Notes préliminaires sur l'exemple de Mérida." In P. A. Fevrier & P. Leveau (eds.), *Villes et campagnes dans l'Empire romain.* Aix-en-Provence, 1982, 101–110.

Graham, A. J. "The Authenticity of the ὅρκιον τῶν οἰκιστήρων of Cyrene." *JHS* lxxx (1960), 94–111.

Grandjean, Y. *Une nouvelle arétalogie d'Isis à Maronée*. Leiden, 1975.

Green, W. M. "Augustine's Use of Punic." In *Semitic and Oriental Studies: A Volume Presented to William Popper* (U. of Calif. Publications in Semitic Philology xi). Berkeley, 1951, 179–190.

Gregory, C. R. *Canon and Text of the New Testament*. New York, 1912.

Grier, E. *Accounting in the Zenon Papyri*. New York, 1934.

Griffin, M. "The Elder Seneca and Spain." *JRS* lxii (1972), 1–19.

Grundmann, H. "Litteratus—illiteratus." *Archiv für Kulturgeschichte* xl (1958), 1–65.

Guarducci, M. "Poeti vaganti e conferenzieri dell'età ellenistica." *Mem.Acc. Linc.* ser.6 ii (1929), 629–665.

———. *Epigrafia greca*. Vols. i–iv. Rome, 1967–1978.

———. "La cosiddetta fibula praenestina." *Mem.Acc.Linc.* ser.8 xxiv (1980), 413–574.

Guéraud, O., & P. Jouguet. *Un livre d'écolier du IIIᵉ siècle avant J.-C.* Cairo, 1938.

Guillemin, A.-M. *Le public et la vie littéraire à Rome*. Paris, 1937.

Haas, O. *Die phrygischen Sprachdenkmäler*. Sofia, 1966.

Habicht, C. "Falsche Urkunden zur Geschichte Athens im Zeitalter der Perserkriege." *Hermes* lxxxix (1961), 1–35.

Häusle, H. *Das Denkmal als Garant des Nachruhms*. Munich, 1980.

Hall, U. "Voting Procedure in Roman Assemblies." *Historia* xiii (1964), 267–306.

Hands, A. R. *Charities and Social Aid in Greece and Rome*. London, 1968.

Hansen, M. H. "*Nomos* and *Psephisma* in Fourth-Century Athens." *GRBS* xix (1978), 315–330. Reprinted in *The Athenian Ecclesia*. Copenhagen, 1983, 161–176.

———. *Demography and Democracy. The Number of Athenian Citizens in the Fourth Century B.C.* Herning, 1986.

Harmand, J. *L'armée et le soldat à Rome de 107 à 50 av.n.è.* Paris, 1967.

Harrauer, H., & R. Seider. "Ein neuer lateinischer Schuldschein, P.Vindob. L135." *ZPE* xxxvi (1979), 109–120.

Harris, W. V. *Rome in Etruria and Umbria*. Oxford, 1971.

———. "Roman Terracotta Lamps. The Organization of an Industry." *JRS* lxx (1980), 126–145.

Harrison, A. R. W. *The Law of Athens*. Vols. i–ii. Oxford, 1968–1971.

Hartog, F. *Le miroir d'Hérodote*. Paris, 1980.

Harvey, F. D. Review of Havelock, *Origins of Western Literacy*. *CR* xxviii (1978), 130–131.

Hasebroek, J. "Zum griechischen Bankwesen der klassischen Zeit." *Hermes* lv (1920), 113–173.

————. "Die Betriebsformen des griechischen Handels im IV. Jahrh." *Hermes* lviii (1923), 393–425.

Hassall, M. W. C., et al. "Roman Britain in 1978, II. Inscriptions." *Britannia* x (1979), 339–356.

Hassall, M., M. Crawford & J. Reynolds. "Rome and the Eastern Provinces at the End of the Second Century B.C." *JRS* lxiv (1974), 195–220.

Haussoullier, B. *La vie municipale en Attique*. Paris, 1884.

Havelock, E. A. *Preface to Plato*. Cambridge, Mass., 1963.

————. "Preliteracy and the Presocratics." *BICS* xiii (1966), 44–67. Reprinted in *The Literate Revolution* (see below), 220–260.

————. *Prologue to Greek Literacy*. Cincinnati, 1973.

————. *The Origins of Western Literacy*. Toronto, 1976.

————. "The Preliteracy of the Greeks." *New Literary History* viii (1976–77), 369–391. Reprinted in *The Literate Revolution* (see below), 185–207.

————. *The Literate Revolution in Greece and Its Cultural Consequences*. Princeton, 1982.

Helbig, W. *Wandgemälde der von Vesuv verschütteten Städte Campaniens*. Leipzig, 1868.

Hellebrand, W. *Das Prozesszeugnis im Rechte der gräko-ägyptischen Papyri*. Munich, 1934.

Helmbold, W. C., & E. N. O'Neil. *Plutarch's Quotations*. Baltimore, 1959.

Herman, J. "Du latin épigraphique au latin provincial." In *Etrennes de Septantaine. Travaux de linguistique et de grammaire comparée offerts à Michel Lejeune*. Paris, 1978, 99–114.

————. "La langue latine dans la Gaule romaine." In *ANRW* ii.29.2 (1983), 1045–60.

Herrmann, P. "Teos und Abdera im 5. Jahrhundert v. Chr." *Chiron* xi (1981), 1–30.

Héron de Villefosse, A. "Un peson de fuseau, portant une inscription latine incisée, trouvé à Sens." *BACT* 1914, 213–230.

Heubeck, A. *Schrift* (= *Archaeologia Homerica* iii.X). Göttingen, 1979.

————. "Die Würzburger Alphabettafel." *WJA* xii (1986), 7–20.

Hignett, C. *A History of the Athenian Constitution*. Oxford, 1952.

Hinard, F. "Remarques sur les *praecones* et le *praeconium* dans la Rome de la fin de la République." *Latomus* xxxv (1976), 730–746.

Hodder, I. "The Spatial Distribution of Romano-British Small Towns." In W. Rodwell & T. Rowley (eds.), *The "Small Towns" of Roman Britain*. Oxford, 1975, 67–74.

Hölscher, T. *Staatsdenkmal und Publikum*. Konstanz, 1984.

Holl, K. "Das Fortleben der Volkssprachen in Kleinasien in nachchristlicher Zeit." *Hermes* xliii (1908), 240–254.

Hombert, M., & C. Préaux. "Recherches sur le *prosangelma* à l'époque archaïque." *Cd'E* xvii (1942), 259–286.

———. *Recherches sur le recensement dans l'Egypte romaine.* Leiden, 1952.

Honoré, T. "The Making of the Theodosian Code." *ZSS* ciii (1986), 133–222.

Hope-Simpson, R. "The Analysis of Data from Surface Surveys." *JFA* xi (1984), 115–117.

Hornshöj-Möller, S. "Die Beziehung zwischen der älteren und der jüngeren römischen Kursivschrift. Versuch einer kulturhistorischen Deutung." *Aegyptus* lx (1980), 161–223.

Hudson-Williams, H. L. "Isocrates and Recitations." *CQ* xliii (1949), 65–69.

Humphreys, S. C. "Family Tombs and Tomb Cult in Ancient Athens. Tradition or Traditionalism?" *JHS* c (1980), 96–126. Reprinted in *The Family, Women and Death. Comparative Studies.* London, 1983, 79–130.

Immerwahr, H. R. "Book Rolls on Attic Vases." In *Classical, Mediaeval and Renaissance Studies in Honor of Berthold Louis Ullman.* Rome, 1964, i.17–48.

———. "More Book Rolls on Attic Vases." *Antike Kunst* xvi (1973), 143–147.

Isserlin, B. S. J. "The Antiquity of the Greek Alphabet." *Kadmos* xxii (1983), 151–163.

Jacques, F. "Les cens en Gaule au IIᵉ siècle et dans la première moitié du IIIᵉ siècle." *Ktema* ii (1977), 285–328.

Janko, R. "Forgetfulness in the Golden Tablets of Memory." *CQ* xxxiv (1984), 89–100.

Jeffery, L. H. "Further Comments on Archaic Greek Inscriptions." *ABSA* l (1955), 67–84.

———. *The Local Scripts of Archaic Greece.* Oxford, 1961.

———. "Ἀρχαῖα γράμματα: Some Ancient Greek Views." In *Europa. Studien zur Geschichte und Epigraphik der frühen Aegaeis. Festschrift für Ernst Grumach.* Berlin, 1967, 152–166.

———. "Greek Alphabetic Writing." In *Cambridge Ancient History.* 3d ed. Vol. iii.l. Cambridge, 1982, 819–833.

Jeffery, L. H., & A. Morpurgo-Davies. "Ποινικαστὰς and Ποινικάζειν. BM 1969 4-2, 1, a New Archaic Inscription from Crete." *Kadmos* ix (1970), 118–154.

Johnson, A. C. *Roman Egypt* (= T. Frank [ed.], *An Economic Survey of Ancient Rome* ii). Baltimore, 1936.

Johnston, A. W. "A Fourth Century Graffito from the Kerameikos." *Ath. Mitt.* c (1985), 293–307.

Jones, A. H. M. *The Greek City from Alexander to Justinian.* Oxford, 1940.

———. *The Athenian Democracy.* Oxford, 1957.

———. *The Later Roman Empire, 284–602.* Vols. i–iii. Oxford, 1964.

———. *The Decline of the Ancient World.* London, 1966.

Jones, J. W. *The Law and Legal Theory of the Greeks.* Oxford, 1956.

Jordan, D. R. "A Survey of Greek Defixiones Not Included in the Special Corpora." *GRBS* xxvi (1985), 151–197.

Judge, E. A., & S. R. Pickering. "Biblical Papyri Prior to Constantine: Some Cultural Implications of their Physical Form." *Prudentia* x (1978), 1–13.

Kaster, R. A. "Notes on 'Primary' and 'Secondary' Schools in Late Antiquity." *TAPhA* cxiii (1983), 323–346.

Katičić, R. "Die Balkanprovinzen." In Neumann & Untermann (see below), 103–120.

Keaney, J. J., & A. E. Raubitschek. "A Late Byzantine Account of Ostracism." *AJPh* xciii (1972), 87–91.

Kelly, T. "The Spartan Scytale." In *The Craft of the Ancient Historian: Essays in Honor of Chester G. Starr.* Lanham, Md., 1985, 141–169.

Kenyon, F. G. "Two Greek School-Tablets." *JHS* xxix (1909), 29–40.

———. *Books and Readers in Ancient Greece and Rome.* 2d ed. Oxford, 1951.

Kim, C.-H. "Index of Greek Papyrus Letters." In J. L. White (ed.), *Studies in Ancient Letter Writing* (= *Semeia* xxii). Chico, Calif., 1982, 107–112.

Kirk, G. S., & J. E. Raven. *The Presocratic Philosophers.* Cambridge, 1957.

Klaffenbach, G. *Bemerkungen zum griechischen Urkundenwesen* (= *SB Berlin* 1960, vi).

Kleberg, T. *Buchhandel und Verlagswesen in der Antike.* Trans. E. Zunker. Darmstadt, 1967. Originally published as *Bokhandel och Bokförlag i antiken.* Stockholm, 1962.

Kneppe, A. *Untersuchungen zur städtischen Plebs des 4. Jahrhunderts n. Chr.* Bonn, 1979.

Knibbe, D. "Quandocumque suis trium virorum rei publicae . . ." *ZPE* xliv (1981), 1–10.

Knox, B. M. W. "Silent Reading in Antiquity." *GRBS* ix (1968), 421–435.

———. "Books and Readers in the Greek World. 1. From the Beginnings to Alexandria." In *Cambridge History of Classical Literature.* Vol. i. Cambridge, 1985, 1–16.

Koskenniemi, H. *Studien zur Idee und Phraseologie des griechischen Briefes bis 400 n. Chr.* Helsinki, 1956.

Kraemer, M. *Res libraria cadentis antiquitatis Ausonii et Apollinaris Sidonii exemplis illustratur.* Marburg, 1909.

Kroll, J. H. *Athenian Bronze Allotment Plates.* Cambridge, Mass., 1972.

Kubitschek, W. "Census." In *RE* (1899), cols. 1914–24.

Kübler, B. "Subscriptio." In *RE* (1931), cols. 490–501.

Lahusen, G. *Untersuchungen zur Ehrenstatue in Rom.* Rome, 1983.

Lallemand, J. *L'administration civile de l'Egypte de l'avènement de Dioclétien à la création du diocèse (284–382).* Brussels, 1964.

Lambrinudakis, W., & M. Wörrle. "Ein hellenistisches Reformgesetz über das öffentliche Urkundenwesen von Paros." *Chiron* xiii (1983), 283–368.

Lang, M. *Graffiti and Dipinti* (= *The Athenian Agora* xxi). Princeton, 1976.

Lang, M., & M. Crosby. *Weights, Measures, and Tokens* (= *The Athenian Agora* x). Princeton, 1964.

Langdon, M. K. *A Sanctuary of Zeus on Mount Hymettos* (= *Hesperia* suppl. xvi). Princeton, 1976.

Langhammer, W. *Die rechtliche und soziale Stellung der Magistratus municipales und der Decuriones.* Wiesbaden, 1973.

Larfeld, W. *Handbuch der griechischen Epigraphik.* Vols. i–ii. Leipzig, 1902–1907.

Lauffer, S. (ed.), *Diokletians Preisedikt.* Berlin, 1971.

Laur-Belart, R. "Ueber die Schreibkunst beim römischen Militär." *Jahresbericht der Gesellschaft Pro Vindonissa* 1942/43, 32–39.

Lavelle, B. M. "Hipparchos' Herms." *Echos du monde classique* xxix (1985), 411–420.

Lavency, M. "La préparation du discours dans la rhétorique primitive." *LEC* xxvii (1959), 353–361.

Leipoldt, J., & S. Morenz. *Heilige Schriften.* Leipzig, 1953.

Leisi, E. *Der Zeuge im attischen Recht.* Frauenfeld, 1908.

Lejeune, M. "Sur les abécédaires grecs archaïques." *RPh* lvii (1983), 7–12.

Lejeune, M., et al. "Textes gaulois et gallo-romains en cursive latine: 3. Le plomb du Larzac." *Etudes celtiques* xxii (1985), 95–177.

Lemerle, P. *Le premier humanisme byzantin.* Paris, 1971.

Leo, F. *Geschichte der römischen Literatur.* Vol. i. Berlin, 1913.

Lepelley, C. *Les cités de l'Afrique romaine au Bas-Empire.* Vols. i–ii. Paris, 1979–1981.

Levick, B. M. "Propaganda and the Imperial Coinage." *Antichthon* xvi (1982), 104–116.

Levin, D. N. "To Whom Did the Ancient Novelists Address Themselves?" *Rivista di studi classici* xxv (1977), 18–29.

Lewis, N. *Papyrus in Classical Antiquity.* Oxford, 1974.

———. *Life in Egypt under Roman Rule.* Oxford, 1983.

———. *Greeks in Ptolemaic Egypt.* Oxford, 1986.

———. "The Process of Promulgation in Rome's Eastern Provinces." In *Studies in Roman Law in Memory of A. Arthur Schiller.* Leiden, 1986, 127–139.

Linderski, J. "The libri reconditi." *HSCPh* lxxxix (1985), 207–234.

———. "The Augural Law." In *ANRW* ii.16.3 (1986), 2146–2312.

Littmann, E. *Thamūd und Ṣafā. Studien zur altnordarabischen Inschriftenkunde.* Leipzig, 1940.

Lloyd, G. E. R. *Magic, Reason and Experience.* Cambridge, 1979.

———. *Science, Folklore and Ideology.* Cambridge, 1983.

Longo, O. "Scrivere in Tucidide: Comunicazione e ideologia." In *Studi in onore di Anthos Ardizzoni*. Rome, 1978, i.519–554.

———. *Tecniche della comunicazione nella Grecia antica*. Naples, 1981.

Lonie, I. M. "Literacy and the Development of Hippocratic Medicine." In F. Lasserre & P. Mudry (eds.), *Formes de pensée dans la collection hippocratique*. Geneva, 1983, 145–161.

Lord, A. B. *The Singer of Tales*. Cambridge, Mass., 1960.

Lullies, R. "Die lesende Sphinx." In *Festschrift zum sechzigsten Geburtstag von Bernhard Schweitzer*. Stuttgart, 1954, 140–146.

Luschnat, O. "Thukydides der Historiker." In *RE* Suppl. xii (1971), cols. 1085–1354.

MacDowell, D. M. *The Law in Classical Athens*. London, 1978.

MacMullen, R. "Provincial Languages in the Roman Empire." *AJPh* lxxxvii (1966), 1–14.

———. *Soldier and Civilian in the Later Roman Empire*. Cambridge, Mass., 1967.

———. "Sfiducia nell'intelletto nel quarto secolo." *RSI* lxxxiv (1972), 5–16.

———. "How Many Romans Voted?" *Athenaeum* lviii (1980), 454–457.

———. *Paganism in the Roman Empire*. New Haven, 1981.

———. "The Epigraphic Habit in the Roman Empire." *AJPh* ciii (1982), 233–246.

———. "What Difference Did Christianity Make?" *Historia* xxxv (1986), 322–343.

———. "Frequency of Inscriptions in Roman Lydia." *ZPE* lxv (1986), 237–238.

Maiuri, A. "Tabulae ceratae Herculanenses." *Par.Pass.* i (1946), 373–379.

Manca Masciadri, M., & O. Montevecchi. *I contratti di baliatico*. Milan, 1984.

Mann, J. C. "Epigraphic Consciousness." *JRS* lxxv (1985), 204–206.

Marganne, M.-H. *Inventaire analytique des papyrus grecs de médecine*. Geneva, 1981.

Marichal, R. *L'occupation romaine de la Basse Egypte*. Paris, 1945.

———. "L'écriture latine et la civilisation du Ier au XVIe siècle." In *L'écriture et la psychologie des peuples (XXIIe semaine de Synthèse)*. Paris, 1963, 199–247.

———. "Nouvelles fouilles et nouveaux graffites de la Graufesenque." *CRAI* 1981, 244–272.

Marquardt, J. *Das Privatleben der Römer*. 2d ed. Leipzig, 1886.

Marrou, H. I. ΜΟΥΣΙΚΟΣ ΑΝΗΡ. Paris, 1938.

McDonnell, M. "*Ambitus* and Plautus' *Amphitruo* 65–81." *AJPh* cvii (1986), 564–576.

McDowell, R. H. *Stamped and Inscribed Objects from Seleucia on Tigris*. Ann Arbor, 1935.

Meeks, W. A. *The First Urban Christians: The Social World of the Apostle Paul*. New Haven, 1983.

Meid, W. *Gallisch oder Lateinisch? Soziolinguistische und andere Bemerkungen zu populären gallo-lateinischen Inschriften*. Innsbruck, 1980. Another version in *ANRW* ii.29.2 (1983), 1019–44.

Meiggs, R., & D. M. Lewis. *A Selection of Greek Historical Inscriptions*. Oxford, 1969.

Mélèze-Modrzejewski, J. "Le document grec dans l'Egypte ptolémaïque." In *Atti del XVII Congresso internazionale di papirologia*. Naples, 1984, iii.1171–87.

Meritt, B. D. *Athenian Financial Documents of the Fifth Century*. Ann Arbor, 1932.

———. *Epigraphica Attica*. Cambridge, Mass., 1940.

Meyer, C. *Die Urkunden im Geschichtswerk des Thukydides*. Munich, 1955.

Michell, H. *The Economics of Ancient Greece*. 2d ed. Cambridge, 1957.

Millar, F. "Local Cultures in the Roman Empire: Libyan, Punic and Latin in Roman Africa." *JRS* lviii (1968), 126–134.

———. *The Emperor in the Roman World*. London, 1977.

Millett, P. "The Attic *Horoi* Reconsidered in the Light of Recent Discoveries." *Opus* i (1982), 219–249.

Minton, W. W. "Homer's Invocations of the Muses: Traditional Patterns." *TAPhA* xci (1960), 292–309.

Mitteis, L., & U. Wilcken. *Grundzüge und Chrestomathie der Papyruskunde*. Vols. i–iv. Leipzig & Berlin, 1912.

Mócsy, A. "Die Unkenntnis des Lebensalters im römischen Reich." *AAASH* xiv (1966), 387–421.

———. *Gesellschaft und Romanisation in der römischen Provinz Moesia Superior*. Amsterdam, 1970.

———. *Pannonia and Upper Moesia*. London, 1974.

———. "The Civilized Pannonians of Velleius." In *Rome and Her Northern Provinces. Papers Presented to Sheppard Frere*. Gloucester, 1983, 169–178.

Momigliano, A. "The Place of Herodotus in the History of Historiography." In *Secondo contributo alla storia degli studi classici*. Rome, 1960, 29–44. Reprinted in *Studies in Historiography*. London, 1966, 127–142.

———. *Alien Wisdom*. Cambridge, 1975.

———. "Storiografia greca." *RSI* lxxxvii (1975), 17–46. Reprinted in *Sesto contributo alla storia degli studi classici e del mondo antico*. Rome, 1980, 23–32.

———. "The Historians of the Classical World and Their Audiences: Some Suggestions." *ASNSP* ser.3 viii (1978), 59–75. Reprinted in *Sesto contributo*, 361–376.

———. "An Inscription from Lyons and the Language Situation in Gaul in the Third and Fourth Centuries A.D." *ASNSP* ser. 3 xii (1982), 1105–15. Reprinted in *Settimo contributo alla storia degli studi classici e del mondo antico*. Rome, 1984, 463–473.

Mommsen, T. "Die pompeianischen Quittungstafeln des L. Caecilius Jucundus." *Hermes* xii (1877), 88–141. Reprinted in *Gesammelte Schriften*. Vol. iii. Berlin, 1907, 221–274.

———. *Römisches Staatsrecht*. Vols. i–iii. Leipzig, 1887.

———. *Römisches Strafrecht*. Leipzig, 1899.

Montevecchi, O. "Ricerche di sociologia nei documenti dell'Egitto greco-romano, I. I Testamenti." *Aegyptus* xv (1935), 67–121.

———. "Ricerche di sociologia nei documenti dell'Egitto greco-romano, II. I contratti di matrimonio e gli atti di divorzio." *Aegyptus* xvi (1936), 3–83.

———. "Ricerche di sociologia nei documenti dell'Egitto greco-romano, III. I contratti di compra-vendita." *Aegyptus* xix (1939), 11–53; xxi (1941), 93–151; xxiii (1943), 11–89, 244–261.

———. *I contratti di lavoro e di servizio nell'Egitto greco romano e bizantino*. Milan, 1950.

———. *La papirologia*. Turin, 1973.

———. "Il censimento romano d'Egitto. Precisazioni." *Aevum* l (1976), 72–84.

Mrozek, S. "A propos de la répartition chronologique des inscriptions latines dans le Haut-Empire." *Epigraphica* xxxv (1973), 113–118.

Muciaccia, G. "In tema di repressione delle opere infamanti (Dio 55.27)." In *Studi in onore di Arnaldo Biscardi*. Milan, 1984, v.61–78.

Murray, O. *Early Greece*. Brighton, 1980.

Nellen, D. *Viri litterati; gebildetes Beamtentum und spätrömisches Reich im Westen*. Bochum, 1977.

Neumann, G. "Kleinasien." In Neumann & Untermann (see below), 167–185.

Neumann, G., & J. Untermann (eds.). *Die Sprachen im römischen Reich der Kaiserzeit* (Bonner Jahrbücher Beiheft xl). Cologne & Bonn, 1980.

Nicolet, C. *Le métier de citoyen dans la Rome républicaine*. Paris, 1976.

———. "Centralisation d'état et problème du recensement dans le monde gréco-romain." In *Culture et idéologie dans la genèse de l'état moderne*. Rome, 1985, 9–24.

Nielsen, M. "The Lid Sculptures of Volaterran Cinerary Urns." In P. Bruun (ed.), *Studies in the Romanization of Etruria*. Rome, 1975, 263–404.

Nilsson, M. P. *Die hellenistische Schule*. Munich, 1955.

———. *Geschichte der griechischen Religion*. Vols. i–ii. 3d ed. Munich, 1967–1974.

Nock, A. D. *Conversion*. Oxford, 1933.

Norman, A. F. "The Book Trade in Fourth-Century Antioch." *JHS* lxxx (1960), 122–126.

Norsa, M. *Scrittura letteraria greca dal secolo IV a.C. all'VIII d.C.* Florence, 1939.

Notopoulos, J. A. "Mnemosyne in Oral Literature." *TAPhA* lxix (1938), 465–493.

Ogilvie, R. M. *The Library of Lactantius*. Oxford, 1978.

Osborne, R. "Buildings and Residence on the Land in Classical and Hellenistic Greece. The Contribution of Epigraphy." *ABSA* lxxx (1985), 119–128.

———. *Classical Landscape with Figures*. London, 1987.

Pack, R. A. *The Greek and Latin Literary Texts from Greco-Roman Egypt*. 2d ed. Ann Arbor, 1965.

Page, D. L. "Thucydides' Description of the Great Plague at Athens." *CQ* iii (1953), 97–119.

Painter, K. "A Roman Writing Tablet from London." *BMQ* xxxi (1966–67), 101–110.

Panciera, S. "Catilina e Catone su due coppette romane." In φιλίας χάριν. *Miscellanea in onore di Eugenio Manni*. Rome, 1979, v.1635–51.

Papanikolaou, A. D. *Chariton-Studien. Untersuchungen zur Sprache und Chronologie der griechischen Romane*. Göttingen, 1973.

Parca, M. "Prosangelmata ptolémaïques, une mise à jour." *Cd'E* lx (1985), 240–247.

Pasquali, G. "Commercianti ateniesi analfabeti." *SIFC* vii (1929), 243–249.

Patlagean, E. *Pauvreté économique et pauvreté sociale à Byzance, 4ᵉ–7ᵉ siècles*. Paris & The Hague, 1977.

Payne, H. *Archaic Marble Sculpture from the Acropolis*. 2d ed. Oxford, 1950.

Pecorella Longo, C. "La bulé e la procedura dell'ostracismo: Considerazioni su Vat.Gr. 1144." *Historia* xxix (1980), 257–281.

Peremans, W. "Egyptiens et étrangers dans l'Egypte ptolémaïque." *EFH* viii (1962), 121–155.

———. "Le bilinguisme dans les relations gréco-égyptiennes sous les Lagides." In E. Van't Dack et al. (eds.), *Egypt and the Hellenistic World. Proceedings of the International Colloquium, Leuven, 24–26 May 1982*. Louvain, 1983, 253–280.

Perna, R. *L'originalità di Plauto*. Bari, 1955.

Pestman, P. W. *L'archivio di Amenothes, figlio di Horos (P.Tor. Amenothes)*. Milan, 1981.

———. *A Guide to the Zenon Archive*. Leiden, 1981.

Petit, P. "Recherches sur la publication et la diffusion des discours de Libanius." *Historia* v (1956), 479–509.

Petitmengin, P., & B. Flusin. "Le livre antique et la dictée. Nouvelles recherches." In *Mémorial André-Jean Festugière*. Geneva, 1984, 247–262.

Petrucci, A. "Per la storia della scrittura romana: I graffiti di Condatomagus." *Bullettino dell'Archivio paleografico italiano* ser.3 i (1962), 85–132.

——— (ed.). "Epigrafia e paleografia. Inchiesta sui rapporti fra due discipline." *S & C* v (1981), 265–312.

Pfeiffer, R. *A History of Classical Scholarship*. Vols. i–ii. Oxford, 1968–1976.

Pfohl, G. (ed.). *Das Alphabet. Entstehung und Entwicklung der griechischen Schrift*. Darmstadt, 1968.

Pfuhl, E., & H. Möbius. *Die ostgriechischen Grabreliefs*. 2 vols. Mainz, 1977–1979.

Philonenko, M. "Le collège des 'officiales tabularii legionis' dans le camp de Lambèse." *Revue africaine* lxix (1928), 429–435.

Picard, G. C. "Observations sur la condition des populations rurales dans l'Empire romain, en Gaule et en Afrique." In *ANRW* ii.3 (1975), 98–111.

Pierce, R. H. "Grapheion, Catalogue, and Library in Roman Egypt." *Symb. Osl.* xliii (1968), 68–83.

Le pitture antiche d'Ercolano e contorni incise con qualche spiegazione. Vols. i–v. Naples, 1757–1779.

Poccetti, P. "Nomi di lingua e nomi di popolo nell'Italia antica tra etnografia, glossografia e retorica." *AION (ling)* vi (1984), 137–160.

Polomé, E. C. "The Linguistic Situation in the Western Provinces of the Roman Empire." In *ANRW* ii.29.2 (1983), 509–553.

Pomeroy, S. B. "Technikai kai Mousikai." *AJAH* ii (1977), 51–68.

———. "Women in Roman Egypt (A Preliminary Study Based on Papyri)." In H. P. Foley (ed.), *Reflections of Women in Antiquity*. London, 1981, 303–321.

———. *Women in Hellenistic Egypt*. New York, 1984.

Posner, E. *Archives in the Ancient World*. Cambridge, Mass., 1972.

Préaux, C. "La preuve à l'époque hellénistique, principalement dans l'Egypte grecque." In *Recueils de la Société Jean Bodin* xvi (1964) (= *La preuve* i), 161–222.

Pringsheim, F. *The Greek Law of Sale*. Weimar, 1950.

———. "The Transition from Witnessed to Written Transactions at Athens." In *Aequitas und Bona Fides. Festgabe zum 70. Geburtstag von August Simonius*. Basel, 1955, 287–297. Reprinted in *Gesammelte Abhandlungen*. Heidelberg, 1961, ii.401–411.

Pugliese, G. "La preuve dans le procès romain de l'époque classique." In *Recueils de la Société Jean Bodin* xvi (1964) (= *La Preuve* i), 277–348.

Pugliese Carratelli, G. "L'instrumentum scriptorium nei monumenti pompeiani ed ercolanesi." In *Pompeiana. Raccolta di studi per il secondo centenario degli scavi di Pompei*. Naples, 1950, 266–278.

Purpura, G. "Tabulae Pompeianae 13 e 34: Due documenti relativi al prestito marittimo." In *Atti del XVII Congresso internazionale di papirologia.* Naples, 1984, iii.1245–66.

Ramsay, W. M. "Inscriptions en langue pisidienne." *Revue des Universités du Midi* i (1895), 353–362.

Raskin, G. *Handelsreclame en soortgelijke praktijken bij Grieken en Romeinen.* Louvain, 1936.

Raubitschek, A. E. *Dedications from the Athenian Akropolis.* Cambridge, Mass., 1949.

Rebuffat, R., & R. Marichal. "Les *ostraca* de Bu Njem." *REL* li (1973), 281–286.

Reed, R. *Ancient Skins, Parchments and Leathers.* London & New York, 1972.

Reeve, M. D. "Hiatus in the Greek Novelists." *CQ* xxi (1971), 514–539.

Rémondon, R. "Problèmes de bilinguisme dans l'Egypte lagide (UPZ I 148)." *Cd'E* xxxix (1964), 126–146.

———. "L'Egypte au 5ᵉ siècle de notre ère: Les sources papyrologiques et leur problèmes." In *Atti dell'XI Congresso internazionale di papirologia.* Milan, 1966, 135–148.

Renfrew, C., & M. Wagstaff (eds.). *An Island Polity. The Archaeology of Exploitation in Melos.* Cambridge, 1982.

Rhodes, P. J. *The Athenian Boule.* Oxford, 1972.

———. "Ephebi, bouleutae and the Population of Athens." *ZPE* xxxviii (1980), 191–201.

———. *A Commentary on the Aristotelian Athenaion Politeia.* Oxford, 1981.

Riché, P. *Education et culture dans l'Occident barbare, VI–VIIIᵉ siècles.* Paris, 1962.

Riepl, W. *Das Nachrichtenwesen des Altertums.* Leipzig & Berlin, 1913.

Robb, K. "The Poetic Sources of the Greek Alphabet: Rhythm and Abecedarium from Phoenician to Greek." In E. A. Havelock & J. P. Hershbell (eds.), *Communication Arts in the Ancient World.* New York, 1978, 23–36.

Robert, L. *Etudes anatoliennes.* Paris, 1937.

———. *Hellenica.* Vol. vii. Paris, 1949.

———. "Une épigramme de Carie." *RPh* ser.3 xxxi (1957), 7–22. Reprinted in *Opera Minora Selecta.* Amsterdam, 1969, i.373–388.

———. "Documents d'Asie Mineure." *BCH* ci (1977), 43–132.

Roberts, C. H. *Manuscript, Society and Belief in Early Christian Egypt.* London, 1979.

———. "Books in the Graeco-Roman World and in the New Testament." In *Cambridge History of the Bible.* Vol. i. Cambridge, 1970, 48–66.

Roberts, C. H. & T. C. Skeat. *The Birth of the Codex.* London, 1983.

Rocco, A. "Caleni, vasi." In *EAA* (1959), 271–272.

Rodríguez Almeida, E. *Il Monte Testaccio*. Rome, 1984.

Röllig, W. "Das Punische im Römischen Reich." In Neumann & Untermann (see above), 285–299.

Rössler, O. "Libyen von der Cyrenaica bis zur Mauretania Tingitana." In Neumann & Untermann (see above), 267–284.

Roma Medio Repubblicana. Rome, 1973.

Rossi, F. *I papiri copti del Museo Egizio di Torino*. Turin, 1887.

Rostovtzeff, M. I. *A Large Estate in Egypt in the Third Century B.C.* Madison, Wis., 1922.

———. *The Social and Economic History of the Hellenistic World*. Vols. i–iii. Oxford, 1941.

———. *The Social and Economic History of the Roman Empire*. Vols. i–ii. 2d ed. Oxford, 1957.

Rotondi, G. *Leges Publicae Populi Romani*. Milan, 1912.

———. *Scritti giuridici*. Vols. i–ii. Milan, 1922, i.433–489.

Rougé, J. *Recherches sur l'organisation du commerce maritime en Méditerranée sous l'empire romain*. Paris, 1966.

Roux, G. "Commentaires à l'Orestie." *REG* lxxxvii (1974), 33–79.

Ruschenbusch, E. ΣΟΛΩΝΟΣ ΝΟΜΟΙ. Wiesbaden, 1969.

———. "Epheben, Buleuten und die Bürgerzahl von Athen um 330 v. Chr." *ZPE* xli (1981), 103–105.

———. "Die Diaitctenliste IG II/III² 1927." *ZPE* xlix (1982), 267–281.

———. "Die Diaiteteninschrift vom Jahre 371 v.Chr. . . ." *ZPE* liv (1984), 247–252.

Ryle, G. *Plato's Progress*. Cambridge, 1966.

Sachers, E. "Tabula." In *RE* (1932), cols. 1881–86.

Saglio, E. "Praeco." In C. Daremberg & E. Saglio, *Dictionnaire des antiquités grecques et romaines* (1907), 607–610.

Sanmartí, E., and R. A. Santiago. "Une lettre grecque sur plomb trouvée à Emporion (Fouilles 1985)." *ZPE* lxviii (1987), 119–127.

Saward, J. *Perfect Fools*. Oxford, 1980.

Sbordone, F. "Prcambolo per l'edizione critica delle tavolette cerate di Pompei." *RAAN* li (1976), 145–168.

Scheele, J. "Buch und Bibliothek bei Augustinus." *Bibliothek und Wissenschaft* xii (1978), 14–114.

Schefold, K. *Die Wände Pompejis*. Berlin, 1957.

Schmidt, K. H. "Gallien und Britannien." In Neumann & Untermann (see above), 19–44.

Schmitt, R. "Die Ostgrenze von Armenien über Mesopotamien, Syrien bis Arabien." In Neumann & Untermann (see above), 187–214.

Schmoll, U. *Die südlusitanischen Inschriften*. Wiesbaden, 1961.

Schnapp-Gourbeillon, A. "Naissance de l'écriture et fonction poétique en Grèce archaïque. Quelques points de repère." *Annales E.S.C.* xxvii (1982), 714–723.

Schubart, W. *Das Buch bei den Griechen und Römern.* 2d ed. Berlin & Leipzig, 1921.

Schulten, A. *Numantia.* Vols. i–iv. Munich, 1914–1931.

Schulz, F. "Roman Registers of Birth Certificates." *JRS* xxxii (1942), 78–91; xxxiii (1943), 55–64.

Schürer, E. *The History of the Jewish People in the Age of Christ.* Rev. ed. G. Vermes et al. Vol. ii. Edinburgh, 1979.

Scobie, A. *Aspects of the Ancient Romance and Its Heritage.* Meisenheim, 1969.

———. "Storytellers, Storytelling and the Novel in Graeco-Roman Antiquity." *RhM* cxxii (1979), 229–259.

Segal, C. P. "Greek Tragedy: Writing, Truth, and the Representation of the Self." In *Mnemai: Classical Studies in Memory of Karl K. Hulley.* Chico, Calif., 1984, 41–67.

Seidl, E. *Ptolemäische Rechtsgeschichte.* Glückstadt, 1962.

Seston, W., & M. Euzennat. "Un dossier de la Chancellerie romaine, la Tabula Banasitana. Etude de diplomatique." *CRAI* 1971, 468–490.

Shaw, B. D. "Bandits in the Roman Empire." *P & P* cv (1984), 3–52.

———. "The Family in Late Antiquity: The Experience of Augustine." *P & P* cxv (1987), 3–51.

Shear, T. L. "The Monument of the Eponymous Heroes in the Athenian Agora." *Hesperia* xxxix (1970), 145–222.

Sherk, R. K. *Roman Documents from the Greek East.* Baltimore, 1969.

Sherwin-White, A. N. *The Letters of Pliny. A Historical and Social Commentary.* Oxford, 1966.

Siewert, P. "Die angebliche Uebernahme solonischer Gesetze in die Zwölftafeln. Ursprung und Ausgestaltung einer Legende." *Chiron* viii (1978), 331–344.

Skeat, T. C. "The Use of Dictation in Ancient Book Production." *PBA* xlii (1956), 179–208.

———. "Early Christian Book-Production: Papyri and Manuscripts." In *Cambridge History of the Bible.* Vol. ii. Cambridge, 1969, 54–79.

———. "The Length of the Standard Papyrus Roll and the Cost-Advantage of the Codex." *ZPE* xlv (1982), 169–175.

Smith, C. C. "Vulgar Latin in Roman Britain: Epigraphic and Other Evidence." In *ANRW* ii.29.2 (1983), 893–948.

Smith, M. "The Eighth Book of Moses and How It Grew (PLeid. J 395)." In *Atti del XVII Congresso internazionale di papirologia.* Naples, 1984, ii.683–693.

Smith, M. F. "Fifty-five New Fragments of Diogenes of Oenoanda." *Anatolian Studies* xxviii (1978), 39–92.

Sofer, J. "Die Hieronymuszeugnis über die Sprachen der Galater und Treverer." *Wiener Studien* lv (1937), 148–158.

Sokolowski, F. *Lois sacrées des cités grecques. Supplément.* Paris, 1962.

Solin, H. *L'interpretazione delle iscrizioni parietali. Note e discussioni.* Faenza, 1970.

———. "Die herkulanensischen Wandinschriften. Ein soziologischer Versuch." *Cronache ercolanesi* iii (1973), 97–103.

———. In A. Petrucci (ed.) (see above), *S & C* v (1981), 304–311.

Solin, H., & M. Itkonen-Kaila. *Paedagogium* (= V. Väänänen [ed.], *Graffiti del Palatino* i = Acta Instituti Romani Finlandiae iii). Helsinki, 1966.

Solmsen, F. Review of E. A. Havelock, *Preface to Plato. AJPh* lxxxvii (1966), 99–105.

Sommer, R. "T. Pomponius Atticus und die Verbreitung von Ciceros Werken." *Hermes* lxi (1926), 389–422.

Speidel, M. "Legionaries from Asia Minor." In *ANRW* ii.7.2 (1980), 730–746. Reprinted in *Roman Army Studies.* Amsterdam, 1984, i.45–63.

Speyer, W. *Bücherfunde in der Glaubenswerbung der Antike.* Göttingen, 1970.

———. *Büchervernichtung und Zensur des Geistes bei Heiden, Juden und Christen.* Stuttgart, 1981.

Starr, R. J. "The Circulation of Literary Texts in the Roman World." *CQ* xxxvii (1987), 213–223.

Steinacker, H. *Die antiken Grundlagen der frühmittelalterlichen Privaturkunde.* Leipzig & Berlin, 1927.

Stella, L. A. *Tradizione micenea e poesia dell'Iliade.* Rome, 1978.

Stibbe, C. M., et al. *Lapis Satricanus* (= Archeologische Studiën van het Nederlands Instituut te Rome, Scripta Minora V). The Hague, 1980.

Susini, G. "Problematica dell'epigrafia classica nella regione apula e salentina." *Arch.Stor.Pugl.* xxii (1969), 38–48.

Syme, R. *History in Ovid.* Oxford, 1978.

Szegedy-Maszak, A. *The Nomoi of Theophrastus.* New York, 1981.

Talamanca, M. "Documentazione e documento (diritto romano)." In *Enciclopedia del diritto* (1964), 548–560.

Tanzer, H. H. *The Common People of Pompeii: A Study of the Graffiti.* Baltimore, 1939.

Tarn, W. W. *Hellenistic Civilisation.* 3d ed. London, 1952.

Taubenschlag, R. *The Law of Greco-Roman Egypt in the Light of the Papyri.* New York, 1944.

Taylor, L. R. *Roman Voting Assemblies.* Ann Arbor, 1966.

Thesleff, H. "Scientific and Technical Style in Early Greek Prose." *Arctos* n.s. iv (1966), 89–113.

Thomas, J. D. "Aspects of the Ptolemaic Civil Service: The Dioiketes and the Nomarch." In H. Maehler & V. M. Strocka (eds.), *Das ptolemäische Aegypten*. Mainz, 1978, 187–194.

Thompson, D. L. "Painted Portraiture at Pompeii." In *Pompeii and the Vesuvian Landscape*. Washington, D.C., 1979, 78–92.

Thompson, H. A. "The Excavations of the Athenian Agora. Twelfth Season, 1947." *Hesperia* xvii (1948), 149–196.

Thompson, W. E. "Athenian Attitudes towards Wills." *Prudentia* xiii (1981), 13–23.

Thomsen, R. *The Origin of Ostracism.* Copenhagen, 1972.

Tibiletti, G. *Le lettere private nei papiri greci del III e IV secolo d.C.* Milan, 1979.

Torelli, M. *The Typology and Structure of Roman Historical Reliefs.* Ann Arbor, 1982.

———. *Lavinio e Roma.* Rome, 1984.

Tovar, A. "Las inscripciones celtibéricas de Peñalba de Villastar." *Emerita* xxvii (1959), 349–365.

———. "A Research Report on Vulgar Latin and Its Local Variations." *Kratylos* ix (1964), 113–134. Reprinted in R. Kontzi (ed.), *Zur Entstehung der romanischen Sprachen.* Darmstadt, 1978, 410–435.

Tozzi, P. L. *Saggi di topografia antica.* Florence, 1974.

Turner, E. G. *Athenian Books in the Fifth and Fourth Centuries B.C.* London, 1952.

———. *Greek Papyri. An Introduction.* Oxford, 1968.

———. "Oxyrhynchus and Rome." *HSCPh* lxxix (1975), 1–24.

———. *The Typology of the Early Codex.* Philadelphia, 1977.

Untermann, J. "Alpen-Donau-Hadria." In Neumann & Untermann (see above), 45–63.

———. "Die althispanischen Sprachen." In *ANRW* ii.29.2 (1983), 791–818.

Väänänen, V. *La latin vulgaire des inscriptions pompéiennes.* Rev. ed. Berlin, 1958.

van Compernolle, R. "Le droit à l'éducation dans le monde grec aux époques archaïque et classique." *Recueils de la Société Jean Bodin* xxxix (1975) (*L'enfant* v), 95–99.

van den Branden, A. *Les inscriptions thamoudéennes.* Louvain, 1950.

Vanderpool, E. *Ostracism at Athens.* Cincinnati, 1970.

Vanderpool, E., & W. P. Wallace. "The Sixth Century Laws from Eretria." *Hesperia* xxxiii (1964), 381–391.

van Effenterre, H. "Le contrat de travail du scribe Spensithios." *BCH* xcvii (1973), 31–46.

Vetter, E. *Handbuch der italischen Dialekte.* Heidelberg, 1953.

Veyne, P. "Titulus praelatus, offrande, solennisation et publicité dans les ex-votos gréco-romains." *Rev.arch.* 1983, 281–300.

Vinogradov, Y. G. "Drevneisheye grecheskoye pismo s ostrova Berezan." *VDI* cxviii (1971), 74–100.

von Harnack, A. *Ueber den privaten Gebrauch der Heiligen Schriften in der alten Kirche (Beiträge zur Einleitung in das Neue Testament* v). Leipzig, 1912.

von Schwind, F. *Zur Frage der Publikation im römischen Recht.* Munich, 1940.

von Wilamowitz-Moellendorff, U., et al. *Staat und Gesellschaft der Griechen und Römer.* 2d ed. Leipzig & Berlin, 1923.

Wade-Gery, H. T. *The Poet of the Iliad.* Cambridge, 1952.

Walke, N. *Das römische Donaukastell Straubing-Sorviodurum.* Berlin, 1965.

Wallace, S. L. *Taxation in Egypt from Augustus to Diocletian.* Princeton, 1938.

Watson, A. *The Law of Obligations in the Later Roman Republic.* Oxford, 1965.

———. *Roman Private Law around 200 B.C.* Edinburgh, 1971.

———. *The Law of Succession under the Later Roman Republic.* Oxford, 1971.

———. *Law Making in the Later Roman Republic.* Oxford, 1974.

———. *Rome of the XII Tables: Persons and Property.* Princeton, 1975.

Watson, G. R. "Documentation in the Roman Army." In *ANRW* ii.1 (1974), 493–507.

Weaver, P. R. C. *Familia Caesaris.* Cambridge, 1972.

Weil, R. "Lire dans Thucydide." In *Le monde grec. Hommages à Claire Préaux.* Brussels, 1975, 162–168.

Weiss, E. *Griechisches Privatrecht.* Vol. i. Leipzig, 1923.

Welles, C. B. *Royal Correspondence in the Hellenistic Period.* London, 1934.

Wendel, C. "Bibliothek." In *RLAC* (1954), cols. 231–274. Reprinted in *Kleine Schriften zum antiken Buch- und Bibliothekswesen.* Cologne, 1974, 165–199.

Wenger, L. *Die Quellen des römischen Rechts.* Vienna, 1953.

West, M. L. *Hesiod, Works and Days.* Oxford, 1978.

———. "The Metre of Arius' *Thalia*." *JThS* xxxiii (1982), 98–105.

West, S. "Herodotus' Epigraphical Interests." *CQ* xxxv (1985), 278–305.

Whatmough, J. Κελτικά. *HSCPh* lv (1944), 1–85. Reprinted in *The Dialects of Ancient Gaul.*

———. *The Dialects of Ancient Gaul.* Cambridge, Mass., 1970.

White, J. L. "The Greek Documentary Letter Tradition Third Century B.C.E. to Third Century A.D." In White (ed.), *Studies in Ancient Letter Writing* (= *Semeia* xxii). Chico, Calif., 1982, 89–106.

Whitehead, D. *The Demes of Attica, 508/7–ca. 250 B.C.* Princeton, 1986.

Whittaker, C. R. "Labour Supply in the Later Roman Empire." *Opus* i (1982), 171–179.

———. "Late Roman Trade and Traders." In P. Garnsey, K. Hopkins & C. R. Whittaker (eds.), *Trade in the Ancient Economy*. London, 1983, 163–180.

Widmann, H. "Herstellung und Vertrieb des Buches in der griechisch-römischen Welt." *Archiv für Geschichte des Buchwesens* viii (1967), 545–640.

Wieacker, F. *Textstufen klassischer Juristen* (= *Abh.Gött.* ser.3 xlv). Göttingen, 1960.

———. "Die XII Tafeln in ihrem Jahrhundert." *EFH* xiii (1966), 293–356.

Wilcken, U. *Griechische Ostraka aus Aegypten und Nubien*. Leipzig, 1899.

———. "Zu den Florentiner und den Leipziger Papyri." *Archiv für Papyrusforschung* iv (1908), 423–486.

———. "Ueber antike Urkundenlehre." In *Papyri und Altertumswissenschaft. Vorträge des 3. Internationalen Papyrologentages* (1933). Munich, 1935, 42–61.

Wilhelm, A. *Neue Beiträge zur griechischen Inschriftenkunde*. Vol. i (= *SBAW Wien* clxvi.1). 1910.

Will, E. L. "The Roman Amphoras." In A. M. McCann (ed.), *The Roman Port and Fishery of Cosa*. Princeton, 1987, 171–220.

Willetts, R. F. *The Law Code of Gortyn* (= *Kadmos* Suppl. i).

Williamson, C. "Law-Making in the Comitia of Republican Rome." Ph.D. diss., London, 1983.

———. "Monuments of Bronze: Roman Legal Documents on Bronze Tablets." *Classical Antiquity* vi (1987), 160–183.

Willis, W. H. "A Census of Literary Papyri from Egypt." *GRBS* ix (1968), 205–241.

Winnett, F. V. *Safaitic Inscriptions from Jordan*. Toronto, 1957.

Winnett, F. V., & G. L. Harding. *Inscriptions from Fifty Safaitic Cairns*. Toronto, 1978.

Wolff, H. J. *Das Recht der griechischen Papyri Aegyptens*. Vol. ii. Munich, 1978.

Woodward, A. M. "Notes on Some Attic Decrees." *ABSA* l (1955), 271–274.

Worp, K. A. *Das Aurelia Charite Archiv*. Zutphen, 1980.

Wycherley, R. E. *Literary and Epigraphical Testimonia* (= *The Athenian Agora* iii). Princeton, 1957.

Young, R. S. "Excavation on Mount Hymettos, 1939." *AJA* xliv (1940), 1–9.

Youtie, H. C. "Records of a Roman Bath in Upper Egypt." *AJA* liii (1949), 268–270. Reprinted in *Scriptiunculae*. Amsterdam, 1973, ii.990–993.

———. "P.Mich. inv. 855: Letter from Herakleides to Nemesion." *ZPE* xxvii (1977), 147–150. Reprinted in *Scriptiunculae Posteriores*. Bonn, 1981, i.429–432.

Zalateo, G. "Papiri scolastici." *Aegyptus* xli (1961), 160–235.

Zambon, A. Διδασκαλικαί. *Aegyptus* xv (1935), 3–66.

Zgusta, L. "Die epichorische pisidische Anthroponymie und Sprache." *Archiv Orientálni* xxxi (1963), 470–482.

Ziegler, K. "Plutarchstudien." *RhM* lxxxi (1932), 51–87.

III. Selected Works on Literacy in Other Cultures

Ascher, M., & R. Ascher. *Code of the Quipu: A Study in Media, Mathematics, and Culture.* Ann Arbor, 1981.

Aston, M. "Lollardy and Literacy." *History* lxii (1977), 347–371.

Baines, J. "Literacy and Ancient Egyptian Society." *Man* xviii (1983), 572–599.

Baines, J., & C. J. Eyre. "Four Notes on Literacy." *Göttinger Miszellen* lxi (1983), 65–96.

Beales, R. W. "Studying Literacy at the Community Level: A Research Note." *JIH* ix (1978–79), 93–102.

Bozzolo, C., D. Coq & E. Ornato. "La production du livre en quelques pays d'Europe occidentale aux XIVᵉ et XVᵉ siècles." *S & C* viii (1984), 129–160.

Chall, J. Contribution to "Illiteracy in America: A Symposium." *Harvard Educational Review* xl (1970), 264–276.

Chartier, R., M. M. Compère & D. Julia. *L'éducation en France du XVIᵐᵉ au XVIIIᵐᵉ siècle.* Paris, 1976.

Cipolla, C. *Literacy and Development in the West.* Harmondsworth, 1969.

Clanchy, M. T. *From Memory to Written Record: England, 1066–1307.* Cambridge, Mass., 1979.

Collinson, P. "The Significance of Signatures." *Times Literary Supplement* 8 January 1981, 31.

Cressy, D. *Literacy and the Social Order. Reading and Writing in Tudor and Stuart England.* Cambridge, 1980.

Davis, N. Z. *Society and Culture in Early Modern France.* Stanford, 1975.

de Chabrol de Volvic, G. J. G. "Essai sur les moeurs des habitants modernes de l'Egypte." In *Description de l'Egypte.* Vol. xviii. 2d ed. Paris, 1826, 62–65.

Dore, R. P. *Education in Tokugawa Japan.* London, 1965.

Duverdier, G. "La pénétration du livre dans une société de culture orale: Le cas de Tahiti." *Revue française d'histoire du livre* xlii (1971), 27–49.

Eisenstein, E. *The Printing Press as an Agent of Change.* Vols. i–ii. Cambridge, 1979.

Franklin, S. "Literacy and Documentation in Early Medieval Russia." *Speculum* lx (1985), 1–38.

Furet, F., & W. Sachs. "La croissance de l'alphabétisation en France, XVIIIᵉ–XIXᵉ siècle." *Annales E.S.C.* xxix (1974), 715–721.

Gawthrop, R., & G. Strauss. "Protestantism and Literacy in Early Modern Germany." *P & P* civ (1984), 31–55.

Golden, H. H. "Literacy." In *International Encyclopedia of the Social Sciences*. New York, 1968, 412–417.

Goody, J. *The Domestication of the Savage Mind*. Cambridge, 1977.

———. "Paths to Knowledge in Oral and Written Cultures." In D. Tannen (ed.), *Spoken and Written Language: Exploring Orality and Literacy*. Norwood, N.J., 1982, 201–215.

———. *The Logic of Writing and the Organization of Society*. Cambridge, 1986.

Goody, J., & I. Watt. "The Consequences of Literacy." *CSSH* v (1962–63), 304–345. Reprinted in Goody (ed.), *Literacy in Traditional Societies*. Cambridge, 1968, 27–68.

Graff, H. J. *The Literacy Myth: Literacy and the Social Structure in the Nineteenth-Century City*. New York, 1979.

———. *The Legacies of Literacy*. Bloomington, Ind., 1987.

———. (ed.). *Literacy and Social Development in the West: A Reader*. Cambridge, 1981.

Grafton, A. T. Review of E. Eisenstein, *The Printing Press as an Agent of Change*. *JIH* xi (1980–81), 265–286.

Gruneberg, M. M., P. E. Morris & R. N. Sykes (eds.). *Practical Aspects of Memory*. London, 1978.

Hajdu, H. *Lesen und Schreiben im Spätmittelalter*. Pécs, 1931.

Hallpike, C. R. *The Foundations of Primitive Thought*. Oxford, 1979.

Harman, D. "Illiteracy: An Overview." *Harvard Educational Review* xl (1970), 226–244.

Hibbert, C. *The Great Mutiny*. London, 1978.

Houston, R. "Literacy and Society in the West, 1500–1850." *Social History* viii (1983), 269–293.

Johansson, E. "The History of Literacy in Sweden." In H. J. Graff (ed.), *Literacy and Social Development in the West: A Reader*. Cambridge, 1981, 151–182.

Kirsch, I. S., & A. Jungeblut. *Literacy: Profiles of America's Young Adults* (Educational Testing Service Report no. 16-PL-02). Princeton, 1986.

Kozol, J. *Illiterate America*. New York, 1985.

Laqueur, T. W. "The Cultural Origins of Popular Literacy in England 1500–1850." *Oxford Review of Education* ii (1976), 255–275.

Lockridge, K. A. *Literacy in Colonial New England*. New York, 1974.

———. "L'alphabétisation en Amérique, 1650–1800." *Annales E.S.C.* xxxii (1977), 503–518.

Lülfing, H. *Johannes Gutenberg und das Buchwesen des 14. und 15. Jahrhunderts*. Munich, 1969.

Murra, J. V. *Formaciones económicas y políticas del mundo andino.* Lima, 1975.

Naveh, J. *The Early History of the Alphabet.* Jerusalem & Leiden, 1982.

Nickerson, R. S. "Adult Literacy and Technology." *Visible Language* xix (1985), 311–355.

Ong, W. J. *Orality and Literacy. The Technologizing of the Word.* London, 1982.

Parkes, M. B. "The Literacy of the Laity." In D. Daiches & A. Thorlby (eds.), *The Mediaeval World.* London, 1973, 555–577.

Pattison, R. *On Literacy. The Politics of the Word from Homer to the Age of Rock.* Oxford, 1982.

Petrucci, A. "Scrittura e libro nell'Italia altomedievale. Il sesto secolo." *Studi medievali* x.2 (1970), 157–213.

Safrai, S. "Elementary Education, Its Religious and Social Significance in the Talmudic Period." In H. H. Ben-Sasson & S. Ettinger (eds.), *Jewish Society through the Ages.* New York, 1969, 148–169.

Sanderson, M. "Literacy and Social Mobility in the Industrial Revolution in England." *P & P* lvi (1972), 75–104.

Scribner, S., & M. Cole. *The Psychology of Literacy.* Cambridge, Mass., 1981.

Seppilli, A. *La memoria e l'assenza. Tradizione orale e civiltà della scrittura nell'America dei Conquistadores.* Bologna, 1979.

Steinmann, F. "Wie gross war die Zahl der schreibkundigen Kopten?" *Klio* liii (1971), 353–360.

Stone, L. "Literacy and Education in England, 1640–1900." *P & P* xlii (1969), 69–139.

Street, B. V. *Literacy in Theory and Practice.* Cambridge, 1984.

Stubbs, M. *Language and Literacy. The Sociolinguistics of Reading and Writing.* London, 1980.

[UNESCO]. *Statistics of Educational Attainment and Illiteracy 1945–1974* (Unesco Statistical Reports and Studies no. 22). Paris, 1977.

Vansina, J. *Oral Tradition as History.* Madison, Wis., 1985.

Yates, F. A. *The Art of Memory.* London, 1966.

Index